THE SACRAMENT OF HOLY ORDERS

THE SACRAMENT OF
HOLY ORDERS

*Some Papers and Discussions concerning
Holy Orders at a Session of the
Centre de Pastorale Liturgique, 1955*

Translates Études sur le sac de l'ordre
(Lex orandi #22)

**THE LITURGICAL PRESS
COLLEGEVILLE, MINNESOTA**

PRINTED IN ENGLAND

First published by Les Editions du Cerf, Paris, 1957

This edition © Aquin Press, 1962

Nihil obstat: *Hubertus Richards, S.T.L., L.S.S. Censor deputatus*
Imprimatur: *E. Morrogh Bernard, Vic. Gen. Westmonasterii, die*
7a Junii, 1962

.

Printed for Bloomsbury Publishing Co Ltd, London, by
The Garden City Press Limited, Letchworth, Hertfordshire

PRINTED IN ENGLAND

CONTENTS

Taking part in the discussions were:

M. BASSEVILLE, Superior of the Seminary at Lyons.
M. BOULARD, National Chaplain to the A.C.R.
FR BOUYER, of the Catholic Institute, Paris.
DOM BOTTE, from Mont César, Louvain.
RT REV. DOM CAPELLE, Abbot of Mont César.
M. CHAMBOUNAUD, from the Seminary of the Mission de France.
M. CHAVASSE, University of Strassbourg.
FR CONGAR, O.P., from Le Saulchoir.
A. CRUIZIAT.
FR DALMAIS, O.P.
FR DANIÉLOU, S.J., of the Catholic Institute, Paris.
V. REV. FR FORESTIER, O.P., Prior of Le Saulchoir.
FR GELIN, P.S.S., Superior of the Maison Saint-Jean.
FR GELINEAU, S.J., of the C.P.L.
M. GIRAULD, from the Seminary at Poitiers.
FR GY, O.P., from Le Saulchoir.
M. IDIART, from the National Centre for Research.
FR LÉCUYER, C.S.SP., Director of the French Seminary in Rome.
M. LeLUBRE, Chaplain of Chapelle Saint-Louis d'Alfortville.
M. LE SOURD, from Saint Sulpice.
FR LIÉGÉ, O.P., from Faubourg Saint Honoré, Paris.
FR LOUVEL, O.P., Editor of *Fêtes et Saisons* of the C.P.L.
REV. CANON MANCENCAU, from Bordeaux.
M. MARTIMOT, University of Toulouse.
M. OSTER, from Offendorf, Bas-Rhin.
M. PERROT, from Notre Dame des Champs, Paris 6.
M. RAUCH, from Ottersthal, Bas-Rhin.
FR RÉGAMEY, O.P., Paris.
FR ROGUET, O.P., Director of the C.P.L.
FR ROQUETTE, Editor of this volume.
DOM ROUSSEAU, from Chevetogne, Editor of *Irenikon*.
M. SAUVAGE, Superior of the Seminary of Lille.
M. VINATIER, Vicar General of the Mission de France.

PREFACE

IN his admirable prayer for the clergy of France, M. Paris asked God for 'old priests in new men'.[1]

This great master of the priestly life wanted modern priests who would subscribe to the unbroken tradition, the school of divine wisdom and sanctity. He wanted them to be heirs and continuers of that venerable 'presbyterium' extolled so lyrically by Ignatius of Antioch at the dawn of the early Church. He implored them also 'not to adulterate the imperishable newness of the gospel of Christ with transient opinions'.

But he believed that the old tradition of the priesthood must live again in modern men, the 'messengers of a universal and eternal truth'; he expected them to 'know how to present that truth to the men of their own generation, to their own countrymen'. He expressed the ardent hope that they would 'understand and speak the language of their times'. Above all he urged them to draw from their daily celebration of the Mass 'a solicitude for the salvation of their brethren and for the salvation of the world'.

I have often thought that these two essential facets of the Catholic priesthood could not be brought out in a better way.

Because he is the man of God and the man of an Incarnate God, the priest is both 'the man of every age' and 'the man of today'.

Once this is admitted, it is easy to see that, while remaining true to itself, the Catholic priesthood has, in the course of the centuries, presented different aspects in each age and civilisation.

Any objective study which enables us to perceive some of its

1. cf. *Oeuvres de M. Paris, prêtre de Saint-Sulpice, aumonier des Universitaires Catholiques*, Paris, Letouzey, 1946, vol. 1, p. 509.

immutable features through the many manifestations of its unique mission is a valuable contribution to the theology of priesthood.

This is the purpose of the present work from the Centre of Pastoral Liturgy. Its contents are the result of two sessions of study.

As its title indicates, it is a modest attempt to present a series of studies on the sacrament of Orders, without claiming to exhaust the subject or to construct an exclusive synthesis.

The chief interest of these studies lies in the fact that they were pursued without preconceived ideas and by specialists speaking on their own subjects.

They delve deep into the treasures of the liturgy and the bible, the tradition of the Fathers and the life of the Church, particularly into its successive legislative codes. Such an extensive inquiry could hardly disregard indirect contribution such as, for example, the recent discoveries at Qumran, the careful examination of ancient vocabulary, or the findings of the contemporary study of comparative religion.

Some may be surprised to find so little about the seventeenth century French school, but the reason for this is the existing abundance and fulness of the literature on this subject.

This new volume in the *Lex Orandi* collection seems wholly to merit the approval which the Sovereign Pontiff recently bestowed on the members of the last international congress of Pastoral Liturgy:

'The attitude of the liturgical centres to the past seems to us, in general, to be quite correct – they look into it, they study it conscientiously, they cherish what is really praiseworthy without actually going to extremes.'[1]

This legitimate preoccupation with the past by no means prevents the members of C.P.L. from having a justifiable solicitude for the present and the future.

At a time when the activity of real Christians is having more and more influence on those concerned with the building of a new type of world, some people are wondering if the promotion of the laity into an organised apostolate might not lead to a

1. *Doc. Cath.*, no. 1236 (14–10–56), col. 1298.

depreciation of the vocation of the priest and of his role in the Christian community.

It is instructive to see from their spontaneous remarks and actions what the militants or the ordinary practising Christians really think about this.

But we must remind ourselves here that in defining the tasks proper to the laity in the apostolate of today, the Catholic hierarchy, far from minimising the activities of the priesthood, reasserts in all its doctrinal statements the pre-eminent place of the priest in the 'City', and his irreplaceable role in the economy of salvation, by putting the accent unfailingly on his essentially priestly functions, particularly on his concern for evangelisation, and on the necessity for giving spiritual 'animation' to an adult laity.

As the rediscovery of the grandeur of the sacrament of matrimony by many of the faithful has in no way detracted from the sublime character of consecrated virginity – rather the contrary – so a conscientious appraisal of the nature of that mission which the Church entrusts to lay apostles ought normally to lead them to a more intelligent understanding of the unfathomable riches of the grace which their priests, and the priesthood alone, can bring them.

Now it is not the least interesting feature of these various studies on the sacrament of Orders that they provide some valuable answers, drawn from the well of ecclesiastical tradition itself, to the aspirations of present-day apostles or to the demands made by their apostolate. There are some traditional aspects of the priesthood which correspond so perfectly to the urgent pastoral needs of today that we might have thought that they were invented to meet our own case – such as the corporate character of the presbyterate and episcopate.[1]

Perhaps I may apply to the clergy of today the words which His Holiness Pius XII addressed to young Catholics throughout the world:

Custodians of a tradition, you are not the blind and selfish upholders

1. cf. Dom Botte's study: *The Collegiate Character of the Presbyterate and Episcopate.*

of outmoded forms, but the possessors of a treasure whence are drawn
things new and old for the benefit of the whole Community.[1]

'Old priests', yes – but 'in new men'.

✠ JEAN GUYOT
Bishop of Coutances

1. Message of His Holiness Pius XII to those taking part in the
second *Assemblée du Mouvement international de la jeunesse agricole et
rurale catholique.*

CHAPTER I

HOLY ORDERS IN THE ORDINATION PRAYERS

DOM B. BOTTE, O.S.B.

THE contribution which I have to make at the beginning of this session is of rather a factual nature. I do not propose to construct a theological synthesis from the liturgical texts but simply to collect the data which might prove helpful to the discussions of this gathering. And I cannot quote all the texts, much less comment on them – they are far too numerous. Some choice must be made and as I would not wish it to be capricious I shall confine myself to the texts which concern the episcopate, the priesthood and the diaconate, and to the earliest examples of these in the three great patriarchates of Rome, Antioch and Alexandria. In doing this I do not mean to deny the theological interest of the rites and the prayers which were added later, but since limits are necessary it seemed to me preferable to keep to those representing the most ancient and universal tradition. This also explains why, in setting limits to my subject on one side I have broadened it on the other to include the Eastern rites. In doing so I follow the example of Pius XII, who has reminded us in the *Sacramentum Ordinis*[1] that in this matter it is necessary to respect what has to be done 'always and everywhere'. Perhaps the comparison of the Eastern tradition with that of the West will throw out some valuable suggestions.

I shall, therefore, deal first with the earliest Western texts and then with those of the East. I shall then try to enunciate some general conclusions which seem to me to follow from these texts.

1. cf. B. Botte, 'La Constitution Apostolique "Sacramentum Ordinis"' in *La Maison-Dieu* 16 (1948), pp 124–9.

1. THE WESTERN RITES

The first Roman rite of ordination and the earliest of them all is to be found in the apostolic tradition attributed to St Hippolytus.[1] It is important to remember that this is of consequence not only for the West, but that it has exercised a profound influence in the East. Its formulae, for example, are still in use in the patriarchate of Alexandria.

After the election of the bishop by the people, the bishops present laid their hands on the elect, while all prayed 'for the descent of the Spirit'. Then one of the bishops, at the request of them all, laid his hand upon him while pronouncing a prayer. I am not going to give the full text, which is fairly well known; it may be summarised as follows: God is asked to shed upon the elect the sovereign Spirit, *spiritum principalem*,[2] which he gave, through Christ, to his apostles who established the Church in the place of the temple to the honour of his name. The prayer goes on to indicate what the bishop must do; feed the holy flock (a biblical image recalling John 21, 15–17 and 1 Peter 3, 2); exercise the sovereign priesthood by serving God night and day; make propitious, and offer, the gifts of holy Church; remit sins, dispense the portions, and loose all bonds by virtue of the power given to the apostles.

None of the later formulae possesses such wealth or clarity. The bishop stands out clearly as the successor of the apostles; he receives their spirit and exercises their functions; he is charged with feeding the holy flock, and with exercising the sovereign priesthood.

In the ordination of a priest both the bishop and the priests

1. Text in Hippolytus of Rome, *La tradition apostolique*, ed. B. Botte, Paris 1946, pp 26–30 and 37–41. The text of the prayer for the consecration of a bishop is preserved in the original language – Greek; cf. *ibid.*, pp 77–8. See also the excellent commentary by J. Lécuyer, 'Episcopat et Presbyterat dans les écrits d'Hippolyte de Rome' in *Recherches de Science religieuse*, 41 (1953), pp 30–50.

2. On the meaning of this word, see the reservations I have expressed on the subject of Fr J. Lécuyer's interpretation, *art. cit.* in *Bulletin de Théol. anc. et médiév.*, v, vi, no. 2000. After a conversation with Fr Lécuyer I have come to the conclusion that we are fundamentally in agreement but that Fr Lécuyer had simply expressed himself rather ambiguously.

lay on their hands, but the bishop alone pronounces the formula. He asks that the elect may have counsel and strength to share in the government of the Church. We are put in mind here of the elders chosen by Moses, who were filled with his spirit. The analogy suggests that the priests partake of the same spirit as the bishop. The formula concludes with a prayer for the whole presbyterate – that they may all preserve the spirit of grace and be worthy to serve God with faith in all simplicity of heart.

And so in this way the elect is incorporated into the sacerdotal body which is responsible, together with the bishop, for the government of the people. The priest participates in the *sacerdotium* of the bishop, while the deacon is ordained in *ministerio episcopi*, and not *in sacerdotio*.[1] But the formula does not enumerate the functions of the priest whereas the episcopal functions are named in the prayer for the consecration of a bishop.

Finally, in the case of the deacon, the bishop alone imposes his hands, since the deacon is not ordained for the *sacerdotium*, but for the service of the bishop. He is his servant and must do as the bishop commands him, so he does not receive the spirit common to the priesthood. The bishop invokes the spirit of grace, of zeal and of diligence to come upon this servant chosen by God to serve the Church and to carry the gifts to the altar, so that when he has performed his ministry well he may be rewarded with a higher degree. Here for the first time is found the allusion to 1 Tim. 3, 13, which recurs in almost all the later formulae: *Qui enim bene ministraverit gradum bonum sibi acquirit.*

In Hippolytus the priesthood and the diaconate are therefore defined by reference to the episcopate. The bishop is the pastor and the high priest. The priests participate in his priesthood and form a sacerdotal body which acts with him in governing the Church just as much as in celebrating the eucharist, and we see that immediately after their ordination they concelebrate with

1. *Tradition Apostolique*, 9, p. 39. 'Sicut et praecipimus, in diacono ordinando solus episcopus imponat manus propterea quia non in sacerdotio ordinatur, sed in ministerio episcopi ut faciat ea quae ab ipso iubentur.' The expression is found again in the Roman pontifical, but the word *episcopi* has been suppressed, and *ministerio* occurs on its own. This alteration was made by the redactor of the *Statuta ecclesiae antiqua*. On this collection, see p. 10, note 2.

him. The deacon is the servant of the bishop – he assists the bishop at the altar by bringing up the gifts; and he is under his orders.

We have to wait several centuries from the time of the apostolic tradition before we meet fresh liturgical documents on ordination. The pure Roman rite is represented by the Leonine sacramentary and the Gregorian sacramentary.[1] There are no indications of rites in them but only forms of prayers and there is simply a prayer and preface for each ordination. Let us briefly consider three well-known prefaces.

Only a single idea is retained[2] in the preface for an episcopal consecration – the bishop is the high priest of the new testament. The ordination of Aaron required two rites – he was clothed with sumptuous vestments and he was anointed. This was the figure of what happens at the consecration of the Christian high priest in a spiritual manner. By divine benediction his soul receives an adornment more splendid than Aaron's, and an unction of the Holy Spirit which pervades his whole being. Unction and vesting are here purely symbolic, and definitely exclude the physical actions which were introduced later in places other than Rome. If there had been an actual anointing, a bath full of oil would have been necessary, for the redactor has taken *ora vestimenti* (Ps. **132**, 2) to mean the hem of the garment, and the anointing to have touched the very feet. An interpolation of non-Roman origin,[3] which survives in the pontifical,

1. cf. *Sacramentarium Leonianum*, ed. C. L. Feltoe, Cambridge 1896, pp 119–22. *The Gregorian Sacramentary*, ed. H. A. Wilson, London 1915, pp 5–8.

2. In this formula the following alterations should be noted. The beginning *Deus honor omnium dignitatum* does not correspond to any of the early examples, which have *Deus honorum omnium Deus omnium dignitatum*. This reading is perhaps not entirely satisfactory, and it is probable that, following the analogy of the formulae for the priesthood and the diaconate, we must supply one word: *Deus omnium honorum, Deus omnium dignitatum quae sacratis famulantur ordinibus **distributor***. In any case, the reading in the pontifical has no acceptable meaning. In place of *rore sanctifica* in the preface we should read *fluore sanctifica*, attested by all the early evidence in the erroneous form *flore sanctifica*.

3. It is to be found in the old Gelasian, cf. *The Gelasian Sacramentary*, ed. H. A. Wilson, Oxford 1894, pp 151–2, and in the *Missale Francorum*; cf. *Thomasius, Opera Omnia*, ed. Vezzosi, vol. vi, p. 350.

introduces a series of biblical quotations illustrating the function of the bishop (the preaching of the gospel and the ministry of reconciliation); but the pure Roman rite contains nothing like this. All that can be found is an allusion to his role as intercessor (*ad exorandam semper misericordiam tuam*).

The preface for the ordination of priests is divided into three parts. The first establishes a general principle. It is God himself who organises the hierarchy of sacred functions. The second applies this principle to the old testament (Moses and the seventy elders, Aaron and his two sons), then to the new testament (the disciples associated with the apostles). The third part contains the invocation made to God by the bishop who also has need of helpers. The role of the priests is clearly defined: *ut cum pontifices summos regendis populis praefecisses, ad eorum societatis et operis adiumentum sequentis ordinis viros et secundae dignitatis eligeres.* We cannot fail to be struck by this insistence on the priest's subordination to the bishop:

> *sequentis ordinis viros*
> *secundae dignitatis*
> *secundi meriti munus.*

Following the sources, we must add *secundis praedicatoribus*,[1] which in the pontifical has become *secundis praedicationibus*.

In my opinion, this insistence can only be understood as a kind of protest against a tendency which had arisen at the end of the fourth century, which St Jerome is one of the first to show – i.e. to think of the bishop only as a *primus inter pares* among the priests.[2] A statement as solemn as this, in a liturgical document which probably goes back to the fifth century, seems to have some theological significance. We should also bear in mind that the custom of the popular election of priests and other clerks was no longer known at Rome. The Gelasian formula[3]

1. This is the reading in the early versions, and it is sustained by the context. By making use of disciples who were associated with them as preachers of the second degree, the apostles made their voice heard to the ends of the earth.

2. On this question, see B. Botte, *Secundi meriti munus* in *Questions liturgiques et paroissiales*, 21 (1936), pp 84–8.

3. *The Gelasian Sacramentary*, ed. Wilson, p. 22. The conclusion of this formula has been superseded by the exhortation *Quoniam dilectissimi*, which comes from the *Missale Francorum* (Thomasius-Vezzosi,

Auxiliante, which is certainly of Roman origin is clear: *eligimus in ordine diaconii sive presbyterii*. The people can raise objections, but it is the bishop who makes the choice.

The formula for the diaconate begins by expressing the same principle as in the priesthood. It is God himself who organises the hierarchy of sacred functions in Christ's body the Church, in the three orders fighting for his name. Then, after recalling the levites of the ancient law, the prayer asks God to send the Holy Spirit so that the deacons might exercise their ministry in the seven gifts of his grace, and it enumerates the virtues which they ought to possess, if the people are to be moved to imitate them.[1]

In early times the Roman rite contained nothing more than these prayers, with the imposition of hands. But as it spread beyond Rome foreign elements crept in, and new developments were added which ended by taking root in Rome itself, thanks to the Romano-Germanic pontifical. They survive in the Roman pontifical today. I will describe the most important. The imposition of the gospels occurs at the consecration of a bishop. This is attested in Syria from the end of the fourth century, and it was accepted at Rome for the consecration of the pope; it is difficult to say exactly when, but probably before St Gregory, and under Syrian influence. But it was the *Statuta Ecclesiae Antiqua*,[2] through the agency of the Gelasian sacramentary,

---

vol. vi, pp 345–6). The Roman formula: *Si quis habet aliquid*, etc. has not the same emphasis at all as the original text: *Et ideo electionem vestram debetis voce publica profiteri*.

1. cf. B. Botte, 'Imitation' in *Archivum latinitatis medii aevi*, 16 (1942), pp 149–54. The original reading is certainly: *imitationem sanctae plebis acquirant* and not the Gregorian reading: *imitationem sancta plebs acquirat*. The present reading: *imitationem sanctam plebs acquirat* is still unknown in the first printed pontificals, and is meaningless.

2. On this collection which has exercised a preponderant influence on ordination rites, see B. Botte, 'Le Rituel d'ordination des Statuta Ecclesiae antiqua' in *Recherches de théologie anc. et médiév.* 11 (1939), pp 223–41. It is wrong to think of this collection as an example of the Gallican liturgy. In fact it is an apocrypha, partly inspired by the Apostolic Tradition of St Hippolytus. This can be seen, for example, in the ordination of the deacon. The redactor has changed the formula *quia non in sacerdotio sed in ministerio episcopi* into *quia non ad sacerdotium sed ad ministerium*, by suppressing the word *episcopi*. This is in

that caused this custom to spread. In this apocryphal writing, however, the redactor has replaced the deacons, who originally held the gospels, by two bishops, in conformity with the anti-diaconal tendencies of this writing. There is no formula to express the significance of the rite. The pontifical imposes the book *super cervicem et scapulas*; but in the early documents it is laid on the head. I shall return to this point later.

The anointing of the head was introduced into the preface under the influence of symbolism. But it is not attested before the ninth century, and it was still unknown at Rome at this period.[1] The anointing of the hands is also due to the influence of the old testament (Lev. 16, 32), and was probably only practised in consecrations when the bishop had not been anointed at the time of his ordination to the priesthood. The second formula, *Deus et Pater Domini nostri Jesu Christi*, was accompanied by an anointing of the thumb in episcopal consecrations only.

In the case of the priesthood, we must notice a formula of non-Roman origin, *Sanctificationum Auctor*,[2] an ancient consecratory preface from another rite. It prays for divine grace, so that by the gravity of their conduct and the severity of their life, the new priests should prove themselves to be *seniores*. It is in this prayer that the following beautiful formula is found: *Quod legerint credant, quod crediderint doceant, quod docuerint imitentur*. Liturgical functions are referred to only in the words: *per obsequium plebis tuae corpus et sanguinem Filii tui immaculata benedictione transforment*.[3] The anointing of the hands, as well as the vesting, appeared in Gaul with the eighth-century Gelasian

---

conformity with his tendencies, for in canon 57 he says explicitly that the deacon is the minister of the priest as well as the bishop. But the formula of Hippolytus has as a result lost its meaning.

1. On the rites of anointing, cf. G. Ellard, *Ordination Anointing in the Eastern Church before 1000 A.D.*, Cambridge, Mass., 1935; P. Batiffol, 'La liturgie du sacre des évêques', in *Revue d'histoire ecclésiastique* 23 (1927), pp 733–63; M. Andrieu, 'L'onction des mains dans le sacre épiscopal', *ibid.*, 26 (1930), pp 343–7.

2. cf. *Gelasian Sacramentary*, p. 24, and *Missale Francorum* (Thomasius-Vezzosi), vol. vi, p. 347.

3. This is actually the early formula, which has been modified in the Roman pontifical.

sacramentary. The tradition of the instruments comes much later, doubtless through analogy with the minor Orders. Finally, in the thirteenth century, the last imposition of hands was introduced.[1]

For the diaconate we have a formula parallel to that of the *Sanctificationum* in the ordination of priests – *Deus sancte Pater spei*. It is very short. It is God who ordains the ministry of the angels in heaven and on earth; may he look especially (*speciali ... aspectu* and not *spiritali . . . affectu*[2] as in the pontifical) upon the candidates, that they may be pure ministers of the altar and worthy of those first deacons appointed by the apostles under the inspiration of the Holy Spirit. The vesting and the tradition of the gospels are clearly additional rites.

So, beside the Roman formulae, the pontifical contains two ordination prayers of foreign origin for the diaconate and the priesthood. They may be Gallican. They would seem to be almost the only survivals of this early rite.

We possess nothing which concerns the consecration of a bishop from the Church in Spain. The formula for the diaconate is only an adaptation of the Roman text.[3] Only the formula for the priesthood is original. It is very short, and not very explicit: *Doctor plebium et rector subiectorum teneat ordinate catholicam fidem et cunctis annuntiet veram salutem.*[4] That is all we are told of the functions of the priest. After ordination, the bishop said to the priest: *Ecce, frater, factus es ad docendum ministeria* (read *mysteria*) *Christi collega ordinis nostri. Habeto ergo aditum et*

1. This ceremony, unknown in the early pontificals, had become general by the end of the thirteenth century, thanks to the pontifical of Durandus of Mende. The unction of the hands appears in the old Gelasian sacramentary, but not in its normal place, after the ordination of the subdeacons; cf. *Gelasian Sacramentary* p. 148. It is also found in the *Missale Francorum*, cf. Thomasius-Vezzosi, vol. vi, p. 347. The vesting is prescribed by the Gelasians of the eighth century, cf. *Le Sacramentaire gélasien d'Angoulême*, ed. P. Cagin, Angouleme, 1919, f. 152 v.

2. *Aspectu* must be taken in its active sense – the action of regarding. The emendator who changed *aspectu* into *affectu* did not understand this.

3. cf. M. Ferotin, *Le Liber ordinum en usage dans l'Eglise wisigothique et mozarabe d'Espagne*, Paris 1912, p. 49.

4. *ibid.*, pp 54–5.

potestatem accedere ad altare. Vide ut sancta mysteria sanctificans corde et ore conficiens cunctis fidelibus distribuas.[1]

2. THE EASTERN RITES

We now pass from the patriarchate of Rome to that of Antioch. The earliest document from this area is to be found in the Apostolic Constitutions,[2] an apocryphal compilation dating from the end of the fourth or the beginning of the fifth century. The ordination ritual is only an amplification of that in Hippolytus. The only original element which deserves notice is the imposition of the gospel at the consecration of a bishop, without any formula to signify its meaning. It certainly represents the actual usage of the Church in Antioch, for St John Chrysostom and, later the pseudo-Dionysius, both allude to it. It is to be found in all rites of the Syrian group.

In this group we can distinguish two types. The first is the West Syrian type, comprising the Byzantine rite (to which the Armenian rite is closely related at least in the matter with which we are concerned[3]) and the Syrian rite of Antioch, used by the Jacobites and the Uniate Syrians of this patriarchate and also the Maronites, who have some very remarkable usages of their own. The second type is the East Syrian rite used by the Nestorians, the Chaldeans and the Christians of Malabar. In spite of some notable differences in the formulae these rites are related by elements which appear to be very ancient.

In the consecration of a bishop, the elements which appear to me to be early, apart from the imposition of the gospels, are an indicatory formula and a deprecatory formula, this latter being afterwards duplicated in a second, perhaps more recent, prayer. The indicatory formula is: Divine grace which heals all that is infirm and supplies what is wanting chooses N. as bishop of N.

---

1. cf. Ferotin, *op. cit.*, p. 55.

2. *Constitutions Apost.*, VIII, 4–5; 16–17. cf. *Didascalia et Constitutiones Apostolorum*, ed. Funk, Paderborn 1905, vol. 1, pp 470–8 (episcopate) and 520–5 (priesthood and diaconate).

3. I am referring to the early Armenian rite before it was subjected to Latin influences, for the Armenian Church subsequently adopted Latin ritual and orders.

Let us pray for him, that the grace of the Most Holy Spirit may come upon him.[1] That is actually the Byzantine formula but it is almost identical with the other rites.

The Byzantine deprecatory formula runs:

O Sovereign Lord and our God, who by thine apostle Paul didst set up the hierarchy of degrees and orders for the service of thy most pure mysteries at thy holy altar – first apostles, then prophets, then doctors; do thou strengthen, O sovereign of the universe, by the coming, power and grace of thy Holy Spirit, him whom thou hast judged worthy to receive the yoke of the gospel and the dignity of the high priesthood by the hand of me, a sinner, and of those who celebrate with me, as thou didst strengthen the apostles and prophets, as thou didst anoint kings and sanctify high priests. Make him to be a high priest without reproach and adorned with all dignity; make him to be holy so that he may be worthy to intercede for the salvation of the people and to be heard by thee[2]

This is the only formula which indicates the meaning of the imposition of the gospels. One may well ask if this is really the earliest meaning, for if it is a *yoke* why is it placed on the head? Would not the early sense be rather that the power of the gospel should fill the elect?[3] After a litany, the bishop pronounces a second formula, probably less ancient:

O Lord our God, who, since the nature of man cannot sustain the essence of thy divinity, didst by thy dispensation raise up doctors subject to the same passions as ourselves, who approach thy throne to offer the sacrifice and the oblation for thy people; do thou, O Lord, thou, the true Pastor who didst give thy life for the flock, make him who has been appointed a dispenser of the grace of the sovereign priesthood to be thine imitator, a guide to the blind, a light in the darkness, a teacher of the foolish, a tutor of little ones, a lamp shining in the world, so that after he has formed the souls who have been entrusted to him in this life, he may stand before thy tribunal without shame, and may receive the great reward which thou hast prepared for those who have striven to preach thy gospel.[4]

1. cf. J. Goar, Εὐχολόγιον *sive Rituale Graecorum*, Venice 1730, p. 250 (244 twice in error).
2. *ibid.*, p. 250.
3. For this sense see the text of Severian de Gabala preserved in a series P.G. 125, 533; cf. J. Lécuyer, 'La Grace de la consecration episcopal' in *Revue des sciences philos. et théol.* 36 (1952), p. 40.
4. cf. Goar, p. 251. Instead of 'who approach thy throne', Goar has *tuum thronum obtinentes*, which is an obvious mistranslation.

These formulae are found in the *Euchology Barberini* 336;[1] they are certainly very ancient but it is impossible to fix even an approximate date. It is even more difficult to determine the date of the other Syrian rites which have come down to us in some much more recent manuscripts. The indicatory formula *Divine Grace* is substantially the same in the other rites, but the texts of the prayers are different. I will summarise those of the East Syrian rites, which seem to me to be early. For all three orders we find a basically identical formula. The text of that for the priesthood (which appears to have been originally used at the consecration of a bishop) I will give later. Its principal ideas are[2]: following the tradition which has come down to them from generation to generation through the imposition of hands, the bishops are mediators of the divine graces which God bestows on his Church. They present to God him who has been set apart and chosen as bishop, and they ask that the grace of the Holy Spirit may come upon him through the descent of his presence, that it may make him perfect, that it may sanctify him and consecrate him in the perfect good work which this great and excellent ministry is. It gives no further details about the function of the bishop, except in a second prayer which recalls, like the Byzantine rite, the *charismata* of the new testament (prophets, apostles, doctors). The only liturgical acts which are mentioned are the ordination of clerks, the healing of the sick by the imposition of hands, and the power to bind and loose. The rest of the formula bears on his government of the people – he must visit, preach the word, gather his flock together, and provide for it and increase it.

We will pass on to the priesthood. The Byzantine rite takes up the indicatory formula *Divine Grace*. Then comes a first prayer.

1. On this MS. see A. Strittmatter, 'The "Barberinum S. Marci" of Jacques Goar' in *Ephemerides liturgicae* (1933), pp 329–67. For the ordination prayers in particular, cf. p. 353, with its references to the incomplete editions of the text.

2. cf. J. A. Assemani, *Codex liturgicus Ecclesiae universae*, vol. XIII, Paris 1902, pp 63–5; J. Morinus, *Commentarius de sacris Ecclesiae ordinationibus*, Paris 1655, pp 468–71.

O God, who hast neither beginning nor end, who art more ancient than all creation and hast honoured with the name of elders those who have been deemed worthy to exercise the sacred ministry of the word of thy truth in this order; O Thou who hast been pleased to choose through me this man of irreproachable conduct and steadfast faith, may it also please thee to give him the great grace of the Holy Spirit; make thy servant perfect; may he please thee in all things, and order his ways in a manner worthy of this great grace of the priesthood that he has received in thy providential power.[1]

There are no sacred functions named except in a second prayer: to stand at the altar, to proclaim the gospel of the kingdom, to exercise the sacred ministry of the word,[2] to offer spiritual gifts and sacrifices, to renew the people in the 'bath of regeneration'.

Among the East Syrians the deprecatory formula is, as we have seen, fundamentally the same as for the episcopate. Its translation runs:

O good God, our merciful King ... by thy grace thou didst appoint us mediators of thy divine gifts, that we might in thy name distribute the talents of the ministry of the Spirit to the ministers of thy mysteries; and, following the apostolic tradition which has come down to us through the imposition of hands by the ministry of the Church, we do here present unto thee these servants, that they may be chosen priests in thy holy Church; and we all pray for them – that the grace of the Holy Spirit may come upon them to consecrate them and to make them perfect in the good work of the priestly ministry for which they are now presented.[3]

As in the consecration of a bishop there is a second prayer which names the sacerdotal functions – to lay hands on the sick, to offer spiritual oblations, to consecrate the baptismal water, to adorn the sons of the holy Church with the works of justice.

I will just mention the ordination of the deacon. In the Byzantine rite, as well as the formula *Divine Grace*, which was used for all ordinations we also have two prayers accompanying the imposition of hands. In the first, the deacon appears as the minister of the holy mysteries, and it asks that he may fulfil his

1. cf. Goar, *op. cit.*, p. 242.
2. The word ἱερουργεῖν is normally used for the eucharist. The context seems to me to exclude this meaning here.
3. cf. Assemani, *op. cit.*, pp 37–8; Morinus, *op. cit.*, pp 456–7.

ministry holding the mystery of faith in a pure conscience (cf.
1 Tim. 3, 9), and that he may receive the same grace as St
Stephen. Again, at the end, we find the quotation from 1 Tim.
3, 13. In the second prayer there is a fresh allusion to St Stephen,
and God is asked to fill the elect with faith, charity, strength
and sanctity.[1]

Among the East Syrians the first prayer is, as we have seen,
very similar to that used for the bishop and the priest. In it the
Holy Spirit is asked to consecrate the elect so that he may exercise the ministry for which he is presented. Similarly the second
prayer, at the beginning, is analogous to that used at the consecration of bishops and the ordination of priests, with the following addition:

As thou didst choose Stephen and his companions, so now give to
thy servants the grace of the Holy Spirit, that they may be chosen
ministers in thy holy Church, and that they may serve at thy holy
altar with a pure heart and a good conscience, and that they may
shine with works of justice in serving thy divine and life-giving
mysteries.[2]

I myself feel that this very ancient rite originally had only
one formulary and that it was applied with some modifications
to each of the three orders respectively. We find also that, in this
rite, after each ordination the proclamation: 'N. is set apart,
sanctified, made perfect, consecrated to stand in the ministry
of . . .'[3] is made.

Any study of the rites of the patriarchate of Antioch must also
include the Jacobite and Maronite texts. I do not think in their
essential formulae they contain any new elements. The Maronite
ritual is much more developed and contains elements which are
absent from the other Syrian rites, but these do not belong to
the earliest texts. I think that an examination of the two rites
which have the best guarantee of antiquity, the Byzantine and
the Nestorian, will be sufficient to give us an idea of ordinations
in the patriarchate of Antioch.

1. cf. Goar, *op. cit.*, pp 208–9.
2. cf. Assemani, *op. cit.*, pp 22–3; Morinus, *op. cit.*, pp 449–50.
3. cf. Assemani, *op. cit.*, p. 25. The word used (*perasch*) is the equivalent of the Hebrew word from which Pharisee (separated) is derived.

There remain two rites of the patriarchate of Alexandria.

The earliest document is the *Sacramentary* of Serapion. I myself do not think that this collection, as such, goes back to the time of St Athanasius. It is accepted as the work of Serapion of Thmuis because there are two prayers bearing his name. But this seems to me to indicate that the rest is not his. It becomes increasingly clear that the anaphora attributed to him has been worked over. Serapion was thought to have adapted an earlier anaphora. It is much more likely that a later redactor has worked over Serapion's work, in the interests of a theology which is not that of the fourth century. Nevertheless, the collection is very ancient, and deserves to be placed side by side with the old Syrian rituals.

The prayer for the consecration of a bishop is as follows:

Thou who didst send the Lord Jesus Christ for the good of the whole world, who didst, through him, choose the apostles, and, from generation to generation ordain holy bishops; make of this man, O Lord, a zealous bishop (literally, 'living'), a holy bishop in the succession of the apostles, and give him the grace thou didst give to all thy true servants, prophets and patriarchs. Make him worthy to shepherd thy flock, and grant that he may persevere without reproach and offence in his episcopate.[1]

For the ordination of priests:

O Lord God of the heavens, Father of thine only-begotten Son, we stretch forth our hand upon this man, and pray that the Spirit of truth may come upon him. Give him prudence, knowledge, and a good heart. May he have the divine Spirit within him to rule thy people, to be a steward of thy divine oracles and to reconcile thy people to thee, O uncreated God. Thou who didst give of the spirit of Moses (Holy Spirit) to thine elect, give also a portion of the Spirit of thine only Son to this man, that he may have the grace of wisdom and a right faith, that he may serve thee with a pure conscience.[2]

Finally, for the deacon:

O Father of the Only-begotten, who didst send thine only Son,

1. cf. Funk, *op. cit.*, vol. II, pp 190–1. The absence of the article precludes the translation 'make of this living bishop a holy bishop'. 'Living' must therefore be given a derivative meaning, unless the text of the only manuscript is corrupt. But I cannot see any correction which is really probable.   2. cf. *ibid.*, pp 188–91.

and didst ordain institutions upon earth and give rules for thy Church, and didst appoint orders for the good and the salvation of the flock, and didst choose bishops, priests and deacons for the ministry of thy Catholic Church; ordain this man also a deacon in thy Catholic Church, and give to him the spirit of knowledge and discernment, that in the midst of the holy people he may serve this ministry in purity and without reproach.[1]

In spite of the reservations I have about attributing these formulae to Serapion, their simplicity is striking. If we except certain expressions derived from the particular theology of the redactor, it is probable that these prayers represent a very early usage in one of the Egyptian churches.

Apart from this euchology the rituals which we find in the patriarchate of Alexandria show no new elements. The sacramental formulae are borrowed substantially from St Hippolytus's Apostolic Tradition[2] and need not detain us. But it is important to remember that these formulae, which now have only documentary interest, for centuries formed part of a living liturgy. So they are not merely the expression of the personal opinions of St Hippolytus; they passed into the living tradition of the Church, and testified to the faith of one of its great patriarchates.

3. CONCLUSIONS

Can we draw any conclusions from such a limited inquiry? As I said at the beginning, we have no right to minimise the importance of the rites which were added in the course of the centuries. They also are the expression of the authentic mind of the Church, and they have legitimately made more explicit what was implicitly contained in the simpler rituals of antiquity. Nor do I deny the value of theological speculation, provided it rests on the authentic tradition of the Church. But I have no intention of extracting a whole theology of the sacrament of Orders from the texts I have quoted. My object is simpler and less ambitious. From a comparison of the documents belonging to different

1. cf. Funk, *op. cit.*, pp 188–9.
2. The Coptic rite of ordination can be found in H. Denzinger, *Ritus Orientalium*, Wurtzburg, 1864, vol. ii, pp 7–18, and Morinus, *op. cit.*, pp 505–8.

parts of the Church I should like to be able to state what fundamental convictions about Orders are found everywhere and the
Church recognised as her own from the earliest times. I do not
pretend to be putting forward anything new and I leave the
task of drawing more definite conclusions to theologians more
acute than myself. I will restrict myself to four points on which
the documents seem to be in particularly clear agreement.

1. Bishops, priests and deacons form the hierarchical structure of the Church, the body of Christ; and this hierarchy is
willed by God – its members are chosen by him. Whichever
method is used for the election of a particular person, it is the
divine grace which chooses him, and this choice operates in the
act of ordination itself through the agency of the members of
this hierarchy. I must insist on this point here, which I noted in
passing à propos St Hippolytus. At an episcopal consecration all
the bishops present lay on their hands. This is a universal tradition. The number three has never been any more than a minimum, and this direction was never the answer to scruples about
sacramental validity. Episcopal consecration is not a purely
personal act by which one individual communicates the powers
he possesses to another individual. It is the collective act of the
episcopal body incorporating the newly elect into the *ordo
episcoporum*. From that moment, he enters into this order, and
ensures, together with his colleagues, the stability and the growth
of the body of Christ which is the Church. The priest is no
more an isolated individual than the bishop: he is incorporated
into the *presbyterium* which assists the bishop in his ministry.
The deacon, for his part, is subject to the bishop. The bishop
with his priests and his deacons constitute the supporting framework of the local church, just as the order of bishops constitutes
the supporting framework of the universal Church. The members of this hierarchy are not delegates chosen by the community.
They hold their powers from God alone, who has chosen them
by his grace to ensure the life and growth of the Church.

2. The bishops are the successors of the apostles. This is
strongly asserted by all the rites. The gift of the Holy Spirit,
necessary for ruling the Church and continuing apostolic work,
is conveyed from age to age through the imposition of hands. It

is the bishops who are the *mediators of the divine gifts*, as the ritual of the East Syrian rite says. They are the true high priests of the new covenant as well as the successors of the apostles.

3. The priests are associated with the priesthood of the bishop, while the deacon is but a servant. How far, and with what limits? The liturgical texts do not say, and it would be fruitless to look for minute detail in them. Liturgical texts are neither canonical decisions nor theological dissertations, but prayers. However, what is clearly affirmed, and with particular insistence in the Roman rite, is the subordination of the priests to the bishop. They participate in his priesthood, but in a lower rank. They form a second order (*secundi meriti munus, secunda dignitas, sequens ordo*) whose activity is subordinated to that of the bishop (*cooperatores ordinis nostri*). We have seen that in the circumstances in which these formulae were composed, this insistence is the equivalent of an official declaration and of an argument from tradition.

4. Bishops, priests and deacons are not simply 'ministers of worship'. The additional rites have thrown the liturgical functions of the sacred Orders increasingly into prominence – the tradition of the instruments, the anointings, the vestings; all these ceremonies are more striking than the ancient prayers which form the essential element of the rite of ordination. The typology of the old testament has, especially in the Roman rite, influenced Christian thought in the same direction. However this ritual element has never been exclusive and we cannot fail to be struck by the fact that it has no place in the basic pattern of the vast majority of the early texts. The typology of the old testament is only an imperfect analogy, and has never been the means of an adequate definition of Christian priesthood. Alongside this typology there is always the affirmation that bishops are the successors of the apostles, and that they continue their apostolic work. Their essential mission is to *govern the Church and feed the flock*. They are not only high priests, but also – one might say supremely – pastors and doctors. Ordination is not simply the transmission of juridical and liturgical powers; it is a sacramental act which confers sanctifying grace. The members of the hierarchy are consecrated to

the service of God, they are *set apart*, as the East Syrian rite
says. The grace of the Holy Spirit must transform their soul;
it is to help them fulfil their mission by preaching as much by
example as by word. Sanctity – a sanctity which surpasses that
of the ordinary faithful – is imposed upon them through the
consciousness both of the grace they have received, and of the
responsibilities they have assumed at the call of God.

There is nothing about the bishops and priests of the Roman
sacerdos – officials of a public cult, who had simply to perform
certain ritual functions. Nor is there much more in them of the
old testament priest, for his charge of the temple was a
hereditary one, and his sanctity was above all of a *ritual* kind.
In spite of typology Christian priesthood is of a different order –
it is charismatic and spiritual. And when juridical and liturgical
prerogatives are involved they are the evidence of this fact, since
the *charisma* cannot be transmitted save by a liturgical action.
But to see this aspect only is to risk impoverishing the conception of Christian priesthood. In the early documents, episcopate,
priesthood and diaconate appear not so much ritual functions as
charismata designed to edify the Church. But – and it is important to note this – these *charismata* are not purely individual;
they assume the form of hierarchical orders, furnishing the
actual structure and ensuring its growth and the sanctification
of its members. Even before the juridical organisation of the
Church was complete, before the Council of Nicaea, bishops
had always been conscious of their solidarity, to which the
Apostolic Tradition of St Hippolytus had testified in the collective consecration of the newly elect. The priests are no more
isolated individuals than the bishop. They form a sacerdotal
body around the bishop, they participate with him and under
his direction, in the government of the people, and they concelebrate with him. The deacons, even outside their liturgical functions, are at the service of the bishop, and later of the priest.
The gift of the Spirit, which they have all received, makes them
fit subjects to continue, each in his own sphere, the work of the
apostles.

Perhaps these conclusions seem disappointing, lacking both
the detail of the canons and the definiteness of theological pro-

positions, and other articles will doubtless shed light on matters which are outside the scope of this one. But I can only present what I have discovered, namely that in the early documents holy Orders are regarded less from the angle of the detailed rights and duties of the ordinands than from the standpoint of the universal Church, a living body in which everyone has his rightful place. Without the gift of the Spirit, which Christ communicated to his apostles, and which is conveyed from age to age through the imposition of hands, there would be nothing but a miscellaneous collection of individuals in the Church; there would be no Church. That is the fundamental and supreme conviction expressed in the ancient liturgical texts, and which gripped the conscience of the Church at a very early date. Another conviction, of which the Church was no less strongly aware, is that the *full* effectiveness of sacred functions is conditional upon the sanctity of those who exercise them. The grace of the Holy Spirit had not been given to them merely to ensure the juridical or sacramental validity of certain actions, but also to enable them to acquire a sanctity which might serve as a pattern for the Christian people.

That history is all too full of betrayals of this ideal is a matter I cannot deal with here. One can no more deny the priestly ideals of the Church on the grounds that there may have been more bad, mediocre or perfunctory priests than holy priests, than one can deny the gospel ideal because it is scarcely practised by the majority of Christians. Consecrated, set apart, by virtue of the gift of the Spirit which has been given him, the priest can neither give up the mission which has been entrusted to him through the call of God, nor the ideals which the tradition of the Church puts before him. Whatever form his apostolate may take – and this can vary with times and circumstances – the priest must remain faithful to those ideals which represent not merely the mind of one epoch or of one land, but the tradition of the universal Church. *Quod ubique, quod semper.*

DISCUSSION

Fr Gy: I would like to ask Dom Botte – and Fr Lécuyer – a question. I have not really grasped what the exact significance of the imposition of the gospel originally was?

Dom Botte: I do not know whether this is correct or not, I am simply putting forward a hypothesis; but is there not a sort of power of the gospel which comes to fill the ordinand when the Holy Spirit is invoked upon him? But I have no proof of this.

Fr Lécuyer: I should like to refer to a text in Severian of Gabala, which is not sufficiently well known; it is one of the earliest texts on this subject and it does give one interpretation.

According to Severian, the imposition of the gospel on the head represents the same sign as the tongues of fire upon the heads of the apostles on the day of Pentecost. The explanation he gives is that it is like a tongue because the word of the gospel is a tongue, and it is a tongue 'of fire' because the Holy Spirit is the fire of love.

This is the most interesting text I have found on this point.

Dom Botte: I think it is much more significant than the comparison with a yoke. St John Chrysostom speaks of it as well. Sometimes he sees the gospel as a diadem, and at others he gives a different interpretation, and so we realise that the exact sense had by then been lost, and we have to look to the rite itself. That does happen from time to time.

Dom Capelle: This passage in Severian of Gabala is an explanation of the idea of the yoke.

Fr Lécuyer: This is the actual text:

'Since the descent of the Holy Spirit is invisible, the book of the gospel is laid on the head of him who is to be ordained high priest, and in this book thus imposed we must see none other than a tongue of fire. A tongue, because of the preaching (of the gospel), and a tongue of fire because it is written: "I am come to bring fire upon the earth".'

But it is a very difficult text to find. It is a fragment of a commentary by Severian of Gabala on the Acts of the Apostles, or rather, a homily on the Acts. I have written an article on this subject in *Ephemerides liturgicae.*

Fr Gy: The medievals changed the symbolism of the imposition of the gospel. They saw in it a symbol of the evangelical responsibility of preaching which was laid on the bishop.

Dom Botte: The symbolism was given by Amalarius. That influenced the pontifical. But I believe that the saints on Eastern ikons always have the gospel on their heads, as in the *Statuta Ecclesiae Antiqua.*

Fr Louvel: But is the gospel also lowered from the head on to the shoulders in the Eastern rites?

Dom Botte: No, I don't think so. It is kept on the head.

M. Chavasse: You said that Orders confer a *charisma* which is a gift of personal, and not merely of functional, sanctity. I would like to ask, if it is not impertinent, if this is not a modern reaction to the early texts, in which, fundamentally, the distinction between interior disposition and ritual and canonical commitments does not exist.

Is it not because we are so accustomed to 'interiorise' grace purely and simply, that we confer a kind of 'exteriority' on ritual and liturgical functions? As a matter of fact, did not the ancients regard the *charisma* as being inseparably bound both to the institution and to the disposition of the soul? Is not this 'exteriorisation' of functions a modern distortion?

Dom Botte: Yes, obviously.

M. Chavasse: Basically, in Orders, grace is not the grace of personal sanctification in the sense in which we speak of saving grace. It is a grace of personal sanctification channelled and directed by the function. Consequently, it is the function which reacts on the particular style of one's Christian life, and gives it a different nuance, but it is not a grace given purely and simply for personal sanctification.

This is very important in view of its theological consequences.

Dom Botte: I must leave the theologians to attend to the necessary detail – I do not feel that I am altogether qualified to deal with this point.

M. Martimort: I would like to raise a point about the typology of the old testament; I was rather worried by something Dom Botte said about it.

I see no difficulty in the ritual of the ordination of priests, which speaks of the elders who received the spirit of Moses, but I find the repeated allusions to Aaron, and, in respect of priests, to the sons of Aaron, somewhat disturbing.

You gave us to understand that this typology was an accretion, and that we need not pay too much attention to it. But I am a little disturbed to see it crop up so frequently. What do you think about it?

Dom Botte: It is especially in the Roman rite in the consecration of a bishop that the typology of Aaron is developed. And there, almost only in the great preface.

In the other rites it seems to be much less developed. If we take the Byzantine or Syrian rites, the typology of the old testament has remained in what appears to me to be a relatively modest place. There is much more insistence on the apostolic character of the mission.

This typology is perfectly legitimate, but it is not the only thing we have to consider. That is all I wanted to stress. It is the image particularly that remains – so that from spiritual unction we progress to material unction. In certain sacramentaries during the preface, when anointing is mentioned, *fluore sanctifica* – it is not exactly a dew – the sign of the Cross was made to indicate that an anointing was taking place. So it is the spiritual symbolism which has been materialised.

Fr Gy: The typology of Moses and the seventy elders which appears to be more constant than that of Aaron draws us towards a 'non-ritual' sense, since the elders are not priests.

Dom Botte: I think there is often too much stress laid on this aspect in the presentation of the subject, and people remember images rather than their application.

M. Martimort: In the prayer for the consecration of a bishop in Hippolytus, Moses is not named, but it seems to me that he is present all the time in the thoughts of the one who is offering the prayer, since the subject of 'intercession' looms large, and he actually makes use of the same formula employed by the Septuagint to describe the steps taken by Moses after the episode of the golden calf. So the thought of Moses is always present although he is not mentioned by name.

It seems to me to be very important all the same, for the characters of Moses and Aaron are very different, and consequently the picture that is given us of the bishop will be very different. If we start with the figure of Aaron, his function will be especially of a ritual character, and the Middle Ages did not restrain the attempt to clothe the high priest in old testament vestments. If we start with the figure of Moses, then we have a picture of a leader of the people much more than of a ritual function.

That is why these questions of typology seem to me to be of considerable importance for the picture of Orders that will be formed in our minds.

Fr Lécuyer: Could not the allusion to Moses and the seventy presbyters at the consecration of priests in Hippolytus signify – at least as its simple and original meaning – that it is the same spirit that is being given? . . .

Dom Botte: Yes.

Fr Lécuyer: . . . without directly asserting the appropriate character of either Moses or Aaron.

On the other hand – and this is certainly true, as you stressed just now – it is in the bishop that the powers attributed to Moses have been concentrated. In him is found both the priest and the leader of the people, for he is a priest, and it is he who confers the priesthood.

It is on these lines, I think, that an answer can perhaps be found to your question.

M. Girault: Is there in the ordination prayers, or in any of the rituals, an explicit allusion to the bishop's function of proclaiming the gospel to the heathen?

Dom Botte: They do not say anything about the pagans, but they do speak of preaching the gospel, which is evangelisation.

Fr Roguet: They also speak of 'increasing the flock'.

Dom Botte: The preaching of the gospel is not done only at Sunday Mass. And a distinction is made between the preaching of the gospel and the sacred ministry of the word, which represents the ministry of preaching itself.

M. Martimort: But in Hippolytus there is also the idea of the building up of the Church, of which the ancient temple was only the figure.

M. Le Sourd: You also quoted a text in which there is a reference to the mission of the Son as being for the good of the whole world.

Dom Botte: Yes, it is in Serapion.

Dom Rousseau: I was struck when I read this sentence in the excellent little commentary by M. Cazelles on Leviticus: 'The glory of Yahweh is that all-powerful and transcendent presence which the clergy are now responsible for giving to the people'.

This seemed to me to be very suggestive. It is a fact that for people even today, the priest possesses this power. It is not magic, as was the case in the pagan religions. In the Jewish religion there is the power of Yahweh, but even there, there is this element as well. In the Christian religion, it is the power of Christ which is contained in the Church (the power to remit sins, etc.).

I have been thinking about this while you have been speaking about the difference between the exercise of power and sacred character. For Christian people generally, the priest is valued especially because he is qualified to do things which are beyond the power of men, because he possesses the power of Christ. The other, less 'sympathetic', mark is that he keeps the Church going, and tends to be the dictator. This dominates the sacerdotal world very strongly, almost too strongly, to the detriment of the first mark.

M. Chavasse: I would like to ask a question. We were asking just now if Christian priesthood was to be related to Moses or Aaron.

Has not the kind of choice which the liturgical texts have made come about precisely because the sense of the priesthood of kingship had been lost in ancient Judaism? For, in the old testament, there is something still more important – the person of the king. The king, by possessing the royal character, is a 'type' of the messianic king. He destroys the temple. He builds it again. His office is above that of the high priest.

Dom Botte: Yes, but in Jewish tradition Moses has become a king.

There are two passages, one in the *Vita Moysi* of Philo, the other in his *De Praemiis*, in which the idea that Moses was king, lawgiver, high priest and prophet is developed.

M. Chavasse: At heart, is it not the explanation of something which is a fundamental doctrine? We get the impression that the king is the 'source' of his people, that all the people spring out of him from God, and when Christ appears he takes his functions.

M. Gelin: I would say that Moses has been prophetically 're-thought' as a 'super-prophet', if you like, and I think that the thought of the prophet as well as the mediator is not absent in the epistle to the Hebrews. Christ does not enter into a purely sacerdotal setting, in a liturgical sense. The epistle to the Hebrews is evidence of this. In this epistle, reference is made to the levite, certainly, but also to the king-priest and to the prophet as mediator.

CHAPTER II

THE PRIESTHOOD OF CHRIST IN THE EPISTLE TO THE HEBREWS

A. GELIN, P.S.S.

'Now of the things which we have spoken this is the sum: We have such a high priest, who is set on the right hand of the throne of majesty in the heavens; A minister of the holies, and of the true tabernacle, which the Lord hath pitched, and not man.' (Heb. **8**, 1–2).

This assertion was launched into an environment prepared to receive it.

From the time of Ezechiel, the promoter of priestly theocracy, the advancement of the priesthood was a fact, manifestly redolent of messianism.[1] Indeed, the post-exilic fragment Jer. **33**, 14–22 had combined the future glory of the Davidic and Levitical lines; Ben Sira is the echo of a school which depressed the first to exalt the second, notably in the quasi-polemical passage Ecclus. **44**, 24–6 (cf. **49**, 4), and although his Alexandrian translator moderated his grandfather's zealous enthusiasm[2] he did not fail in **36**, 19 to make God's blessing upon his people be conveyed by Aaron. These clerical preferences are displayed in the complex literature which is increasingly being ascribed to the Essene movement. The 'Testament of the Twelve Patriarchs' proclaims the primacy of Levi over Juda; and the latter

1. The classical proof of this is to be found in Za. **6**, 9–14, where the name of the high priest Joshua has been substituted for that of Zorobabel. The events of history having brought the advancement of the priesthood to Jerusalem, the scribe would harmonise prophecy with history.

2. In Ecclus. **50**, 24, where Ben Sira had written: 'May the grace of God remain faithfully with Simon; may the covenant of Phineas be effectual in him, may it not be taken away from him nor his posterity so long as the heavens endure.'

himself says: 'To me God gave the kingdom, and to Levi the priesthood, and he has subjected the kingdom to the priesthood. To me he gave the things of this earth, but to him the things of heaven.' (T. Juda, 21, 2–4). The doctrine of the two Messias, the Aaronic Messias and the King Messias, projected this dissonance into the future, while harmonising it in this way; we find this expectation in the testaments,[1] in the Damascus document[2] and in the 'Manual of Discipline' which speaks expressly of the coming of the two Messias of Aaron and of Israel.[3] The Qumran sect, where this teaching was handed down, made use of the name of Sadoc, who was priest at the time of David and Solomon (2 Kings 8, 17; 3 Kings 1, 38). The sect was clerical in structure; numerous reforming priests who had broken with the official priesthood at Jerusalem claimed to preserve the flame of true priesthood, which would one day emerge from the shadows. Priestly messianism formed part of their faith, and it is certainly possible that a good number of them were converted to Christianity.

The first Christians were quick to explain the fact of Christ in terms of sacrifice, priesthood and cult.[4] The supper recalled the sacrifice of the covenant (Mk 14, 24; cf. Ex. 24, 8); the Cross, that of propitiation (Rom. 3, 25). The Johannine catechesis, which seems to have influenced the writer of the epistle

1. See R. Eppel, *Le piétisme juif dans les Testaments des Douze patriarches*, 1930, pp 44–52. The texts have been collected by G. B. Bensley-Murray, 'The Two Messiahs in the Testaments of the Twelve Patriarchs' in the *Journal of Theological Studies*, XLVIII, 1947, pp 1–11. See also A. J. B. Higgins, 'Priest and Messiah' in *Vet. Testament*, 1953, pp 321–36.

2. The formula 'the Messias of Aaron and of Israel' occurs in 12, 23 and 14, 19. This is the work of a later copyist who made an orthodox correction. See *Rev. biblique*, 1953, p. 291.

3. IX, 11. For the whole of the messianic thought of Qumran, see J. T. Milik, *Rev. biblique*, 1953, pp 290–1. On priesthood in the documents of Kh. Qumran, see M. Delcor, *Rev. de l'histoire des religions*, CXLIV, 1953, pp 5–14.

4. If the theory defended by Mlle Jaubert (in *Rev. de l'histoire des religions*, 1954, pp 140–73) is correct, the decision of Jesus to celebrate the paschal meal on Holy Thursday, following an ancient calendar which did not correspond with that of official Judaism, could mean that he was making a sacerdotal claim.

to the Hebrews, contains a certain number of significant suggestions. In John 2, 19 the destruction of the temple is related to
the death of Christ (see Heb. 9, 23); in the sacerdotal prayer the
term ἁγιάζω is applied to the sacrifice of Christ (John 17, 19;
see Heb. 2, 11; 10, 10); in John 19, 23 the robe of Jesus is the
same as that of the high priest.[1] The outline of a sacerdotal
theology of Christ is there – the value of the epistle is that it
carries it to perfection.

Our purpose here is not to reconstruct the processes leading
to the formation of the writer's thought. This has recently been
done in a masterly fashion by Fr Spicq, who, favouring the
authorship of Apollos (Acts 18, 24–6), has stressed his Alexandrian affinities. Philo drew his attention to the mediator of the
old covenant, Moses, who is presumed to possess the priesthood, and this portrait provides Apollos with a pattern for
tracing its antithesis in Christ.[2]

Apollos's method is essentially scriptural. He refers continually to the words of the old testament, deemed to be uttered
by God (1,1,5,6,13; 5,5), Christ (2, 12–13; 10, 5), or the
Holy Spirit (3, 7; 10, 15), and quoted from the Septuagint. The
Greek bible is his inspired text. He writes with this bible open
before him, 'and everything it contains is there, under his very
eyes, alive and present' (Goguel)[3], especially the institutions and
the cultus of the wilderness, as they are described in the pages
of Exodus and Leviticus. It has been observed that the interest
of the Alexandrian writers readily centred around the memories
of the Exodus; it is so in the case of the author of 'Wisdom', of

1. C. Spicq, *L'Epître aux Hébreux*, 1 (1952), p. 134. The author
observes that the epistle to the Hebrews in turn must have influenced the Johannine catechesis. The heavenly temple described in
the Apocalypse could have been inspired by the epistle.

2. *op. cit.*, pp 66–72. Perhaps it should be noted that Alexandria was
a centre where Essenian thought, such as we have described, had been
translated and disseminated. A. M. Dubarle has recently shown this in
considering the Instruction on the two minds (*Manual of Discipline* III,
13 – IV) as one of the sources of Wisdom – 'Une source du Livre de
la Sagesse' in *Revue des sc. philos. et théolog.* 1953, pp 425–43.

3. According to Windisch 'a mark of the exegesis of the normal text
is that it takes place in the present' (Quoted in Spicq, *op. cit.*, i, p. 256).

Philo, and of the tragic Ezechiel writing his Exagoge.[1] The sacred text is full of suggestive starting points which are exploited by him. Furthermore, by the disposition of God, the persons and events of the ancient economy prefigure those of the new; God has marked out the road of salvation so that both its continuity and its discontinuity are felt. Throughout the whole epistle, a typology, with some notes of allegory, is used.

But some new lines of thought are introduced which reveal the Alexandrian mentality. The traditional eschatological formulae are reinterpreted: 'for here we have no permanent city, but we seek one to come' (**13**, 14); the formula must not be understood in its temporal aspect (future), but in its qualitative aspect (heavenly). It is not the present which is opposed to the future, but the earth, whose 'character' is that of a shadow (σκία), which is opposed to the heavens. Eschatology has become transcendental, as in Wisdom.[2] The centre of gravity in Pauline doctrine, which was Jesus crucified and risen, here becomes Jesus ascended into heaven and sitting at the right hand of Majesty,[3] as πρόδρομος (**6**, 20) of the caravan of those marching by the light of the star, and λειτουργὸς (**8**, 2) of the people of God.

For it is in the setting of a heavenly liturgy that the triumphal ἔχομεν ἀρχιέρεα (**4**, 14, 15; **8**, 1), the major theme of this epistle, must be understood.[4] Two priestly institutions evidenced by the old testament serve as the starting points for his reflections – the levitical priesthood and the royal priesthood.

---

1. Lagrange, *Le Judaisme avant Jesus-Christ*, 1931, p. 516. It may well be asked if there is a single allusion – at least, direct – to the temple at Jerusalem in the whole epistle, and if Spicq's hypothesis that the people to whom the epistle was written were convert Jewish priests cut off from their temple and regretting the loss of its liturgy – is not superfluous. (*op. cit.* 1, p. 229.)

2. J. Cambier, *Eschatologie ou hellénisme dans l'epître aux Hébreux: une étude sur* μένειν *et l'exhortation finale de l'epître*, Desclée de Brouwer, 1949.

3. Note the similarity in point of view with the epistle to the Ephesians.

4. Compare the tone of the 'Invenimus Messiam' in John **1**, 41.

I. THE LEVITICAL PRIESTHOOD

As the epistle says (7, 11), the theocracy was built upon this. The structure and activities of this priesthood are described in detail in the Priestly Code (P.) and in the work of the Chronicler. After the exile the hierarchy is divided into clearly defined ranks comprising the high priest, the Aaronite priests – sixteen orders of these are traced back to Eleazar, Aaron's elder son, and eight to Ithamar, his younger son – then the levites, who were responsible for all tasks on the circumference of the sacred actions, such as guards, choir, preparation of the sacrifices. This section of the clergy derived from an eponymous ancestor, Levi, the son of Jacob.

In fact, this clear systematisation is the outcome of a complex history[1] which can only be briefly summarised here.

In the oldest document which refers to them (Deut. 33, 8–11) the levites appear to be connected with the covenant; the casting of lots as means of enquiring of God, the approach to God through sacrifice, teaching to sustain fidelity – these are the priestly privileges these professionals were acknowledged to possess. Did they form a tribe or a corporation? Their privileges were not enjoyed without opposition (5, 11), but the old narrative Judges 17–18 proves that they were sought out as sanctuary priests because of their descent from Moses (Judges 18, 30). Judges 17, 7 and Deuteronomy show them as having gone back into the villages. This last book contains a programme of reform; it wishes to see the dispersed levites admitted to the temple at Jerusalem, and thus to suppress the country sanctuaries where they performed their functions. The Deuteronomic programme was not accepted as normal as a result of the efforts either of Ezechias in the eighth century or of Josias in the seventh. The high places, sanctuaries which were insufficiently 'Yahvised', resisted all reform. In the eyes of Ezechiel they were the major

---

1. There is a considerable bibliography. The essential works are listed in Spicq, *op. cit.*, ii, pp 137–9. 'Levitique (organisation)', by A. Lefèvre in *Supplem. au Dict. de la Bible* vol. v, c. 389–97 should be added.

prevarication, and their priests – the levites – are, in the provisions of the Torah which he worked out in exile (Ez. 44, 10–14), peremptorily degraded. The levitical family of Sadoc alone, which had served the national temple faithfully since the time of David, would keep their sacerdotal privileges (Ez. 44, 15–16).[1]

Mingling as they did with all the people, the levites shaped the character of pre-exilic society. Custodians of the rites and the sacred legends, teachers of the law and doctrine, they renewed in the villages the presence of the God of the covenant through liturgies which have now been lost.

Following the exile and the return, interest was centred on the one lawful temple; indeed, post-exilic Israel was simply a religious community grouped around a Holy City. According to the principles of the Priestly Code (P.) and of the Chronicler, lawful priests were descended from Aaron. The latter's prerogatives were only slowly recognised, and it can be established that this idea spread between the period of Esdras (fifth century) and that of the Chronicler (fourth century). Genealogies, which are not biological studies but explanations of a theological and legal system, made Aaron the 'rallying point' of the Jerusalem priesthood.[2] All the other descendants of Levi are considered to have performed only subordinate functions from the very beginning.

There was a hierarchy at the temple in Jerusalem, as at Ras Shamra before the exile (4 Kings 25, 18). But the majestic figure of the high priest, who was consecrated with holy oil (Ex. 29, 7; Za. 4, 14), who bore the symbolism of the twelve tribes on his vestments (Ex. 28, 9–12), and officiated on the Day of Atonement to restore his people to covenant relationship (Lev. 16; Ecclus 50; 'Kippur' first mentioned in Za. 3, 9), is one of the splendours of post-exilic times. His line of succession from Aaron passing through Sadoc is uninterrupted.[3] We are aware

1. Birth was not the only way of entering the levitical order; it could be achieved by means of a vow (cf. Samuel) or a legal contract. This was perhaps the case with Sadoc, though 'there is no documentary evidence to prove it' (A. Lefèvre, art. cit., c. 396).
2. A. Lefèvre, art. cit., c. 396–7. This priesthood was not comprised only of Sadokite elements.
3. Th. Chary. O.F.M., Le culte chez les prophètes à partir de l'Exil, Tournai 1955, makes a detailed study of the links in this chain.

that this sequence was broken by the religious policy of Antiochus, who removed Onias II in 175 B.C. From that moment the story of the sovereign pontificate becomes very complicated. From 172–162 Menelaus, who was not even of priestly family, held the office. Between 160 and 153 there were no high priests. Then the Hasmoneans, who were not Sadokites, assumed the office from 153 to 37. In the eyes of the traditionalists this was a deviation on the part of the Maccabean movement which would be the source of deep resentment by the Qumran sectaries.[1] From 37 B.C. to A.D. 70 there were actually twenty-eight high priests, of whom twenty-five were of priestly families with no right to the office.

This succession perhaps helps us to understand the πλείονες of Hebrews 7, 23.

2. THE ROYAL PRIESTHOOD

Priesthood has not always been left to professionals. It falls naturally on the father of the family, or the patriarch; that is to say on the born representatives of the group, which possesses its *baraka* and its stability from them. The old expression 'father and priest' (Judges 17, 10; 18, 19) has its origin in this. We see that Job offers sacrifices (Job 1, 5; 42, 8 ff), and also Gedeon of Manasse (Judges 6, 26–7), Manoah of Dan (Judges 13, 19) and Mika of Ephraim (Judges 17, 5). Perhaps the immolation of the paschal lamb by the head of the family (Ex. 12, 6 ff (P.)) is a survival of this state of affairs which had atrophied in this way – *nasik*, for example, signifies both a chief and a pourer of libations.

Royal priesthood is the normal extension of this natural priesthood. The institution existed e.g., in Assyro-Babylonia,[2] where the king was the true priest. But he was assisted by a professional clergy who guided him through the labyrinth of the rites. Within the pages of the bible itself we find Melchisedech, the king-

---

1. G. Vermès, *Les manuscripts du Desert de Juda*, 1953, p. 93 ff.
2. The indispensable work is R. Labat's *Le caractère religieux de la royauté assyro-babylonienne*, 1939. See also Dhorme, *La religion assyro-babylonienne*, 1910, pp 146–50.

priest of Salem;[1] he pronounced a blessing on Abraham who had asked for protected status from him, and this benediction followed a covenant rite over a meal (Gen. **14**, 18–20). Melchisedech, the priest of El Elyon the Most High God, appears as a custodian of the monotheistic idea outside Israel. In Israel likewise there is clear evidence of the royal priesthood; David is the first king of Israel to exercise the priesthood with splendour, and he does so for the first time when the ark is translated to Zion, with the whole nation around him, in primitive priestly vestments (2 Kings **6**, 14; **16**, 20; cf. 1 Kings **2**, 18 and Ex. **20**, 26). He offers sacrifices (2 Kings **6**, 13, 17) and blesses the people (*ibid.* **6**, 18), though this was the prerogative of the priest (Num. **6**, 22–7; Lev. **9**, 22–3). His sons are priests (2 Kings **8**, 18), Solomon in turn offers sacrifices (3 Kings **3**, 4, 15), blesses the people (**8**, 14–15, 55) and prays for them (**8**, 30 ff); he appoints and removes priests (**2**, 26–7, 35) who are his officials (**4**, 2–4).[2] Similar traits are evident again in Jeroboam I (3 Kings **12**, 33) and Achaz (4 Kings **16**, 12ff), and Ezechiel's polemic against encroachments upon the cultus by future princes (Ez. **46**) is closely bound up with his knowledge of past history.

We can now consider the portrait of Christ the High Priest bearing in mind these typological components.

It was first necessary to establish the parallelism between Melchisedech and Jesus. A leading text serves as the basis, and chapter **7** is simply an exegesis of Psalm **109**, 4, in which the Messias is proclaimed a priest for ever according to the order of Melchisedech.[3]

This emphasis enables the writer to assert:

(*a*) the messianic character of the priesthood of Jesus, or, if preferred, to integrate the sacerdotal note into his royal messianism. Now the kingship of Christ, according to Hebrews, is

---

1. Salem is used in Gen. **14**, 18, and in Psalm **76**, 2, instead of Jerusalem to 'eliminate an offensive concept'. Jerusalem means in fact Foundation of (the god) Salem (L. N. Vincent, 'Abraham à Jérusalem' in *Rev. biblique*, 1951, p. 364).

2. E. Podechard, *Le Psautier, II. Psaumes 76–100*, Lyon 1954, p. 174.

3. The author is engrossed with Psalm **109**: (see **1**, 3, 13; **5**, 6, 10; **6**, 20). It has been observed that the Hasmonaeans took the title of 'High Priests of the Most High God' (Josephus, *Antiquities* xvi, vi, 2), thus laying claim to Melchisedech (M. Delcor, *art. cit.*, pp 13–14).

eschatological just as his priesthood is heavenly. The two dignities go together and must be asserted simultaneously. It is noteworthy that on several occasions our Lord made use of Psalm 109, especially in a discussion with the Pharisees (Matt. 22, 41–6) and in his most solemn declaration before Caiaphas (Mk 14, 62), to suggest the transcendental character of his messianism. Hebrews simply lights up his thought and frames it more explicitly.

(b) the fully human character of the priesthood of Jesus. There had been a prototype and a pattern 'on the fringe of the official institutions of the religion of Israel, and before they had finally taken shape'.[1] The order of Melchisedech implies universalism: 'the narrow confines of Judaism are broken down'.[2] In the old testament God calls Nebuchadnosor his servant (Jer. 25, 9), and Cyrus his anointed (Is 45, 1). Job, his servant, is not an Israelite (Job 1, 8). Melchisedech represents an authentic religious value outside Israel; he was taken into the history of salvation and was to enjoy an extraordinary position in it.

(c) the transcendent character of the priesthood of Jesus. A most careful exegesis of what Genesis 14 actually says, and does not say, would fall a long way short of proving that the King-Priest of Salem was 'likened unto the Son of God' (7, 3). But there is an intense faith at the heart of this exegesis. Just as Paul had magnified the first Adam to accommodate his theology of the Second Adam (Rom. 5, 14), so Apollos urges the similarity between Melchisedech and Jesus to the extent of telescoping them. He knew full well that Christ alone could bring priesthood to its perfection (τελείωσις) because of his dignity as the Son of God, but, not being a Greek – if he had been, he would have described such a priesthood in an abstract way, in its own terms – but a biblical writer, he searched the scriptures and discerned there a living reference to Christ radiant with his glory.

Secondly the sacerdotal office, down to its last detail, had

1. M. Simon, *Verus Israel*, 1948, p. 110.
2. Spicq, *op. cit.*, 11, p. 211. St Paul uses the same method in tracing messianism back to Adam by the theologoumenon of the New Adam (cf. 1 Cor. 15; Rom. 5).

been committed to priests of the levitical order and Hebrews first establishes its abolition (ἀθέτησις) and the revelation of a new dimension of priesthood and then, paradoxically, it shows Christ effectively taking up the work in which the old priesthood failed.

(a) Levitical priesthood must give way to a higher priesthood. Levi was still in the loins of his great-grandfather Abraham when he bowed before Melchisedech, and this act of humility bound his descendants (7, 4–10). Coming after the priesthood of Melchisedech, levitical priesthood is based on the principle of heredity (7, 16), while the new priesthood rests on a divine oath – the declaration in Psalm 109 (7, 20–1); to the multiplicity and the succession of levitical priests is opposed, in 'Jesus-Melchisedech' the fact of a unique, sufficient and intransmissible priesthood, which is eternal.

The old priesthood had been powerless to set men free from sin. It was itself entangled in sin (7, 28). In its worship it merely effected an annual remembrance of guilt (10, 3) but it did not succeed in triumphantly effacing all secret traces of it from the conscience (9, 9; 10, 2). These repetitions of the same rites of purification, these continual efforts to restore the covenant relationship, these attempts at propitiation which form the substance of the post-exilic liturgy, this red symphony of the hecatombs, these long lamentations over the past (Neh. 9; Dan. 9), and, finally, this dream of the Messianic spring which will cleanse the soul (Za. 13, 1) and of the conclusive abolition of sin (Dan. 9, 24); all this spiritual effort, all these deep aspirations of the ancient economy pass before our eyes in that rapid and disillusioning review in Hebrews. The old priesthood can never come to the end of its struggle with sin (5, 1). It belongs to the order of purely human things, the order of the σκία the σαρξ and the τύπος; it cannot get to grips with the root of evil (7, 16; 9, 13; 10, 11).

(b) However, it is through levitical institutions – and by contrast with them – that Hebrews goes on to describe the work of Christ. The climax of the ancient liturgy was the autumn feast of the Atonement (Kippur), through which the people of Israel, considered *per modum unius*, was restored to covenant relationship. The writer refers to the pattern of Kippur[1] with evident relish.

This feast contained the following elements: the slaying of a bull, which served as the propitiatory victim for the high priest and his household; the slaying of a he-goat, which fulfilled the same purpose for Israel (Lev. 16, 6, 15), and the entry of the high priest into the holy of holies (Lev. 16, 14–15); there he sprinkled the mercy seat above the Ark with the blood of the two victims, thus making atonement for his own sins and for those of the people; after the exile 'the sprinkling of blood was made on a stone which had replaced the Ark' (Lesêtre); the purification of the holy place by the blood of the two victims (Lev. 16, 17–19); the sending of the scapegoat away into the wilderness (Lev. 16, 20–2); and finally, outside the camp, the destruction of the two propitiatory victims (Lev. 16, 27–8).

So, as the high priest entered once a year into the holiest part of the temple to anoint with strange blood[2] the place of divine pardon and seat of the Shekinah, so Christ entered once for all (ἐφάπαξ) into heaven to offer his blood there (9, 12), to offer himself there (9, 25), so that, as Priest and Victim he rendered the atoning power of his death fruitful and is now endlessly presenting an acceptable offering to God.

The focal point of the epistle is certainly the entry of Jesus into heaven.[3] It is at this moment that the priesthood which was

1. He also refers to the sacrifice which inaugurated the covenant (Ex. 24, 1–11; Heb. 9, 15–22). But this is in connection with the new covenant proclaimed by Jeremias. And he does not make so much use of this reference – perhaps because the idea of sin was not thrown into prominence in Ex. 24, 1–11, where God was concerned with forming his people and not with their redemption. However, the idea of the new covenant fits in very well with the writer's preoccupation with sin, and thus ties up with the thought of Kippur.

2. Blood had been used by Yahwism and so became a kind of universal sacrament. Hence its place in rites of covenant, protection, expiation, purification and consecration (Ex. 29, 20). With Christ, blood has become a divinised reality: *glorioso sanguine redemisti*. In addition, we should note that under the old covenant, it is not the immolation of the victim, but the offering of the blood which constitutes the sacrifice.

3. The pattern of Kippur is employed in detail. There is the allusion to the offering of the blood (9, 12), to the purification of heaven – which corresponds to the holy place (9, 23), and even to the consuming

imparted to him at the incarnation (*sacerdotium nativum*) was ratified (*ratum*).[1]

The writer has now only to indicate in terms of the cult – which we must be careful not to take too literally, but must always spiritualise – the salutary effects of our Kippur; inner purification ($\mathbf{1}$, 3; $\mathbf{9}$, 14; καθαρίζω); pardon (ἄφεσις $\mathbf{10}$, 18) or redemption (λύτρωσις $\mathbf{9}$, 12) from sins; sanctification, that is to say consecration to God through sacrifice ($\mathbf{10}$, 10, 29; ἁγιάζω); perfection ($\mathbf{10}$, 1, 14; τελείωσις). All these things designed for our eternal salvation have been won in principle ($\mathbf{5}$, 9).

In the portrait of our priest, however, there are some touches which do not fall directly into the typology we have examined so far, but relate rather to the experience of the prophets.[2]

Prophecy is the revelation to us of a new style of mediation. And men do exist who are by vocation responsible for their brethren. They do not always feel born to this charge, and bit by bit they discover its real burden. In the case of Jeremias or Ezechiel, loving one's brethren consists in doing everything possible to put them in touch with the divine message; in being, at heart, constantly preoccupied with their sins and in making intercession for them (Jer. $\mathbf{15}$, 11); in feeling that God will ask him to render an account for the blood of each one of them (Ez. $\mathbf{3}$, 20; $\mathbf{33}$, 8); in facing loathing and discouragement, for suffering is the price of so great a spiritual dignity. It is through his failures that he measures the extent to which this vocation effects his solidarity with others and yet keeps him a solitary amongst them; that he realises that friendship with God, who separates him from sinners, is the ultimate source of the things that happen to him:

Thy words were found, and I did eat them: and thy word was

---

of the victim outside the camp ($\mathbf{13}$, 11–12). The text 9, 23 is difficult to explain. Perhaps it can be related to the belief that certain evil powers have their dwelling-place in heaven (J. Hering). Finally, we note that Hebrews has no reference to the scapegoat, a delicate touch which an allegorist such as pseudo-Barnabas does not possess. (vii, 6 ff).

1. Traditional texts in M. de la Taille, *Mysterium Fidei*, 3rd ed. 1931, p. 136 ff.

2. Spicq, *op. cit.*, 1, pp 288, 297, has noticed these affinities without making use of them.

to me a joy and gladness of my heart, for thy name is called upon me, O Lord God of hosts.

I sat not in the assembly of jesters, nor did I make a boast of the presence of thy hand:

Why is my sorrow become perpetual? . . . It is become to me as the falsehood of deceitful waters that cannot be trusted.

Therefore thus saith the Lord: If thou wilt be converted, I will convert thee, and thou shalt stand before my face. . . . They shall be turned to thee . . .

In the scattered community of the exile, the prophets were the rallying points; they provided a new structure for the people of God at the very time when the earlier institutions had, for all practical purposes, been wiped out, with the king a captive and the priest redundant.

In this soil the messianic hope which found expression in the songs of the servant of the Lord[1] sprang up. This figure is the eschatological projection of an ideal which had been embodied in Jeremias and Ezechiel.[2] His ministry, like theirs, would be one of intercession (Is 53, 12); he would be doomed to denial, and yet devoted to the service of the divine word even to martyrdom (Jer. 26); but while Ezechiel bore the sins of his people merely symbolically (Ez. 4, 4–8), the servant bears their wounds in his flesh (Is 53, 5), and makes atonement for them. Faithfully he makes the offering of his life in expiation (Is 53, 10). This propitiatory sacrifice ('asham), which fulfils the purpose of God, is a ritual commentary on the martyrdom of the servant. This was the line taken by primitive Christianity – and by Christ himself – when confronted by the fact of the passion. The analogy is very close, and in both cases we are reminded of the imagery of Kippur.

Hebrews 9, 28 quotes a phrase from Is 53, 12. This is enough to show that the writer has looked in the direction I have intimated. Indeed we get the very same impression when we see Hebrews stress the part played by suffering in leading our priest to the ὑπακοή ('anawah), i.e. the heroism of submission

---

1. Is 42, 1–4; 49, 1–6; 50, 4–9; 52, 13–53, 12.
2. In the picture of the Servant there are also some traits borrowed from Moses. But it must not be forgotten that he had become a prophet, and even the prototype of the prophets, in tradition.

and sympathy,[1] and also the innocence which equips him for his mission (7, 26), and the fraternal character of that mission (2, 7).

Perhaps I may stress these two points:

(a) The priesthood of Christ is not presented as a purely 'ritual' thing; it possesses royal and prophetic aspects as well. The attentive reader cannot fail to be moved by the touching undertones of the latter. It must also be remembered that the cult can only use words to describe the mission of redemption. The priesthood of Christ is not shut up inside the temple; it is 'according to the order of Melchisedech'.

(b) The question of our own priesthood does not arise in Hebrews, nor does the eucharist.[2] It can only be with the greatest caution that any conclusions can be drawn about priestly spirituality from this epistle.

1. See my *Pauvres de Yahve*, 1954, p. 63.
2. Recent commentators agree in seeing an implicit reference to the eucharist in 13, 10, but it remains outside the scope of the epistle.

DISCUSSION

M. Chavasse: I would like to ask M. Gelin why, in speaking about the epistle to the Hebrews, he seemed to lay so much stress particularly on its prophetic aspect, and on the prophet's solidarity with men? Were the king-priest and the ministerial priest (levitical or otherwise) not also one with the people?

M. Gelin: In speaking of spiritual solidarity I undoubtedly expressed myself badly. What I wanted to say was that the prophets envisaged a 'new' people. The old community of Israel had been a racial one. Like Deuteronomy, the great prophets spoke of a spiritual community specifically based on vocation.

M. Chavasse: Must we then understand the word spiritual as meaning free from all institution?

M. Gelin: You are well aware that Jeremias severely criticised institutionalism as he knew it, but did not for that reason reject institutions. His messianic teaching is proof of this. He insisted on this point precisely because the community of the future would be spiritual. And Ezechiel, who inherited this outlook from Jeremias, did not abandon all thought of institutions.

Fr Chavasse is really reproaching me for having abandoned institutionalism. Isn't that it?

M. Chavasse: No, I will not go so far as to say that you have abandoned it, but I think the word spiritual, when we really understand it, takes on a very different sense from what it had in the prophets. It strikes me very forcibly that Ezechiel is the author of an authentic code of sanctity which is also a ritual code.

In other words, I am wondering if this insistence on the purely spiritual aspect of prophetic thought might not be a return to a kind of liberal protestantism which equates religion with a code of morality, and in which the rite is a sort of method by which a religious flavour is given to a code of morality?

And I am asking myself if, as a result of prophecy, Israel did not begin to discover a higher form of unity among men than social, economic or political unity, a new unity, which I will call spiritual in the sense in which you have used the word, I think, but which is a spiritual thing embodied in an institution which transcends mere temporal institutions.

For myself, I would call the exilic community a ritual and priestly community, which was, as it were, the foreshadowing of that great upheaval which Christ would effect when he refashioned the religious ordinances of the world in his own kingdom.

M. Gelin: Have you realised that Jeremias and Ezechiel, who are really behind what you are saying, were priests themselves?

M. Chavasse: That strikes me very forcibly, now you mention it. That is why I think Christ's solidarity with men is affirmed perhaps just as much from the priestly – as opposed to the prophetic – angle, as from the royal angle. For when, finally, he symbolically destroys the temple by his own death, and refounds religion in himself, Christ performs an act which had always been regarded as the privilege of the king. When the king-messias refounds his people, he destroys the temple, and causes a new stream to spring forth which will flow thence into Jerusalem and the new land.

I would, therefore, regard this solidarity as taking different forms in the priestly, prophetic and royal traditions, but it does exist in all three of them. I don't know whether I am mistaken from the historical point of view. There I would prefer to ask questions rather than make assertions.

M. Gelin: Any explanation which brings together, rather than separates, the various points of view, is obviously to be preferred.

M. Chavasse: Yes, but historically, am I right?

M. Gelin: I rather think that historically the royal priesthood had long been forgotten.

M. Chavasse: When they talk about the king who is coming to rebuild Jerusalem, starting with the temple, it is obviously the contemporary king-priest of the Maccabean type, but in the end it is really rather the other type which is taken up.

M. Gelin: Who is going to rebuild Jerusalem from the temple?

M. Chavasse: It was one of Fr Spicq's remarks which made me say that. I do not know what historical validity it has but in an article in the *Mélanges Goguel* à propos the seamless robe he says: 'Christ, in putting on the seamless robe, openly declares that he is king-priest'.

M. Gelin: Yes, it is from Philo.

M. Chavasse: But historically, would it have this significance for his contemporaries when they saw him in this seamless robe?

M. Gelin: It certainly has significance in St John's gospel, for everything means something there.

M. Chavasse: St John's gospel is an extremely ritual and priestly gospel.

Fr Lécuyer: Could it be that a particular emphasis which is certainly present in tradition, especially in the East, but in the West as well, has its origin in views similar to those of M. Chavasse? In Zacharias 3 there is a passage about Josue, the son of Josedech, which is a prophecy of messianic times; it is a difficult text which foretells a priesthood which really will bring purification from all sin. Now, tradition altered the texts in chapter 6, and the royal crown was placed on the head of Josue the son of Josedech, i.e. the high priest, and not on the head of Zorobabel.

M. Gelin: Tradition changed the reading in this way because originally it was the Messias Zorobabel who was to wear the crown. Josue was put in his place.

Fr Lécuyer: Yes, that is so; but surely this clearly demonstrates that in Jewish thought at the time of Christ there was this tendency to assert the royalty of priesthood itself.

M. Gelin: Undoubtedly. The exegete will see this emendation as a way of getting over a historical fraud (i.e. the failure of Zorobabel), and of squaring the text with the history of the fifth and fourth centuries. On this hypothesis, the altered text is in fact evidence of the promotion of the priesthood, certainly after the exile. We must study post-exilic priesthood very closely – its role in purification indicated, and its function of teaching emphasised, for example, by Malachi and finally, its promotion of messianism itself.

M. Martimort: If I take it upon myself to speak for those who, one might say, are the non-specialists in the audience, I think we should first of all observe the following point in this discussion. After this paper on the epistle to the Hebrews and the little exchanges which have just taken place between M. Chavasse and Fr Lécuyer, it seems that Aaron, the levitical priest, occupies only a small place in that interpretation of the old testament as a whole which enables us to understand Christ, in comparison with all the other elements furnished by the epistle to the Hebrews – the Melchisedech typology, which brings in the figure of the king, and its very important prophetic elements.

Consequently, in speaking of the priesthood of Christ, if, like the epistle to the Hebrews, we have to affirm the ritual aspect of priesthood against those who perhaps denied it then and who deny it now, yet this ritual aspect ought always to be taken in a very broad sense, which brings together in the same priestly physiognomy, the kingly and prophetic aspects, as well as its liturgical aspect. Am I misinterpreting you?

M. Gelin: I don't think so, but Aaron has a very real place, none the less. Could it not be as a pattern and a contrast? Jesus has done perfectly the work of cleansing from sin and of establishing the covenant.

M. Martimort: Which Aaron could not do.

Fr Louvel: But apart from the text you have quoted from the Last Supper, does not Christ sometimes present himself in the gospel as priest? He presents himself as a prophet, as a son of David. . . .

M. Gelin: He does not present himself as a son of David. . . .

Fr Louvel: He is greeted as the Son of David. He refuses the kingship and at the same time claims to be king.

M. Gelin: His messianic 'ego' synthesised all these expectations.

Fr Lécuyer: To return to what M. Martimort said – can we not say that it is precisely because of his sacrifice, which realises the levitical type of sacrifice, and yet realises it effectually, so that it passes into the true sanctuary, and so, because of the true sacrifice and by one single indivisible act Christ is priest and king? For in his sacrifice he leads humanity back to the true promised land, thus making a reality of his title of king by leading the people to their true goal.

Therefore, it is in the act of sacrifice itself that he performs both these functions. He is priest because he offers a sacrifice and enters into the true sanctuary; he is king because the sacrifice is the very act by which he draws the people he saves back to their true destiny, to their true promised land, just as Moses their leader had of old led the people to the promised land.

This is perhaps a little too theological, but it does not seem to me to be going beyond the standpoint of the epistle to the Hebrews.

M. Gelin: Yes, the epistle to the Hebrews calls him the 'prodromos', and shows him taking his seat at the right hand of God. He is king because he is seated, because he is victorious, and his kingship is eschatological.

Fr. Lécuyer: Yes, and because he continues to lead the people, to bring them to God.

M. Gelin: I don't think that is the way Hebrews looks at it.

Fr Lécuyer: Fr Spicq has strongly urged the view that the epistle to the Hebrews regards the priest as a leader of the people. In fact, the first chapters speak to us of Moses and Jesus as well, and at the end of chapter 4, the few verses on Josue. . . .

M. Gelin: Yes, but that has nothing to do with the author's thought about priesthood.

Fr Lécuyer: On the contrary, does not this chapter with its reference to Josue end with a text about priesthood? 'For if Josue had given them rest he would never have afterwards spoken of another day'. Then there are some hortatory verses... 'For the word of God is living and effectual . . .', concluding thus: '{Having, therefore, a great high priest, who hath penetrated the heavens . . . let us hold fast our confession . . . for we have not a high priest who cannot have compassion on our infirmities . . .'.

M. Gelin: You said yourself that there was an hortatory interlude there, but the verse you quote forms no part of it. It is an exhortation about rest.

M. Martimort: The promised land.

Fr Lécuyer: Exactly. And the conclusion is that 'we have one who has already entered into the promised land, as Josue did aforetime, one who is the great high priest, and who can indeed have compassion on our infirmities'.

M. Gelin: But it does not follow that Josue can be called a priest, does it?

Fr Lécuyer: No.

M. Martimort: No, but I think I can see the bearing of the discussion and its importance for our work; the mediation of Christ as presented in the epistle to the Hebrews is not limited to its purely sacerdotal aspect in the way in which we usually think of priesthood in the old testament. We must always have in mind a combination of all these types of mediation if we are to have a right conception of the priesthood of Christ as it appears in the new testament. I think this is the point of the discussion, isn't it?

Fr Lécuyer: Yes, but perhaps in the epistle to the Hebrews the ideas of king and priest do not simply occur side by side, but actually pervade each other the whole time in the mind of the writer. That is my impression.

M. Gelin: Yes, he is trying to convey his highly 'synthesised' conception of Christ.

Fr Lécuyer: Which actually realises what each of the old testament types only realised in a very limited way. All the themes pervade each other.

M. Sauvage: I would like to ask Fr Gelin if he would explain the aspect he has stressed so much in connection with what he calls the 'prophetic vibrations' of the epistle to the Hebrews – the aloneness of Christ, even in the exercise of the prophetic function itself. In what does this alone-ness consist?

M. Gelin: He is alone in the sense that he has no fellowship with sin. He is completely identified with us, sin excepted. His innocence, if you like, sets him utterly apart, and forms, if I may venture to say so, a zone of solitude around him. He is like the suffering servant, completely innocent in the midst of a sinful world. He resembles the Jeremias of chapter **15**.

The work of the prophets, while identifying them with the people, demands such a great perfection that it lifts them, as it were, right out of the world. Sanctity is an actual requirement of their work, if I may say so; and they can only rightly accomplish it (since it is a work relative to sin and salvation) by being outside the world of sin. It is St John's *non estis de mundo sed estis in mundo*.

M. Sauvage: Yes, I feel that it would be interesting to go more deeply into this, because it avoids that purely ritual separation of the priest, to which exception is sometimes taken.

In the actual performance of his prophetic mission, what is it that makes Christ the High Priest, alone and separate, and why?

M. Gelin: It is simply the certainty that he has of belonging to a sinful world, in which he must be immersed, and in which he must be the real presence of God.

M. Sauvage: And you think that the epistle to the Hebrews considers it essential for his mission?

M. Gelin: The great prophets are examples of it. They lived among the people, mixed with them, totally immersed in their world – Jeremias, for instance. It seems to me that this is the inspiration behind certain passages of Hebrews. I do not see how they can be understood otherwise. Especially when a real theology of suffering is not easily found other than in the prophets, beginning with Jeremias, and in the Psalms which follow Jeremias and in Job which copies him in the same way.

M. Martimort: There would seem to be, in some ways, a sort of paradox – the need for this one-ness creates an alone-ness. Is that what you have in mind?

M. Gelin: Yes.

Fr Gelineau: Have we not here one of the essential components of the Holy One? God cannot appear on this earth without being unique. When we speak of the Holy One we automatically imply a setting apart.

So it is not arbitrary to oppose ritual separation and ontological separation, when the very consequence of the appearance of the Holy One in this world is to reveal a break between the world of sin and the world of sanctity. The rite is one of the privileged expressions of this rupture, but it is quite clear that the actual life of the priest must also express it in some way.

Another point – is it possible that in the life of the priest, who is one set apart, there is a distinction between his general ministry, which is that of the priest as such, and his ritual ministry? I cannot see any other alternative.

M. Sauvage: We must recognise, all the same, that there is a whole aspect of the priest's ministry which is completely liturgical in character, and in which he is even more set apart.

Fr Gelineau: And which is the privileged expression of his separation; but there is also a common or general expression of that separation in his life as a whole. The role of the rite in human life is to inaugurate in a particular and formal action something which has to be reflected in the whole of life.

M. Basseville: I would like to ask if the separation which appears in Hebrews essentially as a separation from sin, or the holiness of Christ in relation to a world of sinners, has not some connection with that separation subsequently spoken of in tradition, and which is something very different – a separation of the spiritual functions of the priest as opposed to a world whose business it is to create the temporal city, while the priest is the builder of the spiritual city. Has this any basis in the epistle to the Hebrews, or is it a much later idea?

M. Gelin: I don't think that the epistle to the Hebrews raises the question at all.

M. Chavasse: Hebrews does not even broach the subject since it speaks only of Christ, and not of ministerial priesthood – which is what we possess. Moreover, the distinction between temporal functions – I am not very fond of the expression *creation,* for the idea of creation is very ambiguous – and ministerial functions only begins to have meaning with Christ; it could certainly have no meaning before Christ. If we can find any origin for it all, it is in that kind of initial transposition effected by the Judaic community after the exile in comparison with what the people of God was before the exile.

So I think it would be futile to look for clarification of these distinctions (which are made within the Christian religion) in passages either of the old or the new testament apart from perhaps the Acts of the Apostles. The synoptists (and St John, and the Apocalypse and Hebrews) are only concerned with Christ and his priesthood, and, fundamentally, the problem of priesthood has been resolved. Henceforward there can be no question of anything more than a ministry through which Christ simply prolongs his own activity in time and on earth.

This is the view ratified by the Council of Trent at the beginning of the chapter on sacrifice.

And so I think it would be useless to look for the elucidation of ministerial priesthood in what took place before Christ, or even in those things which speak to us of Christ, except in the sense that ministerial priesthood must be explained by reference to the principle from which it springs in Christ himself.

I may be mistaken, but it seems to me that we are faced with this problem. I am not putting forward a solution; but it does seem that this problematical view of the subject is forced on us.

Fr Roguet: But on the other hand, could we not say that in the Apocalypse, in St Peter and the Acts, it is the community as a whole which is priestly in character, and that consequently the question of separation does not arise?

M. Chavasse: Now there we are faced with the question of the mystical body. No one has ever thought of Christ without his mystical body, but our own priesthood is a special function within the mystical body; and to solve the problem of the worship offered by the total Church, head and body, is not to solve the problem of our own priesthood. I don't know whether you agree with me? I think this problem is the problem of Christ, head and body, procuring for himself the priestly instrument he needs. St Augustine rightly puts it in these words: 'We ourselves are ministers of Christ, head and body'.

M. Mansencau: If I have followed you correctly, we must start with the Acts of the Apostles for the historical development of the sacrament of Orders?

M. Chavasse: Yes.

Fr Lécuyer: But, nevertheless, I think it is impossible to study the sacrament of Orders, i.e. sacramental priesthood, without having previously thoroughly examined the priesthood of Christ, whose sacrament we are. That is why such a study is so very important.

M. Mansencau: Yes, but if I understand this properly, it is in the Acts of the Apostles itself that the sacramental development found there begins. But we are all agreed that the rest must have been studied previously.

M. Martimort: What must be avoided is any attempt to make deductions from the idea of the priesthood of Christ either from Hebrews, or still less from the old testament.

Fr Gelineau: Would it be possible to formulate and to set out the work of Christ as priest? What is his priestly work? Is it to consecrate the old creation so that it may pass into the new? What is it? Certain examples of Christ fulfilling his priestly role have been put forward by way of illustration, but what is that priestly 'work' of Christ which really sums up his mission?

We do not see Christ in perspective through the figures of the old testament (Melchisedech, Aaron or the levitical priesthood), but these figures are seen in perspective by reference to Christ. How does Christ fulfil all these figures? What is the priestly work of Christ the Priest? Separation is a manifestation of this work, but it does not explain it.

M. Martimort: Yes, but I think we should speak of the work of Christ, and not merely of his priestly work.

M. Gelin: Yes, but let us proceed from the fundamental principles which the epistle gives us. It asserts that the law rests on priesthood and is established above (7, 11). Similarly, Christianity is built on Christ certainly, but on Christ the Priest.

Fr Gelineau: Yes. Is it possible to distinguish the work of Christ from the priestly work of Christ?

M. Martimort: The priestly work alone might narrow the field of our inquiry too much.

Fr Gelineau: But if we define it as M. Gelin has done, it is all there.

M. Chavasse: Have we the right even to raise the question? Is there actually any work of Christ which is priestly to the extent of excluding all others? Is it not rather that with Christ everything has been re-cast in such a new mould that we can no longer even ask if he has a specifically priestly function? He is himself the meeting-place with God – that is the incarnation – he is, in his very person, at-one-ness with God. And if this conjunction takes on all the attraction of a human act, it is because he is not a thing; he has a conscience in which he adheres to this ontological meeting between men and God that he himself is.

I think that to look for a particular function would be to look for something which does not exist. If the theologians have tried to find a function of Christ, it is because they have thought out the priesthood of Christ on the eucharistic level. But this does not explain to me fully what Christ is as man's at-one-ment with God.

M. Martimort: Do you think it is exclusively on the level of the eucharistic act? I think that it is rather on the level of the paschal mystery.

M. Chavasse: Granted, but it is the whole being of Christ, the whole of his life, which is thrown into that. *It is not a function.* For the act of death is not an act coming from within man's life – the whole man passes through it.

M. Rauch: But now the question arises – how are we going to proceed from this priesthood of Christ? Are we going to pass straight from Christ to his mystical body, and only thence to our own ministerial priesthood, or if not, in what direction are we going to proceed now?

Dom Capelle: The idea expressed by M. Chavasse is undoubtedly right, but there is nevertheless in the exercise of Christ's priesthood a definite act which corresponds to what is the normal and principal exercise of priesthood – sacrifice. Now of all the facts relating to Christ, the new testament singles out the shedding of his blood as an act of definitive importance. His death is, therefore, the priestly act in as much as we combine the priestly with the sacrificial idea.

M. Chavasse: I am in complete agreement with you, but for me his death is not just one isolated act among others.

Dom Capelle: The death is nevertheless the shedding of blood in the thought of St Paul.

M. Chavasse: If you want to give the word act a very simple meaning and to say that death is the act which drains life from man, it is not an act in which a function is exercised, it is the act in which the whole value and dignity of life is drained away; it is, as it were, its crown.

Dom Capelle: True enough, but it is not merely a completion. This act has a particular value when it involves the shedding of blood.

M. Chavasse: I would go further than you, and say that it is only in death that a man can perform the highest spiritual act of his life, an act of renunciation and charity (always intimately bound up with each other) – which is what you are expressing through the image of the shedding of blood.

Dom Capelle: Yes, but the concept of priesthood is not a purely spiritual idea, but a ritual one as well. So there is at least one element which makes the death of Christ a ritual act.

M. Chavasse: But is it a ritual act?

Fr Gelineau: Yes, in so far as it is a *sacramentum* expressing a *res*. We have got to know whether we are approaching the death from the point of view of a sign, or from the point of view of reality.

M. Chavasse: Yes, but we are playing with the word ritual. When being is thrown into an act, there is no more rite. . . . I don't know.

M. Martimort: I have the impression that the difficulty is we cannot easily take in at once the whole range of the relevant scriptural texts. On the one hand there is the whole current of prophetic thought which bids us get above sacrifice to the *spiritus contribulatus*, the sacrifice of the will, the sacrifice of love; on the other hand, the new testament continually shows us that the act through which Christ makes his own self-offering is an act with ritual significance. It is the blood of the covenant, the pasch. It is always the ritual sign. The two things are inseparable.

Fr Roguet: I think in all this there is a difficulty which arises from the fact that in speaking of a priestly work of Christ we cannot avoid thinking in terms of a human priestly work which we then attribute to Christ. Yet for the priest his sacrificial act is only of a partial and not total character.

This, to my mind, introduces a most interesting distinction: Christ is both priest, victim and the altar of his own sacrifice – it is a total act; whereas when a human priest offers sacrifice he does not give his own self, either on the sacramental or on the redemptive level.

M. Martimort: I think there is still more to be said. When we speak of priesthood as we see it either in the old testament or elsewhere, we do not get beyond the category of priesthood. But the priestly act of Christ is, if you like, the act of the feast of purification, but it is at the same time the entry into the promised land, the leading of a people and the ratifying of the covenant.

That is why I asked just now if it was right to speak of the priestly act of Christ, for this word to our minds seems to imply some limitation when compared with the wealth and variety of the imagery we must take into account at the same time, if we are to understand Christ.

Fr Roguet: Yes, when we apply them to Christ, the words priestly act do not permit of any limitation, for Christ is wholly priest, and I would say nothing other than priest, but we must give the word its full meaning.

Fr Lécuyer: Yet could we not say in spite of all this the sacrifice of Christ in the strict sense of the word, i.e. the passion, resurrection and, perhaps supremely, the ascension, which is the entrance of the victim into the heavenly sanctuary is the consummation of his priesthood, the *teleiosis*, because it is the culminating point of everything else in his life, which, from the very beginning, as Hebrews 10 says, is an offering?

If I am not mistaken, the word *teleiosis* had a priestly sense as well – it was the priestly unction, the consecration of the High Priest.

I think Dom Dupont once wrote an article on this subject. There would thus be a fulfilment of the priesthood of Christ himself as well as a fulfilment of his priestly activity.

Dom Capelle: It is certain that there is an efficacy in the blood of Christ – this is very marked in scripture. And the blood of Christ means the blood shed on the Cross.

M. Chavasse: But the blood as it is presented by the Risen Christ. The Risen Christ ever crucified. The Risen Christ, bearing even now the marks of the wounds, of the fourth gospel.

M. Martimort: The Lamb that has been slain, of the Apocalypse.

Dom Capelle: Yes, but the act itself was finished when we were redeemed by the precious blood, as St Paul says. That seems to indicate that our ransom took place at that moment, and that the precious blood means the blood as it was actually shed.

M. Gelin: But it is the resurrection that gives this moment its meaning.

Dom Capelle: Quite, but all the same it has, if I may say so, the central place in the redeeming mystery of the Incarnate Word. It is clear that it is impossible to separate it either from what preceded or what followed it.

Fr Forestier: 'No man taketh (my life) away from me, but I lay it down of myself.'

M. Martimort: Yes, but with our method of thought and subsequent preaching in mind, should we not carefully preserve all various angles of these biblical images without diminishing them, and is not all attempt at systematisation in itself a diminution and an impoverishment?

M. Mansencau: Yes, but perhaps it is possible to present the subject without systematising it?

M. Martimort: That is also a question which I should like to put to the preachers as much as to the liturgists, for they have to live the riches and the permanent sparkle of the texts, and this results in a synthesis which is not logic or system, but more profound.

M. Chavasse: I do not altogether agree with M. Martimort when he says that on the one hand there is the prophetic, spiritual and interior stratum, and on the other the more ritual or sensible stratum – a ritual, visible sacrifice.

Personally, I avoid the dilemma by saying that an act is as much a corporal as a spiritual thing. Fundamentally, the distinction between spiritual and corporal has no real meaning. Let us admit that the act of the Cross is a ritual act, if by that we mean that it is a sensible act, an act of blood-shedding; but at the same time the soul of Christ is utterly committed to this act of blood-shedding itself, to the act of death.

M. Martimort: I fully agree.

Dom Capelle: It is through the obedience of Christ, as St Paul says.

M. Chavasse: I think the shedding of blood is, as it were, the bones of this obedience, which would not exist as such without this act of death; so that with Christ we transcend both the purely spiritual and the purely ritual, which is only a stepping-stone compared with the reality which is Christ.

I confess that I have always been shocked by the expression the ritual sacrifice of the Cross. If by that is meant a sensible sacrifice which affects the total being of Christ and not only some dispositions of his soul – one wonders how these could exist outside this utter commitment of the being of Christ – then I will allow the expression, but it is very ambiguous.

Dom Capelle: Yes, but that does not prevent it from representing a reality, for it is the supreme act of Christ as Priest. So we must not reduce the profound importance of the word ritual, since it expresses, even if imperfectly, a reality of the priestly and sacrificial order.

M. Chavasse: I think the act of death does more than merely express; for it is in the act of death itself – that is to say, in the separation of the soul from the body – that a complete consummation is effected. Christ is made perfect in this act, in separating himself not only from the whole of creation but from himself as Creator; he is re-united with God in a decisive fashion, since he could not have been a perfect Saviour, possessing the Holy Spirit in its fulness, as Acts says, without his death.

Dom Capelle: The distinction is not essential.

M. Martimort: We must rigorously maintain the different aspects.

M. Chavasse: But is it necessary to proceed from these images at all, to understand what Christ is – even when he performs an act of sacrificial priesthood? Ought we not to get inside what the Church, transcending these images, has helped us to penetrate by faith – that is to say, the mystery of the incarnation and the mystery of that human life which is fulfilled on the Cross, and to understand then that all images would tend towards this kind of light which infinitely surpasses them, and that the death of Christ is an act which no image of any sort could ever completely contain?

M. Martimort: Each image by itself is powerless to grasp and explain it, but in taking them all at once. . . .

M. Chavasse: . . . as a whole.

Fr Gelineau: But can we transcend images and attain reality?

We are searching for the reality of Christ's act, but we cannot reach it save through images, and we find that each image aspires to express the whole truth in itself. It is quite different from the way we express concepts, in which a part of reality is expressed by each concept. Each one of the images relevant to the mystery of the revelation can, by itself, express the totality of the act of Christ.

M. Sauvage: All the same, there is something partial and incomplete in borrowed images.

Fr Gelineau: Every image is necessarily always incomplete. Yet the purpose of an image is to reveal the plenitude of the mystery.

M. Martimort: Yes, but we must remember that these are biblical images, and they have evolved in the course of history. They are not images which have atrophied, they are alive and they converge on Christ. For example the covenant is not an image settled once for all; it is an image which goes on growing right up to the time of Christ. And each one thoroughly appreciated helps us to come nearer to the mystery of Christ, but on its own is not sufficient and needs the others. There is the spiritual sacrifice of Jeremias and the suffering servant. All these images taken together are far more than metaphors.

M. Gelin: They are the result of real spiritual experience.

M. Martimort: They are alive and continually developing.

Fr Gelineau: The image is not something independent of the reality, it is an actual expression of it.

It is impossible here to distinguish the spiritual and the corporal. Revelation is rightly expressed through images. And can we say that understanding is possible by transcending images? In other words, is not the expression of the dogma of the redemption in theology always given through images, and would it ever be possible to dispense with these revealed images?

M. Martimort: They will always be there in the biblical themes.

Fr Gelineau: I am using the word image here very definitely in its sense of a biblical theme.

M. Idiart: The history of religions and the general structure of sacrifice, may help to give some answer to the problem raised by M. Chavasse, in this way: we could regard the sacrifice of Christ as not being a ritual sacrifice at all, since a rite is essentially something derived, something which is repeated and the sacrifice of Christ is something absolutely unique and original. It is neither ritual in the sense of founding a rite, the ritual repetition of which follows it, on the one hand, nor yet because it explains and fulfils the rites which have preceded it.

It seems to me that the general category which corresponds most closely to the place occupied by the sacrifice of Christ is that of myth, which has just this character of both interior and exterior reality, and which postulates an undeniable bond between a certain interior and a certain exterior aspect in such a way that the rite, by repeating the exterior part of the mythical act, will re-establish, re-enact and recover its interior aspect.

The sacrifice of Christ seems to me somewhat analogous. It is a sacrifice which is historical and therefore not a myth in the modern sense of the word – but the modern sense has been distorted. But it is also an act which is trans-historical; it has an absolute value which explains what has gone before and what comes after it which re-enters into *illud tempus* (as Eliade says) but which is above history; which is at once transcendent and immanent in history.

M. Martimort: It is mystery in its Christian dress.

CHAPTER III

JEWISH PRIESTHOOD AND CHRISTIAN HIERARCHY IN THE EARLY PALESTINIAN COMMUNITIES

J. SCHMITT

THE levitical priesthood was the heart of the Jewish theocracy set up after the exile; at the end of the age of the apostles,[1] an entity comparable in purpose as well as in name, the Christian priesthood, made its appearance as the foundation of the new worshipping community, the Church. In spite of their differences in many essential points we can establish with certainty a continuity between the two institutions, or at any rate a development from the one to the other; the priesthood of the Church is really the spiritualised and purified replica, the eschatological fulfilment of the Jewish priesthood in different terms.

Now this continuity itself raises a problem which has a definite bearing on our subject. In what way and how far can we say that the Christian institution succeeded the Jewish? More specifically, under what Jewish influences did the apostolic Church – very quickly conscious of its uniqueness – come to assume some sort of messianic priesthood, and what Jewish

1. Applied at first to the Church as a whole (cf. 1 Peter 2, 5, 9; Apoc. 1, 6; 5, 10; Justin of Rome *Dialogue with Trypho*, cxvi, 3; Irenaeus, *Contra Haereses*, iv, viii, 3). It was not long before the title ιερευς or αρχιερεύς was conferred in a particular sense on the élite of the community, the martyrs (cf. Apoc. 20, 6), and the hierarchy (cf. *Didache*, xiii, 3; Clement of Rome, *Cor.*, xl – xli; Tertullian, *De Baptismo*, xvii; Hippolytus of Rome, *Refutatio*, i, 6).
The doctrine of Christ the Priest expounded in the epistle to the Hebrews (cf. 2, 17; 3, 1; 4, 14, 15 . . .; cf. Clement of Rome, *Cor.*, xxxvi, 1; lxi, 3; Ignatius of Antioch, *Philad.*, ix, 1 . . .) seems at first to have been but a theme parallel to the priesthood of the Church. The two theologies were to be brought together in the patristic period to give prominence to the presbyteral priesthood.

ideas inspired the way in which she shaped its forms and its functions?

There are two aspects of this question; one historical and the other in a sense doctrinal.

To take first the spiritual angle. The early Judaeo-Christian centres seem to have adopted positions vis-à-vis the Jewish priesthood which were, to say the least, very varied. To start with they had to make a very clear distinction between the conforming priesthood which was inextricably bound up with the sacrificial cult of the temple, and closely associated with the party of the Sadducees, and the pietistic priesthood of the Palestinian diaspora, which professed open adherence to the prophetic ideal of the perfect theocracy, and which, for almost two centuries had provided the various messianic and reforming movements in Judaism with their leaders and their rank and file.[1] And those new testament texts with an archaic flavour taken together reveal two rather opposed tendencies. While the parable of the Samaritan (cf. Luke 10, 30–7),[2] for example, is evidence of a negative criticism of the Jewish priesthood in its two principal orders,[3] put forward in the very name of the law

1. This distinction notwithstanding, the new testament is evidence in its way of the complexity of the religious tendencies which asserted themselves in messianistic Judaism. The groups of Jewish priests who played some part in Christian origins certainly all belonged to the broad current of pietism. According to the gospels and Acts their opinions on the great cultural values of Israel were very varied. Some condemned the temple and its liturgy (cf. Acts 6, 8, ff; cf. 6, 7; others, on the contrary, frequented it and even participated in the sacrificial cult (cf. Luke 1, 5 ff).

2. See especially verses 31 and 32, and compare verses 34–5. Compare also the numerous texts relative to the hostility of the official priesthood to Christ (cf. Mk 11, 18 par; 10, 33 par; 14, 1 ff par; Matt. 2, 4; John 7, 32, 45) and the disciples (cf. Acts 4, 1, 6, 23 . . .; 7, 1; 9, 1).

The passages Mk 1, 44 par; 2, 26 par; Matt. 12, 5; Luke 17, 14 are, on the other hand, of a rather neutral character – in them Jesus clearly recognises certain ritual prerogatives declared by the Mosaic law to belong to the priesthood.

3. This verdict is plainly general in scope, as indeed is the contemporary popular opinion to which it undoubtedly alludes (cf. H. Strack-P. Billerbeck, *Kommentar zum Neuen Testament aus Talmud und Midrash* vol. 2, Munich, 1924, p. 182). But did it really apply to the Palestinian priesthood as a whole? I do not think so. At the time of Jesus and his apostles the pietist priesthood was still too imbued with

and of its major precept, other passages – and these are the most
striking – indicate an essentially favourable appreciation of the
messianist priesthood.

By way of illustration I will quote one of the first Judaeo-
Christian documents of a particularly anti-Jewish and doctrinal
character – the discourse of Stephen (Acts, **7**, 2–53 in conjunction with **6**, 8–14). Before the Sanhedrin and the people St
Stephen in effect plainly foretells the fall of the Torah, the
temple and its cult. Did he also proclaim the abolition of priesthood? There is no indisputable indication although both the
allusion to the sacrifices formerly offered by the fathers to idols
(cf. **7**, 42–3), and (more convincingly) the admitted superiority
of the tabernacle of the testimony in the desert over the houses
made with hands might point to it (cf. **7**. 44–50). Considered
in the light of its historic context as it were, the silence of the
disciple on this subject is hardly likely to be fortuitous. Stephen
came of the diaspora, probably from Egypt (cf. **6**, 9).[1] So he
leaves out none of the themes dear to the hellenistic groups whose
spokesman and indeed theologian he was; he includes both the
principle of continuity between the ancient theocracy of Juda
and the true eschatological assembly (cf. **7**, 35 ff), and the theme
of the essentially worshipping character of the messianic community (cf. v. 8). Furthermore, there is no doubt he was from
the very beginning an influential member of the Church at
Jerusalem. As a result of this, whatever his own reformist connections, he must have known the important place held in the

---

the old Judaic ideas concerning poverty and mercy – conditions of
likeness to God – to be exposed to the unbridled criticism of the people.
Moreover, whatever may have been the exact point of verses 31 and
32 in the original version of the parable (compare Deut. **19**, 15), the
pietist priesthood can scarcely have been in the mind of the evangelist,
since it is the object of such favourable quotation in Luke (cf. **1**, 5 ff)
and in Acts (cf. **4**, 36; **6**, 7).

1. The frequent traces of Alexandrianisms and even of Philonisms
in the discourse in chapter 7 (cf. C. Spicq, *Le philonisme de l'Epître aux
Hébreux* in 'Revue biblique' vol. lvi, 1949, pp 542–72; vol. lvii,
1950, pp 212–44; *Alexandrinismes dans l'Epître aux Hébreux* in 'Revue
biblique' vol. lviii, pp 481–502; W. Manson, *The Epistle to the
Hebrews. An historical and theological reconsideration*, London 1951)
illustrate the general tenor of this passage.

apostolic community by Jewish levites and priests who had been converted to the gospel. In particular – to give just one example in support of this assertion[1] – he must have known Barnabas, the leader of the men of Cyprus and Cyrene (cf. 11, 20), who is introduced by the writer of Acts as a levite, a Cyprian born (cf. 4, 36) and as one on whom Peter and the disciples could rely (cf. 11, 22–30; 4, 36).

The approbation thus expressed of certain movements within the Jewish priesthood is significant from many points of view. It does not merely show that Stephen and the first Judaeo-Christian centres generally were anxious to point out that it was the messianist priests and levites, the representatives of the spiritual élite of Israel, who did, in a sense, guarantee the continuity between the two covenants by their conversion and their role in the Church. As we have seen it lights the historical problems of the origins and features of the hierarchy in the early Palestinian churches from a particular and partly fresh angle.

In fact early Christianity and its institutions flow largely from messianist Judaism. Whichever stream of 'baptist' thought and practice he comes from, John, the forerunner, and in one sense the initiator, of the Christian movement is at any rate of priestly extraction (cf. Luke 1, 5 ff) and reformist background.[2] As for John the apostle and author of the Johannine writings, he does not seem to be exceptional among the disciples in having had 'baptist' training (cf. John 1, 35 ff) and priestly connections (cf. 18, 16).[3] A last and still more decisive point – the evidence

1. The probability is also strengthened by the similarity in basic thought and form between Acts 7, 2–53 and the epistle to the Hebrews (see especially W. Manson, *op. cit.*). I shall point out later the various possible sacerdotal affinities of the epistle.

2. This inference which had already been drawn from the 'baptist' provenance of John's 'washings' seems now to have been confirmed and clarified by the similarities to the message of the Forerunner in the Qumran scrolls. The text John 1, 23 (cf. Mk 1, 2–3 par) relating to the central place of Isaias 40, 3 ff in St John's eschatology corresponds with fragments 1 QS, VIII, 13–17 and IX, 19–20. Similarly, Mk 1, 8 and parallels on the final purification 'in the Spirit' (cf. also John 1, 26–7) apparently assumes its real sense only in the light of the texts 1 QS, IV, 21–2 and III, 7–8, concerning the 'Holy Spirit, the purifier'.

3. I must add that in the opinion of the critics (cf. E. Stauffer,

of Acts (cf. **4**, 36; **6**, 7 in conjunction with **3**, 1–5, 42), which is corroborated by the literary criticism both of this writing and of the gospels, shows that numerous messianist groups, consisting of well-born priests and laity, seem from the very first to have gone over to the new Judaeo-Christian communities because they recognised in the spiritual kingdom of Christ the fulfilment of their eschatological aspirations.[1]

Now, in being admitted into the churches they enriched them with religious ideas and practices and with institutions and social forms, which were Jewish in character. What was their contribution to the organisation and life of the churches? And what part did they play in the ministries by which these communities were built? It seems to me that by studying these questions in the light of both Jewish and apostolic Palestinian texts it should be possible to define, if not to describe in detail, an experience through which the Church passed; an experience which some have already suspected but whose historical importance still seems all too frequently to be disregarded.

The recent discovery of the site of the ancient Jewish community on the north-west shores of the Dead Sea and the unearthing of the last remnants of its religious library in the rocks of Qumran have made it possible for us to have a better understanding of the truly Jewish framework of primitive Christianity and in particular, the precise part which the best elements of the Jewish priesthood played in the life and organisation of certain messianist centres at the time of Jesus and his apostles.

Theologie des Neuen Testament, Stuttgart and Berlin 1941, pp 323–5) Johannine thought and writings show many affinities with pietist literature, especially with the *Testament of the Twelve Patriarchs*, composed in priestly centres (cf. R. Eppel, *Le pietisme juif dans les Testaments des douze Patriarches*, Paris 1930, pp 178–88) similar to the community at Qumran. On the 'baptist' background of certain members of the apostolic group see John **1**, 35 ff and R. Gylleberg, 'Die Anfange der johannischen Tradition' in *Neutestamentliche Studien für R. Bultmann*, Berlin 1954, pp 144–7.

1. This is the view held by A. Bea, 'Neue Handschriftenfunde in Palestina' in *Stimmen der Zeit* LXXVIII, 1953, pp 248–53, and of J. Bonsirven, 'Genres littéraires dans la littérature juive post-biblique' in *Biblica* XXXV, 1954, pp 344–5.

Now, the reformist community of Khirbet Qumran was largely a *qehillah* or priestly church. The priests[1] and the levites[2] although they did not live apart from the laity did not merely represent an important section of its effective members – they were its élite. It was for this reason, and this reason alone, that they had precedence over the other members of the group, and also provided its officialdom. The guards and the officers were taken from their ranks, men who were responsible for the religious training of the catechumens, as well as for the spiritual progress of the admitted members.[3] And it was also from them that in all probability the hierarchs of the assembly were chosen, from the *maskil* or master of wisdom, whose business it was to keep the proficients continually alert to their adherence to the light or the truth,[4] to the *mebaqqer* or overseer, whose task it was to supervise the faithful prosecution of the common ideal by priests, levites and laity alike, by means of periodic inspections and tests.[5]

The priesthood of Qumran was also a school of perfection and, more accurately, of the perfection of the community. There are two points which illustrate this and they are both apparent in the *Manual of Discipline* or, to use a designation more in line with the terminology of the centre, *The Rule of the Community*. Though compiled as a result of successive revisions by representatives of the priesthood at Qumran, this writing nevertheless reveals a very clear tendency to overlook the more ritual functions of the priests and levites at the plenary assemblies, such as purifications and common meals, which it mentions but does not describe.[6] Moreover – and this speaks volumes for the development of the idea of sacrifice in Palestinian Judaism – a highly evolved spiritualisation of the idea of sacrifice is implicit in it. Certainly, like their opposite numbers at Jerusalem, the

1. cf. 1QS, I, 18–19, 21–2; II, 1 ff, 11 ff, 19–20; III, 8 . . .
2. cf. 1QS, I, 18–19, 23; II, 4 ff, 11 ff, 20 . . .
3. cf. 1QS, II, 21–2; V, 2, 9; IX, 7–8; VI, 2–5; VIII, 1–4.
4. cf. 1QS, III, 13 – IV, 26; IX, 12, 21; the Damascus Document, XII, 21.
5. cf. 1QS, VI, 11–12, 19–20; the Damascus Document, X, 10; 1QS, VI, 13–15.
6. cf. 1QS, I, 21 – II, 20; III, 4–5, 8–9; V, 13–14; VI, 2–5, 20–1.

priests of Qumran, who displayed great pride in their priest-hood, were vitally conscious of the essential connection between the notion of sacrifice and the idea of priesthood. Yet, as distinct from their colleagues at Jerusalem, they condemned the sacri-ficial cult of the temple in the name of a spiritual purification which alone was effective and which God would henceforward grant to his elect.[1] And to safeguard their priestly dignity they thought out the idea of sacrifice afresh. True sacrifice, the authentic expression of divine praise and the unfailing pledge of saving justice is, in the words of the psalmist,[2] that generosity of heart which moves the priest and the levites, and in their train the other members of the community, to make the offering of their lives so that the perfect theocratic order may be brought about in their midst and preparation made for the assembly of the last days.[3] To this end priests and laity alike faithfully ob-served – under pain of sanctions which could go so far as excom-munication – the law of the triple communism of knowledge, work and goods, which, according to the documents is the essential condition to all search for God.[4] Let us note this point in passing. The ideal of a priesthood which in the final stages of the preparation for supreme salvation was to share in some measure the poverty and toil of the humble and poor is un-doubtedly very ancient. On the evidence of the Qumran texts it marks the spiritual testament, so to speak, bequeathed by the reformist Jewish priesthood before it was swallowed up in the avalanche of A.D. 70.

Was such a spiritual priesthood, as the keystone of eschato-logical perfection, peculiar to what some rather inappropriately call the 'sect' of Khirbet Qumran or did it also exist, even if in different forms, in other centres of messianist Judaism? This latter hypothesis is not improbable. It fits in very well with the rather complex character of the beliefs and rites of the Qumran

---

1. cf. 1QS, VIII, 3–4, 5–10; IX, 3–5, 5–6, 23–6; X, 1–8.
2. cf. Ps. 51, 14a (*ruah nedybah*); 54, 8.
3. The expression the generous ones (*hndbym*) is one of the most characteristic titles of the members of the community; cf. 1QS, I, 7, 11; V, 1, 6, 8, 9–10.
4. QS, I, 1–2; II, 17; cf. I, 11–13; II, 24; V, 4.

community. It is to some extent supported by the actual writings of the group, especially the *Manual of Discipline* in which practices and religious themes which were apparently current are repeatedly interpreted and evaluated in a new sense.[1] But the very large gaps in our information preclude the question's being definitely decided. In any case it is only incidental to our own problem, despite the interest it holds for the historian in other respects. However prevalent and varied it was in Palestinian Judaism, priesthood of the Qumran type certainly seems to have exercised a very considerable influence on the life and the original structure of the early Judaeo-Christian churches. The many parallels at present being elucidated between certain passages in the new testament and the principal Qumran MSS afford sufficiently strong grounds for this hypothesis. Without mentioning them all we can at least note the principal points which exegesis now considers reasonably well established.

1. The office of the *mebaqqer* at Qumran is clearly parallel to the apostolic institution of the *episkopos*. And this similarity is both complete and exclusive. Not only is there no example of it in the other spiritual streams of contemporary Judaism but both the offices in question share the same salient features. In both there is the same duty of spiritual vigilance and disciplinary oversight, the same precedence in a hierarchy more or less limited to advisers, and both are even called by the same name. In the opinion of the critics[2] the identity of the two institutions at this point is clear and the reformist dignity is in all probability the source of its Christian counterpart. Moreover in some ways the new testament writings themselves suggest this. While the episcopate is mentioned only occasionally in the passages recording St Paul's utterances (cf. Phil. 1, 1, Acts 20, 28) it is, on the other hand, given particular prominence in the documents of a more emphatic Judaeo-Christian character (cf. 1 Peter 2, 25; 1 Timothy 3, 2; Titus 1, 7). From this we must conclude that the office of the *episkopos* was not peculiar to the pagan-Christian

1. cf. 1QS, VIII, 12–16; Isaias 2, 7–11; 4, 1–3; John 1, 23; Mk 1, 2–3.

2. cf. J. Jeremias, P. Benoit, G. Kuhn, to quote only the most representative of those who have reached this conclusion, which is scarcely disputed.

churches, or to the Pauline communities, but was a mark of at least some of the Palestinian churches from the beginning.

2. Besides furnishing the young Church with its structure, Judaism of the type to be found at Qumran was largely responsible for providing the pattern for its community life. Two passages, related in purpose and provenance, make this clear: Acts 4, 32–5, 11 (cf. 2, 42 and 6, 1–6) on the community of goods in the apostolic Church, and the words of Jesus to the rich young man (Matt. 19, 21) concerning eschatological perfection through the renunciation of riches in favour of the poor, i.e. the members of the messianic Church.[1] Notwithstanding some differences these fragments can be traced to very ancient traditions. They are undeniably reformist in tone. The book of Acts, for instance, savours so much of Qumran in its most striking element, the account of Ananias and Sapphira (cf. 5, 1–11), that it can only be fully understood in the light of the parallels in the *Manual of Discipline*. For the fault of which the two members of the Church at Jerusalem were guilty by violating the law of community had been foreseen previously, and penalised in the law of the community at Khirbet.[2] Furthermore, the destruction of these two prevaricators by God himself as guardian of the essential holiness of his Church (cf. 3, 23) corresponds in every detail to one of the most striking principles of the messianist community.[3] Such facts, which it would be easy to support with others, leave little room for doubt. The pattern of community life in certain Judaeo-Christian centres is largely reformist in inspiration. And – and this last point illustrates my contention – it was the converts coming from the messianist priesthood who appear to have been behind it. This is suggested in the Matthaean passage by the reformist and communal character of the tradition which he re-echoes. The account in Acts is more explicit, and emphasises it with vigour and originality: the

1. cf. M. W. Davies, 'Knowledge in the Dead Sea Scrolls and Matt. 11, 25–30' in *The Harvard Theological Review*, XLVI, 1953, pp 115–16. I find it difficult however, to accept the writer's view that, contrary to its recognised messianic connotation in the first gospel, the word πτωχόι here only applies to the needy in the economic sense.

2. cf. 1QS, VI, 24–5; VII, 3–4, 5.

3. cf. 1QS, IV, 18–19; V, 19; II, 11–17; V, 10–13.

example of Barnabas, the levite from Cyprus, who sells his property so that he may deliver its price to the apostles (cf. 4, 36–7) is deliberately contrasted with the sin of Ananias and Sapphira (cf. 5, 1–11), in whom it is certainly not too far fetched to see some of the laity and perhaps even some of the Hebrews.[1]

3. Like the priesthood of Qumran the leaders of the Judaeo-Christian churches also had their rule and ecclesial code. The community or ecclesiastical discourse in St Matthew's gospel (cf. 18, 1–35) corresponds to the *Manual of Discipline* in several ways. Together with real differences which indicate the originality of Christianity and its superiority over its sources, these documents do in fact possess numerous elements and features in common. The same type of leadership for the community, without any real parallel in other parts of the new testament; the same insistence on the duties of the leaders to the faithful – respect for their spiritual poverty, and watchful care over their spiritual progress;[2] finally, the same practice of fraternal correction,[3] which can hardly be said to be attested in other centres of Palestinian Judaism. The divergencies between the parallel features of the two passages are more in the nature of differences of nuance and emphasis. On the whole the discourse in Matthew shows deeper insight and a more spiritual conception of the subject. In particular the divine principle underlying the standards of pastoral conduct is more marked there than in the reformist text.[4] In short, comparing the Judaeo-Christian document with its parallel from Qumran, it would appear that it is a conflation,

1. This suggestive presentation of the incidents, noted by early criticism but questioned in recent exegesis, is not merely elucidated by the Qumran texts; it appears to be largely corroborated by the narrative in VI, 1–6, and particularly by the note in VI, 1 on the dissensions between Greeks and Hebrews in the matter of the daily ministration, to which the excerpt IV, 32 – V, 11 is a preface and introduction in conformity with the compiler's method of anticipation.

2. cf. Matt. 18, 1–14; v, 3 ff; 1QS, III, 8; IV, 2; V, 3, 25. The pastoral epistles do not correspond to 1QS and Matthew either in theme or content.

3. cf. 1QS, V, 23 – VI, 1; Matt. 18, 15–17. See Strack-Billerbeck, *op. cit.*, 1, Munich 1922, pp 787–92.

4. cf. Matt. 18, 12–14; Luke 15, 3–7; J. Jeremias, *Die Gleichnisse Jesu*, Zurich 1947, pp 20–1; C. H. Dodd, *The Parables of the Kingdom*, London 1952, p. 119.

in which certain themes of a Jewish character are mingled with the properly evangelical traditions, such as would be effected by church leaders familiar with the communal customs and ideas of groups which were, to say the least, similar to that at Qumran.

4. We know that the epistle to the Hebrews is, in a sense, the most sacerdotal document in the new testament. Could it not also be one of the most 'reformist'? Doubtless it was addressed to some convert Jerusalem priests, who in spite of their conversion seem to have retained an acute nostalgia for the old levitical cult. But once the Pauline character of the epistle has been safely established, could we not say that the writer of the epistle himself might have been a leader of the community who had come over from the messianist priesthood? Admittedly this explanation is conjectural, but it does account for all the various special characteristics of the epistle. The writer certainly knew the temple, but hardly as one who had been directly connected with its liturgy. Moreover the principal sources of his thought are Jewish and sacerdotal rather than Christian. For example, chapter 18 of the *Testament of Levi*, in which the priestly theme of a Messias of levitical descent and heavenly rank is put forward, certainly inspires his whole exposition; and, like other Jewish apocalypses, this one must have held a rather high place in the life and thought of the reformist priests and levites. Finally, the very purpose of the epistle is strongly reminiscent of the most characteristic ideas of the messianist priesthood; in showing that, by his oblation on the Cross and his glorious ascension Jesus accomplished the ideal sacrifice and is now the heavenly high priest, did not the writer in point of fact wish to signify to his readers that the major spiritual aspirations of the Jewish priestly élite had been realised in Christ? I repeat this is hypothetical but it seems the most satisfying of the numerous explanations put forward up to now. It is also one of the most suggestive. Should it prove right the epistle to the Hebrews would then appear to be documentary evidence of the meeting within the apostolic Church of the two Jewish priesthoods – reformist and official.

Admittedly this evidence is far from complete. But it is no less conducive to those who are aware of the lacunal and indefinite character of the data furnished by the writings of the new testament on the communal life and experience of the first Judaeo-Christian churches. By exemplifying the doctrinal postulates concerning the collapse of Jewish institutions, they do show, as we have said, that there is a remarkable continuity between the priesthood of the old covenant and the Christian priesthood. Primarily by their tendency to spiritualise the ideas of sacrifice and priesthood, and by their conversion and subsequent work in the *ecclesia*, Jewish priests and levites coming from the various contemporary reformist or messianist movements guaranteed in the historic order the unity of the two priestly and theocratic communities. And it is not perhaps too rash to add to this fundamental conclusion, which can be taken as certain, another which is only probable. If the hypothesis about the writer of the epistle to the Hebrews is correct, there would also be converts from the messianist priesthood, who, by developing the ideas of the gospel story and of nascent apostolic thought, contributed to the wealth of the doctrine of the transcendent and unique priesthood of Christ.

In joining the early Palestinian churches Jewish priests of the reformist school brought with them, as we have seen, various doctrinal, cultural, religious and disciplinary traditions. And, from the very beginning, they bore witness to a remarkably keen sense of the actual eschatological condition, the transcendent faith and life, and the already traditional institutions of these churches. The reason for this is apparent. Through their adherence to the community of Christ, they saw that the election and mission of the Jewish priesthood had been achieved in it. Consequently there was no eschatological salvation save through the ministry of the Church. Whatever their precise rank in the local communities they spontaneously assumed a share in the functions or diaconies of the Church.

What, according to our texts, were these functions?

The first part of Acts and the community discourse of Matthew, which are in many ways the most suggestive sources for this subject, enable us to draw these two fundamental conclusions; each of the churches at Jerusalem, Antioch, Caesarea and Damascus was, by the very fact of its eschatological character, the organ of the Spirit, the principle of salvation shed abroad in the world. Because of this, each had a kerygmatic or missionary function of world wide scope, which it fulfilled first by preaching the gospel – which is both *kerugma* and *didache*, the message of salvation and the moral rule – and second by its own radiance.

Subordinate to this there appear to have been various functions directed rather towards the community, whose chief purpose was according to the later expression of St Paul, the support of the churches. Although the texts are hardly definite on this point, and we cannot entirely preclude the danger of inaccuracy it is nevertheless possible to distinguish three groups of ministries. On the one hand there are the functions of liturgy and worship, the ritual or prayer (Acts 2, 42) in the biblical and complex meaning of the word, the forms and themes of which were, especially at the beginning, clearly Jewish in inspiration. Then there are also, and in strongly marked prominence, what the Church later called the sacraments, i.e. baptism, remission of sins, and imposition of hands, the conferring of the Spirit. Finally there was the eucharist (cf. *ibid*. 2, 41; 8, 14–17). There can be little doubt that these functions were primitive and, in a sense, fundamental. Yet very soon under the influence of Judaism, and particularly the messianist movements, a dual pastoral ministry of teaching and discipline was added to them. The disciplinary functions were aimed at the spiritual development of the communities and the preservation of their eschatological sanctity; within the Church's organisation they made possible religious vigilance and, when necessary, the policing, in some way, of sin as well as of error (cf. 5, 1–11). The ministry of teaching, a typical feature of the first Judaeo-Christian communities, finds its most outstanding and most normal expression in the *paraklesis* or exhortation (cf. 4, 36; Heb. 13, 22) which very quickly took on rather stereotyped forms and which was indeed coloured for a long time by a Jewish tinge.

However the apportionment and the hierarchy of ecclesiastical functions suggested by such a survey are only apparent. In fact all the diaconies of the community are marked by an essential unity, and by an inspiration flowing from the worship, or as we should say from the liturgical climate. The Palestinian Church was keenly aware of being the community of the 'last days'. Following the best scriptural tradition it recognised that its essential mission was to proclaim the *megaleia* or wonderful works of God (cf. Acts 2, 11; 10, 46). From the first it fulfilled this under the impulse of the Spirit by a preaching which centred on the story of salvation (7, 2–53), by the sacramental repetition of the supper as the memorial of the passion and the resurrection, and by its own experience of salvation.

It follows that from the supreme ministry of the word to the most humble disciplinary function, fraternal correction, for example, all the diaconies are proper to the community as such, and that, according to an actual though imperfect formula, they stipulate the participation of the faithful. What then is the role of the *hegoumenoi* or leaders (cf. Hebrews 13, 7, 17, 24; Luke 22, 26; Acts 15, 22) in the work of the Church? One thing relative to this question transpires from the rare early texts. Whatever their rank or special ministry the leaders are in a sense the embodiment of the eschatological order seen in its saving fulness. Consequently they are, as it were, the expression of the community. More precisely, they are both its foundation and organ, its guide and its conscience.

It is on these grounds that they assumed the various ecclesial functions in a very special way, and in particular that of witness for which they were equipped by their historic contact with the Risen Christ (Acts 4, 20) or, failing this, by their character as guardians of the tradition as well as by the experience of the Spirit of Christ which the community had.

It is also on these grounds that they discharged the liturgical functions in worship, presided at the prayer, and performed the various eschatological rites. And a certain hierarchy of sacraments seems to have been established from the beginning. The imposition of hands is in certain respects the major rite, because by it is conferred, for the various ministries and conditions, the Holy Spirit, who is the 'form' of messianic salvation itself. The eucharist is moreover, especially for the converts from Judaism, the sublimation and fulfilment of the old custom of community meals; it is by definition the sacrament of the *koinônia* or community, by which the unity of the faithful amongst themselves and with the glorified Christ is shown forth and intensified. Finally, baptism remits sins and incorporates into the Church; because of its cleansing reference and its character as a preparation to the conclusive work of the Spirit, and also because of its natural significance as the parallel of Jewish circumcision, it remained for long a basic but merely preliminary rite.

Nevertheless in spite of the importance conceded to these various functions in the cult, the hierarchy of the early Palestinian communities is seen to be supremely and completely pastoral in character. The consideration in fact which inspired and dominated it was the safeguarding of the holiness of the Church and particularly of its proper spiritual perfection. The hierarchy felt bound to embody the numerous moral and religious requirements of plenary salvation, of which it was the conscious and essential expression. It never wavered on this principle. In fact it can hardly be said to have lost any time in striving to ensure its permanence. Certainly it seems true that at the beginning a keen sense of eschatological realities and also, to a great extent, the rigorist influence of the reformist movements had prevented its members from wavering. As the ideal of messianic poverty was lost, and the Judaeo-Christian tendency to de-radicalise the moral teaching of Christ and his disciples a reaction set in. On the evidence of the new testament this manifested itself in the tendency to catalogue, and even to codify, the elementary virtues required in those aspiring to office within the community. The pastoral epistles reflect the logical consequence of this tendency. But to the historian they are also evidence of the moral crisis experienced by the early hierarchy in certain of its representatives, and of the apostolic effort made to safeguard the law of the essential sanctity of the Church, her leaders and her faithful.

CHAPTER IV

COLLEGIATE CHARACTER OF THE PRESBYTERATE AND EPISCOPATE

DOM B. BOTTE, O.S.B.

EXAMINATION of the earliest ordination prayers in the rites of East and West alike has led us to the conclusion that early tradition did not think of Orders so much as the detailed powers of each ministry as from the standpoint of their function in the growth of the Church. Holy Orders with its degrees of bishop, priest and deacon, appeared as a *charisma* transmitted from the time of the apostles, whose purpose was to edify Christ's body, the Church, and to ensure its growth, continuity and unity. This ecclesial view of Orders as it appears in the ancient documents should broaden our vision and help us to pin-point the problem we have undertaken to study.

Since I have been asked to return to this subject, I shall now explain what the primitive Church understood by the terms *presbyterium* and *ordo episcoporum*. I shall not deal with the information given in the new testament, which is studied separately, and I shall stop at the Council of Chalcedon, i.e. the point where the Church, at the same time as she defined the essential dogmas of Christianity, obtained for herself a completed juridical structure. I am well aware that the development of the Church and of her institutions did not stop there, and I am not pretending to represent this period as the ideal age to which we must return. I am simply concerned to gather from this embryonic period those traditional elements which might help to provide a theological synthesis.

I. PRESBYTERIUM

By the end of the first century we see from St Ignatius of Antioch that the churches had at their head a bishop surrounded by his presbyterate. Submission to the bishop and presbyterate is one of the most frequent exhortations in the letters of Ignatius: 'Be minded to do all things in divine concord, for the bishop presides in the place of God, and the priests in place of the council of the apostles'.[1] To the Ephesians he writes that their presbytery is (as) fitted to the bishop as the strings are to the lyre.[2] So the presbyterate exists to assist the bishop. It forms a priestly body around him, or rather with him, and shares in his charge of ruling the Christian people. But it does not do so on an equal footing. It is the bishop who is the head and Ignatius brings out the distinction well in the passage I have just quoted and lays down the principle which will be accepted by the councils later on. 'Without the bishop let no one do anything that concerns the Church.'[3] He even adds: 'He who does anything without the bishop's knowledge, serves the devil'.[4]

The Apostolic Tradition of St Hippolytus gives us more detail. The presbyterate appears when the bishop is elected.[5] It takes part, with the people, in the election but not in the ordination. Only the bishops who are present lay their hands on the elect and the passage expressly states that the presbyterate does not intervene at this moment. Immediately after the ordination the priests take their place around the new bishop and, with him, extend their hands over the gifts while he alone says the

1. *Magn.* 6, 1.
2. *Eph.* 4, 1. See the other Ignatian texts: *Magn.* 3, 1–2; 13, 2; *Eph.* 5, 3–6, 2; *Trall.* 2, 1–2; *Phil.* 4, 1; *Smyrn.* 8, 1, and the excellent introduction by T. Camelot, *Ignace d'Antioche, Lettres,* 2nd ed., Paris 1951, pp 43–7.
3. *Smyrn.* 8, 1. cf. Council of Laodicaea, c. 37; *Mansi* II, 574. Council of Toledo (438), c. 20; *Mansi* III, 1002. 'Canons des Apôtres' 39 (Funk, *Didascalia et Constitutiones apostolorum,* Paderborn 1905, p. 572) 'Let the priests and deacons do nothing without the counsel of the bishop, for it is to him that the people of the Lord are committed, and it is he who will have to render an account for their souls.'
4. *Smyrn.* 9, 3.
5. *Tradition apostolique,* 2, ed. B. Botte, Paris 1946, p. 27.

anaphora.[1] Here they are performing a sacerdotal act. Indeed Hippolytus says later that they are ordained for the priesthood.[2] But the presbyterate does not confer his powers on the bishop. He holds these from the other bishops who impart to him 'the sovereign Spirit that Christ gave to his apostles'.[3] In this way he is chosen to 'govern the holy flock and to exercise the sovereign priesthood'. It pertains to him to offer the gifts of holy Church, to remit sins, to apportion the lots, i.e. the offices of the Church, in a word he is the pastor and high priest of the Church.

However in carrying out this charge he is assisted by a college of priests. These are ordained for the priesthood and the ordination prayers define their mission – to govern the people of God. They are like the seventy elders to whom Moses imparted his spirit.[4] They share in the common spirit of the presbyterate. No positive details are given as to their powers. Hippolytus excludes only the ordination of priests, which is reserved to the bishop.[5] However, when a new priest is ordained, they lay their hands on him with the bishop 'because of the common and like spirit of their charge'. They are not isolated individuals, each having a particular mission of his own; they form a college sharing the bishop's burdens.

It is also as a college gathered around the bishop that the presbyterate appears to us during the time of Pope Cornelius, some years later. He wrote to St Cyprian to say that he had called the presbyterate together so that they might arrive at a

1. *B. Botte, op. cit.*, 4, p. 30.
2. *ibid.*, 9, p. 39. With regard to the deacon, Hippolytus notes that the priests do not lay their hands on him because, unlike the priest, he is not ordained *in sacerdotio.*
3. *ibid.*, 3, p. 28. Nunc effunde eam virtutem quae a te est principalis spiritus quem dedisti dilecto filio tuo Iesu Christo quod donavit sanctis apostolis.
4. *ibid.*, 8, p. 38. Respice super servum tuum istum et impartire spiritum gratiae et consilii praesbyteris (b.; presbyterii) ut adiuvet et gubernet plebem tuam in corde mundo, sicut respexisti super populum electionis tuae et praecepisti Moisi ut elegeret praesbyteros quos replesti de spiritu tuo quod tu donasti famulo tuo. The typology of Moses and the seventy elders reappears in the Roman ordination prayers.
5. *ibid.*, 9, pp 39–40.

common decision about the Roman schism.[1] St Cyprian acted
in the same way. He wrote to his priests that at the beginning
of his episcopate he had decided to do nothing without their
counsel and the consensus of the people.[2] But this seemingly
very democratic declaration must not mislead us. Cyprian was
fully aware that his status was very different from that of president of a legislative assembly. He was the successor of the
apostles, and it was from them that he held his authority. I
shall return to this point later. Cyprian defines the Church as
the people united to its bishop (*sacerdos*), and the flock adhering
to its pastor. And he adds: 'Wherefore, know this, the bishop
is in the Church, and the Church is in the bishop; and those
who are not with the bishop are not in the Church.'[3] It is the
bishop who represents Christ and guarantees the unity of the
Church. 'Heresies have arisen, schisms have been born, for
the sole reason that the priesthood of God (*sacerdos*) was not
obeyed, and because it had been forgotten that there must be
one priest at once in the Church, one judge in place of Christ.'[4]

The schismatic Roman priests who returned to unity under

1. Letter to Cyprian, ap. Cyp., *Epist.* 49, 2 (ed. Hartel, p. 610):
'omni actu ad me perlato, placuit contrahi presbyterium. Adfuerunt
etiam episcopi quinque qui eo die praesentes fuerunt, ut firmato
consilio quid circa personam eorum observari deberet consensu
omnium statueretur.' Priests continued to sit on the Roman councils,
as we can see, for example, from that which took place in 431 under
Pope Hilary: *Mansi* VII, 959: 'residentibus etiam universis presbyteris,
adstantibus quoque diaconibus'. The custom was the same at
Alexandria. Bishop Alexander called the presbytery together during
the controversy with Arius, cf. Epiphanius, *Adv. Haer.* II, 69, 3, P.G.
42, 208.

2. *Epist.* 14, 4 (ed. Hartel, p. 512): 'Ad id quod scripserunt mihi
conpresbyteri nostri Donatus et Fortunatus et Novatus et Gordius,
solus rescribere nihil potui, quando a primordiis episcopatus mei
statuerim nihil sine consilio vestro et sine consensu plebis mea privata
sententia gerere.'

3. *Epist.* 66, 9 (ed. Hartel, p. 733): 'Et illi sunt ecclesia plebs
sacerdoti unita et pastori suo grex adhaerens. Unde scire debes
episcopum in ecclesia esse et ecclesiam in episcopo; et si qui cum
episcopo non sint, in ecclesia non esse.'

4. *Epist.* 59, 5 (ed. Hartel, pp 671–2): 'Neque enim aliunde haereses
obortae sunt aut nata sunt schismata quam quando sacerdoti Dei non
obtemperatur, nec unus in ecclesia ad tempus sacerdos et ad tempus
iudex vice Christi cogitatur.' Note that in Cyprian, *sacerdos* signifies
the bishop.

Pope Cornelius were of the same opinion; they recognised that there could only be one God, one Lord Christ, whom they had confessed, one Holy Spirit, one bishop in the Catholic Church.[1] A century later the same thing will be heard in an acclamation of the Roman people. The Emperor Constantius wished to set up two bishops at Rome. The people cried out: 'One God, one Christ, one bishop.'[2] There is not, then, a presbyterate side by side with the bishop but having distinct powers; there is a presbyterate *around* the bishop, who actually calls the priests his *cum presbyteri*. But he is their head; it is he who constitutes the unity of the presbyterate, as of the whole Church.

These are not abstract theories. They are translated into the concrete facts of the liturgy and discipline. When the bishop is present, it is he who celebrates the eucharist; the priests con-celebrate with him.[3] It is he also who presides at the rites of

1. In a letter from Pope Cornelius, ap. Cypr., *Epist.* 49, 2, (ed. Hartel, p. 611): 'Nec ignoramus unum verum deum esse et unum esse Christum dominum quem confessi sumus, unum sanctum spiritum, unum episcopum in catholica esse debere.'

2. Theodoret, *Hist. eccl.* II, 17, 6 (ed. Parmentier, p. 137). The case of coadjutor bishops is only an apparent exception to the rule. The first example we know of is that of Alexander, a contemporary of Origen, who was chosen to assist Narcissus, the bishop of Jerusalem, whose age prevented him from performing his duties, cf. Eusebius, *Hist. eccl.* VI, 1–3. In the fourth century, Senecion, coadjutor of Bassus, can be cited, cf. Pseudo-Ambrose, *Epist.* 56 (twice), P.L. 16, 1224. St Augustine was chosen by Valerius and consecrated during his lifetime, cf. Possidius, *Vita Aug.* 8, P.L. 32, 39; Augustine, *Epist.* 31, 4, P.L. 33, 23. But Augustine recognised that this was contrary to the Council of Nicaea. When he chose his successor, Eraclius, he had him elected by the people, but was content with ordaining him priest. He could only become bishop after Augustine's death. See the report of the election, *Epist.* 213, P.L. 33, 966–8. The temporary compromise proposed by the Catholics at the conference at Carthage, by which the Donatist would have sat with the Catholic bishop, was contrary to the Council of Nicaea, cf. Collatio Carthaginensis, *Mansi* IV, 61–2. The Council of Nicaea, Canon 8, *Mansi* II, 672, decided that Catharist bishops (Novatianists) returning to unity should perform the functions of priests or *chorepiscopi*. On the latter, see E. Kirsten, Art. Chorcischof in *Reallexikon fur Antike und Christentum*, II, Stuttgart 1954, c. 1105–14.

3. See Ignatius, *Philad.* 4, 1: 'Take heed to hold but one eucharist; for there is only one flesh of our Lord Jesus Christ, and one chalice to unite us to his blood, one altar, as there is one bishop with the presbytery and the deacons, my companions in service.' *Smyrn.* 8, 1: 'Without the bishop let no one do anything that concerns the Church.

initiation.[1] All the early rituals are pontificals, if we may be permitted this anachronism. The bishop reserved to himself the task of preparing the catechumens. The priests assisted him. They performed some part of the rites but everything was done under the presidency of the bishop. Just as there is only one altar so there is only one *cathedra*.[2] The priests are seated around the bishop but in lower places. They are 'of the second throne' as Constantine said at a convocation.[3] The bishop, successor of the apostles, is the sole doctor. It is to him that the teaching of the people pertains. When the old bishop of Hippo, Valerius, made St Augustine, then a simple priest, preach before him, there was a great fuss in Africa where nothing like it had been heard of before.[4] The custom had already spread to the East, but

Let that eucharist alone be regarded as lawful which is done under the presidency of the bishop, or of him to whom he has entrusted it. For where the bishop is, there let the community be; even as where Jesus Christ is, there is the Catholic Church.' The custom of the single Mass was maintained for long in the East and in the West; see St Leo's letter to the patriarch of Alexandria, *Epist.* 9, 2, P.L. 54, 926–7.

1. cf. Ignatius, *Smyrn.* 8, 2: 'It is not lawful, without the bishop, either to baptise or to hold *agape*.' Tertullian, *De bapt.* 17, 1 (ed. Refoulé, Paris 1952, pp 89–90): 'Dandi quidem summum habet ius summus sacerdos, si qui est, episcopus; dehinc presbyteri et diaconi, non tamen sine episcopi auctoritate, propter ecclesiae honorem quo salvo salva pax est.' The rite described by St Ambrose in *De Sacramentis* is an episcopal rite, but the priests take part in the ceremonies. It is the same in Hippolytus's *Apostolic Tradition*. The numerous homilies of the Fathers, such as St Augustine, Peter Chrysologus, Maximus of Turin, addressed to catechumens, show the care taken by the bishops in the preparation of candidates for baptism. A large proportion of the treatises of St Ambrose have their origin in this preaching.

2. For St Cyprian, there is only one *cathedra*, as there is only one altar, cf. *Epist.* 43, 5 (ed. Hartel, p. 594): 'Deus unus est et Christus unus et una ecclesia et cathedra una super Petrum domini voce fundata.' He reproaches the schismatics for wanting to set up another chair: 'Cathedram sibi constituere . . . conantur (*Epist.* 69, 8, Hartel, p. 757), profanum altare erigere et adulteram cathedram collocare' (*Epist.* 68, 2, Hartel, p. 745). The *cathedra* still appears in the Roman rite today as the symbol of the teaching office of the bishop: 'Tribue ei cathedram episcopalem.'

3. Letter to Chrestus, ap. Eusebius, *Hist. eccl.* X, 5, 23. See also *Statuta Ecclesiae antiqua*, P.L. 56, 880: 'Ut episcopus in ecclesia in consessu presbyterorum sublimior sedeat.'

4. Possidius, *Vita Aug.* 5, P.L. 32, 37: 'Eidem presbytero potestatem dedit coram se in ecclesia evangelium praedicandi ac frequen-

the Africans, attached to the old ways, could not understand why a simple priest should teach in the presence of him who was the doctor of the Church. It is the bishop also who reconciles penitents; he is the sole judge, as St Cyprian said in the passage already quoted.[1]

The bishop, however, could not be everywhere. As urban and rural churches were multiplied the needs of the Christian people grew and the bishop was compelled to delegate priests to the various churches. In these, especially when they were a great distance from the town, the priests themselves exercised the ministry of the word and sacraments. Nevertheless certain points of discipline are always there to remind us that this was by way of being a substitute. No Christian initiation was completed without the bishop; confirmation was reserved to him (the normal discipline in the West) or at any rate it was necessary to have holy chrism blessed by him.[2] The priests of the Roman titles celebrated the eucharist for a section of the people, but the sending of the *fermentum*, bread consecrated at the bishop's Mass, marked the link with the episcopal eucharist.[3] Moreover – and this is a more general discipline, which lasted a long time – the priests had to come into the episcopal city to take part in the bishop's Mass.[4] I shall not speak of penance,

---

tissime tractandi contra usum quidem et consuetudinem Africanarum ecclesiarum. Unde etiam nonnulli episcopi detrahebant.'

1. This is clear in the case of public penance, the only form of which there is evidence in the early Church. The reconciliation of penitents still remains an episcopal rite in the Roman pontifical.

2. Already in St Cyprian, *Epist.* 73, 9 (ed. Hartel, p. 785): 'Quod nunc quoque apud nos geritur, ut qui in ecclesia baptizantur praepositis ecclesiae offerantur et per nostram orationem ac manus impositionem spiritum sanctum consequantur et signaculo dominico consummentur.' cf. Innocent I, *Epist.* 25, III, 6, P.L. 20, 554. In the Eastern Church the custom of confirmation by a simple priest has become general but the blessing of the holy chrism remains a most solemn pontifical rite; cf. J. Goar, *Euchologion sive Rituale Graecorum*, Venice 1730, pp 501–16.

3. cf. Innocent I, *Epist.* 25, V, 8, P.L. 20, 556. On the meaning of this and analogous customs, see J. A. Jungmann, 'Fermentum' in *Colligere fragments*, Beuron, 1952, pp 185–90.

4. cf. Council of Auvergne (535), c. 15, *Mansi* VIII, 862; Council of Mâcon (581), c. 10, *Mansi* IX, 933.

since even today no priest can absolve the faithful without jurisdiction given him by the Ordinary of the place.

So the bishop is not simply the honourable president of a college, like the dean of a chapter or an administrator dealing with disciplinary matters. He is the true pastor of his people. A little illustration serves to show how keenly aware a great bishop was of his obligations. Forty miles from Hippo there was a very important locality, Fussala, which contained a good number of Donatists to be brought back into unity. St Augustine stated that distance prevented him from dealing with the matter personally. What did he do? He wrote to the primate of Numidia to ask him if he would go and set up a bishop there.[1] It was in his eyes too important a task of his ministry to be entrusted to a simple priest.

Towards the end of the fourth century, however, there was a presbyterian movement. In the East we note Aerius, an Arian; in the West, St Jerome,[2] who had such an influence on the theology of the Middle Ages. The priest, it was said, could do almost everything the bishop did apart from ordination and certain rites of consecration. And indeed the terminology of the new testament is fluid. The bishop should be but a *primus inter pares*. The *Statuta Ecclesiae Antiqua*, an apocryphal writing of the fifth century, the presbyterian tendencies of which are obvious, attempted to limit the prerogatives of bishops; but the move was too timid. It was content to direct the bishop to do nothing without the advice of his clergy, and he was reminded that, although he occupied a higher place in church, he must consider the priests as his colleagues when he was at home. In the end priests were allowed to ordain *chanters* which seems to have been a phantom order in the West.[3] For the rest, all episcopal prerogatives were respected. In short St Jerome's opinion had no

1. Augustine, *Epist.* 209, 2, P.L. 33, 953.
2. On Aerius, cf. Epiphanius, *Adv. haer.* III, 73, P.G. 42, 505–12. For St Jerome, see *Comm. in Tit.* P.L. 26, 596–8; *Epist.* 69, 3, P.L. 22, 656. See also the pseudo-Jeromite treatise *De septem ordinibus*, P.L. 30, 152–9.
3. On the Statuta see B. Botte, 'Le rituel d'ordination des Statuta Ecclesiae antiqua', in *Recherches de théologie ancienne et médiévale* 11, 1939, pp 223–41.

effect at all on the *discipline* of the Church; it remained a private opinion which was unable to prevail against a well-established tradition. But it influenced the medieval theologians. Taken up by Rabanus Maurus and Amalarius, the passages from St Jerome re-orientated theological speculation by making it start with the priesthood and not with the episcopate. *Sacerdos* no longer normally signified the bishop, as it did up to the fourth century. It became synonymous with *presbyter*. And so attempts to define the *sacerdotium* began with the priesthood and it was then asked what more the bishop could have than the priest. Furthermore the episcopate as such disappeared from the list of Orders.

Yet the constitution of the Church did not change. The liturgical texts are always there to affirm that priests are co-operators with the order of bishops. Neither did the canonical direction change, at least in substance. Canon 329 of the *Codex Iuris Canonici* still states: '*Episcopi sunt successores apostolorum atque ex divina institutione peculiaribus ecclesiis praeficiuntur quas cum potestate ordinaria regunt sub auctoritate Pontificis Romani.*' Apart from the last clause, this is exactly St Cyprian's doctrine. Later enactments may have restricted episcopal privileges but they have changed nothing that is essential. Relations between priests and bishops may have been modified in certain points of detail, but from the theological point of view they have remained the same. So what we find in the first four centuries remains valid for determining what priesthood is. The presbyterate remains a priestly body, assisting and supplying for the bishop in his charge of governing the people of God.

2. ORDO EPISCOPORUM

Looking at the local church of the first centuries our immediate impression is of a patriarchal society living very much on its own resources. There are no liturgical books and no codified law. The bishop is the sole legislator for his community. He lives very close to his people, consults his presbyters on important matters, and even seeks the consensus of the people. But he is dependent on no one. He is the head of the community. Some historians regard it as the golden age. But it changed when the conciliar period opened with the Council of Nicaea. The Church began to shape its constitution after the pattern of the Roman Empire and acquired a juridical structure which, with its metropolitans and patriarchs, became more and more rigid. A whole system of decisions of ecumenical and local councils began to enclose the bishop and his community in a network of directions and minutiae, until the interventions of the Roman See (which became more and more frequent) made the Church an absolute monarchy. So from the fourth century the political influence of the Empire, together with Roman legalism, transformed the Church by firmly securing the little primitive autonomous communities in the iron collar of a gigantic juridical machine. It is quite certain that the juridical structure of the Church was only developed in stages, and it was only gradually that the autonomy of the bishop found itself reduced. Indeed no one has ever dreamed of denying it. But it is not true to say that this organisation was imposed from without or that it only began with the conciliar period. It emerged, in fact, much earlier because the bishops were conscious of belonging to an *ordo episcoporum*.

This expression can be taken in two ways – in its historical sense and in its hierarchical sense.

In its historical sense, *ordo episcoporum* indicates the succession of bishops through whom the apostolic tradition is conveyed, as well as the *charisma* bestowed by the imposition of hands. The expression is first found in Tertullian.[1] But St Irenaeus had previously expressed the same idea. To meet sectarian pretensions of preserving secret traditions Irenaeus pleaded the tradition of the apostolic churches. He confined himself in particular to the Church of Rome but this was only in the interests of brevity; an enquiry into the other apostolic

---

1. *Adv. Marc.* iv, 5, P.L. 2, 395; 'Habemus et Ioannis alumnas ecclesias. Nam etsi Apocalypsim eius Marcion respuit, ordo tamen episcoporum ad originem recensus in Ioannem stabit auctorem.' *De praescr.* 32, P.L. 2, 52: 'Edant ergo origines ecclesiarum suarum, evolvant ordinem episcoporum suorum ita per successiones ab initio decurrentem, ut primus ille episcopus aliquem ex apostolis vel apostolicis viris . . . habuerit auctorem et antecessorem. Hoc enim modo ecclesiae apostolicae census suos deferunt.'

churches would have produced the same results. In the churches, then, the transmission of the deposit of faith was guaranteed by an uninterrupted succession of bishops.[1] This succession must not be thought of in an unspiritual way, but as though every bishop has ordained his successor although in fact he was usually ordained by neighbouring bishops. As a rule he was chosen by the people within the community itself and there are texts which definitely show that this was still the rule in the fourth century.[2] The bishop was chosen to continue the work of his predecessor and he was equipped for it by consecration. Irenaeus is the first to formulate the *theory* of apostolic succession but there is nothing to show that he invented it. In fact, episcopal lists were in existence before his time as evidenced by Hegesippus (middle of the second century). The historical accuracy of these lists is of small moment. They evidence the conviction of the Christian people that the catholicity of the Church was bound up with its continuity, itself guaranteed by the succession of the *ordo episcoporum*.

As we have seen Tertullian took up the same ideas as Irenaeus, and actually made use of the expression *ordo episcoporum*.[3] But above all the bishops themselves were conscious of being the successors of the apostles. Thus Firmilian of Caesaraea in Cappadocia, writing to St Cyprian, speaks of the Catholic Church 'in which we are, we, who have succeeded the apostles'.[4] Cyprian, for his part, writing to Pope Cornelius says: 'We work, and we must work, to preserve the unity handed down by the

1. Irenaeus, *Adv. haer.* iii, 2 (ed. Harvey, vol. ii, pp 8–9). Hegesippus had already discovered the elements of these lists of bishops before him.

2. See Cyprian, *Epist.* 57, 5 (ed. Hartel, p. 739). In the fourth century, Pope Julius mentions among the canonical irregularities attending the election of Gregory as bishop of Alexandria, that he had not been baptised in that church, that he had not been asked for, either by clergy or people, and that he had been consecrated at Antioch. cf. Athanasius, *Apol.* 30, P.G. 25, 297.

3. See texts quoted.

4. Letter to Cyprian, ap. Cypr., *Epist.* 75, 16 (ed. Hartel, p. 821): 'Potestas ergo peccatorum remittendorum apostolis data est et ecclesiis quas illi a Christo missi constituerunt et episcopis qui eis ordinatione vicaria successerunt.'

Lord through the apostles to us, their successors.'[1] Examples
could be multiplied. Even St Jerome, though tending to limit
the power of bishops, supports the tradition: 'Wherever there
is a bishop, whether he be of Rome, Gubbio, Constantinople,
Reggio, Alexandria or Tanis, there is the same dignity, the same
priesthood . . . they are all successors of the apostles'.[2] The
bishop, on taking up his charge, is therefore aware that he is not
the leader of a kind of community that he can fashion according
to his pleasure. He enters into a succession whose origin leads
him back to the apostles, and he becomes a link in this *ordo*
which guarantees the continuity of the Church. This conviction,
as we have seen, is expressed in the ordination prayers of the
various rites.

There is, however, a second sense of *ordo episcoporum* which
I have called hierarchic. In an organised society not every person
possesses the same rank, and various classes are formed. For
example, the Romans had their *ordo senatorius* and their *ordo
equestris*. It is the same in the Church. There is an *ordo episcoporum*. It is in this sense that the old Roman ordination prayers
describe priests as *cooperatores ordinis nostri*.

It is not merely a question of individuals possessing the same
dignity without any link between them. The *ordo episcoporum*
forms a body, a college. These are the expressions used by St
Cyprian, although he set himself up as the champion of episcopal autonomy:

There are many bishops in the body; they are joined together by
the cement of mutual concord and the bond of unity, so that if any
one of our college attempts to frame a heresy, to wound and worry the

---

1. *Epist.* 45, 3 (ed. Hartel, p. 602): 'Hoc enim vel maxime, frater,
et laboramus et laborare debemus ut unitatem a domino et per
apostolos nobis successoribus traditam, quantum possumus, obtinere
curemus.' See also the sentence of Clarus, *Sententiae episcoporum* (ed.
Hartel, p. 459): 'Manifesta est sententia domini nostri Iesu Christi
apostolos suos mittentis et ipsis solis potestatem a patre sibi datam
permittentis, quibus nos successimus eadem potestate ecclesiam
domini gubernantes.'

2. *Epist.* 146, P.L. 1194: 'Ubicumque fuerit episcopus sive Romae
sive Eugubii sive Constantinopoli sive Rhegii sive Alexandriae sive
Tanis, eiusdem meriti est et sacerdotii . . . Ceterum omnes successores
apostolorum sunt.'

flock of Christ, the others come to the rescue ... for although we are many pastors, we feed the one flock, and we must gather together and care for all the sheep Christ won by his blood and passion.[1]

So the bishop is conscious not only of being admitted into the succession of the apostles but also of being a member of a body, a college, an order entrusted with the care of feeding the Lord's flock. And this conviction was expressed in acts.

First of all there is episcopal consecration itself. It is performed, not by the presbyterate, but by the bishops present according to the apostolic tradition. Hippolytus does not say who these bishops are. St Cyprian is more definite and says that according to African custom and that of the majority of the provinces all the neighbouring bishops of the province gathered together in the community which desired to elect a bishop, and that the election was held in the presence of the people.[2] This discipline must, therefore, have been in force for a long time, since Cyprian considers it to be quasi-universal. The Council of Nicaea made no innovations; it merely put the seal on an existing custom when it made this ruling on the matter:

It is most expedient that a bishop be set up by all the bishops of the province. However, if this proves to be difficult because of urgency or distance, let the ordination be performed after three of them have met together, those who are absent taking part in the election by writing.[3]

The number three which is mentioned in subsequent texts

1. *Epist.* 68, 3–4 (ed. Hartel, pp 746–7): 'Copiosum corpus est sacerdotum concordiae mutuae glutino atque unitatis vinculo copulatum, ut si quis ex collegio nostro haeresim facere et gregem Christi lacerare et vastare temptaverit, subveniant ceteri qua pastores utiles et misericordes oves dominicas in gregem colligant ... Nam etsi pastores multi sumus, unum tamen gregem pascimus et oves universas quas Christus sanguine suo et passione quaesivit colligere et fovere debemus.'

2. *Epist.* 67, 5 (ed. Hartel, p. 739): 'Propter quod diligenter de traditione divina et apostolica observatione servandum est et tenendum, quod apud nos quoque et fere per provincias universas tenetur, ut ad ordinationes rite celebrandas ad eam plebem cui praepositus ordinatur episcopi eiusdem provinciae proximi quique conveniant et episcopus deligatur plebe presente quae singulorum vitam plenissime novit et uniuscuiusque actum de eius conversatione perspexit.'

3. *Mansi* II, 669.

was never more than a minimum. The purpose of the direction was never to ensure sacramental validity[1] but because the election of a bishop is not a matter for the community alone but concerns the whole Church. The candidate is incorporated into the *ordo episcoporum* by a collegial act.

This was no simple juridical formality. To exercise his authority lawfully the bishop must remain in communion with his colleagues. This communion is expressed in eucharistic communion but it presupposes a common faith. St Irenaeus gives an account of Polycarp's interview with Pope Anicetus, and to show that the paschal question did not possess the importance that Pope Victor wished to attribute to it, he stresses that the Pope 'yielded the celebration of the eucharist to him', and that they communicated together.[2] Had it been an important question which might have imperilled the unity of the Church the Pope would not have acted in this way. This is clearly what is in St Irenaeus's mind. Hegesippus, about the middle of the second century, relates that in the course of his voyage to Rome, where he stayed during the pontificates of Anicetus and Eleutherius, he met many bishops and found that they all held the same doctrine.[3] This unity of faith, at a time when sects were springing up like mushrooms, can only be understood in the light of the relations which the bishops, who had the unity of the Church at heart, maintained with each other. The preservation of the tradition was only possible through the various local churches comparing their particular customs. Personal relationships, such as that of Polycarp and Pope Anicetus, were doubtless exceptional, but contact by correspondence was much more common. Dionysius of Corinth wrote to the communities of Athens, Lacedemonea, Gortyne, Amastris, Pontus, Cnossus and Rome. The bishop of Cnossus replied to him, and asked him to write again.[4] Not every bishop had the epistolary talents of

1. Council of Arles (314), *Mansi* I, 473: 'Si non potuerint septem, sine tribus fratribus non praesumant ordinare.' At the third Council of Carthage (393), *Mansi* III, 883, two bishops demanded the retention of the custom requiring twelve bishops. The council simply accepted the Nicaean directions.

2. Eusebius, *Hist. eccl.*, V, 24, 16–17.

3. *ibid.*, IV, 22, 1.   4. *ibid.*, IV, 23, 1–13.

Dionysius but they all shared his solicitude for the unity of the Church. A question had only to crop up and the bishops of the whole region met to discuss it. We have an example of this in the paschal question.[1] This was dealt with chiefly by the bishops of the most important sees, such as Rome, Alexandria, Antioch, Ephesus, but we observe that the bishops of the various regions met to examine the traditions of their respective churches in this matter.

In the third century these contacts were multiplied. The Novatian schism was not a purely Roman concern: it could only succeed if Novatian managed to obtain recognition from the other bishops. A council of sixty bishops met at Rome[2] and another was held at Antioch.[3] St Cyprian took part personally,[4] as did Dionysius of Alexandria who exhorted Novatian to bear witness to the unity of the Church 'which is no less great than to bear witness to the faith'.[5] A short while after this the controversy concerning Paul of Samosata broke out – he was bishop of Antioch, one of the most important churches, and the first centre of the spread of Christianity after Jerusalem. Now, by departing from the rule of faith, Paul had forfeited his right to his bishopric, and a synod which met at Antioch deposed him and put Domnus in his place. The members of the synod wrote a letter addressed to the bishops of Rome and Alexandria, which was also to be communicated to the other bishops requesting them to receive 'letters of communion' from Domnus, and to reply to them.[6]

From this we infer that these 'letters of communion' were already an established custom. However, Paul of Samosata refused to surrender the church buildings. Having no power of coercion, the bishops approached the Emperor Aurelian, who decided to give the buildings to the one recognised as the true head of the community by the bishops of Italy.[7] So, in the eyes of

1. See the whole dossier collected by Eusebius, *Hist. eccl.* V, 24–35; cf. B. Botte 'La question pascale' in *La Maison Dieu*, no. 41 (1955), pp 84–95.
2. Eusebius, *Hist. eccl.* VI, 43, 2.   3. *ibid.*, VI, 43, 3.
4. See especially letters 44, 52, 55, 59, 60, 68 in Hartel's edition.
5. Eusebius, *Hist. eccl.* VI, 45.
6. *ibid.*, VII, 30, 14–19.   7. *ibid.*, 19.

a pagan emperor, there were not only local churches but a Catholic Church whose unity was guaranteed by the communion of bishops.

It might seem, however, that this unity was precarious and superficial. The manuals of ecclesiastical history give the impression that the life of the Church during these first centuries was no more than a long sequence of disputes asserting local particularism. This is because our manuals are too frequently of the 'war story' type. They lay so much stress on the conflicts that there is no space left to speak of the profound life of the Church. Yet the controversies are only small matters in comparison with the essential principles on which there was complete agreement – the canon of scripture, the rule of faith, moral discipline and sacramental life. And all this at a period when Christianity was in danger of dissipation through gnostic speculation or montanist illuminism. What gave the young Church this cohesion in face of the sects? It could not have been the support of the Empire which even when it was not persecuting was indifferent. It could not have been the superiority of its apologists, for the sects also had some very clever doctors. Nor could it have been the hierarchical structure as such, for the sects had their organisation as well. It could only be the profound conviction of being the Catholic Church founded on the apostles and prophets. And its apostolicity was guaranteed by the succession of bishops who had received, through the imposition of hands, the charge to continue the work of the apostles, and who, through their concord, maintained the Church's unity. They were not great writers: there are perhaps a dozen of them, at most, who have left some trace of literary work. But it is chiefly they who were in the forefront of the battle for the defence of the tradition – much more so than the apologists. History has hardly preserved their memory. Most are just names in a list or signatures at the foot of documents, e.g. those on the letter of Serapion against the Montanists.[1] But it is impossible that these men who wrote

1. Eusebius, *Hist. eccl.*, V, 19, 3–4: 'And in this letter of Serapion there are preserved in the signatures of various bishops, of whom one signed himself "I, Aurelius Cyrenaeus, a martyr, pray for your welfare". Another as follows: "I, Aelius Publius Julius, bishop of Debeltum, a colony of Thrace. As God lives in the heavens, the blessed Sotas in

and met to decide the paschal question should not have had the very foundations of Christianity, which were threatened by the sects, much more at heart. The very fact that they discussed together proves that they wished to agree and that they had a sense of unity.

We must recognise, however, that on certain points such as the paschal question and of the baptism of heretics there was no progress and everyone held to his own position. And soon other thorny questions arose and the period of the great theological controversies began. A way to preserve the unity of the faith had to be found and thus began the great ecumenical councils, which were to determine not only the formularies of the faith but also the law of the Church.

This period has not had a good press, as I have said, among many non-Catholic historians and theologians. It was the time when Roman legalism was introduced into the Church, after the pattern and with the help of the Empire, doing away with the ecclesiastical autonomy of the first centuries. The sphere of the metropolitan and patriarch was to be determined by the pattern provided by the Roman province; decrees were to be promulgated which would have the force of law throughout the whole Church; in other words it was to be given a juridical constitution.

In all this there is some truth, but much exaggeration. It is quite true that the emperors were greatly interested in seeing the conflicts settled and both favoured the councils and intervened in a way which was often inopportune. But it is utterly wrong to suppose that the conciliar movement and the organisation of the Church were due only to the influence of the Empire. Both arose because the *ordo episcoporum* was deeply conscious of the unity of the Church, a conviction which was already present in the second century. St Irenaeus says: 'The Church preserves this faith with great care, and although she is dispersed throughout the whole world, it is as if she occupied but one

---

Anchialus wished to drive the devil out of Priscilla, and the hypocrites would not let him." The autograph signatures of many other bishops who agreed with them are also preserved in the above-mentioned writing.' (trs. Kirsopp Lake, Heinemann 1926.)

house. She believes these things as if she had a single heart and a single soul; she preaches and teaches and passes them down with perfect harmony, as if she had but one mouth.'[1] And St Cyprian: 'The Catholic Church is one; she is organised and united by the cement of the bishops who are joined one to another.'[2] It was this awareness of being the 'cement' of the Catholic Church which led to the convocation of the ecumenical councils. The peace of the Church and the facilities of the imperial post made it possible where it had not been so in previous centuries, but there was no break with the past; it was merely a logical and necessary development from what had gone before.

As to hierarchical organisation, although it is true that political factors determined the constitution of the patriarchate to a certain extent, it would be wrong to think that it was due simply to the intrusion of the political element in the life of the Church. Organisation had begun before Nicaea. The Council explicitly refers to a previous tradition, and we note that the jurisdiction of the bishop of Alexandria extended practically over the whole of Egypt.[3]

Finally what happened in the period of the great councils is only a confirmation of what is found in preceding centuries. The ecumenical council is nothing more than the *ordo episcoporum* meeting to fulfil in unanimity and concord its office of governing the Church of God.

3. CONCLUSIONS

This account only serves to illustrate what the ordination prayers have already revealed – the collegiate character of the episcopate and priesthood. So I could conclude now and leave

1. *Adv. haer.* I, X, 2 (ed. Harvey, vol. 1, p. 92).
2. *Epist.* 66, 8 (ed. Hartel, p. 733): 'quando ecclesia quae catholica una est, scissa non sit, sed utique conexa et cohaerentium sibi invicem sacerdotum glutino copulata'.
3. *Mansi* II, 669–72. See also the commentary in Hefele-Leclercq, *Histoire des conciles*, 1, Paris 1907, pp 552–69. The council did no more than codify a position which had been reached in fact and in law. The Council of Chalcedon made some modifications in the organisation of the patriarchates but did not introduce a completely new law.

to others the task of discovering what light it throws on the whole problem with which we are concerned. I will, however, permit myself some reflections which have no purpose other than to give a lead to the discussion.

Our object is not to put forward some reform of the Church, nor even to seek, at any rate immediately, a solution to present-day difficulties. Our proper and immediate object is to work out a theology of priesthood. I think we all agree that we can only establish this theology on the solid basis of tradition and not on the shifting sands of purely abstract speculation. But of course there is some ambiguity about the meaning of the word 'tradition'. Certain theologians appear to regard tradition as a series of intellectual utterances, principles or theories passed from mouth to mouth, and which were one day committed to writing, and to think that we have only to stir the dust of scholasticism, to shake up the texts of the Fathers and ecclesiastical writers, to discover the lost theory. As a result of this rummaging, passages completely isolated from any context are brought to light, and a phrase from Clement of Alexandria is tacked on to one from St Cyril, a third from Pseudo-Dionysius, a fourth from St Gregory or St Bernard, and this assortment is then advanced as an argument from tradition in favour of some theological theory which is obtruding itself – or almost – on the Christian faith.

This kind of research can only result in theories which are not likely to survive and whose only effect is to clutter up our libraries, since they spring from a false idea of tradition. Tradition is not an abstract theory circulating by word of mouth. It is lived before being formulated, and it is formulated before it is rationally explained. The Mass was lived as a sacrifice before anyone could dream of expressing it clearly, and its sacrificial character was defined before an explanation of it had been given; in fact even today no conclusive explanation of it has been found to satisfy everyone. So true tradition is not to be found exclusively in intellectual utterances but is made concrete in attitudes, usages, acts and institutions. And among the utterances of ecclesiastical writers there is a certain amount of sorting out to be done for not everything has the same value. The words of a St Augustine when he is speaking as a bishop, and in the name of a tradition whose guardian he is, have more weight than the theories of St Jerome or Pseudo-Dionysius, which only express a personal opinion. A burst of oratory in a sermon has not the same value as a sentence uttered at a council and we must not mix them up, or ideas will become confused. I think this is particularly important for the question we are now considering for there is a danger in elaborating an abstract theory of priesthood from utterances gleaned here and there – the priest, mediator between God and men. Then alongside this theory is placed an ecclesiastical discipline, since a certain order is absolutely necessary in any society. But that has nothing to do with theology – it is canon law. This is emptied of all theological content, so that in it is seen only an amalgam of decisions, more or less valid, according to circumstances, without distinguishing between the essential and the accessory. Yet by this very fact theology is also emptied of one part of its traditional substance. It is paradoxical that the episcopate does not figure in the list of orders: one synopsis of dogmatic theology devotes a chapter to the sacrament of Orders without naming the episcopate, except in an appendix. *Sacerdotium* is defined by reference to the priesthood as the sacrament which confers the spiritual power and grace to celebrate the eucharist and perform the other ecclesiastical functions. A dual power is conferred in Orders: the one, over the eucharistic body of Christ, to consecrate it; the other, over his mystical body, to prepare the souls of the faithful to receive the eucharist.

All this is perhaps right in itself, but it must be recognised that, away from its ecclesiological context, it is somewhat incomplete. The eucharist has the appearance of being an end in itself, and, in spite of the expression 'mystical body' – put in for its parallelism – the perspective is rather individualistic; there is the priest on the one hand, and the souls of the faithful on the other. And if anyone with a little curiosity asks what the episcopate is, he will find, in the appendix I mentioned, an account of the discussions of the theologians – does the episcopate imprint a new character, or is it merely the extension of the priestly character for other purposes? Let us note, in passing, that this sacramental character which spreads like a wine-stain is one of

the most convenient devices of modern theology! The episcopate is indeed treated in this manual, but we have to refer to
the chapter *De Ecclesia* to find it: apparently it has no connection with the sacrament of Orders.

Is there any need to add that a theology as curtailed as this,
added to that simplification which ideas always undergo, ends
by becoming a veritable caricature? If we wish to make a valid
theological synthesis of priesthood we must give it a broader and
more solid basis in tradition, and take into account not only the
theories but also the living tradition.

Some of you will have said to yourselves in the course of this
paper: 'This is all very well but it is about the history of institutions or canon law: what has that to do with theology?' This
is quite true but it is in the history of institutions, much more
than in theories, that the Church's sense of priesthood is expressed
in act. Now this sense has two roots – the conviction that she is
apostolic, and the conviction that she is one and Catholic. She
is apostolic because her bishops have, with the deposit of tradition, passed on from age to age a *charisma* which comes to them
from the apostles and, in the last analysis, from Christ himself.
She is one and Catholic because her bishops are in solidarity one
with another and because the *ordo episcoporum* maintains,
through its communion, the unity of the Church spread abroad
over the whole earth.

This invites us to construct a synthesis, not on the basis of
the ritual powers of each particular priest, but from the point of
view of the *ecclesia* as a whole – priesthood is the principle of
the growth, organisation and unity of the body of Christ – the
same conclusion to which we were led by the study of the liturgical prayers.

The presbyterate, then, is not an autonomous organism placed
side by side with the bishop. It has no special domain assigned
to it outside the bishop's sphere. It is there to advise and assist
him and to deputise for him in his absence. But it is the bishop
who is the pastor of his people *par excellence*. In the first centuries he did indeed live very close to them and he knew them
and was known by them. It is the bishop who is the principle of
unity in his church not only in disciplinary but in sacramental

and doctrinal matters. Although he is assisted by a presbyterate he is fully cognisant of being the head, and of representing the apostolic power in himself alone. The presbyterate shares his power, but in unity and submission.

However the bishop is no dictator, imposing an arbitrary law on his community without any restraint. Above him are the gospel and tradition. He must therefore remain in contact with the other churches. Should he violate the rule of faith he will forfeit his rights. Here again, the ideal of the early Church is an ideal of unity. Certainly there were strains on this unity – but the conflicts and schisms only served to underline, sometimes tragically, the conviction that there could only be one Church, one faith, one communion. The idea of intercommunion never occurred to anyone in the early Church: nothing was more foreign to the early episcopate than insularity. Doubtless each bishop held on to his own customs – unity must not be confused with uniformity – but the bishops had an acute sense of their duty towards the universal Church because they were aware of belonging to the order on which the apostolicity and unity of the Church rested. They felt responsible as a body for what happened in the whole Church.

I am not pretending that the picture of the Church of the early centuries represents an ideal to which we must substantially return. For the Church was organised in a more definite way through conciliar legislation, and then as a result of the intervention of the apostolic see of Rome, which claimed and exercised in an increasingly effective manner its right to jurisdiction over the whole Church; and in the last place there has been the definition of pontifical infallibility at the Vatican Council. Furthermore, the conditions under which the priesthood is exercised today in our vast dioceses are not the same as in the tiny episcopal cities of the first centuries. Yet in spite of all these changes the constitution of the Church has not changed. The code of canon law still proclaims that the bishops are the successors of the apostles, and that their jurisdiction is by divine right. The ordination prayers inculcate the same doctrine. We are ordained to be *collaborators*, fellow-workers, with the order of bishops. The ideal of unity is no less alive now than it was in the early centuries. It seems to me clear that the fundamental principles which were lived and proclaimed in former days are as valid as ever, and that a theology of the priesthood must take the *ordo episcoporum* as its starting point, not only in the sense of a narrow legalism which sees in it merely an external discipline, but in the theological sense of the word. It is because of a *charisma*, conveyed through the imposition of hands, that the bishops, assisted by their presbyterate, have built up the Church. It is through them that she must still grow.

Of course the hierarchy is not the Church. But without it there would be no Church. There has been a reaction, and rightly, against a presentation of the Church which placed the accent so strongly on the hierarchy that it appeared to be rather like a fleshless skeleton. But the opposite error would be even more dangerous. If we disposed of the skeleton, there would be nothing left but an invertebrate. No longer must anyone think of placing an invisible Church side by side with the visible, as two distinct entities which coincide only by chance. That there are men of good will outside the Church who form part of the Church no one can possibly doubt – but that is one of God's secrets. The mission which Christ gave to his apostles is to unite all men in a visible society having the same faith, the same hope, partaking in the same eucharist and living in the same charity. It is towards this unity that the efforts of the apostles and those who have continued their work have been directed. It is for this unity that the priesthood of today must strive. Not only to sanctify souls, as our manual of theology says, each on his own account, but to form a living Church. Such, it seems to me, is the angle from which we must study the priesthood and to this end the theology of the episcopate must be given first place. The episcopate is not a juridical organism superimposed on the priesthood: it is the very principle of priesthood, and therefore of the Church itself – at any rate unless the Church has been mistaken for the last nineteen hundred years. But for us who believe in the Church as one, holy, catholic, and apostolic, there is no room for doubt about this.

CHAPTER V

NOTES ON THE EARLY TERMINOLOGY OF CHRISTIAN PRIESTHOOD

P.M. GY, O.P.

DOCTRINAL historians have been so concerned with the vocabulary of priesthood in the new testament that they have frequently neglected the study of the realities to which this vocabulary is applied.[1] The present paper is the result of a different approach. Following the method suggested by the encyclical *Humani Generis*,[2] I should like to throw the light of tradition on the two terms which are foreign to new testament usage, but which are employed in the theology of the Latin Church at the present day with reference to priesthood – *ordo* and *sacerdos*. On several occasions the epistle to the Hebrews effectively quotes the phrase in psalm **109** which describes Christ as priest after the order of Melchisedech, but the use of *ordo* – τάξις recurs in no part of the new testament outside chapters 5–7 of this epistle. The term ἱερευς, which is translated by *sacerdos* is still not regarded as the equivalent of πρεσβύτερος – presbyter in the new testament, but is reserved to Christ, who transcends the ἱερεῖς of the old testament and the pagan cults.

I. ORDO, ORDINARE, ORDINATIO

Ordo has quite a definite sense in the institutions of ancient Rome,[3] where it used to describe colleges or definite social

---

1. J. Colson, *L'Église dans les communautés primitives*, Paris 1951, marks a healthy reaction in this respect.
2. A.A.S. 42 (1950), p. 568.
3. On *ordo* in antiquity, the essential work is a study by B. Kuebler in Pauly-Wissowa-Kroll, xviii-1, Stuttgart 1939, col. 930–4. Through

classes. At Rome itself the highest *ordo*, *ordo amplissimus*, was the senate, which looked after the welfare of the *res publica* and of the *populus romanus*. During the period of the Gracci a new social and political body arose, known as the *equites*, which ranked between the senatorial order and the *populus romanus*. From that time *ordo uterque* was used to denote both senators and equestrians. It is quite improper to refer to the *plebs* as an *ordo* although the code of Theodosius does mention once those who had been reduced to the order of the plebs, *rejecti in ordinem plebeiorum*.[1]

The combination of *ordo et plebs*[2] was found outside the capital of the Empire in the municipalities and the colonies, where the *ordo* was the body of men governing the town, the order of the *decurions*.

With the emergence of Christian Latin in Tertullian we see that the analogy of the *ordo* and the people of the city of Rome was taken up to describe the relationship of the clergy to the people of God. It would be beyond the scope of these reflections on terminology to show that the position of the clergy does not stand out in such clear outlines in the new testament, and that there had been a real development of institutions. But at any rate I must point out that a profane term such as *ordo* would not meet with the same feelings of disapproval among Christian people as the terminology of the pagan religions. Tertullian used it as a generic term for the clergy, correlative to the *plebs sancta*.[3] And since, in profane speech, we sometimes come across *ordo et plebs*, and sometimes *ordo et populus*, Mgr Schrijnen and

---

the kindness of the management of *Thesaurus Linguae Latinae* I have had access to the index of the article *Ordo* in the Thesaurus.

1. *Cod. Theod.* ix, 45, 5. In fact the *Lex Aurelia iudiciaria* (75 B.C.) associates a third order – *tribuni aerarii* – with the senators and equestrians. Kuebler, col. 932.

2. Kuebler, col. 931. For *ordo populusque*, cf. *Inscr. Not. d. Scavi*, 1915, p. 32; 1922, p. 154; 1923, p. 405. Corp. xiv *Suppl. Ost.* 4449 (fourth century), *ordo et populus civitatis*.

3. Differentiam inter ordinem et plebem constituit Ecclesiae auctoritas (*De exhort. cast.* 7, Oehler i, 747). Other references in A. Harnack, *Entstehung und Entwickelung der Kirchenverfassung und des Kirchenrechts in den zwei ersten Jahrhunderten*, Leipzig 1910, p. 82.

Miss Mohrmann[1] have observed that where African Christians used *plebs* to translate λαός the 'holy people' of the bible, Rome, from the time of Pope Cornelius, more naturally used *populus*. The Roman sacramentaries and the missal itself confirm this preference,[2] in spite of the *nos et plebs tua sancta*, which, in the Canon of the Mass, marks the highest point of participation by the holy people in the celebration of the liturgy.

To return to clergy and *ordo*; after the peace of the Church, we meet a new tripartite arrangement in the city of Rome combining the clergy with the order of senators or with the decurions. So, at the time of the synod of 501, Theodoric sent a letter to the clergy, senate and people of Rome, *clero, senatui et Romano populo*.[3] Although the word *ordo* does not occur here we know that in the sixth century both the Roman clergy and the senate assumed the title of sacred order, *sacer ordo*.[4] St Gregory, writing at the end of the century, has left us numerous letters addressed jointly to the clergy, the *ordo*, and people of such and such an Italian city.[5] The Pope speaks indifferently of 'such a city' or of 'such a church', since the people of the city as a whole had now become a *populus christianus*; they were no longer *gentes*, the Gentiles having been admitted into the people of God, and the order of decurions had become the most dignified section of the laity.

Most frequently the word *ordo* is applied to the various orders into which the clergy were divided. Thus St Leo calls the order of subdeacon 'fourth from the head', *quartus a capite*, and above it he numbers the *leviticus* and the *presbyteralis honor* and the *episcopalis excellentia*.[6] Furthermore, in a Holy Week sermon in

---

1. J. Schrijnen and C. Mohrmann, *Studien zur Syntax der Briefe des hl. Cyprian*, 1, Nijmegen 1936, p. 58.
2. cf. P. Bruylants, *Concordance verbale du sacramentaire léonien*, Louvain 1946; *Les oraisons du missel romain*, Louvain 1952.
3. In Cass., *Varia*, ed. Mommsen, p. 421. *Ecclesiasticus ordo* in Roman law is attested in 395 (*Cod. Theod.* 16, 26).
4. For the senate cf. Cass., *Varia* i, 31 (Mommsen), p. 37; iii, 33, p. 96; iv, 21, p. 125, etc. For the clergy cf. *Constitutum* of Vigilius, 20 in *Collectio Avellana* (C.S.E.L. 35) p. 234; *Leonine sacramentary*, ed. Feltoe, p. 119.
5. *Ep.* i, 81 (P.L. 77, 535A); ii, 6 (542A); 9 (545A); 11 (547A), etc.
6. *Ip* 14, 4 (P.L. 54, 672B–C).

which he contrasts the new priesthood springing from the Cross with the priesthood of the old law, he proclaims: '. . . now the order of levites is more glorious, the dignity of the elders greater, the unction of the priests more sacred' – '. . . *nunc etenim et ordo clarior levitarum, et dignitas amplior seniorum, et sacratior est unctio sacerdotum*'.[1] The *seniores* here are the priests, and the *sacerdotes* the bishops. But we ought to notice especially the words *honor* and *dignitas* which are found in the Roman ordination prefaces down to our own times. Like *ordo*, they are applied to the different orders, and in addition to this they have a technical significance in reference to the hierarchy of the imperial officials.[2] In fact it seems that from the time of Constantine, bishops, priests and deacons had their place in the strictly hierarchic gradations of Lower-Empire officialdom. They rejoiced in the titles *clarissime, illustre, gloriosissime*, and in the insignia of their rank, among which were the pallium, the stole, the sandals and probably also the maniple.[3] In addition, according to M. Le Bras's conjecture, the prohibition of ordinations *per saltum* and the obligation to proceed through all the degrees would be borrowed in the fourth century from the rules of advancement pertaining to the civil service.[4]

As distinct from *dignitas* and *honor, ordo* has a collective

1. *Serm.* 60, 7 (P.L. 54, 341B).
2. cf. H. E. Dirksen, *Manuale latinitatis fontium iuris civilis Romanorum*, Berlin 1837, pp 285 and 419.
3. This has been shown by T. Klauser, *Der Ursprung der bischöflichen Insignien und Ehrenrechte*, 2nd ed., Krefeld 1953, which should be qualified by an article by his pupil, E. Stommel, 'Die bischöfliche Kathedra im christlichen Altertum' in *Munch. Theol. Zeitschr.* 3 (1952), pp 17–32.
4. 'The prohibition of ordinations *per saltum*, the requirement of proceeding through the intervening degrees, the premium on seniority, which the Council of Sardica, the decretals of Siricius and Zosimus insisted so strongly upon, were modelled on the *cursus honorum*, the *ordo promotionis*, which jurists and emperors strictly upheld.' Digeste L, 4, 11, p. 4, 14, 5. C.–Th. viii, 7, 1 (G. Le bras, 'Le droit romain au service de la domination pontificale' in *Rev. d'hist. du dr. fr. et etr.*, 27 (1949), p. 380, n. 7). G. Dix saw in this a more administrative and less organic conception of ecclesiastical orders than pertained in the ante-Nicene Church. (cf. his article 'The Ministry in the Early Church', in *The Apostolic Ministry*, Hodder and Stoughton 1946, p. 284.)

significance. Sometimes an order is said to be 'received',[1] but much more frequently one is 'admitted into' it. This collective character is particularly striking in the case of the priesthood, for the abstract term *presbyteratus* is rare in the patristic period, and we normally meet the expression *ordo presbyterii*, the order of the presbyterium. At ordinations in the Gelasian rite the Pope announces to the people: 'We have chosen the subdeacon (or the deacon) N. of such and such a title for the order of the diaconate (or the presbyterate).' And further on the rubric adds: 'After having received the benediction – i.e. ordination – they stand in their order, *stant in ordine suo*.'[2]

It was in the twelfth century, at the time when the theological treatment of the sacraments was elaborated, that Hugh of St Victor and Peter Lombard introduced a definite distinction between *ordo* and *dignitas*, thus isolating what they called orders (sacramental), which, for them, ranged from the door-keeper to the priest, the episcopate or the archdiaconate being but a *dignitas in ordine*.[3] These words had long lost the precise juridical connotation they bore in the fourth century, and so a new technical significance could be given them. It was, if one may say so, from within this technicalisation of terminology, and by it, that the idea of sacramental order was worked out. Hugh of St Victor was led to use the word *ordo* for this purpose, partly because it had preserved greater consistency in ecclesiastical language, but largely because of the influence of the terminology and ecclesiology of Pseudo-Dionysius the Areopagite, who saw the Church in heaven and on earth as an immense hierarchy of angelic and ecclesiastical orders.[4]

1. St Gregory, *Dial*, iv, 12 (Moricca, p. 243).
2. *The Gelasian Sacramentary*, ed. Wilson p. 22: 'Elegimus in ordine diaconii siue presbyterii illum sudiaconum siue diaconum de titulum illum. Si quis autem habet aliquid contra hos viros . . . Stant in ordine suo benedictione percepta.' cf. the expression 'homo ordinis mei' in St Avitus with reference to a bishop (*Opera*, ed. Peiper, p. 58), and in St Jerome with reference to a priest, *Ep*. 22, 28 (Hilberg, p. 185).
3. The idea was already there in St Peter Damain's *Liber Gratissimus*, c. 15 (v. Heinemann, p. 36), but the distinction of terms appears with Hugh in *De sacramentis* ii, 2, 5 (P.L. 176, 419).
4. cf. the various recent German studies associated with the name of P. H. Weisweiler, who gives a bibliography in his article 'Sakrament als Symbol und Teilhabe. Der Einfluss des Ps. – Dionysius auf die

The terminology of Hugh of St Victor was taken up by Peter Lombard and met with immediate and general success. In less than fifty years the order of the episcopate had almost ceased to be spoken of, except by canonists, who found it necessary at this period directly to manipulate the texts concerning the early discipline of the Church. *Ordinare* and *ordinatio*, which in antiquity had a broader sense than *ordo*,[1] and which were applied without difficulty during the high Middle Ages to kings, abbots and abbesses, supplanted the synonyms *consecrare* and *benedicere*, and became the technical terms correlative to sacramental *ordo;* conversely, it was customary to speak of consecration of bishops and of the benediction of abbots. With Innocent III, the pontifical of the Roman Curia adopted and sanctioned this terminology, and the canonists themselves extended its use at the beginning of the thirteenth century by making the great and fruitful distinction between the power of Order and the power of Jurisdiction.[2]

At this stage we can ask ourselves what enrichment the early conception of ecclesiastical orders is capable of bringing to our own theology of the sacrament of Orders. It seems that antiquity can here draw our attention firstly to the organic function of Orders within the body of the Church, and secondly to the collegiate or corporate character of the presbyteral priesthood. Scholastic theology did not recognise this collegiate character; in the Middle Ages it was more concerned with the place of Orders in the organic structure of the body of Christ's Church, but it has not laid so much stress on it since then. It is certainly worth the trouble of giving more thought to these aspects in our theological consideration. Moreover, numerous utterances of

---

allgemeine Sakramentenlehre Hugos von St Viktor', in *Scholastik* 27 (1952), pp 321–43; it was the same Dionysian influence that led theologians like William of Auxerre to affirm the existence of nine orders of the ecclesiastical hierarchy.

1. At Rome, *ordinatio* was the technical term for the nomination of imperial officials. cf. O. Hirschfeld, *Die kaiserlichen Verwaltungsbeamten bis auf Diocletian*, 2nd ed., Berlin 1905, p. 443.

2. cf. the very searching study by M. Van De Kerckhove, 'La notion de juridiction dans la doctrine des décrétistes et des premiers décrétalistes de Gratien (1140) à Bernard de Bottone (1250)', in *Etudes francisc.* 49 (1937), p. 438.

Pius XII urge us to do this – utterances which on the one hand revive the early terminology, and on the other prudently encourage certain new positions in theology. The constitution *Sacramentum Ordinis* restores the title of 'Order', sacred Order, to the episcopate, and even seems to suggest that the title of sacred Order should be reserved to the sacramental Orders alone.[1] Moreover, the Pope reinstates the expression *ordo laicorum* – the order of laity – which was common in moral and ecclesiological thought from the Carolingian era until the eve of scholasticism;[2] it is clear that this expression has never had, and has not now, a sacramental significance, but it denotes perhaps better than *plebs sancta* the organic character of the incorporation of the laity into the mystical body. It is up to us not to allow it to be buried in the documents of the Magisterium.

Another and very remarkable use of the word *ordo* is made by Pius XII. Since 1946 a series of apostolic constitutions have set up the episcopal hierarchy in various missionary lands. In the constitution of 25th March, 1953, the expression *hierarchia episcopalis* is replaced by *ordo episcoporum*. The title of the constitution is: 'The order of Catholic bishops is set up in the countries of Kenya, Uganda and Tanganyika – *catholicorum ordo episcoporum constituitur* – and the expression 'order of bishops' is repeated in the text of the Bull.[3] In these missionary countries, let us note, there were already persons enjoying the episcopal character, bishops, but they were there only as individuals, not yet forming an episcopal order as the *ordo episcoporum* exists in Italy, France and all those countries where the

1. A.A.S. 40 (1948), pp 6–7.
2. The expression *ordo laicalis* appears for the first time in a letter from St Gregory to Augustine of Canterbury, probably apocryphal, but already known to Bede (P.L. 77, 1351A). *Ordo laicalis* is current during the Carolingian period (cf. Delaruelle, *Rev. hist. Egl. de Fr.*, 38 (1952), pp 66 and 68). A text from Nicholas I was quoted by Gratian (*sive ex clero sive ex laicali ordine*; iv, Q. i, c. 2; Friedberg, 537) and thence it is accepted into the canonical tradition. cf. the encyclical *Evangelii Praecones*, A.A.S. 43 (1951), p. 510.
3. A.A.S. 45 (1953), p. 705; unhappily the terminology loses its fine theological sharpness in the two constitutions of 1st January 1955 for Burma (A.A.S. 47 (1955), p. 263) and Southern Rhodesia (*ibid.*, p. 369). The first is entitled 'In Unione Foederali Birmana Ecclesiarum atque Episcoporum Ordo constituitur, quae est Episcopalis Hierarchia'.

hierarchy has already been established. Is there not here an example and, as it were, a prudent invitation to us to give a larger place in our language, our theology and our Church life to the organic and corporate character of the episcopal order, as well as the order of priests, the presbyterium?

2. SACERDOS, SACERDOTIUM

Except for the period from the second to the fourth century there has been scarcely any study of the application of the terms *sacerdos* and ἱερεύς to bishops and priests. The present norm in the use of these words was achieved in the twelfth century when the scholastic treatment of the sacraments began to take shape. I am going to try to survey certain stages, beginning with the twelfth century, but without pretending to do more than fix some points on the graph, which others will add to, so that we shall then be in a position really accurately to draw the curve of the world's history.

1. During the first stage – in the eleventh century for example – bishops and priests were normally called *episcopi et sacerdotes* rather than *episcopi et presbyteri*. Thus a contemporary witness relates that in 1073 the deacon Hildebrand on becoming Pope Gregory VII, *ordinatus est sacerdos*, was ordained priest at Embertide in Pentecost, then *consecratus est in episcopum*, was consecrated bishop on the feast of the Holy Apostles.[1] We will note in passing that of the many deacons who had been elected Pope, Gregory VII was the first to be ordained priest before being consecrated bishop – St Leo, St Gregory the Great proceeded immediately from the diaconate to the fulness of the priesthood.[2]

Thanks to the use of biblical typology, and the anthologies of patristic texts, the eleventh century kept relatively alive the idea that bishops and priests were both *sacerdotes*; the whole century was taken up with that great dispute which opposed priesthood,

1. Bonizon de Sutri, *Liber ad Amicum*, i, vii (Duemmler, p. 601).
2. M. Andrieu, 'La carrière ecclésiastique des papes', *Rev. des sciences* rel. 21 (1947), pp 106–7.

the *sacerdotium* – i.e. the ecclesiastical hierarchy and its head the Sovereign Pontiff – to empire. St Peter Damian, who had already formulated with true theological clarity the equation '*sacerdos* = he who has power to consecrate the body of Christ', did not forget to note that despite their privileges the bishops 'because in common with other priests they also possess that which is greatest of all (i.e. the power to consecrate) possess, not without right, the title of priest';[1] the idea that bishops were priests persisted, but the use of the term 'priest' for bishops was well on the way to being lost.

2. In the Carolingian era the distinction between *episcopi* and *sacerdotes* was freely employed. In Gaul it was already ancient; the earliest absolutely clear example I know of it is the little treatise *De officiis septem graduum*, portions of which have been introduced into the Pontifical. The sixth and seventh paragraphs run: 'De presbyteris. Sacerdotem oportet offerre et benedicere, praeesse et praedicare et baptizare. De episcopis. Episcopum oportet iudicare, interpretari et consecrare, consummare, ordinare, offerre et baptizare'.[2] Unfortunately it is very difficult to date this text. Dom Botte thinks that he can trace it back to about the end of the fifth century;[3] for myself, I do not see how it can be earlier than the seventh, for it makes no mention whatsoever of the acolyte.

As to the distinction between *episcopi* and *sacerdotes*, we can safely hold that at this period *sacerdos* referred more naturally to the priest than to the bishop. We ought to add, however, that the idea that the priest possessed his *sacerdotium* through participation with the bishop had practically ceased to be an active force.[4]

1. '. . . quia tamen id, quod omnibus maius est, commune cum reliquis sacerdotibus habent, cum eis etiam et ipsi non immerito sacerdotii nomen tenent.' (*Liber Gratissimus*, c. 15; v. Heinemann, p. 36).
2. Hittorp, *De cath. Eccl. div. officiis*, Rome 1591, p. 63.
3. B. Botte, 'Le rituel d'ordination des Statuta Ecclesiae Antiqua' in *Rech. Théol. anc. et méd.* 11 (1939), p. 235.
4. This evolution of ideas is bound up with the development of the regulations governing ordinations. Typical in this respect is the astonishment expressed by Aeneas, bishop of Paris, at the Roman

The word presbyter continued to be used side by side with *sacerdos*. But *sacerdos* is always used in speaking of the celebrant at Mass, whether in liturgical commentaries (*expositiones missae*) or in the rubrics of the *ordines romani*. This latter case is particularly interesting, and Mgr Andrieu has observed in his edition that in those places where the *ordines* compiled at Rome itself speak of *presbyteri*, the *ordines* of Frankish redaction deriving from Roman sources replace this word by *sacerdotes*.[1]

Sacerdos was still however applied to bishops as well as to priests. Thus in 744 a council at Soissons stressed the importance of a canon by saying that it had been promulgated by twenty-three bishops 'with the other *priests, cum aliis sacerdotibus*'.[2] The words *episcopus* and *sacerdos* came to be used interchangeably – witness the account of the obsequies of St Cuthbert in Amalarius.[3] Other uses, for example, in the addressing of letters, merely continued a stereotyped custom. The matter of Elipand of Toledo and the Council of Frankfurt (794) led to a correspondence between the Pope, the bishop of Toledo and Charlemagne; at Rome, in Spain and in the Frankish Empire a bishop to whom a letter was sent was called *sacerdos*.[4] The Pope, however, did not describe himself as *sacerdos* but *pontifex: sanctae catholicae atque apostolicae primaeque pontifex sedis*.[5]

---

practice mentioned to the Frankish bishops by Pope Nicholas I (P.L. 119, 1115), of ordaining deacons directly to the episcopate: 'De hoc ... quod queritur quare apud Roman plerumque diaconus quodam saltu non percepta presbyterali benedictione in episcopum subito consecretur.' Such a practice does not rest on scripture, and no reason can be given for it. By way of hypothesis Aeneas suggests its traditional significance: '... forte illi qui istiusce ordinationi assentiunt, hoc intelligi velint, quia qui benedictione pontificali perfungitur, reliquarum benedictionum honore decoretur, sive quia in consecratione corporis Christi et sanguinis officium praesulis ac presbyteri mystice uniatur' (*Liber adv. Graecos*, c. 210; P.L. 121, 759–60). Similarly, the bishops of Germany declared that in their country no one was ever raised immediately from the diaconate to the episcopate: 'pene nos hoc nunquam accidisse' (P.L. 119, 1212).

1. *Les Ordines Romani du haut moyen âge*, iii, Louvain 1951, p. 66.
2. *Concilia Aevi Karolini* T. i (1906), p. 36.
3. *De Off.* iv, 41, 1 (Hanssens, T. ii, p. 531).
4. *Conc. aev. kar.*, T. i, pp 111, 158, 165; cf. p. 171: 'ut nulli episcoporum et sacerdotum liceat sacris ignorare'.
5. *ibid.*, p. 122.

I have already alluded to the divergence between the Frankish and Roman terminologies, the latter making more use of the word *presbyter*. The Gregorian Sacramentary, which was sent to Charlemagne so that he might make it the official book of his empire, enables us to make a detailed analysis of Roman liturgical usage at this period. Occasionally *sacerdos* is applied to the priest in the anniversary Mass of his ordination: 'upon us, though unworthy, thou dost confer the priestly dignity – *nobis indignis sacerdotalem confers dignitatem*'.[1] The prayer of ordination states indirectly that priests are prefigured in the *sacredotes* of the old testament.[2] Sometimes *sacerdos* is also applied to the Pope; at his funeral there is a prayer 'for the soul of Bishop N., thy servant and sacerdos – *pro anima famuli et sacerdotis tui illius episcopi*'.[3] Here *episcopus* is the essential term – *sacerdos* is a description of one of its aspects rather than its exact equivalent. The same duplication is found in another prayer for a deceased Pope in the Leonine Sacramentary, which runs as follows: *Deus qui inter apostolicos sacerdotes famulum tuum illum fecisti vigere pontificem*...[4] N. is Pontiff, and God has numbered him among the *sacerdotes* (i.e. in this case the bishops) who occupy the see of the apostle Peter; more simply, in everyday speech, the Pope was called the *Apostolicus*.[5] In the great prayer of episcopal ordination, at the place where it petitions God for him who has been chosen for the 'ministry of the sovereign priesthood', there is a clause proper to the ordination of a Bishop of Rome, which adds 'whom thou hast given to be *praesul* and primate of all *sacerdotes* upon earth, and to be doctor of thy universal Church'.[6]

A comparison of the Gregorian with the Leonine and Gelasian sacramentaries shows us that the vocabulary of priesthood remained more or less stable in the Roman liturgical texts between the sixth (perhaps even the fifth) and the eighth and

1. *Gregorian Sacramentary*, ed. Wilson, p. 120.
2. *ibid.*, p. 7.   3. *ibid.*, p. 142.
4. cf. the text and its variants in P. Bruylants, *Les oraisons du missel romain*, Louvain 1952, ii, p. 102.
5. cf. L. M. Dewailly, 'Notes sur l'histoire de l'adjectif apostolique', *Mél. de sc. rel.* 5 (1948), p. 146.
6. *Gregorian Sacramentary*, ed. Wilson, p. 143.

ninth centuries. Furthermore, it can be seen that the Leonine only calls priests *sacerdotes* in an indirect way,[1] and that the Gregorian abandons the use of the word *sacerdos* in the collect for the feasts of holy bishops.[2] Generally the Roman sacramentaries refrain from referring to priests and bishops simultaneously as *sacerdotes*.[3]

3. The second half of the fourth century and the fifth century present us with a whole collection of texts where *sacerdos* normally means the bishop,[4] but also, on occasion, the priest. Innocent I used it so, formally, when he explained to the bishop of Gubbio that priests could not bestow the sacrament of confirmation: 'As to the signing of children, it is clear that it cannot be performed by anyone other than a bishop; for priests, although they may be *sacerdotes* of the second degree – *licet secundi sint sacerdotes* – have not reached the apex of the pontificate – *pontificatus tamen apicem non habent*.[5] St Leo, in turn, observes in a

---

1. *Leonine Sacramentary*, ed. Feltoe, p. 122 (preface for the ordination of priests).
2. cf. the Masses of St Sixtus and St Clement in Gelasian ii, 40, 1 and 3; ii, 65, 1 (Wilson, pp 188 and 205). Per contra, this designation reappears in the Roman missal for St Apollinarius (23rd July), and it survives in the Ambrosian liturgy.
3. Undoubtedly we must see a Gallican interpolation in a rubric in the Gelasian Sacramentary concerning the ordination of the deacon: 'Solus episcopus . . . manum super caput ejus ponat: **reliqui vero sacerdotes** juxta manum episcopi caput ejus ponant' (I, 95; ed. Wilson, p. 144). cf. the classical distinction between *sacerdotes* (i.e. bishops and priests) and *ministri* (i.e. deacons), which had already appeared in an Imperial Edict of 398 (Th. C. xii, 2, c. 31); it is to be found in the liturgies of the Mass, at Rome in that of Gelasius (B. Capelle, 'Le Kyrie de la messe et le papa Gelase', *Rév Bén.* 46 (1934), p. 136); at Milan in the second litany of Lent (*ibid.*, p. 131); cf. in Gaul the solemn collects of the Paschal Vigil, which correspond to the Roman solemn collects on Good Friday, *Missale gothicum* 33 (P.L. 72, 271); *Gallicanum vetus* 24 (P.L. 72, 366).
4. At this period *sacerdos* even seems to be superseding *episcopus*. Thus, Rufinus, translating Eusebius's *Ecclesiastical History*, quite naturally renders the Greek ἐπίσκοπος by *sacerdos* (*Hist. Eccl.*, v, 24, 5) (*Mommsen* i, p. 493); vii, 30, 19 (*ibid.*, ii, p. 715), and ἐπισκοπή by *sacerdotium* or *locus sacerdotii*: vi, 35 (*Mommsen* ii, pp 590–1); vii, 30 (*ibid.*, i, p. 714).
5. *Ep.* 25, 3; Denzinger 98; Zosimus *Ep.* 9, 3 (P.L. 20, 673A) speaks of the *presbyterii sacerdotium*.

Lenten sermon that preparation for Easter and the purification of the spiritual temple is not only the concern of *summos antistites* (prelates) or the *sacerdotes secundi ordinis* (the priests), nor yet of the ministers of the sacraments (the deacons) alone, but of the whole body of the Church.[1] At the end of the fifth century the formula used by Innocent I recurs in the letter from John the deacon to Senarius, which combines it with a quotation from Ambrosiaster: 'We can say, in effect, that every pontiff is a *sacerdos*, but not that every *sacerdos* is a pontiff'.[2] Indeed, this idea that priests are *sacerdotes secundi ordinis* provides the theme for the Roman preface at the ordination of priests, which can be traced to the first half of the sixth century, or even the fifth;[3] in it priests are called *secundi ordinis viri, secundi praedicatores*;[4] they possess the *secunda dignitas*, the *secunda meriti munus*, i.e. the office of the second dignity, as the expression retained as essential and sufficient by Pius XII states. The idea of a priesthood of the second order is borrowed from the old testament: *Helciae pontifici et sacerdotibus secundi ordinis* – the king commanded Helcias the high priest, and the priests of the second order (4 Kings, **23**, 4), a passage which Origen had already applied to presbyters.[5]

In Africa the same idea is found in St Augustine, who, quoting Apoc. **20**, 6: 'They shall be priests of God and of Christ and shall reign with him a thousand years', adds: 'This is spoken not only of bishops and presbyters, who are now properly called priests in the Church; but just as we call all (Christians) christs because of the mystical chrism, so are all priests, for they are members of the one Priest.'[6] St Augustine, then,

1. Non enim summos tantum antistites aut secundi ordinis sacerdotes, nec solos sacramentorum ministros sed omne corpus Ecclesiae (*Serm.* 48, 1, P.L. 54, 298).

2. Merito, quia episcopus summi pontificis gradum obtinet, presbyter vero secundi sacerdotii locum retinere cognoscitur. Omnis enim pontifex est sacerdos, non omnis pontifex sacerdos dici potest' (ed. Wilmart, p. 175; cf. Ambrosiaster, in 2 Tim. **3**, 10; P.L. 17, 496).

3. B. Botte, 'Secundi meriti munus', in *Quest. lit. et par.* 21 (1936), pp 84–8.

4. From the tenth century *secundi praedicatores* is replaced by the variant *secundis praedicationibus*.

5. *Hom xi in Exod.*, n. 6; P.G. 12, 380D.

6. *De Civ. Dei*, 20, 10, ed. Hoffmann, ii, p. 455.

describes priests as *sacerdotes* with all the theological sharpness that could be desired, but at the same time both here and elsewhere he intends the *sacerdotium* of the priest to be related to that of Christ, and there is no doubt that he uses the term *sacerdos* much less than his contemporaries in other parts of the Latin Church.[1] However, in Africa itself, Optatus of Milevum (c. 366-7)

1. On this question as a whole, see D. Zaehringer, *Das kirchliche Priestertum nach dem heil. Augustinus*, Paderborn 1931, pp 115-18. As Dom Zaehringer has so clearly observed, the reason behind St Augustine's reluctance to apply the term *sacerdos* to the Christian priest, and his insistence on the unique priesthood of Christ, is the defence of Catholic truth about priesthood which was endangered by the Donatist heresy. St Cyprian had been the first of the Fathers to apply to the Christian priesthood on any large scale the old testament texts concerning the Aaronic priesthood. So, developing the germs which they found in the sacramental theology of St Cyprian, the Donatists turned his moral application of the old testament texts on priesthood into a structural necessity for the Church. For Parmenian, who succeeded Donatus as head of the sect, the *sacerdotium* was one of the six essential *dotes* of the Church, without which the Church would disappear; for him, priesthood was mediatory not only in the Catholic sense that the action of the minister is necessary to bring the sacraments into existence, but also in the sense that the unworthiness of the minister deprives him of all capacity to confer the sacraments – bishops and priests who had lapsed in the persecution, and who afterwards repented, no longer belonged to the Church, and were priests no more.

St Augustine's major criticism of the Donatists was that they made the validity of the sacraments dependent on the worthiness of the minister, and it was in that that their heresy lay; but in addition to this heresy proper he also attacked their loss of the sense of the transcendent action of Christ the sole true priest and only mediator. It is clearly on account of this that, while admitting its fundamental rightness, his use of the word *sacerdos* is so cautious. The Donatist crisis having receded, Latin tradition as a whole was not afraid to make use of *sacerdos* and the old testament passages on priesthood, secure in the kind of permanent corrective provided by the great anti-Donatist texts of St Augustine.

Here are two quite typical passages:

Contra Ep. Parm. 2, 7, 12 (P.L. 43, 57-8): 'Bene quidem de veteribus Libris ista testimonia proponunt. Dicant ergo mihi, cui sancto secundum salutem spiritualem obfuerit, vel in sacerdotibus, vel inter populum constituto, malus aut maculatus sacerdos? Ubi erat Moyses et Aaron, ibi murmuratores sacrilegi, quod Deus a facie sua semper perdere minabatur. Ubi erat Caiphas et ceteri tales, ibi Zacharias, ibi Simeon et ceteri boni; ubi Saul, ibi David; ubi Jeremias, ubi Isaias, ubi Daniel, ubi Ezechiel, ibi sacerdotes mali et populi mali: sed sarcinam suam unusquisque portabat' (Parmenian undoubtedly made

speaks of 'deacons being appointed to the third priesthood, and priests to the second';[1] this is an almost isolated example in tradition of the application of *sacerdotium* to the deacon.

4. Certain Anglican historians have asked if *sacerdos* was applied to priests or only to bishops before the fourth century. Fathers Congar and Lécuyer have thrown much desirable light on this question.[2]

On occasion St Cyprian describes priests as *sacerdotes*. He speaks once of priests 'being associated with the bishop in the honour of priesthood – *cum episcopo presbyteri sacerdotali honore conjuncti*'[3] and, in a context concerned with both bishops and priests, he declares: '*sacerdotes* and *ministers* who serve the altar and the sacrifices must be pure and without spot'.[4] We can see that here and elsewhere in St Cyprian the full use of *sacerdos* has actually made its appearance, and is closely linked with both the old testament and the cult, and especially with the oblation of the sacrifice.[5]

In the last years of the second century and the first years of the third, around 200, at about the same time, the words

---

use of St Cyprian's anthologies, *Ep.* 65, 2; 67, 1; 72, 2). The second text of St Augustine contains an explicit denial of the title *mediator* to the priest; he writes on St John: 'Si vero ita diceret: **haec scripsi vobis ut non peccetis; et si quis peccaverit, mediatorem me habetis ad patrem et exoro pro peccatis vestris** (sicut Parmenianus quodam loco mediatorem posuit episcopum inter populum et Deum), quis eum ferret bonorum atque fidelium christianorum? quis sicut apostolum Christi, et non sicut antichristum? (*Contra Ep. Parm.* 2, 8, 15; P.L. 43, 59–60).

1. I, 13 (ed. Ziwsa, p. 15).

2. Y. Congar, Critical notes accompanying G. Long-Hasselmans, 'Essai sur le sacerdoce catholique', *Rev. des sc. rel.* 25 (1951), pp 289–91, and especially his *Lay people in the Church*, Chapman, 1960. cf. J. Lécuyer, 'Episcopat et presbytérat dans les écrits d'Hippolyte de Rome', *Rech. de sc. rel.* 41 (1953), pp 30–50.

3. *Ep.* 61, 3 (ed. Hartel, ii, pp 696–7).

4. *Ep.* 72, 2 (ed. Hartel, ii, p. 777). cf. B. Poschmann, *Die Sichtbarkeit der Kirche nach der Lehre des hl. Cyprian*, Paderborn 1908, p. 169; S. L. Greenslade, 'Apostolic Ministry' in *Theology* 50 (1947), p. 135; Fathers Congar and Lécuyer cited above.

5. cf. Poschmann, *op. cit.*, p. 168: 'Die Bezeichnung Sacerdos, ein Begriff, welcher mit der des Opfers in engster Beziehung steht . . . '

sacerdos, sacerdotium and ἀρχιερεύς are apparently applied to the bishop. Towards the end of the second century Bishop Polycrates of Ephesus describes St John as ἱερεύς.[1] Tertullian, who does not use *sacerdos*, speaks several times of the sacerdotal function (*sacerdotalia munera*,[2] *sacerdotale officium*).[3] We are indebted to Fr Lécuyer for his extremely detailed analysis of the Greek texts which are contemporaneous with Hippolytus – like Tertullian, Hippolytus speaks rather of the bishop exercising the sovereign priesthood ἀρχιερατεύειν, but on occasion he refers also to the bishop as ἀρχιερύς.[4] Similarly, in a passage which we possess only in its Latin translation, he tells us that, as distinct from the priest, the deacon *non in sacerdotio ordinatur*.[5] Therefore, we can say that even if Hippolytus and Tertullian do not directly describe the priest as ἱερεύς or *sacerdos*, both of them show that they are fully aware that the presbyter shares in the *sacerdotium* of the bishop. The same conclusion follows from a passage from Clement of Rome a century earlier,[6] i.e. the immediate subapostolic age. This passage, which clearly inspires Hippolytus, speaks of the high priest ἀρχιερεύς, of the *sacerdotes* (ἱερεῖς) and of the levites; each has his proper liturgy, in Latin his *munera*; this is the same term which Tertullian uses in connection with the oblation, but with Clement the comparison with old testament 'cultual' terminology seems as yet to have been no more than a comparison; ἀρχιερεύς and ἱερεύς are still not applied to the bishop and Christian priest as properly pertaining to them. We can reasonably conclude from this that sacerdotal terminology, ἀρχιερεύς, ἱερεύς, *sacerdos*, was adopted by Christians to describe their hierarchy in the second century, in the subapostolic age, and that it sprang from old testament typology.

Christians of the subapostolic period nowhere explain why they adopted a terminology with which the new testament had wished to break, but the texts show us clearly that the idea of priesthood was developed at the same time as that of sacrifice,

1. Quoted by Eusebius, *Hist. eccl.* v, 24, 2.
2. *De praescr.* 41.   3. *De virg.* vel. 9.
4. *Trad. apost.*, ed. Botte, pp 41 and 66.
5. *ibid.*, p. 39.   6. xl, 5.

and in conjunction with it. The leading text here is the anamnesis from the Anaphora of Hippolytus: 'Making therefore the memorial of his death and resurrection, we offer unto thee bread and wine, rendering thanks to thee for that thou hast deemed us worthy to stand before thee and to serve thee'.[1] Dom Botte translates the *et tibi minstrare* of the Latin version by 'to serve thee'. The Apostolic Constitutions, supported by the *Testamentum Domini*, have ἱερατεύειν. In the opinion of Dom Connolly, who has attempted to reconstruct the Greek of the Anaphora, there is no reason for rejecting this word;[2] if ἱερατεύιν must be rejected, the only possible Greek word would be λειτουργείν. Now the two verbs are associated in the ordination prayer of a bishop, and the prayer runs 'that he might exercise the sovereign priesthood (ἀρχιερατεύειν) without reproach, serving thee day and night (λειτουργοῦντα); may he render thy countenance propitious, and offer the gifts of thy holy Church'.[3] Fr Jungmann has made it crystal clear that, even if it cannot strictly be proved that the explicit mention of sacrifice had not existed in the Anaphora before Hippolytus and hence from the apostolic age, there was, in the second and third centuries an increasing appreciation of the eucharist as an offering of material gifts by way of reaction against the exaggerated spiritualism of the gnostics.[4] The new testament had to bring out chiefly the uniqueness of the sacrifice of Christ compared with the carnal sacrifices of the old law. Irenaeus and his successors reintroduced, as against the gnostics, the idea that creation is good, and that it forms the subject of an authentic offering to God – in other words, there was a valid side to the priesthood of the old law, which had been integrated into the worship of the new law.

In conclusion, to try to sum up the development of the word *sacerdos* as applied to bishops and priests:

1. Botte, *op. cit.*, p. 42.
2. 'The Eucharistic prayer of Hippolytus' in the *Journal of Theological Studies*, 39 (1938), pp 350–69; cf. E. C. Ratcliff, 'Sanctus and Pattern of early Anaphora', *Journal of Ecclesiastical History*, i (1950), p. 127.   3. Botte, *op. cit.*, pp 29 and 77.
4. *Missarum Sollemnia*, French translation, i, pp 51–3.

(1) In the eleventh century *sacerdos* normally refers to the priest. Men were still aware that theoretically it also applied to the bishop.

(2) In the Carolingian period *sacerdos* refers as much to the priest as to the bishop, but most frequently to the priest. The idea that the priest is *sacerdos* through participation with the bishop is hardly active save at Rome.

(3) Between the second half of the fourth century and the sixth *sacerdos* normally means the bishop, and except where the context indicates the contrary *sacerdos* is synonymous with *episcopus*. But it was also occasionally applied to the priest when he exercised his eucharistic and liturgical powers.

(4) It is about the year 200 that the application of *sacerdos* to the bishop is clearly attested for the first time in connection with his 'cultual' power. From the beginning it was recognised that the priest participated in this power, even if he was not forthwith and directly given the name of *sacerdos*. But even this is attested from the time of St Cyprian.[1]

1. On the significance of the word *sacerdos* in the Carolingian period, a complementary account can be found in 'Autour de Leon d'Ostie et de sa **translatio** S. Clementis', *Analecta Bollandiana*, 74, 1956 by Frs Meyvaert and Devos, especially pp 196 ff, an article I only heard of after I had prepared this study. Relating the visit of the two brothers Cyril and Methodius to Rome, the *Translatio* says: '. . . consecraverunt fratrem eius Methodium in sacerdotem, nec non et ceteros eorum discipulos in presbyteros et diaconos'. There has been much discussion about the meaning of *sacerdos* in this leading passage – is it an account of the ordination of Methodius to the presbyterate or to the episcopate? A comparison with the two Slav lives shows that here it can only be a question of presbyteral ordination. From the point of view of the Latin terminology alone, it would be impossible, in my opinion, to give an adversative value to the combination *sacerdos-presbyteri* in a ninth-century text. For *sacerdos* by that time was much closer to *presbyter* than to *episcopus*.

CHAPTER VI

THE PRIESTLY MINISTRY IN THE GREEK FATHERS

J. DANIÉLOU, S.J.

THE existence within the Christianity of the first centuries of a class (τάξις – *ordo*) of men dedicated to sacred functions and receiving by ordination (χειροτονία) the powers necessary to perform them, is a fact so obvious as to need no proof. Clement of Rome shows us that the apostles after 'proving their first-fruits in the Holy Spirit appointed bishops (ἐπίσκόπους) and deacons for those who should come to believe' (*Epist.* 42, 5). But taken as a whole our information about this priestly ministry is very patchy, and it raises two questions: what is the nature of this ministry? what are its different aspects? I shall try to answer these questions from the Greek Fathers.

It is a very common error of method, in speaking of the Church's ministry, to approach it first of all through one of its particular aspects, and then to seek to fit it in the others. Thus, if the minister is defined as a ἱερεύς because of his sacrificial function we are then involved in the difficult questions of his affinity with the pagan or Jewish priesthood. But priesthood is only one aspect of the ministry. Or if we start with the position of the minister within the community, we can describe him as πρεσβύτερος since he presides over the assembly. But the presbyterate is not the whole role of the minister any more than priesthood. Equally if his connection with apostolate is singled out the ministry will be defined in terms of a theology of the word, and the minister as a missionary. But this is also far from expressing its full significance.

It is obvious that all these definitions are partial and incomplete, and of little help in trying to understand the true nature of the ministry. In fact we have to use a different method, and ask ourselves first what is the purpose of the ministry in the Christian Church. Now the answer to this question seems clear. There is an economy of salvation which is both revelation (λόγος) and action (ἔργον). It is the work of the divine power (δύναμις). Its end is the edification of the people of God. Ministers are the servants of this economy; they are, in St Paul's words – which seem to me to provide the most accurate definition of their work – 'the dispensers (οἰκόνομοι) of the mysteries (μυστήρια) of God' (1 Cor. 4, 1).[1] The ministry is defined essentially by its role in the history of salvation.

So priesthood is to be defined in terms of a theology of mystery. But first I want to elucidate a certain confusion which has obscured the question a good deal. Dom Casel thought it was possible to discover in the Greek Fathers, and especially in St John Chrysostom, a doctrine of mystery common to them and to the Hellenistic religions, and which was essentially referable to the cult. From this point of view, to connect the ministry with mystery would be to define it in terms of its ritual aspect, and to make the Christian minister a kind of ἱερεύς. But G. Fittkau has conclusively shown, as far as St John Chrysostom is concerned,[2] that there is no foundation for this view and that if the Christian ministry has affinities with mystery it is in the Pauline sense of the word – as the 'secret' of the economy of salvation which has been fulfilled in Christ and is being realised in the Church through word and sacrament. To describe the minister as a 'dispenser of the mysteries' in this way is simply to describe him as a servant of the economy of salvation.

I want to show that this is really the thought of the Fathers. The most relevant text is found in Gregory of Nazianzen. The purpose of God's design, he said, is the restoration of the image of God in man: 'It is towards this that the law as a tutor (παιδαγωγός), the prophets as intermediaries between the law and the Christ, and Christ himself as consummation and end of

1. On the subject of the 'economy' in the gospel parables, and its connection with the ministry of the Church, see A. Feuillet, *La synthèse eschatologique de St Mathieu*, R.B., 1950, pp 66–71.

2. *Der Begriff des Mysteriums bei Johannes Chrysostomus*, Bonn 1953. See R.S.R., 1954, 502–605.

the spiritual law do all tend. It is for this that the Godhead humbled himself (κενωθείς), and took flesh. It is for this that we have Christmas and the Virgin, the crib and Bethlehem; the Virgin because of the woman, the crib because of paradise, Bethlehem because of Eden, Christmas because of creation. All these things were God's tutoring, to raise up the old Adam from whence he had fallen, and to give him access to the tree of life.' (P.G. 35, 432B–433B.)

Now, of this healing of humanity, which is the end of God's whole design, we ourselves here and now 'are the ministers (ὑπηρεται) and fellow-workers (συνεργοι); all we who preside over (προκαθεζόμεθα) others' (436A). Moreover; 'The aim (of the priesthood) is to give wings to the soul, to wean it from the world and to present it to God. It consists in preserving the image of God in man, if it exists; in strengthening it if it has become enfeebled; in restoring it if it has become obliterated. Its end is to make Christ dwell in men's hearts through the Spirit, and – this sums up everything – to fashion a god who shares in the blessedness of the heavens out of him who belongs to the heavenly city.' (432B.)

In these passages two points are particularly noteworthy. First, the priesthood is concerned with works which are peculiarly divine. It is this that gives it its pre-eminent grandeur. 'Medical science deals with the body and fragile matter' but 'our solicitude and care reach men in the secret places of their hearts' (429C). In fact the minister is the instrument of a work which can only be divine, since that work is the divinisation of man: 'He restores the creature. He reveals the image. He works for the heavenly world and, greatest of all, he is a god who fashions gods (θεοποιήσοντα)' (481A–B). He is, in effect, the dispenser of that divine energy present in the Church 'through the word and the sacraments (λόγῳ καὶ ἔργῳ)' (432A).

Secondly, the priest is a co-operator in that divine work which, in effect, continues in time through the Church the *mirabilia Dei* of the two testaments. There is an ἔργον which is of God. God is active and at work in our midst. And of this ἔργον the priest is the συνεργός. The word is of great importance. We are aware, as Jaeger has recently reminded us,[1] of its place in eastern spirituality, in which it denotes the co-operation of man in his own sanctification. Now here, in a parallel fashion, it denotes the co-operation of the priest in the edification of the Church. And it emphasises that essential note of the theology of priesthood so misunderstood by Protestantism, that God himself effectively communicates to his spouse the Church, and consequently to priests, who are its concrete expression, powers which are proper to himself, so that they can actually transmit them.

That this dual theme of divinisation and co-operation is one of the essential elements of the Greek theology of priesthood is proved by the fact that it is found elsewhere than in Gregory of Nazianzen. Here I will quote only Pseudo-Dionysius: 'Every hierarch, according to his nature, position and order, is initiated into divine things and divinised, so that he might impart sacred divinisation (θεοποίησις) to those who follow him' (372D). Elsewhere he says: 'The perfection of each one who has received orders (ἱεραρχίαν) is in promoting the imitation of God. Now, among divine things, the highest of them all is to be a fellow-worker (συνεργός) with God' (165B–C).

We are now at the heart of the theology of priesthood. From one point of view the priest is only an instrument: it is God alone who effects (ἐνεργεῖ) the work of divinisation. St John Chrysostom expresses this forcefully in his commentary on the second epistle to Timothy: 'Do you not know what the priest (ἱερεύς) is? He is an angel from the Lord. Are his words his own? If you despise him, it is not him you despise, but the God who ordained (ἐχειροτόνησεν) him. If God does not work (ἐνεργεῖ) through him, then there is no more baptism nor communion in the mysteries, nor blessings; you are no longer a Christian.' (P.G. 62, 610.)

Consequently, a priest, even if he is unworthy, remains a dispenser of grace, since what he bestows is not his own; 'He is unworthy? How does that affect the matter? God has indeed made use of oxen to save his people. It is not the life of the priest, nor his virtues, which accomplish such a thing. Everything springs from grace. The priest has but to open his mouth. But

1. *Two rediscovered works of ancient Christian literature*, 1954, p. 88.

it is God who works all things. Alone he performs the sign (σύμβολον). The oblation (προσφορά) is the same whether it is offered by the first to hand or by Peter or Paul. One is no less than the other, for it is not men who consecrate (ἁγιάζουσι) it, but he himself who bestows sanctification.' (P.G. 62, 612.)

But at the same time this power to dispense the mysteries is itself a work of divine power, a sacrament. In a remarkable passage Gregory of Nyssa, after demonstrating that the other sacraments render things common in themselves, like water, oil, bread and wine, capable of effecting (ἐνεργεῖν) supernatural results, applies the same principle to ordination: 'The same power (δύναμις) of the divine word bestows a pre-eminent dignity on the priest (ἱερεύς), separating him from the ranks of the people by consecration (εὐλογία). Only yesterday he was but one of the throng. But he has been appointed preceptor, president (πρόεδρος), doctor and mystagogue by invisible power and grace (δυνάμει καὶ χάριτι).' (P.G. 46, 581D–584A.)

In thus making the priest a dispenser of the mysteries, of that hidden wealth which the economy of salvation seeks to impart, ordination gives to the priest a share in the mysterious grandeur of this economy: 'If we consider how wondrous it is that a man fashioned of flesh and blood should be able to approach that blessed nature, then we shall see how great is the grace which the Holy Spirit has bestowed upon priests. For it is at their hands that (the holy mysteries) are performed, and other marvels no less great.'[1] The priesthood arouses this fear, this holy trembling (φοβερὰ καὶ φρικωδέστατα) which seizes men when confronted by those divine works which make up the history of salvation (ibid., 642); it is both a fear and a transporting wonder.[2]

We are now in a position to sum up the first conclusions we have reached. Priesthood is defined essentially in its relationship with the history of salvation. This history of salvation is the history of the mirabilia Dei, the wonders of God which are continued in time through the Church. The priest is the minister and dispenser of them and he is this by virtue of that work of

1. John Chrysostom, Sacerd.; P.G. 48, 643.
2. cf. Fittkau, op. cit., p. 133.

divine power which is his very priesthood itself. This makes him participate in the reality of the mystery, of the hidden design of God; and its paradox, its bewildering and amazing character, arouses a sense of the sacred.

Having tried to deduce the essential aspects of the ministry of the Church from the Fathers, we must now consider it as a concrete reality. And what strikes us here first of all is the variety of the designations for it. I mentioned this at the beginning of this article but set it aside as a bad starting point in method. Now we can return to it. The expressions we have met for the minister include ἡγούμενος (Chrys., *Comm. in I Tim.*, 2; *P.G.* 62, 609), πρόεδρος, ἱερεύς, διδάσκαλος, μυσταγωγός (Gregory of Nyssa, *Hom. Bapt.*; *P.G.* 46, 581D). All these descriptions fit him equally well.

If we turn to origins, this variety appears to be still more striking. It is to this period that a charismatic hierarchy of teachers and prophets has sometimes been attributed, a hierarchy distinct from the institutional hierarchy of bishops and presbyters. Campenhausen has proved in masterly fashion that this idea is without foundation.[1] There has never been more than one hierarchy. But the same writer has shown that this hierarchy presented some very varied facets.[2] At Alexandria its principal function, in the Pauline tradition, seems to have been the ministry of the word; the priest was a doctor and a missionary. This is particularly striking in Origen. At Antioch, the minister was the one who offered the sacrifice, the ἱερεύς – as Ignatius of Antioch demonstrates. Finally, the Judaeo-Christian community at Jerusalem, perhaps influenced by Essene organisation, looked on the ministers as elders (πρεσβύτεροι), overseers (ἐπίσκοποι), whose principal function was government. This view is also found in the Roman Church, whose Judaeo-Christian affinities have been demonstrated by Cullmann.[3]

The differentiation must not be pressed too far. It is clear, in fact, that the Antiochene conception, for example in the *Letters*

1. *Kirchliches Amt und geistliche Vollmacht in der ersten drei Jahrhunderten*, p. 214.   2. *ibid.*, p. 131.
3. *Peter: Disciple – Apostle – Martyr*, S.C.M., 1953.

of Ignatius, although it emphasises the minister's function in worship very strongly, also stresses his function in government. Ignatius refers to the presidency (προκαθήμενος) of the bishop, the senate (συνέδριον) and the presbyters (*Magn.* 6, 1). Moreover, even if it was in the Judaeo-Christian community at Jerusalem that organised hierarchical government appeared first of all, it was also there that the prophetic aspect of the ministry received most recognition – both of these actually in an 'extension' of Essenism.

This leads us to the picture of a ministry which is essentially one, but whose functions are varied. And these functions in the end correspond to the dipsensation of the mystery under its various aspects. It is first of all secret, hidden in God and revealed in Christ. The first function of ministers, therefore, is to proclaim it lawfully or, more strictly, the Word of God is at work in the Church, converting, instructing, reproving. Priests are *servants of the Word* (Acts 6, 2). From this angle the priesthood is essentially apostolic. Its mission is evangelisation, the proclamation of the *kerygma* to the whole world. There is no need for me to enlarge on the teaching of the Fathers about the ministry of the word – I have already done this elsewhere.[1] A few notes will suffice here.

First, there is the pre-eminent and even preferential dignity given to this aspect of the ministry by a whole current of opinion. It is there already in St Paul: 'For Christ sent me, not to baptise but to preach the gospel' (1 Cor. 1, 17). Origen is its great exponent: 'Anyone can perform the solemn functions of the liturgy before the people; but there are few men who are learned in doctrine, formed in wisdom, capable of teaching the science of faith' (*Hom. in Lev.*, 6, 6). And it occurs elsewhere. For example Gregory of Nazianzen writes: 'We come now to the dispensation of the word, so that in conclusion we might speak of what comes first in our ministry' (*op. cit.*, 444A).[2]

Secondly there is the priestly character of the ministry of the word. This is not simply a question of persuasion by human

1. 'Parole de Dieu et mission de l'Église' in *Le prêtre ministre de la parole*, 1955, pp 41–54.
2. cf. Chrys., *Sac.*: P.G. 48, 666.

reasoning, but of a divine activity of the Word. Now, the priest is the minister of these divine actions, these mysteries: 'Proclaiming the gospel is priestly work' (Origen, *Com. in Rom.* 10, 2). That is why the ministry of the word is the continuation in the new covenant of the levitical priesthood: 'When you see that the priests and the levites are no longer handling the blood of rams and bulls, but the Word of God by the grace of the Holy Spirit, then you can say that Jesus has taken the place of Moses' (Origen, *Hom. in Jos.*, 2, 1).

Nevertheless, however great the ministry of the word, it is only one aspect of priesthood. The priest is also and on the same level a ἱερεύς because the divine δύναμις is both ἔργον and λόγος. The divine works under this present economy are the sacraments, and the priest is the minister of them. This, in the language of Pseudo-Dionysius (429D), is the *theurgic* side of his ministry in its *theological* aspect. It is in the sacraments that the specifically divine character of the actions of which the priest is minister stands out most. The human role is comparatively great in the ministry of the word, since it makes use of human talents, but in the sacraments the man is but the amazed witness of the works which are performed at his hands.

St John Chrysostom has portrayed the general character of this theurgic ministry in a beautiful passage which runs: 'No one can enter into the kingdom of heaven except he be regenerate by water and the Spirit; and he who does not eat the flesh of the Lord will not have life eternal. Now, it is certain that we cannot receive all these good things save at the consecrated hands of the priest. It is the priests who bring us to spiritual birth through baptism. It is the priests who clothe us with Christ, who bury us with him in the tomb, and bring us to life again with his body. They are not charged merely to wipe out our faults and regenerate us in the waters of baptism. They have also the power to remit faults committed after baptism' (*Sac.;* P.G. 48, 644).[1]

Here again the priest appears as the minister, the instrument of actions which in reality are divine. It is from this point of view

1. cf. Theodore of Mopsuestia, *Hom. catech.*, 16, 14; *Comm. in Psalm.*, 44, 16; *Didaskalia* 7, 20; 8, 5–21.

in particular that light is shed on the difficult question of the relationship of the priest's *sacerdotium* to that of Christ. In reality Christ is the sole priest. In him the reality of priesthood, prefigured in pagan and levitical priesthood, is fulfilled and exhausted. Yet Christ fulfils his priestly activity as head of the whole mystical body, which is 'a royal priesthood, a holy nation' (1 Peter, **2**, 9). But the priest is the minister of its priestly activity, since it is through his agency that it is made effective in the sacraments. He alone offers the sacrifice, that is to say, he is the servant of a mystery in which Christ, the one Priest, offers the sacrifice in the name of the whole body.

There still remains one final aspect of the work of salvation, the leadership of the holy people, the body of Christ. This again is the work of God. He is the one head and is the sum of all royalty as of priesthood. But priests are the ministers of his rule, as of his word and his operation and they therefore have a duty of leadership. Paul mentions among the charismatics: 'He that ruleth' ὁ πρόϊστάμενος (Rom. **12**, 8). It is to this function that the terms *bishop* and *presbyter*, both of them early, are linked. We have met numerous equivalents in πρόεδρος, ἡγούμενος, προκαθήμενος, καθηνεμώυ (P.G. 46, 581D). The Didaskalia says: 'You are princes (ἄρχοντες), leaders (ἡγούμενοι) and kings (βασιλεῖς)' (2, 25, 7). And it sees in the presbyteral body 'the sanhedrin (συνέδριον) and the senate (βουλή) of the Church' (2, 28, 5).

This authority is strongly emphasised by Ignatius of Antioch. It incorporates first of all the idea of the government of the Church: 'It is therefore necessary that nothing be done without the bishop, and that you be subject also to the presbyterate. Without them one cannot even speak of the Church' (*Trall.* 2, 2; cf. *Magn.* 2, 2). This implies a dependence on the part of the rest of the community. 'That, being joined together (ὑποταγή) and subject (ὑποτασσόμενοι) to the bishop and the presbyterate, you may be sanctified in all things' (Eph. **2**, 2). This aspect had been earlier strongly stressed by Clement of Rome; in his case it has a somewhat military ring: 'Not all are prefects or tribunes or centurions, but each one in his own rank carries out the orders he receives' (*Epist.* 37, 3). As Campenhausen noted this was a feature of the Roman community.

This aspect of the ministry, moreover, includes the presidency over the Christian assembly, the ἐκκλησία: 'Let nothing be done without the bishop, in matters concerning the Church', writes Ignatius. 'Let that eucharist alone be regarded as lawful which is done under the presidency of the bishop or of him to whom he has entrusted it. For where the bishop is, there let the community be. It is not lawful, apart from the bishop, either to baptise or to hold *agape*' (*Smyrn.* 8, 1). The relationship of the priest to the eucharist thus appears in a new light – as a sacrifice, he is its minister, and as an assembly, he is its president.

This role of president includes, for the Fathers, the administration of the goods of the community. The Christian community, in effect, is also a community of temporal charity taking care of its poor. And as president of the community the priest must also show solicitude for temporal misfortune. This is also found in Hermas who praises the bishops 'who have never failed to provide shelter for the needy and the widows' (*Sim.* 9, 27, 2) and it recurs throughout the tradition. The Didaskalia says: 'You are appointed the good stewards of God who will require at your hands an account of the stewardship (οἰκονομία) he has entrusted to you . . . So, then, dispense well those things which have been delivered to you as good stewards of God, to the orphans, the widows, the needy and the strangers' (2, 25, 2).

So the Christian ministry amply justifies the definition we gave it at the beginning – the 'dispensation of the mysteries' – and its various facets correspond to the various aspects of these mysteries. The ministry cannot therefore be defined by reference to priesthood or to mystery, as if it were one particular variety of these general categories. If we wish to find its antecedents in paganism and Judaism, we must discover what the instruments of divine activity were at those particular times in the history of salvation. In this sense it can be compared with prophecy and priesthood in the old testament. But the Christian ministry appears to be greater than these because it is the instrument of divine actions which themselves are much higher.

Thus the succession of God's ministers has been ordered in a wonderful sequence. St John Chrysostom illustrates it by referring to Elias on Mount Carmel. He describes the people in silence, the prophet at prayer, and the fire falling from the heavens: 'All these things were wonderful and amazing (θαυμαστά). But today the mysteries exceed all amazement. The priest stands there to cause not fire, but the Holy Spirit, to descend. He prays at length, not so that fire falling from on high may consume the offerings, but that grace, descending on the Host, may reach men's souls and make them brighter than silver that is tried by fire' (Sac; P.G. 48, 642).

Fr Liégé: I would like to put a question about the missionary function expressed by St Paul's words: 'Christ sent me not to baptise, but to preach' (1 Cor. 1, 14). What place within the one priesthood do the Fathers of the Church give to the specifically missionary function – not as opposed to the others, but as a particular activity?

You have laid great stress on the 'word' as having a place in the cult, and as being bound up with the rite, but do the Fathers give the word, as such, a place in the ministry of evangelisation and place catechesis first in their definition of priesthood? Is the ministry of the word exercised by virtue of the priestly character?

Fr Daniélou: I am always surprised, in studying the works of the Fathers, to find that the missionary question is hardly raised at all at that period. They considered themselves, fundamentally, as being placed in a Christian world where everything which was not Christian was of no importance, a state of mind which persisted into the Middle Ages.

Fr von Balthasar has explained this in an article in a recent number of *Dieu Vivant*, where he shows that the realisation that important things do exist outside the Church is of modern origin, and is the reason why the missionary question presents itself to us in such an acute form.

But from the point of view of the early history of Christianity I have never seen the question as such raised at all. There were concrete technical difficulties (those concerned with evangelisation, for example), but these were not questions which gave rise to reflection, and when the Fathers speak of the ministry of the word, it is essentially the word addressed to the community. But as far as the proclamation of the message to non-Christians is concerned I know of no patristic document which deals with this point.

Fr Liégé: Could this imply, then, that it was the laity who performed this function?

Fr Daniélou: I think it was originally performed by laymen. They played an immense part in the first stages of evangelisation. The priest came into the picture at the time of the instruction: it was the layman who effected the first contact with the pagan. The layman, godfather or godmother, brought the pagan who wished to become a convert to the priest, who then took on the instruction.

In a world consisting largely of adults, this is in fact what we normally meet. Contact is made by the layman and the priest gives the instruction.

Dom Rousseau: I would just like to observe that there is one aspect of contact with what is outside the Church in the Jewish question. This we do find discussed in the Fathers. So that that was at any rate one non-Christian world which engaged attention.

Fr Gy: You alluded just now to that sort of apparent autonomy, and even pre-eminence, which the Fathers – and the medievals as well, it seems to me – attributed to the word.

As far as the medievals are concerned, I think that they found the answer to Fr Liégé's query about evangelisation in this. For them, there is a kind of autonomy of the word extending beyond the worshipping order, which can eventually be directed – there is some evidence of this – to those not within the worshipping community.

Is this some sort of indication that when the Fathers speak of the pre-eminence of the word they also have in mind the question of evangelisation?

Fr Daniélou: I do not think so. But in the texts I have examined it is true that the word goes beyond the sacramental.

Fr Gy: In the sense that it 'makes the Church', so to say?

Fr Daniélou: Yes, that is so. It constitutes, in fact, an appeal to faith addressed to those who do not believe. For example sometimes the Fathers speak to the catechumens present in the assembly; but when they do address anyone, it is the catechumens and not the pagans.

They speak to the catechumens, and you know that at this period some of them waited for a very long time, sometimes as much as ten or twenty years before being baptised. There is the classical sermon of Epiphanius which the bishop preached each year to the catechumens, asking them to enrol for baptism at Easter.

We must also bear in mind the occasional allusions to the controversies with the Jews, much of which is in the form of a sermon addressed to the Jews as if they were actually present.

M. Chavasse: But I think we find a specific theory of apostolate in heathen lands in Eusebius of Caesarea, the only theorist who has really elaborated it. He developed a theory which is very interesting for the modern era. I will outline its main features.

In order to establish Christianity, the intervention of the emperor was necessary to effect first of all a *politeia*, which may be more or less translated by *civilisation*. Then, when 'civilisation' had been established, that is, when men had reached a certain level of humanity which made them ready to receive Christianity, he chose the wisest and most holy bishops in the empire, and they were sent to make Christians of those who had thus been prepared for Christianity by the emperor.

There would certainly have been preaching at that time, but there is no written trace of it because we only possess the literary remains of what are called 'organised Christian groups'. But the fact that we have no literary traces of it must not be taken to mean that what was in fact a very conscious function did not exist. For this care in choosing the most wise and saintly bishops means that it was recognised to be an outstanding and difficult task, perhaps more difficult than the ordinary administration of the flock.

M. Girault: I think St Augustine cites the scriptural passage: 'Go . . . teach all nations . . . in the name of the Father, and of the Son, and of the Holy Ghost', about thirty times, but never in a missionary context. What interests him is the 'in the name of the Father, and of the Son, and of the Holy Ghost', and he is speaking about the Trinity.

There are some Fathers, such as Origen and St Augustine, who although they mention the arrival of people from far distant lands who did not appear to have heard of Christianity, do not draw any missionary inferences from it. Others make the deduction: in scripture it is stated that when the whole earth has been evangelised the end of the world will come. Therefore, if some peoples had still not been evangelised, it meant the end of the world was not imminent. On the other hand, when they felt that the world had been almost completely evangelised they said 'it is because the end of the world is now not far off '. It is always in the context of some particular question, which is never that of evangelisation.

Dom Rousseau: But there is one very clear example of an exposition of evangelisation preserved in the annals of ecclesiastical history – that is the evangelisation of England by Gregory the Great.

Bede the historian relates how this was done, without bloodshed, simply by the technique of setting up the monastic life there to sing its office and shed its light by prayer and worship. This is the first very important example. These are isolated examples, no doubt, but they still count. And from this beginning the missionary movement spread throughout the whole of Germany.

Fr Daniélou: But this evangelisation of the barbarian world is very late.

Fr Lécuyer: I do think, though, that it is possible to find if not a completely formed and elaborated theory of the whole matter, at any rate the elements of one, in the homilies on Pentecost, notably on the duty of bishops as successors of the apostles. There is, indeed, a very beautiful discourse by St John Chrysostom on *Aquila and Priscilla*, which contains what I consider to be two very important points bearing especially on the missionary role of the laity.

We find them also in the commentaries on Romans, à propos the last words: 'Salutate . . . etc.'. It ought to be possible to collect a certain number of these points; no doubt they are scattered but they do exist.

Fr Daniélou: There are, in fact, many points on the missionary role of the laity. I merely wanted to say that we have no written traces of a *kerygmatic* preaching.

M. Martimort: There is one conclusion I have drawn from this discussion – we cannot find the exact answer to our own problems in the past. We came to the same conclusion several years ago in connection with first communion. The Church today is becoming increasingly conscious of its own peculiar problems, and although texts from the past help us to analyse and elucidate these problems, they do not give us a complete answer. We cannot put the clock back.

CHAPTER VII

THE MYSTERY OF PENTECOST AND THE APOSTOLIC MISSION OF THE CHURCH

J. LÉCUYER, C.S.SP.

A TALK on the mystery of Pentecost may appear to be somewhat unexpected in a session of studies on Orders; the sacrament of Orders has hardly been brought into relationship with the mystery of the descent of the Holy Spirit in the form of fiery tongues in the upper room, a mystery which itself has still not received sufficient attention. It would not therefore be good method to offer here and now a kind of synthesis of the points of contact between the two mysteries, much less to attempt final conclusions. The purpose of the present paper, then, will be merely to present the documents of tradition, and on this footing to assess as far as possible their theological relevance, and to indicate what the possibilities are for their integration into a complete theology of holy Orders. So this account will be in three parts:

1. A study of the documents of tradition.
2. An assessment of their theological relevance.
3. Provisional conclusions.

I. THE DOCUMENTS OF TRADITION

St Irenaeus

Traces of the teaching with which we are here concerned can be found in *Adversus Haereses*. At the beginning of Book III Irenaeus writes:

The Lord of all gave the power of preaching the gospel to his apostles . . . It is not lawful to say that they preached before they possessed 'perfect knowledge', as some are bold enough to assert, boasting that they are improving on the apostles. For after our Lord arose from the dead the apostles were invested with virtue from on high when the Holy Spirit came down suddenly upon them, were filled with all gifts and had perfect knowledge. Then they departed to the ends of the earth, proclaiming the glad tidings of the good things which God sends us, and preaching the peace of heaven to men. (*Adv. Haer.*, 3, 1, 1.)

The statement that at Pentecost the apostles were granted the grace of perfect knowledge should be compared with another passage which treats of the same mystery. In chapter 17 of the same book, Irenaeus relates how the Holy Spirit descended on Jesus at the river Jordan, and that this same Spirit had been foretold by the prophets, especially by Isaias when he wrote: 'The Spirit of the Lord is upon me, because the Lord hath anointed me', (Isaias **61**, 1); it is the same Spirit that David asked for in Psalm **50**: *Et Spiritu principali confirma me.* Then the writer adds:

It is he also, as Luke tells us, who descended on the disciples at Pentecost after the Lord's ascension, for it is he who has power to admit all nations to the knowledge of life, and to open the new testament to them; that is why, all tongues in harmony, they sang praise to God, the Spirit bringing the scattered races back into unity and offering to the Father the first-fruits of every nation.[1]

We must note first of all how this passage connects the descent of the Holy Spirit at Pentecost with his descent on Jesus at the river Jordan. This became a classical comparison. In the episode at Jordan, Irenaeus invariably sees an anointing of Christ, the very unction which made him the Anointed One, the Christ.[2]

Furthermore, Irenaeus points out the various marks and effects of this descent of the Spirit: 'Power to admit all nations to the knowledge of life and to open the new testament to them'; the return of the dispersed peoples to unity, revealed in the harmony of tongues; the offering to the Father of the first-fruits of all the nations. Here there is a clear allusion to those different aspects of the feast of Pentecost which were already familiar to Jewish

1. *Adv. Haer.*, 3, 17, 2.   2. *ibid.*, 3, 9, 3; 12, 7; 18, 3.

tradition: the escape from the bondage of Egypt which brought them to the promised land; the giving of the covenant on Mount Sinai; the feast of the first-fruits of the harvest. At Pentecost, says Irenaeus, all nations are invited, *ad introitum vitae*, to receive a new covenant, *novum testamentum*; the first-fruits of the harvest are all the first baptised, whatever their origin. To these three principal aspects of Pentecost, he adds a fourth: the return to unity of all peoples, scattered abroad since the confusion of tongues at Babel.

Thus, the Holy Spirit confers on the apostles a grace of light, which Irenaeus, following Gnostic terminology, calls 'perfect knowledge'. It is a grace directed towards the admission of all nations into the people of God, to the formation of a new people under a new covenant, and to the offering of the whole human race in one single sacrifice of first-fruits to God.

Now recalling that this gift of the Spirit was compared with that which Jesus received at the river Jordan, and if the latter was actually the bestowing of an unction on Christ, we may ask if there is not a priestly unction here as well. But since Irenaeus does not actually say this, it is better not to force the texts. But we must note that the terms which are used to compare the apostolate in heathen lands with the offering of the first-fruits of the harvest form part of the terminology of sacrifice, and indeed are reminiscent of St Paul's formulae (Rom. **15**, 16; Phil. **2**, 17; 2 Tim. **4**, 6). Finally we can ask ourselves if the last old testament passage cited by Irenaeus (Ps. **50**: *et Spiritu principali confirma me*), is not an allusion to the ritual at the consecration of a bishop as it appears in the apostolic tradition of Hippolytus which we have already mentioned. Be this as it may, it is certain that bishops, according to Irenaeus, are those who continue to receive the same 'sure charisma of truth' which the apostles received at Pentecost: 'it is necessary to obey the presbyters who are in the Church, who, as we have shown, possess the succession from the apostles; those, who, together with the succession of the episcopate, have received the sure charisma of truth . . .'[1] So the grace received by the apostles at Pentecost

1. *Adv. Haer.*, 4, 26, 2.

corresponds to that received by Jesus at the river Jordan and is the same as that which the bishops, the successors of the apostles, also receive.

Hippolytus of Rome

The same teaching recurs in Hippolytus of Rome. The very lovely prayer for the consecration of a bishop, which he has preserved for us, is well known.[1] The following passage is perhaps the most relevant:

Do thou now shed that power of thine, the sovereign Spirit (*Spiritum principalem*) which thou didst give to thy well-beloved Son Jesus Christ, and which he bestowed upon the holy apostles, who established thy Church in place of thy sanctuary.

The grace sought for the bishop is therefore an outpouring of that sovereign Spirit which had been given to Jesus by the Father, and to the apostles by Jesus; it is clearly a quesion of the Spirit, but of the Spirit imparting a special grace, as is indicated by the expression: *spiritus principalis*, ἡγεμονικὸν πγεῦμα, which is to be translated 'the sovereign Spirit', or better, I think, 'the Spirit of sovereignty'. But what is important for us here is the reference to the communication of this same Spirit to the apostles, and before them to Jesus himself. Hippolytus is undoubtedly alluding to the scene at the baptism of Jesus, as Dom Botte observes, and it is difficult not to think of Pentecost as well. So the consecration of a bishop is related to both these mysteries, and a comparison with the texts from Irenaeus is extremely telling, since here again we have a triple successive outpouring of the 'Spirit of sovereignty' at the baptism of Jesus, at Pentecost and at the consecration of bishops.

This can be confirmed from other passages in Hippolytus where Christ appears as the ἡγούμενος foretold in the Blessing of Jacob, and which the Father's voice at his baptism declared him to be.[2] And apostles are not only those who founded the Church[3] and established it, but also those who, thanks to the

1. cf. my article: 'Épiscopat et presbytérat dans les écrits d'Hippolyte de Rome', in *Recherches de Sciences Religieuses*, xli (1953), pp 30–50.
2. *De Antichristo*, 7 and 9–12.   3. *ibid.*, 61.

power of the Holy Spirit which they have received, remain at the present time its ever firm supports, and who are like those beams in the house of the spouse in Canticles, which, because they are made of cypress wood, will not rot.[1] Similarly, Hippolytus asserts that the chariot of the Church is always driven by the apostles.[2] These similes describe, then, the power received by the apostles, by virtue of the gift of the Spirit, a power which still remains in the Church today; this is easily understood if we see in the grace of Pentecost a grace which corresponds at least partially to that which is bestowed on our bishops.

St Athanasius

A most interesting passage in Athanasius shows that he too held similar views; it occurs in a short commentary on Psalm 132, *Ecce quam bonum*, which has been preserved in the exegetical catenae. The lines with which we are concerned are:

The Psalmist declares that 'when the Church has been gathered together into a kind of community, then both the anointing of the Holy Spirit and the priesthood (ἱεράτευμα) will be bestowed, first upon the head of the Church, which is Christ, then upon the beard adorning the face of the Church, which symbolises the apostles. And finally it will cover the whole body, that is to say, all those who have put on Christ in the Church... At Jerusalem, the life-giving dew of the Holy Spirit was shed upon the apostles, that dew which brings eternal blessing to believers.'[3]

In these lines a triple communication of the Christian priesthood is described: the priesthood of Christ, the head of the body which is the Church; the priesthood conferred upon the apostles on the day of Pentecost, and the priesthood common to all the faithful. The anointing of Christ by the Holy Spirit is developed at length by Athanasius in his first discourse against the Arians;[4] a passage in the first letter to Serapion relates to the mystery of Pentecost the apostles' power to impart the Holy Spirit through the imposition of hands after baptism.[5]

1. *In Cantic.*, 1, 17 (Ed. Bonwetsch, T.u.U., 23, 1902, pp 48–9).
2. *ibid.*, 1, 9 (p. 40).
3. *In Ps.*, 132 (P.G. 27, 524bc).
4. *Orat. I Contra Arianos*, 47 (P.G. 26, 108–12).
5. *Epist. I ad Serapionem*, 6 (P.G. 26, 544a).

There is no direct reference to the episcopate, but the priesthood of the Church is placed in direct dependence on the mystery of Pentecost.

St. John Chrysostom

The thought of St John Chrysostom is not altogether clear. In his Homilies on St John (20, 22) he makes a clear distinction between the two occasions on which the Holy Spirit was imparted to the disciples; after the resurrection when Christ breathed on them and said: 'Receive the Holy Spirit', Jesus gave them:

> a certain power and spiritual grace . . . not to raise the dead or perform miracles, but to remit sins. For there are various spiritual gifts (*charismata*). That is why the evangelist adds: 'whose sins ye shall forgive, they are forgiven', thus indicating the kind of power Christ was giving them. It was only after forty days that they received the power of miracles.[1]

And in the adjoining paragraph Chrysostom goes on to say that this power to remit sins belongs to priests.

So Pentecost gave to the twelve, already equipped with sacerdotal powers, a new outpouring of the Holy Spirit, a new spiritual gift. Here Chrysostom considers that it was the gift of miracles which was added to the gift of remitting sins, a distinction which recurs in other works of the same writer.[2] But elsewhere he also compares the descent of the Spirit in the upper room with the unction which Jesus received at the river Jordan:[3] although the twelve were not the only ones to receive the gift of the Spirit,[4] at any rate they received a special power, notably the power to impart the Holy Spirit to the baptised.[5]

Severian of Gabala

This contemporary – and rival – of Chrysostom has left us a wonderful example in his Homily on Pentecost, which has been preserved almost in its entirety in the exegetical catenae: Severian wishes to explain why the Holy Spirit appeared upon

1. *In Joan.*, Homil., 87 (al. 86), 3 (P.G. 59, 471).
2. *In Act. Ap.*, Homil., 18, 2 (P.G. 60, 143d).
3. *ibid.*, Homil., 1, 5 (P.G. 60, 21).
4. *ibid.*, Homil., 4, 1 (P.G. 60, 43).
5. *ibid.*, Homil., 18, 3 (P.G. 60, 144).

the apostles in tongues of fire, and why these tongues rested on their heads:

But why upon the head? Because the apostles were ordained (ἐχειροτονοῦντο) to be doctors of the whole world; now ordination (χειροτονία) is always performed only on the head. The presence of the tongues on their heads is therefore the sign of an ordination. It is in fact right that ordination is performed on the head as custom has required down to our own times. For, since the descent of the Holy Spirit is invisible, the book of the gospel is laid on the head of him who is to be ordained high priest; and in this imposition we must see nothing less than a tongue of fire resting on the head; a tongue, because of the preaching of the gospel; a tongue of fire because of the words: I am come to bring fire on the earth.[1]

It would be difficult to be more explicit than this. But this example is even more telling if we consider the whole context in which Severian sums up with remarkable clarity and precision the different aspects of the mystery of Pentecost.

He sees it as the giving of the new law fifty days after Easter, as the law of Sinai had been given on the fiftieth day after the exodus from Egypt (col. 529). He tells us that although the new law, which is grace, is written in the heart and received not only by the twelve but by all those present in the Cenacle (*ibid.*, col. 532), the bishop has nevertheless quite a special role to fulfil in this sphere. In the homily *De Legislatore* which J. Zellinger attributes to Severian, we find in fact an extremely interesting passage in which the orator asks why Aaron wore a mitre, and what it signified; he replies that the head of the people must have his head covered as a reminder that, although he is a leader and lawgiver, there is a Law above him:

It is for this reason that in the Church also, at the ordination of priests (τῶν ἱερέων) the book of the gospel is placed on the head of the ordinand, that he may know that he is receiving the true crown of the gospel, that he may also know that, although he is our head, he is none the less subject to these laws; ruling all, but himself ruled by the law; a legislator for all, yet himself under the legislation of the

1. Catena on Acts attributed to Theophylact (P.G. 125, 533ab). But we must not forget, in the case of this reading, the catena of Cramer (pp 22–3) and other sources cited in the article 'Note sur la Liturgie du Sacré des Evêques' in *Eph. Liturg.*, lxvi, 1952, pp 369–70.

Word (of God). . . Consequently the imposition of the gospel upon the high priest means that he is subject to an authority.[1]

We are thus led to the same idea of a power of leadership conferred on the apostles and bishops we previously met in Hippolytus of Rome.

Severian points out a second aspect of the mystery. Pentecost was a feast of the harvest at which the first fruits and the new sheaves were offered. Henceforth it would be the 'sheaves of the souls of every race who would be offered to God by the word of the apostles' (col. 529–32).

By the gift of tongues and a rediscovered unity, Pentecost also reverses the confusion of tongues which took place at the tower of Babel (ibid., col. 534).

These are identical with the themes we have already found in Irenaeus.

One last note – Severian admits that the twelve had already (in John 20) received a first ordination: 'The Saviour had indeed ordained the apostles before, yet not as apostles for the whole world, but only for the whole of Judaea.'[2]

Cyril of Alexandria

Several passages of Cyril of Alexandria bear on the subject. In his commentaries on the minor prophets he refers to the two occasions on which the apostles received the Holy Spirit. On the first occasion, when Jesus breathed on them, the Holy Spirit adorned them with his gifts as with a garment;[3] but the grace bestowed at Pentecost made them 'witnesses of his glory at Jerusalem, in Judaea and to the ends of the earth'.[4]

Cyril returns to this theme at greater length in his Commentary on St John, explaining the words of Jesus: 'Pax vobis. Sicut misit me pater et ego mitto vos' thus:

By these words the Lord Jesus Christ ordained (or appointed: κεχειροτόνηκε) the leaders and teachers of the world, that they may also be dispensers of his divine mysteries' (P.G. 74, 708d).

1. P.G. 56, 404. On this aspect of Pentecost, see 'Penecôte et Loi Nouvelle' in La Vie Spirituelle, May 1953, pp 471–90.
2. This text is preserved in the catena of Cramer.
3. In Joelem, 2, 28–9 (P.G. 71, 376d).
4. In Amos, 4, 6 (P.G. 71, 569d).

Then, a little further on, explaining why Jesus breathed on them and spoke to them of the remission of sins:

After proclaiming their exaltation in the great dignity of the apostolate, and having declared them to be dispensers and priests (ἱερουργούς) of the divine altars, he sanctified them forthwith and gave them his Spirit by breathing visibly upon them' (col. 709).

And Cyril recalls the consecration of Aaron and the Levites, a figure of the truth which is only fulfilled in Christ (col. 712 c). There is, however, a difficulty here – is it actually at this moment or at Pentecost that the apostles received the Holy Spirit (col. 712–13)?

Cyril's answer can be summed up in a few words. The first time, the apostles received, as it were, the first-fruits (ἀπαρχὴν ὥσπερ τινά) of the promise of the Spirit. But at Pentecost they received 'not the beginning of the gift (of the Spirit) . . . but rather the beginning of the Word' (col. 717b). The tongues of fire, in effect, show that it is a special gift directed towards the apostolate, and we actually see that the apostles began to preach at once:

You see . . . they began to preach, not to be sanctified, and tongues are given to them by the action of the Spirit present with them. As when the voice of the Father was heard from heaven bearing witness to his only Son, saying: 'This is my beloved Son, in whom I am well pleased . . .' so likewise God bestows a manifest sign of his grace on the apostles by sending them tongues under the form of flames of fire (col. 717).

Here again we find that comparison between the baptism of Jesus and Pentecost, and the assertion that a new grace was bestowed on the apostles, which directed them to preaching.[1] This grace comes after a first outpouring of the Holy Spirit, which has the marks of being a priestly consecration.

Ammonius of Alexandria

Among the surviving exegetical fragments on St John's gospel attributed to Ammonius of Alexandria, and which, according to Badenhewer, date from the middle of the fifth century, we find

1. cf. *Com. in Luc.*, 24, 45 (Trans. Payne Smith, ii, Oxford, 1859, p. 731).

one short passage which is of interest to us. Once again it is a commentary on John **20**, 22–3:

> It can be said that at this moment they received the charisma of remitting sins, while after Pentecost they received the gift of raising the dead, and other more perfect gifts.[1]

It is clear that we are very close to Chrysostom here.

Pseudo-Dionysius

We must dwell at greater length on the evidence provided by Pseudo-Dionysius. He wishes to show that the initiative in vocation and in the transmission of grace does not lie with the consecrating bishop, but that it is to 'God himself who moves him in all his hierarchical ordinations'. Thus Moses awaited the command of God before consecrating Aaron (Ex. **29**, 4). Thus, according to the epistle to the Hebrews, even Jesus did not confer the priestly dignity upon himself, but received it from his Father (Heb. **5**, 5–6). And he goes on:

> So indeed, he himself, when he purposed to confer sacred ordination on his disciples, although as God he was himself the cause of the sacrament, nevertheless hierarchically refers his act of consecration to his all-holy Father, and the thearchis Spirit, informing his disciples, according to the scriptures, that they were not to leave Jerusalem but should 'wait for the promise of the Father which you have heard by my mouth . . . you shall be baptised with the Holy Ghost'.[2]

ἄγων ἐπὶ τὴν ἱερατικὴν τελείωσιν has been translated by: 'when he purposed to confer sacred ordination'. It seems to me, however, that Pseudo-Dionysius considered that the ordination of the apostles took place entirely at Pentecost. This, at all events, is the interpretation the Greek commentators give to this passage; so also the Scholia bearing the name of St Maximus:

> Notice at what moment the disciples were ordained priests, and that Jesus, although he was God, did not ordain them himself, but promised to send the Holy Spirit from the Father when the tongues of fire appeared (P.G. 4, 165d).

1. P.G. 85, 1517d.
2. *De Eccles. Hier.*, v, Contemplatio, 5 (P.G. 3, 512c).

Similarly, the paraphrase composed by Pachymerus in the thirteenth century states:

Although he was God, he did not, strictly speaking, ordain the disciples himself, but promised to send the Holy Spirit from the Father (P.G. 3, 528c).

This was also the interpretation given by Thomas Gallus, Abbot of Verceil in the thirteenth century.[1]

I do not therefore agree with Thomassin's[2] interpretation, nor with M. de Gandillac's[3] proposed translation; according to these writers, it seems, there was a double ordination, one before the ascension and the other at Pentecost. But it seems to me, on the contrary, that in the opinion of Pseudo-Dionysius the apostles were not ordained except at the time of the latter mystery.

Isho'dad of Merv

Towards the middle of the ninth century we meet an isolated example in the Syrian bishop of Hadatha, Isho'dad of Merv. He writes:

the Spirit descending upon the twelve in the shape of tongues of fire; but upon the seventy, and upon the other men and women, the grace of the Spirit was poured out in the likeness of effused light . . .[4]

There is, therefore, a difference between the gift of the Spirit to the twelve, and that to the rest of the faithful. The first, the writer continues, receive the Spirit in the form of tongues

because . . . they were about to preach to the strange tongues in the world

and also

to show that they were treasurers and guardians of the Spirit, and interpreters and organs of God the Word, as the tongue is to the mind and the sense.

1. See the passage in the *Oeuvres Complètes* of Denys the Carthusian, vol. xv, Tournai, 1902, p. 535.
2. *De Incarnatione Verbi Dei*, lib. x, cap. 29, 15 (Vivès, iv, 1868, p. 457.   3. Ed. Aubier, 1943, pp 302–3.
4. 'The Commentaries of Isho'dad of Marv,' ed. and trans. M. D. Gibson. Commentary on Acts 2, 3 (*Horae Semiticae* x, Cambridge 1913, p. 7).

Furthermore, Isho'dad is not afraid to assert that

the twelve apostles ... received in one hour the great degrees of apostleship, and of priesthood, and of high-priesthood and of prophecy. But the seventy received the degree of eldership in that hour; and these were also called bishops, as of old elders were called bishops.[1]

The writer, however, was aware that there was another point of view. Commenting on the conclusion of St Luke, where Jesus is sending out his apostles, and before ascending to heaven stretches out his hands over them in blessing, he writes:

Others say ... that he gave them the mystery of consecration so that they here received the degree of presbytery, and in the upper room that of apostleship.[2]

It would be easy to show that this connection between Pentecost and the sacrament of Orders was faithfully preserved in the later tradition of the Eastern Church. But it will not be possible to quote more than a few of the writers.

Theophylacte (xi-xii c.), in a short exposition of the Acts of the Apostles, takes up the teaching of Severian of Gabala[3] and makes it his own.

His contemporary Euthymios Zigabene, in his commentary on John 20, 22, also accepts the two communications of the Holy Spirit to the apostles, and indeed follows very closely the thought and expression of Chrysostom.[4]

We also note the very interesting comparison made between the baptism of Christ and Pentecost by Theodore Prodromos in the thirteenth century:

In the form of a dove the Spirit descends on the Master;
In the form of fiery tongues the Spirit descends on the apostles;
For he imparts himself to ministers of the Word
That they may consume the errors of idolatry.[5]

A homily on Pentecost by Gregory Palamas in the fourteenth century contains the following passage:

1. 'The Commentaries of Isho'dad of Merv,' ed. and trans. M. D. Gibson, p. 9.
2. *ibid.*, p. 209.   3. P.G. 125, 849 ff.
4. *Comment. in Joan.*; ed. Mattaeus, Leipzig 1792, pp 639–41.
5. P.G. 133, 1209.

By virtue of the ordination conferred by the apostles on their successors, and by them in turn on their successors, and so on, the grace of the divine Spirit bestowed (at Pentecost) remains to all generations, and enlightens all those who are obedient to their pastors and spiritual teachers.[1]

I will conclude with a fine illustration from Simeon of Thessalonica. Examining the rites of episcopal consecration, the writer explains why the newly elected bishop does not enter into the sanctuary at the same time as the consecrating bishops, who make their entry before him. He writes:

It is, therefore, after the first entrance that this marriage of the Spirit – ordination – takes place; this is because such order has been observed from the beginning; for the Lord was first of all made flesh, then suffered for us, rose again and ascended into heaven – all these mysteries are signified by the first entrance; afterwards, the Holy Spirit alone came down and ordained the disciples of the Saviour, making them participants of the same throne. That is why, when the high priest together with his companions has reached the altar – which is the symbol of heaven – and before he ascends the common throne, which signifies the throne of God, the ordinand is brought to him for consecration, and he thus becomes a participant in the same throne.[2]

Simeon explains himself at greater length in chapter 240. After the transfiguration, he says, Christ appointed (κατέστησε) bishops and priests, and sent them to preach before him. Then he offered himself in sacrifice, gave us the eucharist, reconciled us to the Father by his death and resurrection, and imparted the first-fruits of the Spirit by breathing on the apostles.

But, he adds, 'he ordains (χειροτονεῖ) the disciples in a still more perfect manner after his ascension by those fiery tongues of the Holy Spirit which hovered over them and rested upon each one of them. So they all received the same grace, and were all filled with the Holy Spirit. Therefore the disciples had been chosen from the beginning, they had been sent to the lost sheep, they had received a gift (δωρεάν) and the command to impart it; but they had not yet received perfect consecration.

The reason was because the sacrifice of Jesus had not yet been offered.[3]

1. *Hom.*, 24 (P.G. 151, 316ab).
2. *De Sacris ordinationibus*, cap. 203 (P.G. 155, 112d).
3. *ibid.*, cap. 240 (col. 457–8a).

In rounding off these examples from the Eastern Church, we must bear in mind that the majority of the rituals of episcopal ordination are closely dependent on the apostolic tradition of Hippolytus, and so preserve the allusion to Pentecost in the consecratory prayer.

The Western Tradition

I have to admit that there are not so many examples in the Latin Church, after the time of St Hippolytus, as in the Eastern Church. It would take too long to examine the courses of this difference between East and West, but doubtless it can be largely attributed to the influence of St Jerome's point of view on the subject of the episcopate.[1] Consequently, the few examples we have discovered are all the more valuable.

First of all, I will quote Maximus of Turin, who compares the baptism of Christ with Pentecost: as the operation of the Holy Spirit followed the baptism of Christ, so Pentecost follows the mysteries of the passion and life of the Saviour; the apostles, already purified by the blood and the teaching of the Master, thenceforth received the fulness of the Spirit. ' *Illos nimirum replevit Spiritus, quorum corda adventui ejus sanguis et doctrina Christi purgaverat.*'[2] The Holy Spirit joins together in perfect unity the apostles who had been chosen by the Saviour to celebrate his mysteries. '*Ipsos Paracletus visitat et illustrat, quos mysteriis suis idoneos Salvator elegit.*'[3]

St Augustine, in his sermon (266) against the Donatists, states that the apostles received the power to lay their hands on others on the day of Pentecost – J. Coppens has shown that in its context this refers to confirmation.[4] But we know that St Augustine was of the opinion that only a bishop could confirm.[5]

This comparison between the descent of the Holy Spirit at the baptism of Jesus and his communication to the apostles on

1. cf. my article, 'Aux origines de la théologie thomiste de l'Episcopat' in *Gregorianum* xxxv, 1954, pp 56–89.

2. *Serm.* 50, P.L. 57, 635a.

3. *Serm.* 51, *ibid.*, col. 636c.

4. cf. J. Coppens, *L'imposition des mains et les rites connexes*, Paris 1925, pp 300–8.

5. *De Trinit.* 15, 26, 46 (P.L. 42, 1093).

the day of Pentecost is constantly made by the writers. In both cases the Holy Spirit is the fount of the preaching and proclamation of the kingdom of God. We shall return to these examples later; they are particularly important because the anointing of the Holy Spirit received by Christ at the river Jordan is frequently considered to be a priestly unction but the comparison with the sacrament of Orders and the episcopate is very rarely made.

Peter Damian, however, must be classified separately. He broaches the subject of ordination in his *Liber Gratissimus* written against the Simoniacs in 1052. Since the true bestower of the Holy Spirit at baptism is not the minister but God himself, it is also he who imparts the Holy Spirit to the ordinand.[1] This is shown in particular at the baptism of Christ in the river Jordan and at the anointing of the priesthood:

> In illa namque columba quae super Dominum baptisma descendit, ipse cum sacramento baptismi et veri sacerdotii jura suscepit, fuso videlicet super eum oleo exsultationis . . . Probatur autem Redemptor noster cum baptismo simul et sacerdotii sucepisse mysterium, quia baptizatus mox praedicare, discipulos eligere, novisque coepit miraculis coruscare . . .

It is the same in the case of the apostles:

> Nam et ipsi sancti apostoli non reperiuntur alibi fuisse a Domino consecrati nisi in perceptione baptismi . . . Cum a Domino dictum sit: Johannes quidem baptizavit aqua, vos autem baptizabimini Spiritu Sancto non post multos hos dies, consat eos tunc perfecti baptismatis atque omni genae simul consecrationis accepisse mysterium cum super eos Spiritus Sanctus venit in diversitate linguarum.[2]

A sermon attributed to Hildebert of Mans but ascribed by W. Lampen to Geoffrey Babion (c. 1110) also admits a first reception of the Holy Spirit at the time of Christ's appearance after the resurrection, but sees in the gift to the apostles at Pentecost, the grace proper to bishops – the grace of wisdom in the new law, the grace of holy daring in preaching, and finally,

1. *Liber Gratissimus*, cap. iii, ed. L. de Heinemann, 'Libelli de Lite' i (M.G.H. 31), p. 21.

2. *ibid.*, cap. 4, pp 21–2. In chapter 15 of the same work the writer admits a first ordination of the apostles – corresponding to the presbyterate – on the evening of Easter Sunday.

the grace of the compelling word. All this is signified by the tongues of fire which are at once light, tongue and flame. The writer adds: '*Modo ista nobis (licet indigni vicarii eorum sumus) ad aedificationem data sunt*'.[1] So he compares Pentecost with the theophany on Sinai. In both cases there is the gift of a law, and bishops receive a quite special communication of the new law. As Moses and Aaron alone had the privilege of ascending the mountain while the people remained in the plain, so the 'doctors of the Church', the bishops, receive a higher communication of the mysteries of God. Finally, the writer concludes: '*Haec omnia . . . nobis . . . ex officio convenire debent*'.[2]

Honorius of Autun (c. 1131?) applies the words of Psalm 132 to Pentecost. The priestly unction poured on the head of Aaron, the figure of Christ, descends on the day of Pentecost into his beard, i.e. the apostles; and by the activity of the latter spreads to all the faithful.[3] Honorius compares Pentecost to the baptism of Christ,[4] as so many had done before him. What is particularly interesting in his teaching is the distinction he makes between the apostles and the ordinary faithful in the gift of the Spirit at Pentecost, the former being the instruments by which the heavenly unction was imparted to the others.

Abelard discerns two receptions of the Spirit by the apostles. On the first occasion, when Jesus breathed on them, he gave them only a limited gift, '*ad unum potestatis donum . . . non ad omnia charismata*'; at Pentecost, on the other hand, '*in omni bonorum perfectione sunt consummati*'.[5] And here he points out an analogy with confirmation: '*Cum baptizati a presbyteris confirmantur postmodum ab episcopis . . . haec ipsa eorum confirmatio quaedam est virtutum armatura spiritualis*'.[6] To show that Pentecost has a special connection with the apostles, the first Pentecost, that is the theophany on Sinai, occurred at the twelfth halting-place in the wilderness, and this symbolises the college of the twelve.[7] However, Abelard does not admit that the whole

---

1. *Serm.* 52 (P.L. 171, 593).   2. *ibid.*, col. 594.
3. Honorius of Autun, *Speculum Ecclesiae*, in Pentecostem, P.L. 172, 962cd.   4. *ibid.*, col. 964.
5. *Serm.* xvii (P.L. 178, 502a); cf. *ibid.*, col. 511.
6. *Serm.* xvii, col. 503; cf. *Serm.* xxi, col. 518–19.
7. *ibid.*, col. 504–5.

of the grace received on the day of Pentecost is transmitted to all the successors of the apostles, to all bishops.[1]

One of Richard of St Victor's sermons on Pentecost refers to Psalm 132. The anointing bestowed on Christ, the head of the body of the Church, descends on to the apostles, figured in Aaron's beard; first of all incompletely after the resurrection, then perfectly at Pentecost.[2]

It is a verse from Canticles which provides Robert of Tombelaine (c. 1186) with the opportunity for considering the grace received by the twelve at Pentecost: '*Soror autem parvula ubera non habebat, quando in solis apostolis ecclesia erat, in quibus seipsam vel alos nutrire lacte praedicationis non poterat*'.[3] The grace given to the apostles was therefore before everything else directed towards preaching.

This theme was taken up by Peter of Blois (c. 1200). The Church in heaven is saying that her little earthly sister is as yet too young to nourish children. For this reason the Holy Spirit had to be sent to the apostles.[4] They had, however, already received the Holy Spirit previously, but he must needs be given to them afresh '*ad usum, ad auxilium, ad solatium, ad miraculum, ad acquisitionem gentium, ad salutem omnium populorum*'.[5]

St Martin of Leon (c. 1203) also takes up the image in Canticles. The Church reached maturity at Pentecost, for she became fruitful, bringing forth sons by the apostles' preaching, and nourishing them with the milk of their doctrine.[6] The unction of the Holy Spirit bestowed that day on the Church continues to be imparted to her by Christ.

Absalom of Springskirsbach (c. 1203?) makes a nice distinction between the different degrees of spiritual unction:

This anointing of the Holy Spirit was promised in divers manners – I mean that there was a particular promise, a special promise and a general promise. The particular promise concerned Christ . . . the apostles were given a special promise and received the first-fruits

1. *Serm.* xxii; P.L. 178, 523.
2. *Serm.* 70, in the works of Hugh of St Victor, P.L. 177, 1122.
3. *Super Canticum Expositio*, cap 8, 11 (among the works of St Gregory, P.L. 79, 543cd).   4. *Serm.* 24 (P.L. 207, 631a).
5. *Serm.* 25; *ibid.*, 635a.
6. *Serm.* 32 (P.L. 208, 1253–4).

of the Spirit, as we read in the Acts of the apostles: 'You shall receive the power of the Holy Ghost . . .'. Finally, a general promise was made to all those who should believe in Christ, by these words in Joel: 'I will pour out of my Spirit . . .'.[1]

Lastly St Thomas, so sensitive to all the principles he found in tradition, was aware of that teaching whose signs I have tried to trace:

To the apostles the mission was directed in the form of breathing, to show forth the power of their ministry in the dispensation of the sacraments; and hence it was said, 'Whose sins you shall forgive, they are forgiven' (John 20, 23); and again under the sign of fiery tongues, to show forth the office of teaching (Ia q. 43, a. 7, ad 6).

There were for St Thomas then, two outpourings of the Holy Spirit on the apostles; the first directed towards the administration of the sacraments, the second towards their role as preachers and teachers. He states this also elsewhere, notably in the Commentary on John 20 (*In Joan. cap. 20*, lect. 4).

The Holy Spirit descended upon the apostles first of all through breathing, to indicate the diffusion of grace effected through the sacraments, of which the apostles were the ministers, and that is why Christ said: 'Whose sins you shall forgive, they are forgiven', and again, 'Go ye, therefore . . . baptising them in the name of the Father, and of the Son, and of the Holy Ghost'. He is imparted to them a second time in tongues of fire, to signify the diffusion of grace effected through teaching, and that is why Acts says that after being filled with the Holy Spirit they began to speak forthwith.

St Thomas also compares these two gifts of the Spirit to the apostles with the two manifestations of the Spirit in the life of Christ, one after his baptism by John the Baptist, the other at the transfiguration under the form of a shining cloud.

But I must bring to an end what might seem a tedious list of texts, and try to draw from them some conclusions which may be of interest to the theologian and the pastor.

2. TOWARDS A THEOLOGICAL APPRECIATION OF THE DOCUMENTS

There is one observation forced on us at the outset. The texts I have quoted – and there are many others – tend towards a

1. *Serm.* 37 (P.L. 211, 214b).

study of the sacrament of Orders which may appear, even in its method, to deviate noticeably from the formulae normally approved in theology. I mean that if these pointers are followed the sacrament of Orders will not be considered so much from the outside, as for example in the history of Christian origins or development by an examination of the activity of the clergy, or the often changeable part played by institutions. I hasten to add that these historical researches are frequently of absorbing interest. In particular there are the recent inquiries into the possible influences of contemporary Judaism on the apostles, both on the part of the dissident sects we have learned about through the recent discovery of the Dead Sea Scrolls,[1] and on the part of official Judaism and its institutions, for, as Arnold Ehrhardt[2] has shown, it is difficult to deny their influence on the early institutions of Christianity. Many patristic texts could be quoted to confirm this Judaistic influence on the theology of Christian priesthood, and I shall come back to it later.

But the line of thought which I should like to elucidate gives a very different approach. Here the mystery of the episcopate and of priesthood generally is to be examined from the 'inside', by a direct consideration of the inspired texts and an explanation of their contents. Moreover, this attempt at consideration and explanation is made in the light of analogies from different series of mysteries – those in the life of the Church on the one hand, and those in the life of Christ and in the history of the chosen people on the other. Pentecost will thus be related not only to the old feast of Weeks, but above all to the mystery of the anointing of Christ at the river Jordan.

Pentecost and the Anointing of Christ at the River Jordan

A large number of the examples I have quoted relate Pentecost to the descent of the Holy Spirit on Christ at the river Jordan. We find that this traditional theme occurs very

1. cf. Delcor, 'Le Sacerdoce, les lieux de Culte, les Rites et les Fêtes dans les documents de Khirbet Qumran' in *Rev. de l'hist. des religions*, 144, 1953, pp 5–41. cf. also Fr Schmitt's article in this volume.

2. A. Ehrhardt, *The Apostolic Succession in the first two centuries of the Church*, London, Lutterworth Press, 1953.

frequently and is derived from holy scripture itself; the Saviour had actually been anointed by the Holy Spirit when he came out of the water after his baptism. St Peter already taught this in his great discourse after the conversion of Cornelius: 'You know the word which hath been published through all Judea: for it began from Galilee, after the baptism which John preached Jesus of Nazareth: how God anointed him with the Holy Ghost, and with power; who went about doing good, and healing all that were oppressed by the devil' (Acts **10**, 37–8). And Jesus himself, in the synagogue at Nazareth, applied the words of the book of Isaias to his own mission: 'The Spirit of the Lord is upon me: wherefore he hath anointed me to preach the gospel to the poor; he hath sent me to heal the contrite of heart, to preach deliverance to the captives, and sight to the blind, to set at liberty them that are bruised, to preach the acceptable year of the Lord . . . And he began to say to them: This day is fulfilled this scripture in your ears' (Luke **4**, 18–21). We have only to read this passage and the thought of Pentecost springs to our minds. It is concerned, in fact, with an anointing for the preaching of the good news, of the jubilee year; now the jubilee, which came round every fifty years, was a figure of our Pentecost occurring on the fiftieth day after Easter. The anointing of Christ at the river Jordan is also, like Pentecost, the inauguration of a new law of liberty; until then Christ had remained subject to the requirements of the Jewish law; but henceforth it is the Spirit of God alone who will guide him: 'The law and the prophets were until John: from that time the kingdom of God is preached' (Luke **16**, 16).[1]

There is no need for us to examine here all the examples, for they have already been fully collected together elsewhere;[2] i.e. the examples which go to show that tradition is firmly united on this fundamental point – that the descent of the Holy Spirit on Jesus at the river Jordan is a new anointing bestowed on his human nature, a spiritual unction ordaining the Saviour directly

1. cf. 'La grâce de la consécration épiscopale' in *Revue des Sc. Phil. et Theol.*, xxxvi, 1952, pp 392–3.
2. *art. cit.*, p. 392 ff; cf. 'Essai sur le sacerdoce des fidèles chez les Pères', *La Maison-Dieu* no. 27, 1951, pp 38–41.

for his apostolate, the preaching of the new law. There have indeed been some obvious exaggerations on this point, e.g. the Syriac Fathers, notably Aphraates and St Ephraim, who thought that the anointing at the river Jordan was a participation in the levitical priesthood imparted to the Saviour by John the Baptist, who belonged to the priestly tribe.[1] In this we clearly detect that tendency, which is frequently in evidence and whose roots must be sought in the apocryphal testaments of the twelve patriarchs, to link the priesthood of Christ with that of Aaron – a judaising tendency best refuted by the chapter on Melchisedech in the epistle to the Hebrews.

Christ is indeed a priest, but his priesthood is not the legal priesthood of the old law. Furthermore, he is a priest from the moment of the incarnation, not merely from the time of his baptism. We can and we must speak of the priestly anointing of the Holy Spirit received by Jesus at the very beginning of his earthly existence. In this connection it is sufficient to recall the anathema of Cyril of Alexandria (no. 10) against Nestorius, an anathema included in the Acta of the Council of Ephesus in 431; 'If anyone asserts that it was not the Word of God himself who became our High-Priest and Apostle when he was made flesh and man as we, but a man other and distinct from him, born of a woman . . . let him be anathema'. (Denz. 123).

It seems, then, that we must assume two priestly anointings in the earthly life of Jesus, as well as two births; Jesus is priest from the beginning, he is aware of it and directs himself towards his priestly offering: 'Therefore, coming into the world, he saith: Sacrifice and oblation thou wouldest not, but a body thou hast fitted to me: Holocausts for sin did not please thee . . . Then said I: Behold, I come to do thy will, O God' (Heb. 10, 5–9).

But there is a second birth, and a second priestly anointing – a birth to his public life, an unction visibly bestowed by the descent of the Spirit in the form of a dove, whereas the first had been invisibly effected in Mary's womb.

Now, from the instances quoted above, we are led, in the case

1. Aphraates, *De Persecutione*, 13 (Pater. Syr., I, 1, pp 963–6); St Ephraim, *Comment. on the Diatesseron*, cap. 4 in the Latin translation by Aucher-Moesinger, Venice 1876, p. 42.

of the apostles, to envisage a similar succession of anointings by
the Holy Spirit: one, which the majority of writers place after
the resurrection, when Jesus breathed on the twelve and said:
'Receive the Holy Ghost', and the other at Pentecost.

And, as in the case of Christ, these two anointings correspond
to the two births of the Church parallel to the two births of its
Head: the first birth took place at the paschal mystery, like the
new Eve from the wounded side of the new Adam; from that
moment, as St Ambrose says: '*Domus spiritalis surgit in sacerdotium sanctun*',[1] words which are quoted by Pius XII in the
encyclical *Mystici Corporis* (A.A.S. 35, p. 205). From that
moment the Church was filled with the unction of the Holy
Spirit which made her a sharer in the priesthood of her Head.
Subsequently, after a period of hidden life, there was a new birth,
a new anointing, which was for the Church what the theophany
at Jordan was for Jesus – the starting point of her apostolate
and her manifestation to the world.[2]

But at this point two new problems arise, which we must
briefly deal with.

Analogy with the Problem of Confirmation.

The first concerns the obvious analogy between the question
we are now studying and that of confirmation. The most recent
studies have led theologians to relate confirmation to the mystery
of Pentecost, and consequently to the mystery of the descent of
the Holy Spirit upon Jesus after his baptism by John. I will
mention only M. A. G. Martimort's article in the symposium
Communion solennelle et Profession de foi (Lex Orandi, Paris
1952, pp 159–201), a more recent work by the Anglican theologian L. S. Thornton,[3] and a short article by Fr T. Camelot in
Revue des Sciences Philosophiques et Théologiques.[4]

The difficulty might appear to be so much greater since, as I

1. cf. *La Maison-Dieu* 26, p. 41.
2. cf. *Mystici Corporis* (A.A.S. 35, p. 207).
3. L. S. Thornton, *Confirmation, Its place in the Baptismal Mystery*,
Dacre Press, 1954.
4. Camelot, 'Sur la théologie de la Confirmation' in *Rev. des Sc.
Phil. et Théol.*, 38, 1954, pp 637–57.

showed in *La Maison-Dieu* in 1951,[1] baptism and confirmation have traditionally been considered as a twofold participation by the faithful in the priesthood of Christ. At all events we know St Thomas's teaching. The subject of Pentecost raises afresh the whole problem of the distinction between the priesthood of the hierarchy and the priesthood of the faithful.

The writers I cited above felt this difficulty and, as we saw, some of them sought to explain how, although there was only one single visible outpouring of the Spirit in the upper room, the effects were different in the case of the twelve and in the case of the other disciples.

But the Acts of the Apostles indicates a solution. As he was leaving his apostles, Jesus said: 'But you shall receive the power of the Holy Ghost coming upon you, and you shall be witnesses unto me in Jerusalem, and in all Judea, and Samaria, and even to the uttermost part of the earth' (Acts 1, 8). Now the apostles understood this promise to be addressed in a special way to themselves alone, as is shown in Peter's discourse at the time of the election of Matthias: 'Wherefore of these men who have been with us all the time that the Lord Jesus came in and went out among us, beginning from the baptism of John, until the day wherein he was taken up from us, one of these must be made a *witness* with us of his resurrection' (Acts 1, 21–2). He who was elected in place of Judas would take 'that share of the ministry' left vacant by the traitor, his charge, his 'bishopric' (τὴν ἐπισκοπήν) as Peter's words, which are borrowed from Psalm 108, should be translated (Acts 1, 20). Other disciples, among whom was 'Joseph, called Barsabas, who was surnamed Justus' (Acts 1, 23), who was set aside in the casting of lots, had been *witnesses* of the life of Christ. But the twelve had quite a special claim to this title, and the grace of Pentecost was given to them particularly for this purpose; we see them, in fact, immediately after the descent of the Spirit, filled with that 'power' which had been promised by Jesus. 'And with great power did the apostles give testimony of the resurrection of Jesus Christ our Lord', wrote St Luke (Acts 4, 33).

1. cf. recent article already cited in the *Rev. des Sc. Phil. et Théol.*, 1952, pp 396–7.

11—TSOHO

The same distinction is found again if we examine Pentecost from another traditional angle – that which relates it immediately to the theophany on Sinai. Christian tradition and the liturgy have seen in Pentecost the gift of the new law, the fulfilment of the prophecies of Isaias (2, 3–4) and Micheas (4, 2–3): 'for the law shall go forth out of Sion, and the word of the Lord out of Jerusalem'. We recall that the promulgation of the new law also has its place in the traditional theology of the baptism of Christ: '*Lex et prophetae usque ad Joannem . . .*' This new law is given in two ways. It is first of all (*principaliter*, says St Thomas, Ia, IIae q. 106, a. 1, c) written inwardly in our hearts according to the prophecy of Jeremias (Jer. 31, 33) cited by the epistle to the Hebrews (8, 10; 10, 16) and 2 Corinthians, 3, 3; from this point of view the new law is nothing less than the presence of the Holy Spirit with his gifts of grace and charity in the soul.[1]

But the apostles have quite a special title to the new law, for they are its official witnesses and preachers. This is actually what St Irenaeus states, and he is followed by SS Basil, Chrysostom, Theodoret, etc.[2] Their role is compared with that of Moses the lawgiver and leader of the people.[3] And this prerogative belongs to the episcopal body as well, as Ignatius of Antioch expresses so admirably when he congratulates the deacon Zotion on being 'subject to the bishop as to the grace of God' (Magn. 2, 1). It is not merely invisible grace which guides us, it is the Word, who by his incarnation has become our law,[4] and who is visibly perpetuated on earth through the apostles and

1. cf. S. Lyonnet, 'Liberté chrétienne et loi de l'Esprit selon saint Paul', *Christus*, 4, 1954, pp 1–22; J. Lécuyer, 'Pentecôte et Loi Nouvelle', *La Vie Spirituelle*, May 1953, pp 474–80.

2. Irenaeus, *Adv. Haer.* iv, 34, 4; Basil, *In Isaiam*, 2, 3 (P.G. 30, 240–1); Chrysostom, *In Isaiam*, 2, 3 (P.G. 56, 32); Theodoret, *In Isaiam*, 2, 3 (P.G. 81, 238); *In Mich.* 4, 2 (P.G. 71, 698d).

3. cf. Chrysostom, *In Pentecosten* (P.G. 52, 811, or 64, 420d); Severian of Gabala, *In 2 Cor.*, 3, 7–9 (Staab, pp 284–5); Cyril of Alexandria, *In Mich.* 4, 2 (P.G. 71, 698). The Roman Pontifical compares the bishop with Moses (prayer for the ordination of priests) in a formula which goes back to Hippolytus of Rome.

4. cf. the Kerugma of Peter in a text preserved by Clement of Alexandria (*Eclogae Propheticae*, 58; *Strom.*, i, 28, 82; ii, 15, 58). cf. E. Dobschütz, *Das Kerygma Petri*, T.u.U., xi, 1, p. 18; Justin, *Adv. Tryphonem*, xi, 2.

their successors. When the Holy Spirit descended upon them he taught them not only 'how they themselves shoud act, but also how they ought to instruct others'. This phrase from Atton of Verceil well expresses the distinction that can be discerned in the actual gift of Pentecost itself.[1] There is a dual aspect of Pentecostal grace corresponding to the dual aspect of the new law, which is chiefly 'inward' but which is imparted by sensible and external signs, and expressed in a certain number of external precepts. All the faithful, because they are members of the body of Christ, are anointed by the Spirit and constituted witnesses of the new law, but it is the apostles who give the law in bestowing grace through the sacraments and in making its demands plain.

We can see by this short analysis that it is possible to relate, at the same time and without confusing them, both the sacrament of confirmation and that of the highest degree of Orders, the episcopate, to the mysteries of Pentecost and the anointing of Christ at the river Jordan.

The Council of Trent and the Last Supper

Here a fresh problem arises, which we cannot evade, although a subsequent paper will study the question of the Council of Trent and holy Orders.

We know that the Fathers of the Council in Session XXII on the sacrifice of the Mass declared, in a short parenthesis, that the apostles 'were constituted priests of the new testament' at the last supper on Holy Thursday: '*Quos tunc Novi Testamenti sacerdotes constituebat*' (Denz 938). Canon 2 of the same session is still more definite: '*Si quis dixerit, illis verbis: Hoc facite in meam commemorationem, Christus non instituisse Apostolos sacerdotes, aut non ordinasse ut ipsi aliique sacerdotes offerrent corpus et sanguinem suum*', A.S. (D. 949). These passages call for comment, for the majority of the texts quoted in the first part of this article see the ordination of the apostles as taking place rather at the time when Jesus appeared to the twelve after his resurrection and breathed on them to impart the Holy Spirit to them. It is not really my place to examine the exact meaning of

1. Atton of Verceil, *Sermo xii de Pentecoste* (P.L. 134, 847cd).

the Council of Trent's propositions, but perhaps I may be allowed to make these observations:

(1) The Council states that the apostles were constituted priests at the last supper (*constituebat . . . instituti sunt*); it says nothing directly about the 'sacrament' of Orders in these passages.

(2) In the first draft on the sacrament of Orders put out on the 21st January, 1552 reference was made both to the supper and to the appearance of Jesus after his resurrection:

Itaque Dominum, qui, porrecto sancto pane et calicis benedictione suis apostolis, dixit: Hoc facite in meam commemorationem, insufflasse etiam in illos et dixisse legimus: Accepite Spiritum Sanctum, quorum remiseritis peccata remittuntur eis, et quorum retinueritis retenta sunt, atque ita potestatem illis super utrumque suum corpus et verum et mysticum contulisse.[1]

(3) We are aware of the discussion which was aroused on this precise point on 16th September, 1562. The archbishops of Granada and Brage requested that the moment of the institution of the apostles as priests should not be stated in the canons on the Mass, since, they said, the majority of the Fathers taught that they had been made priests after the resurrection. Many other bishops declared that they were of the same opinion, and a discussion followed – indeed, almost a battle – which was only calmed by the conciliatory statements of Cardinal Hosius, who said:

The opinions of the Fathers can easily be reconciled, for both are true. In Luke 22, 19, Christ gave to his apostles power over his actual body; in John 20, 22 he gave them power over his mystical body.

It was after these conciliatory statements that the canon was adopted,[2] which indicates its limits and restricts its reference to the power of offering the eucharist.

(4) Nevertheless, it remains true that the apostles did receive a sacerdotal power and a communication of the Holy Spirit corresponding to this power, before Pentecost. This was directed towards the eucharist and also towards the remission of sins.

1. J. Le Plat, *Monument. ad Hist. Conc. Trid.*, iv, p. 398.
2. *Conc. Trid. Act.* (ed. Goerres), vol. 8, pp 954–6.

But the Council certainly did not wish to exclude the possibility of a new communication of a priestly grace at Pentecost.

(5) Finally, and most important, let us say quite simply that it is not so much the determination of the precise historical moment when the apostles were ordained (if we can use this term) which concerns us, nor even the precise moment of the institution of the sacrament of Orders. On the contrary, starting out from the faith of the Church, it seems to me of supreme importance to penetrate a little into the inner nature of the sacrament by relating it to the mysteries of the life of Christ and the origins of the Church. This is a standpoint more theological than historical or apologetic, but its importance for the pastoral aspect of the sacraments will not escape any of us. It is this point of view which I should like to outline very briefly in the third part.

3. HOLY ORDERS AND THE APOSTOLIC CHARACTER OF THE CHURCH'S MISSION

If the grace received by bishops at their consecration corresponds to that received by the apostles at Pentecost, it is possible to define what pertains to them by vitue of their episcopal character. And what the apostles especially received, as I have said, was grace to be the official witnesses to Christ throughout the whole world.

(1) So the episcopal body is always a body of witnesses. But what is a witness? Not merely one who has 'seen and heard' (Acts 4, 20), but one who has faithfully retained what he has seen and heard, and understood it sufficiently well for his witness to be a reality. Jesus had specifically promised: 'The Holy Ghost, whom the Father will send in my name, he will teach you all things, and bring all things to your mind, whatsoever I shall have said unto you' (John 14, 26). And again: 'He will teach you all truth' (John 16, 13). The gift of Pentecost is therefore chiefly a grace of light, bestowing a sure knowledge of what the apostles, and after them the bishops, will have to bear witness to. This grace of light, which is in the episcopal body, and particularly in its visible head, is undoubtedly the source

of its infallibility. To be a true witness, courage and strength to bear witness will be necessary; and this is precisely the point of the promise made by Jesus: 'You shall receive . . . power . . . and you shall be witnesses unto me' (Acts 1, 8). Lastly, the witness must speak and that is why the gift of the Spirit is manifested in form of fiery tongues:

> *Ignis vibrante lumine*
> *Linguae figuram detulit*
> *Verbis ut essent proflui . . .*
> (Lauds of Pentecost).

But to whom must this witness of the episcopal body be addressed? The words of Jesus are clear: '*Usque ad ultimum terrae*'. Certain bishops can be given a particular territorial area, but the body of bishops as a whole remains responsible for the evangelisation of the whole world and of every class of society. We might ask ourselves if a consideration of the particular Church, or of the diocese, is actually a proper starting-point for an examination of the theology of episcopacy. At all events, it seems from the stand-point of the sacrament of Orders, that this is only a secondary, perhaps even accidental, aspect. A vicar apostolic, an apostolic administrator, a legate, if he has received episcopal consecration, has received the same grace as a diocesan bishop. His subsequent sphere is perhaps of the canonical rather than the exclusively theological order.

(2) We can go further. For, as I have said, the bishop is no ordinary witness. He receives the deposit of the new law by a special title, and this distinguishes him from those who are simply confirmed – he is its special witness and official representative. The duty of promulgating externally the essential or contingent demands of the law of charity written within the hearts of all the faithful devolves directly on the body of bishops (cf. *Summa Theol* Ia, IIae q. 108, a. 1, c.). Now it is the ruler's role to make known, to promulgate the law. The grace of the episcopate is therefore a grace of leadership, the *spiritus principalis*, as the apostolic tradition of St Hippolytus says.

St Thomas insists strongly on this point: '*Officium docendi commisit eis Christus ut ipsi per se illud exercerent, tamquam principalissimum*' (IIIa, q. 67, a. 3, ad 2 m.). '*In regno Ecclesiae*

*episcopus ungitur tamquam principaliter habens curam regiminis
... principalem accipit curam et quasi regalem' (De perfectione
vitae spiritualis*, c. 24). It will therefore be the function of the
bishop within the Christian community, as official witness of
Christ, to define the obligations incumbent on the faithful, to
direct initiative and to condemn errors. Even the personal
witness which each member of the body of Christ can and must
bear before the world will consequently be under the control of
the bishop, who must 'try the spirits, whether they be of God'
(1 John 4, 1), without, however, 'extinguishing the Spirit' (1
Thess. 5, 19).

(3) But the new law consists chiefly, as St Thomas says, 'in
the grace of the Holy Ghost which is shown forth by faith that
worketh through love' (Ia, IIae, q. 108, a 1). And since the incarnation, this grace has come to us through the human nature of
Christ and the sensible signs of the sacraments. The new law,
visibly bestowed at Pentecost will consequently be conveyed
normally to men through the sacraments, and since the apostles,
like Moses on Mount Sinai, were appointed its witnesses and
official mediators, it is they and their successors who possess the
power to administer the sacraments. The grace of Pentecost,
within the episcopal body, confirms and sets the seal on the
power over the eucharist, penance, baptism and the other sacraments, previously given to the apostles. The episcopal body is
a priestly body which can and must present to God the offering
of the first-fruits which formed part of the rite of Pentecost in the
old law; and not only through the ministry of the word, but also
through that sacrifice which represents and contains, *sub sacramento*, the one sacrifice of Christ, first-fruits of the human race
which he is leading back to the Father in the unity of his Body.

But since we have discovered a twofold priestly unction,
both in the life of Christ and in the mysteries of the nascent
Church, there remains the possibility of the existence within
the Church of a priesthood subordinate to that of the bishop,
which, without enjoying the prerogatives belonging to the head
(and hence under the direction and in dependence on the
bishop), is able to perform sacramental actions.

But not all of them. For any sacrament which bestows a

certain participation in the functions of the head normally remains the bishop's privilege. That is what St Thomas means by:

Per ordinem et confirmationem deputantur fideles Christi ad aliqua specialia officia, quae pertinent ad officium principis et ideo tradere hujusmodi sacramenta pertinet ad solum episcopum qui est quasi princeps in Ecclesia (IIIa, q 65, a. 3, ad 3m).

In the case of the other sacraments, the bishop can, if he thinks it necessary, allow them to be administered by simple priests (cf. IIIa, q. 67, a 2, ad 1m); but he cannot divest himself completely of his teaching role, which stems directly from his mission as official witness and head (*ibid.*), nor normally from the conferring of the sacraments of confirmation and Orders. Although, in exceptional cases, confirmation and certain Orders can be delegated by the body of bishops to simple priests, the actual consecration of a bishop will always remain the inalienable prerogative of the bishops. The grace received by the apostles at Pentecost is only transmitted through their successors.

(4) What, then, are priests of the second degree? Since we have seen that the apostles were already priests before Pentecost, and that tradition connects this mystery with the episcopate, it is hard not to think of linking the presbyterate with the still incomplete sacerdotium received by the twelve in the course of the paschal mystery. Of course this conclusion is not absolutely incontravertible, but it is not out of the question as a working hypothesis and it is the more attractive in that it gives us a striking analogy in the sacerdotal hierarchy both with the priesthood of Christ himself, and with that of the ordinary faithful. In all these cases, priesthood is presented as having two stages; the first is that of the incarnation and the hidden life, of the baptism and the paschal mystery, the threefold mystery of birth, internal growth and sanctification through work and prayer. The second stage, on the other hand, is that of the public life, of confirmation, external growth, of Pentecost and the missionary apostolate properly so-called.

From this stand-point the sacramental grace of the presbyterate is not of itself directed towards an external mission. Like the apostle before Pentecost, and Christ himself before his baptism by John the Baptist, the simple priest will have a function of prayer and internal sanctification within a community of the faithful, for which Nazareth and the Cenacle have previously provided the ideal pattern. Within the fellowship of the members of Christ's Body, who are to unite the offering of their whole life of worship and work with the sacrifice of their Head, the priest sacramentally represents Christ the Priest in his function of offering. Thanks to the priest and to the powers he has received, the sacrifice of Jesus remains present in the Church under the sacramental signs; the incarnation is continued, in that the grace of the Word made flesh, working through the sensible actions of his priests, takes possession of the whole of human life.

In all this, the simple priest remains the bishop's fellow-worker. The new people of God, marching towards the true promised land, are governed by the bishop, who is prefigured in Moses. At the first Pentecost on Mount Sinai, Moses received the law, and bestowed his spirit on the seventy elders he had chosen to govern the people (Num. 11, 25). The Sacramentaries, from Hippolytus's apostolic tradition to the present Roman Pontifical, have all envisaged Moses's act as a prophetic figure of the bishop ordaining simple priests. And so, within the fold of the people of God, it is the priests who convey the new law to the faithful. Now, as we have seen, this law is chiefly sanctifying grace, which is communicated normally through the sacraments. It seems that the priest is to be considered above all in the light of his role as mediator of sacramental grace, and especially through the eucharist. We might ask if the function of the priest as such within an already constituted community is not restricted to this and if the missionary aspect, as directed to those outside, forms no necessary part of his proper vocation.

Such a hypothesis, if it could be sustained, would have the considerable advantage of making it possible to understand the position of priests vowed exclusively to a life of contemplation, prayer, hidden work and liturgical worship, without any real external ministry; for they are not something less than priests and their priesthood, far from being a useless luxury, bears witness within the Church to the indispensable value of hidden sacrifice and of the unseen activity of the sacrifice of Calvary.

It would, moreover, be wrong to conclude from this that such a conception of the priesthood of the second degree would divest it of all apostolic character. For its role in administering the sacraments, if not immediately directed towards apostolic and missionary activity, is always so indirectly and necessarily. It is exercised within a Christian community composed not only of the baptised but of the confirmed, of faithful who have received according to their status as members of Christ's Body, the Spirit of Pentecost. All the faithful are called to be witnesses to Christ and his resurrection before the whole world. The simple priest, who has, of course, received the seal of the sacrament, is by his priesthood the 'animator' of this missionary community, since it is he who, through the eucharist and the other sacraments, fills and sustains it with the life of Christ, the source of all truly supernatural apostolate. The paschal mystery, of which the priest is minister, is directed towards that of Pentecost, in which it finds its fulfilment.

Furthermore, the priest of the second degree is at the immediate service of the episcopal body. Although the bishop clothes him at ordination for the direct ministry of the sacraments, he is also by a subsequent commission to associate him more closely with his own missionary function of preaching the word of God. Yet there are many documents in tradition which might lead us to think that such co-operation, on this particular level, is more relevant to the proper grace of the diaconate than the presbyterate.[1] But this would take us too far, and could not be included within the limits of a study on Pentecost.

1. See the article 'Diaconat' in *Dictionnaire de Spiritualité*. I ought to add, however, that since the presbyterate actually includes the diaconate, the simple priest is found to be the bishop's normal collaborator in this matter.

Additional Note: I must add the following observations in connection with the documents of the Latin tradition mentioned. From the earliest days, the consecration of a bishop took place on a Sunday (cf. P. T. Michels, *Beiträge zur Geschichte des Bischofsweihetages*, Münster i. W., 1927). From the time of St Leo the Great (*Epist.* ix, 1) the reason for this was said to be that the apostles received the gift of the Spirit on a Sunday. This was stated specifically in the Pseudo-Decretals which attributed to St Anacletus a decision fixing 'the third hour of Sunday' for the consecration, i.e. the hour when the Spirit was outpoured on the day of Pentecost (ed. Hinschius, p. 75). This

DISCUSSION

Fr Congar: I would like to say a word, if I may since I am much concerned with all these questions. I am in complete agreement with you about the role you attribute to the anointing of his baptism in the case of Christ, and the anointing of Pentecost in the case of the apostles. Personally I have been teaching for many years that this was their anointing for the ministry. There is the anointing of the incarnation, of the hypostatic union itself. But there is an anointing for the ministry, and the Fathers saw the basis of baptism and, through baptism, the basis of the whole sacramental Orders, in the baptism of Christ.

But personally, I do not so easily agree with you when you appear to confine this relationship to the episcopate, and not to priesthood as such. Apparently you relate the priesthood of simple priests to the anointing of the incarnation, and to the, in some way, secret anointing of the apostles—their 'hidden life', as you say. But does not this lead you to place too much stress on the difference between 'episcopal' priesthood and priesthood as such? This hardly seems in line with present studies.

There is another point. The Fathers, particularly St Cyprian and after him, it seems to me, the whole of the early Middle Ages, saw the birth of the *ordo sacerdotalis* when the power of binding and loosing was bestowed first of all on Peter, and then on the rest of the apostles, a power which when exercised on

---

canonical interpretation was admitted into the medieval collections, notably in those of Burchard of Worms (P.L. 140, 553), Yves of Chartres (P.L. 161, 349 and 1132), and in the Decretum of Gratian (Ia pars, dist. 75, c. 1), and expounded by the early commentators on the Decretum (cf. Rufinus of Assisi, Stephen of Tournai, Summa Parisiensis . . . on this passage), and was preserved even after the addition in the tenth century of feasts of apostles as days on which consecrations might take place. It is partly because he ignored this fact that St Thomas was opposed to the Sacramentality of the episcopate (*In IV Sent*. d. 24, q. 3, a. 2, qla. 2, sed contra).

earth is ratified in heaven. For them, that is the essential significance of the scene at Caesarea Philippi. I think we must bear
this in mind.

Finally, a third observation to bring us back to the real point
of our present study. We have become accustomed, since the
rise of scholasticism – abridged rather, for it does contain other
elements – to relate the priesthood almost entirely to the eucharist, and therefore to its institution on Maundy Thursday. Now,
all the traditional references you have mentioned relate priesthood to apostolate and preaching as well.

I was very struck by what Fr Duval had to say about the
Council of Trent being quite ready to admit the evangelical
ministry, that of 'faith through the word', into the conception of
priesthood itself; it would have done so if it had given more
consideration to the proposition put forward by the Archbishop
of Braga and the other bishop. This is extremely interesting and
important. It is obvious that the new testament includes the
'apostolic' ministry in priesthood itself – see Rom. 15, 16, etc.
For my own part, having worked on these ideas when preparing
Forward the Layman and since, I am more and more in favour of
the ideas put forward for example by Canon Masure. I think we
must concentrate on this point – what does it mean to be a priest
of the new testament? Or, in other words – and this will lead us
still more directly to a solution – what does it mean to be a priest
of the gospel?

Fr Lécuyer: I will answer your first question concerning the
application of the lessons of Pentecost exclusively to bishops, for
I felt rather the same way about it. There are a certain number of
expositors who do, in fact, make this distinction. The apostles
possessed the first degree of the priesthood and afterwards
received the second. I am not absolutely sure that this is right –
hence my hesitation at the conclusion. I admit that I do not see
clearly how it is effected, but perhaps there might be an analogy
to it in the two 'characters' of baptism and confirmation, those
two stages answering to the distinction.

I think this provides us with an instructive analogy, at least in
some respects. It does not explain everything, of course, but it
does show that in all the degrees in which Christian priesthood
is expressed, whether in Christ himself, or in the members
of Christ's body, or on the level of hierarchical priesthood,
we always find these two degrees corresponding to the two

mysteries – the anointing of the incarnation, and the anointing of the apostolic mission.

Must we then not allow the parallel on the level of hierarchical priesthood, reserving it only for the two other cases? I have the impression that the whole force of this stream of thought runs in the opposite direction, to assert it on this level as well.

M. Martimort: Yes, so far as I can see from my own exami-nation of some of the passages you have quoted, there can be no hesitation in applying the two anointings of Christ to the 'bap-tism-confirmation' sequence. I think it is indisputable, and indeed the only way by which a full explanation of the question of the relationship between baptism and confirmation can be given.

But on the other hand I think it is equally indisputable that the second anointing of Christ for his mission at the time of his baptism is to be related to Pentecost, i.e. both to confirmation and to the episcopate.

In fact, the point which seems to me to give rise to discussion, as Fr Congar so rightly said, is the relating of the first anointing of Christ, his 'essential' anointing, to the priesthood of the second degree. It has some foundation, I think, if it is true that radical powers are actually given to this second degree, but some later writers have asked if the episcopal character bestows them for the first time, or if they were already there. And here the distinction between the two positions is not so clear, since the bishop shares part of his apostolic mission, so far as he deems it good to do so, with his priests.

It would seem, then, that the tendency in the Church is to give to priests of the second degree an increasing share in the apostolate of the priesthood of the first degree.

Fr Lécuyer: I had to cut short the conclusion of my paper a little. Perhaps we can rediscover, without abandoning this line of thought, all the possibilities of collaboration by the priest of the second degree in the apostolate, simply by deepening this idea of 'incarnation', or, if you like, of the paschal mystery which cor-responds to the life of the Church. It is, in effect, the mystery of birth, sanctification and, if you wish, divinisation from within.

I had written that another way. Thus, the role of the simple priest would be rather one of some kind of 'hidden life' – I am thinking of his 'character', not of the various charges which can be delegated or committed to him, and not in any negative sense, but rather as a role of prayer, of sanctification from within a community of the faithful, for which Nazareth and the Cenacle had previously provided the ideal pattern.

The simple priest is first of all in the fold of a community of Christ's members. There he is the minister of the sacrifice of Christ, to bring the members, through the eucharist, more and more closely into union with the sacrifice of their Head, through the offering of their whole life of prayer and work. So he represents, sacramentally, Christ the Priest in his function of offering, in his paschal ministry. But it seems he shares this apostolic mission in two ways. For the whole community whose priest he is, is itself a missionary community; it has received the unction of confirmation, and the priest who is there as 'animator', as one who, by the sacraments, preserves, maintains and increases this life of grace, is not indifferent to this witness which all the members of the body must give.

But on the actual level of his priesthood, he can indeed by delegation be associated with the bishop's ministry and with his apostolic role. Once again, I have not got much further than asking these questions.

M. Martimort: Personally, I find difficulty in following you completely on this point. I am at the moment re-reading the preface for the consecration of priests in Hippolytus. This preface possesses added importance in that it is reproduced in the majority of liturgies right down to the present Roman rite. Its value is, therefore, much more than that of a simple patristic text. It compares priests of the second degree with those collaborators given to Moses who were filled with the same spirit which had been given to him, in order to judge the people. It is an anointing of the leaders of the people.

Fr Lécuyer: Yes, but of people who are already Christian. Therefore, it is not directly a missionary function. I think he is the bishop's fellow worker in that too, but in relation to the already constituted people of God.

Dom Capelle: But from all the illustrations you have given us, I see no clear justification for curtailing the priest's mission. We see him as a co-adjutor in the very fact of the development of the Church, because the bishop could not do everything himself, but we do not see any limitation in principle, or that the missionary character so clearly imparted to the bishop is his alone.

Fr Lécuyer: It is an indication, rather, which can be drawn from this twofold communication of the Spirit – the first being directed especially to the administration of the sacraments within the already constituted people; the second, on the other hand, more to the preaching of the word to all nations. The paschal mystery, on the one hand; and on the other the mystery of Pentecost.

If the second corresponds to the episcopate regarded as very priesthood in its supreme degree, and therefore in a degree which surpasses that of the priest of the second degree it seems possible at least to think that the presbyterate corresponds to the first anointing.

Dom Capelle: But don't you think that this responsibility of which you speak might in some way find its justification, if I may say so, passing beyond the state of possibility to the state of reality, if we see there is evidence of it in history?

Fr Lécuyer: History does not approach things from the inside, but from the outside, and I do not think history alone can solve this problem. . .

M. Martimort: Yes, that is something to remember. It is the bishop who is the responsible agent of the apostolate, and if a priest of the second degree receives the apostolic mission, it is a mission delegated to him by the bishop.

Dom Capelle: Completely.

M. Martimort: So much so, that the apostolate, evangelisation, is really a grace proper to the bishop, which he can and does share, but which he could exercise alone.

CHAPTER VIII

PRIESTHOOD AND MONASTICISM

DOM O. ROUSSEAU, O.S.B.

IN the course of the centuries three different relationships are found to have existed between monasticism and priesthood.

I. Priests excluded from the monastic life. This was so in the monasticism of the desert, and is still substantially so in Eastern monasticism.

II. Priests, or at any rate clerks, admitted to the monastic life. This was so in those forms of the monastic life which grew up in the West around several great bishops, e.g. St Augustine. We shall have more to say about them later.

III. A non-monastic priesthood barred (essentially monastic Churches). This form is found in the Celtic Church, in which all the faithful were grouped around the monasteries. It is a form which, as we shall see, had a considerable influence on Western ecclesiastical institutions, just as the previous type had a profound influence on the development of monasticism, and ended in the establishment of non-monastic religious orders.

I shall consider the three forms in turn, and try to draw some conclusions from my observations.

I

John Cassian, who had visited the Egyptian deserts collecting the sentences of the ancients, wrote at the end of the eleventh book of his *Institutions* a chapter entitled *Quod monachus mulieres et episcopos vitare debeat*. He relates this sentence as if it were the current doctrine of his day, i.e. after about a century of monastic development.

Haec est antiquitus Patrum permanens usque nunc sententia, quam proferre sine mea confusione non potero, qui nec germanam (his sister) vitare potui, nec episcopi evadere manus (he is thought to have been ordained priest at Rome), omnimodis monachum fugere debere mulieres et episcopos (P.L. 49, 418).

The relations between early monasticism and the clergy have been studied,[1] and the conclusion arrived at is that, much as the first monks of the desert respected the priesthood and those who had received it, they were adamant in refusing the charge themselves, and considered it a way of life not in harmony with their vocation. In fact, however, it frequently happened that the bishops came to the monasteries to take from them persons who were suitable candidates for the diaconate and the priesthood. Several bishops themselves were former solitaries. Religious frequently fled to escape these charges. We know of three of them who cut off an ear in order to avoid being ordained priests.[2]

However, in the East in the fourth century the custom was introduced of not normally conferring episcopal consecration save on monks, and this custom still prevails today.[3] It is explained by the fact that clerics usually married before their ordination to the diaconate, and were allowed to continue living in the married state, contrary to Western custom in respect of those in major Orders. As the bishop was required to abstain from all marriage relations and to dismiss his wife, it was found more simple to resort to the monasteries to provide the bishops.

None the less, among the first monks opposition to ordination was so great that St Pachomius would not have solitaries accept the clerical state at any price, even in the desert. In the eyes of the Father of coenobitism it appeared to be opposed to the monastic state.[4] Not long after, however, monks were ordained for the service of the communities so that religious would not have to leave their solitude to receive the sacraments. But monastic

1. Dom. J. M. Besse, *Les Moines d'Orient*, Paris, 1900; ch. xviii: 'Les Moines et la cléricature'. 2. *ibid.*, p. 426.
3. Pl. de Meester, *De monachico statu juxta disciplinam byzantinam*, Rome, 1942, p. 389, no. 4.
4. *Vita Pachomii*, ch. XXIV; P.L. 73, 245.

perfection was thought to belong to another type altogether from that of the priesthood. It was essential for the monk to retire from the world to seek God. The vocation of the bishop required him to quit the desert and return to the heart of those things he had left behind – it was a denial of his initial act.

Yet not all early monks must be thought to have been like some examples cited in the biographies. 'The great majority quietly accepted ordination to the priesthood when it was offered to them.'[1] Indeed, some of them went further, and fed their vanity by seeking it, but the legislators always issued a warning to monks against this craving for sacred Orders.

We must observe that the Benedictine rule is still substantially in this tradition. Benedictine monasticism is a Western adaptation of the old monasticism of the desert, to which it is well and truly related. The modifications which are to be found on this point were brought about only so that priests might be available to serve the community itself; there was no thought of any ministry outside it. I am not speaking of the later and more developed Benedictine tradition, but of the rule itself.

This opposition between monasticism and priesthood, unknown to historians today, came as a surprise to scholars in previous centuries. Baronius, submitting to the idea of his age, thought that monasticism had been orientated towards the priesthood from the very beginning.[2] The first great editor of Cassian, Dom Gazet (ca 1626), a Benedictine of Saint-Vaast at Arras, was highly scandalised by the passage from Cassian cited above and endeavoured to explain it in a long note in order to protect his readers against the least edification by it![3] It is still difficult even today to make many people realise that the true character of monasticism in no way presumes access to sacred Orders.

II

We will now pass on to the second stage, or rather, the second relationship – the clergy admitted into the monastic life. Here

1. Dom Besse, *op. cit.*, p. 428.
2. *Annal.*, vol. iii; cit. ap. Gazaeus: Comment. in Cassian. P.L. 49, 413.   3. P.L. 49, 412-13.

we meet a form of the religious life which is hardly in the spirit of Eastern monasticism, but which is, on the other hand, very much in harmony with the hierarchical and liturgical genius of the West.

St Ambrose in his panegyric on St Eusebius, bishop of Verceil, who was a contemporary of St Athanasius, and died in 371, tells us that 'Eusebius, of blessed memory, was the first to combine the monastic with the ecclesiastical life in the West'.[1] Dom Ceillier recapitulates the passages in St Ambrose concerning this form of life thus:

Himself living and causing his clerks to live in the town in almost the same way the monks lived in the desert, he enclosed himself with them in the same house, to which he gave the name of monastery, and which subsequently produced several bishops. Like a celestial and angelic army they drilled night and day; they were permanently occupied in the praising of God, having no other ambition but to render his mercy propitious and to appease his wrath by fervent and continual prayer. They applied their mind at all times to reading or to work. Separated from the conversation of women, they protected one another against temptation.[2]

Moreover, we know that St Augustine, on becoming bishop of Hippo in 395, continued to live within the community whose father he was, as he had loved to do since his ordination to the priesthood. 'I have reached the episcopate; I know that the bishop is obliged to exercise charity towards those who come and go . . . and that is why I wanted to have a monastery of clerks in the bishop's house. *Et ideo volui habere in ista domo episcopii mecum monasterium clericorum.*'[3] Possidius, his biographer, tells us, in effect, that St Augustine 'began to ordain clerks who, with him and under him, and living in the monastery, might serve God in the Church'.[4]

Of course, not all the monastic groups fostered by bishops were invested with this clerical character. For example, the monastery at Marmoutiers near Tours, where its bishop, St Martin, lived, was by no means of this type. Martin, attached to the

1. *Ep.* 63; P.L. 16, 1258.
2. *Histoire générale des auteurs sacrés;* vol. IV, 2nd edition, Paris 1865, p. 271.   3. *Serm.* 355; P.L. 39, 1570.
4. *Ch.* xi; P.L. 32, 42.

monastic life and to his followers, had grouped them together in a retired spot close to his cathedral city, so that he could continue to live amongst them. These men were not clerics at all, but monks living a retired and ascetic life in the Eastern fashion, though the possibility cannot be excluded that some of them may have received Orders to be of assistance to the bishop in his ministry.

St Victrice of Rouen, whose story is related by Paulinus of Nola,[1] his contemporary, multiplied monasteries of men and virgins around his person. He himself seems to fall into the category of those bishops who were seeking some form of monastic life for their clergy. There were others too. This monasticism, which has sometimes been called 'episcopal' or 'urban', originated not in some monk or solitary gathering of disciples around himself, but in a particularly saintly and zealous bishop who wished to raise his clergy to a higher degree of perfection, and who led a common life in celibacy with them.

The chief function of these clerks was to perform the divine office in conjunction with the bishop (liturgical monasticism) and to assist him in his pastoral work, while leading a consecrated life. But it must be remembered that these were only isolated and usually transient instances. The institution was jeopardised when another bishop without the same inclinations succeeded. Down to the eleventh century the Church's legislation made provision for cases where married men were elevated to major Orders – they were allowed to keep their wives on condition that they lived in continence. That is not the monastic system at all.

In the East the bishop alone was thought to have that plenitude of consecration which entailed the life of perfection, and this is shown in the legislation concerning marriage. The Council of Trullo (692) gave its sanction to a custom which was already ancient, when it imposed the obligation of absolute continence on the bishop. If he was married, his wife must leave

1. *Ep.* 18; P.L. 61, 239. cf. the reserve with which Andrieu-Guitrancourt treats Paulinus's account, when dealing with 'Gascon' in *Mélanges Lebreton* (R.S.R., 1952, 1-2), vol. II, pp 90 ff. 'La Vie Ascetique au temps de Saint Victrice'.

the matrimonial home from the time of his consecration, and live in some distant monastery.[1] But the inferior clergy (priests, deacons and those in minor Orders) were allowed to continue in marriages contracted before ordination, subject, however, to a discipline which is somewhat reminiscent of the legal purifications of the old law.

In the West, those in major Orders, i.e. those associated very closely with the bishop, came to share his consecrated state more and more, and the custom which directed the clergy to celibacy finally prevailed.

To sum up: in the West saintly bishops had grouped the clergy together in a certain number of places with considerable resulting benefit, and this form of life undoubtedly influenced, though not in any definite way, the development of clerical institutions. It had, perhaps, much more influence on the evolution of monastic institutions as such. In fact, there is little difficulty in recognising in episcopal monasticism the ancestor of the canonical life, which was to develop particularly as a form of the religious life, and which, from the Carolingian period, followed more and more detailed rules (St Chrodegang), and which received its final shape in the orders of canons regular in the eleventh and twelfth centuries.[2] Canons were vowed to the divine office, to the solemn celebration of the Mass and the other ceremonies of the altar, to the service of sanctuaries and to the subsidiary exercise of a pastoral ministry. Prelates directing these communities of canons presided solemnly at the liturgical worship. Even though they did not follow the *Regula Monachorum*, for they were not, strictly speaking, monks, they followed another rule, which, by and large, is reminiscent of the life of clergy formed into community around their bishop (rule of St Augustine). But these canons are all religious and consequently vowed to celibacy.

Elements of the canonical life very quickly passed into the Benedictine life. The custom of conventual Masses, the more elaborate ceremonial, pontificals for the abbots, and other things, which made the outward life of Benedictine monasteries so

1. C. 48, Mansi, Ac. c. XI, 965.
2. F. Petit, *La spiritualité des Prémontrés*, Paris, 1947, p. 16.

similar to that in the foundations of canons, were largely due to
the inspiration of the canonical life. The monks went with the
stream so far that they became clericalised themselves, and in
many cases it was only through attachment to their rule and the
preservation of their spiritual traditions, no less than their literature, that they were to be distinguished from the canons. In
other matters such as the year of novitiate, profession, ascetical
exercises and the practice of silence, the canons for their part felt
the profound influence of monastic rules and customs.

III

We come now to the third form, the exclusion of the non-
monastic priesthood. It is extremely hard to realise the influence
exercised on the Church in Gaul and even in neighbouring lands
such as Germany, Helvetia, Northern Italy by Celtic monasticism and the Columbanian tradition. The Celtic Church was
constituted around the monasteries; abbots ruled not only the
communities, but the people in the neighbourhood, who were
dependent on them, for there were hardly any other clergy
except monks. What is more it often happened that the abbots
themselves were not bishops, but they had in their service religious who had been consecrated bishops to provide for the needs
of the Church. That suited them better. Urged by the taste for
travelling and the need for apostolate, these monks undertook
the spiritual conquest of parts of the continent, set themselves up
with authority everywhere, haranguing the hierarchy when necessary and entering into conflict with the great. The life of St
Columban, which relates all this at length, is well known. Almost
all the old monastic centres in Gaul owe their origin to these Columbanian foundations: Anegray, Luxeuil, Ste-Croix de Meaux,
Fontenelle, Fécamp, Jumièges, Remiremont, Baume, Thérou-
anne, St-Ghislain, Elnone, Fleury-sur-Loire, St-Aignan, Mar-
bach, and beyond the Alps, Bobbio, St-Galle, Bregenz, and
many others. They subsequently became Benedictine monasteries when the *Regula Monachorum* was imposed everywhere.

Columban and his followers ruled not only men, but their
consciences. They initiated their flocks into the strict confession

of secret sins, and applied a penitential which has remained
famous. Against their opponents, the principle of this penitential
system and the private confession which it assumed, were pronounced to be sound by several councils, and it became a stable
practice. St Columban's letters reveal some informative cases of
conscience, arising, for example, when clerics continued to
cohabit with their lawful wives and yet had to cease all conjugal
relations with them. The lapses in such cases raised a serious
problem of rehabilitation and its solution influenced the Church's
discipline. Can we say that one of the factors leading to the disappearance of a married clergy was the austere and saintly lives of
the Columbanian monks, which discredited it in the eyes of the
people? Certain historians have wanted to say so, but this is
perhaps asking too much of history,[1] for legislation concerning
the celibacy of the clergy (priests and deacons) existed long before this time in the West in many other places quite independently of monasticism and it had become a general tendency in
our Church.

In the eyes of the Easterns, the Latin clergy today are totally
enfeoffed to monasticism because of their general celibacy. For a
member of that Church looking at ours, our clergy seem to be
practically all monks – the position is, in a sense, the logical
fulfilment of the Columbanian ideal. But if we look a little more
closely at it we shall recognise that this is a superficial view. The
absolute rule of ecclesiastical celibacy for the minor Orders and
the simple clergy is recent. It has unquestionably existed since
the promulgation of the new code, which expressly says with
reference to any ordination whatsoever (can. 987, 2): '*Sunt
simpliciter impediti viri uxorem habentes*', and (can 973, 1):
'*Prima tonsura et ordines illis tantum conferendi sunt qui propositum
habent ascendendi ad presbyteratum*'; this implicity assumes that
anyone who has received tonsure cannot honestly contemplate
marriage from the moment he has taken it. This is practically an
acceptance of celibacy, and it is always taken for granted.

In the years between the Council of Trent and the new code,
the number of cases in which this question arose grew steadily

---

1. St Hilpisch, *Geschichte des benediktinischen Mönchtums*, Freiburg, 1929, p. 75.

fewer, but in the nineteenth century it was still frequently discussed in the case of the minor Orders, and opinions differed.

But by the time of the Council of Trent there is tangible evidence that it was otherwise. In chapter seventeen of the decree *De Reformatione* of Session 23, the Council decided to revivify the minor Orders: '*Ut sanctorum ordinum a diaconatu ad ostiarium fonctiones, ab apostolorum temporibus in ecclesia laudabiliter receptae et pluribus in locis aliqamdiu intermissae, in usum juxta sacros canones revocentur, nec ab haereticis tanquam otiosae traducantur, illius pristini moris restituendi desiderio flagrantes, sancta Synodus decernit ut in posterum hujuscemodi ministeria nonnisi per constitutos in dictis ordinibus exerceantur*'; all prelates were asked, or rather enjoined, in so far as it was possible, to re-establish these Orders in cathedrals, colleges and parish churches. The decree continues: '*Quod si ministeriis quatuor minorum ordinum exercendis clerici caelibes praesto non erunt, suffici poterunt etiam conjugati vitae probatae, modo non bigami, ad ea munia obeunda idonei, et qui tonsuram et habitum clericalem ecclesia gestent*'.

The Council of Trent was not merely restoring an old custom. It recognised it as actually in existence, when, in speaking of minor orders, it said: '*In clericis vero conjugatis servetur constitutio Bonifacii VIII, quae incipit "Clerici qui cum unicis"* ', re-establishing for them the '*privilegium fori modo hi clerici alicujus ecclesiae servitio vel ministerio ab episcopo deputati, eidem ecclesiae serviant vel ministrent, et clericali habitu et tonsura utantur*'.[1]

One would hardly have thought, in view of this legislation, that the clerical state would be identified with the monastic or religious state. The fact that there had been bishops in former times who had encouraged their clergy to lead a kind of monastic life merely proves that it is worth while combining the priesthood and all that goes with it on account of its spiritual grandeur, with the perfection of the counsels, but these institutions were usually transitory and were never more than the exception in the

---

1. Sess. XXIII, *De Ref.*, c. 6. The provincial councils subsequently insisted on this decision, e.g. the Council of Rheims in 1564, two years after the conclusion of the Council of Trent. Mansi 1 c., XXXIII, 1295.

case of the secular clergy. It has only been by successive stages since the fourth century – first bishops, then priests and deacons – that the majority of clergy have been required to abstain from all marital relations from the time of their ordination, without necessarily having to send their wives away. In addition, they have been forbidden to contract marriage after receiving Orders. Later subdeacons were brought into line. From the eleventh century the custom spread of not elevating married men to sacred Orders unless the wife left her husband. But inferior clerks have always been allowed to keep their wives and to live in marriage with them. The pontifical text of Pope Benedict XIV, which is sometimes quoted in support of the present discipline, simply says that because they are a step to major Orders and the holy mysteries, minor Orders ought not to be conferred on those whose knowledge or maturity would be inconsistent with their elevation to a higher degree: '*Cumque hinc ad altiores gradus, et sacratissima sit ingressus, nemo iis initietur, quem non scientiae spes, majoribus Ordinibus dignum ostendat*'.[1] We must not read into this text more than it actually says.

My first conclusion, then, is that monasticism and the clerical state (of which the priesthood and the episcopate are the crown) are two different ways of life in the Church, and that the one by no means necessarily calls for the other, except for reasons of convenience.

Monastic celibacy must in no way be confused with the complete continence which from a certain period has been required by the canons of those in higher Orders, and which could be reconciled with married people continuing to live together (as St Leo said: '*De carnali fiat spirituale conjugium*'[2]), a thing which would be unthinkable in the case of the monastic life, since the word 'monk' means precisely 'one who lives alone', who is not married.

Second conclusion. The chief difference between these two states is that the first, monasticism, begins essentially with that renunciation demanded by the evangelical counsels – which consists in leaving all created things behind and going to live where

1. *De ordinibus conferendis*, § 5.
2. *Ep.* 167, inq. III; P.L. 54, 1204.

there are none at all (the desert), and in finding one's 'all' in the Uncreated. This is done in that spirit of renunciation inspired by those incentives given by Christ himself, and through faith in his word: '*Si vis perfectus esse* . . .' But the clerical state is the response to the positive will of Christ or of his ministers (cf. St Paul, who laid his hands on Timothy, 2 Tim. 1, 6), with a view to pastoral responsibilities. He who has been chosen for this must live in a more saintly manner because of the gift he has received. Early tradition generally considered the works of the flesh to be a contamination of this consecrated sanctity, or at least its consequences were thought to be an embarrassment to the minister. This was all the more reason for binding clerks to renounce them. Indeed, this renunciation was occasionally extended to material goods (common life, etc.).

Third conclusion. It was quite natural in times of apathy or when recruitment was difficult, for bishops to appeal to the monasteries to come to the help of their over-worked clergy, either by officiating at nearby shrines or on pilgrimages, or simply by taking pastoral charge of parishes. So ordinations of monks became more frequent, and even when the need for them had disappeared, priests continued to be found in the ranks of the monks, as if some sort of right to ordination had been acquired. Western monks, in the environment of a Church whose development was in the nature of clericalisation and hierarchical order, were never stubborn in refusing sacred Orders – on the contrary. At most, certain reforms, such as the Cistercian (St Bernard excepted) held themselves aloof from an apostolic ministry which would all too easily draw them out of their solitude.

Actually, apart from Cluny where the abbots were auxiliaries of the papacy in movements with a more general scope, such as the reform of the Church, apart from the Crusades, and apart from certain famous personalities such as St Bernard and St Peter Damian, the services rendered to the Church by the monastic orders, as indeed by the canons regular, amounted to no more than a service of the local churches.

Fourth conclusion. If it is an overstatement to say that the intervention of monasticism, particularly of the Columbanian type, was decisive in the matter of clerical celibacy in the West, it must nevertheless be recognised that there was tremendous influence exerted in this direction, not so much by monasticism as by the regular clergy, during those first centuries when the elevation of married men to the simple clerical state had fallen into desuetude. There is, in fact, no doubt that the discipline of the spiritual exercises prescribed for the clergy, the setting up of seminaries – which from some points of view resemble that temporary form of monasticism which was at one time to be found in the Syrian churches – and the training of ordinands, have all served to dispose the clergy more and more towards a spirituality purely and simply borrowed from the great orders or the modern congregations. The efforts of the French Sulpicians apart, the secular clergy have largely become the disciples of the regulars, especially in spirituality and asceticism. This is something which one might deplore, and possibly not without reason, but it is a fact.

Fifth and last conclusion. It has been much less exclusively the lot of the new orders which have arisen since the twelfth century – mendicants, preachers, regular clerks, modern congregations – to serve local churches. These orders, which have always admitted clergy to their ranks or at any rate have accepted them at the first stage of their development like the Franciscans, were constituted around the apostolic see to carry out the mandate received from it. Honorius III gave his sanction to the order of St Dominic when he said to him: '*Nos, attendentes fratres Ordinis tui, futuros pugiles fidei et vera mundi lumina*'.[1] St Francis thought of his religious as subject to the hierarchy in the person of the *Dominus Papa*, and of the superior of the order as his representative. Later the Jesuits likewise put themselves at the disposal of the head of the Church. These religious, having attached themselves to a power other than that of diocesan authority, came to be the auxiliaries of the Holy See in a multitude of new apostolic methods which no longer revolved around the local church, but took their place in the world-wide activity radiating from a more and more centralised Church.

Of course, an apostolate centred on the local church was by no means excluded by these new movements – far from it; often,

1. Potthast, 5402.

and indeed for the most part, it was to be introduced into the Christian life of the diocese, but it remained dependent on directives from a higher quarter. This type of uncloistered and extended monasticism of these religious orders founded since the twelfth century was allied to the clerical state in a new way. Its members constituted a 'regular' clergy, centralised and powerful, alongside the 'local' secular clergy, and often overshadowed them.

Finally, to return to the triple relationship stated at the beginning of this note; it could perhaps be said that the Eastern Church, in conformity with its genius, has preserved in a purer fashion the charismatic element in its monasticism (exclusive tendency towards evangelical perfection). In the West, on the other hand, but also in conformity with its proper genius, this charismatic element is found to have a twofold influence in its relationship with the hierarchy. On the one hand monasticism becomes more and more clericalised, and on the other the priesthood has in some way become monasticised. But the roots of each were firmly fixed in its own particular soil.

There is no doubt that this state of affairs has been largely responsible for a 'partitioning' in our Church and for creating that wide gulf between clergy and laity which is deplored so much today. Could not a powerful means of bridging this gulf be found in the revival of the practice of ordaining inferior clerks from the ranks of the people – in a form adapted to the spirit of the times? The question has been raised in missionary countries, and up to the present Rome has replied with the canons of the new code. The German bishops have also given some attention to this possible expedient. It would perhaps be of some use if in our 'pastoral liturgy' we tried to create a desirable sympathy for this revival in those who have the power to effect it.[1]

1. cf. Fr Congar's excursus on this matter in his *Lay People in the Church* (Geoffrey Chapman, 1960). He refers to W. Croce, S.J., 'Die niederen Weihen und ihre hierarchische Vertung' in *Z. f. k. Theol.* 1948, pp 257–314. Unfortunately, as Fr Croce remarks, the facts reveal that the exercise of these ecclesiastical functions had fallen into desuetude. After the Council of Trent, the minor Orders became simply a step towards the priesthood within the framework of the

DISCUSSION

Fr Dalmais: In this question of the relationships between priesthood and monasticism, Fr Rousseau has laid great stress on the questions of celibacy and continence; he has not broached directly on the question of the divine office at all.

Do you think that there was some interaction there as well? It seems clear to me that at Rome no divine office was known, except that of the monks.

Dom Rousseau: What I can say is that there is a constant tradition in the Church linking celibacy with the divine office.

The use of the entire psalter is, as it were, that angelic praise which pertains to those leading the angelic life, i.e. traditionally the monastic life, in the Church. That is why the divine office is not of obligation among Eastern priests, unlike ourselves. Of course monks within their monasteries say the office, and priests are recommended to say part of it, but this is totally different from our own custom. On this point the canonical connection between the two elements is very remarkable – it is one of the constant factors in the history of the Church.

---

seminaries which had been happily formed as the best remedy for the evils afflicting the clergy. Fr Croce wonders if it would not be better, considering that these functions are out of date, to re-create as their successors new forms of ecclesiastical service adapted to the conditions of our age – a shortage of clergy, an impoverished Church, new opportunities created for Christian *diakonia* by the broad but very incomplete social welfare service, and finally by the needs and difficulties of Christian teaching.

CHAPTER IX

HOLY ORDERS IN EARLY CONCILIAR LEGISLATION
(IVth and Vth centuries)

J. GAUDEMET

WE cannot expect the councils of the fourth and fifth centuries to provide us with a complete answer to all the problems which are raised by the question of Orders and the status of the clergy in the later Roman Empire. They can only throw light on some aspects of this vast problem, and it is not easy to compile an account of what they have to say.

For one thing the history of the councils of this period is by no means clear. Some of them are not well known, and even their dates are not always beyond question: the exact tenor of some of the canons has not been established with certainty and finally we have no good, modern, complete, prescribed and critical edition of these councils.[1]

Yet the period was one of intense conciliar activity. More than seventy-five councils met during the fourth century, at least ten of which were at Rome, and most of them took place in the last quarter of the century, in the fifth century about twenty councils were held at Rome. But the African series holds first place; it began with the Council of Carthage in 348-9, and after 394 others followed in quick succession. From 394 to 426 at least twenty-four councils met in the African capital. The fifth century is also notable for the great councils of the East, Ephesus in 431, and Chalcedon in 451. And the important series of councils

---

1. With Mansi, the most convenient edition remains that of Bruns, *Canones Apostolorum et conciliorum Saec. iv, v, vi, vii*, 2 vols., 183c. But it is very incomplete. Lauchert, *Die canones der wichtigsten altkirchlichen Concilien*, 1896, gives only a very few of the councils.

held in Gaul from the middle of the fifth century, at a time when the invasions had paralysed conciliar activity in Africa and Spain, must not be forgotten.[1]

Of course many of the decisions of these councils were dogmatic, for it was during this period that great theological conflicts were making it necessary to state the faith in more definite terms. But some very important disciplinary decisions are to be found in them as well, and these also are of great interest, for the fourth and fifth centuries were a time of crucial importance for the structural forms of the Church. It was then that they were established as it were in broad daylight, following on the peace of the Church and still more when the Edict of Thessalonica (27th February, 380) required all the peoples of the Empire to follow the religion of the Apostle Peter, and made Christianity the religion of the State. Christians, from being outlaws, became the privileged of the new regime, and as a result evangelisation gained in breadth if not in depth. Its very success presented new problems. Emerging and spreading from conditions of secrecy the growing Christian communities had to adopt more rigid standards in their organisation. Their closer contact with secular society presented them with some precedents, while on the other hand Christian principles penetrated certain spheres of Roman society.

The necessity of facing up to these new problems explains the intensity of this conciliar activity; and many of the resolutions they reached survived in principle, if not in detailed form, long after the ancient world had passed away.

Two false impressions must be dispelled before we begin.

1. The Church in the fourth and fifth centuries was not centralised as it is today. Councils, even those held at Rome, were most frequently local affairs, and the great ecumenical councils were preoccupied with questions of dogma rather than discipline. It is, moreover, impossible to determine with any accuracy the particular area to which the canons of a given council were to be applied. Ecclesiastical boundaries were not then so clearly defined as they subsequently became. The lists of bishops taking

---

1. Riez, 439; Orange, 441; Vaison, 442; Angers, 453; Tours, 461; Arles, 463; Vannes, 465; Bourges, 472; Vienne, 471; 475; etc.

part in these councils provides us with our best clue to this. It can be surely taken for granted that they would see that the decisions they themselves had helped to make were respected in their own dioceses. But we do not possess such lists for all the councils, so it is impossible to state categorically that decisions taken at a particular council would apply to a specified area, much less to the Church as a whole. Prudence counsels us to reckon as purely local the decisions promulgated by the vast majority of the councils.

It is none the less true that the same discipline is often imposed by repeated measures in the different local councils, so that in this way it takes on the character of a general rule.

Indeed, contacts between these communities were frequent, and exchanges possible; it would be quite wrong to think of them as isolated from each other. The lists of the Fathers attending these councils are in themselves evidence of the presence of representatives often from very far afield.[1]

2. The disciplinary decrees lay down rules of law. They cannot be expected to furnish a doctrine of Orders. Their provisions are fragmentary, and cover only points which were causing difficulty so that legislation is incomplete. Moreover, disciplinary canons are as inadequate as legal provisions: they can only determine the form, not the substance, of an institution, For this we must turn to patristics, where the major themes of sacramental doctrine are expounded. Our canons have less breadth, and the lawyer who is by way of being something of a sociologist readily recognises the limitations of his subject. But at least the canons have the merit of solidity and precision.

Now to proceed with my investigation which is principally concerned with two points, the conditions of admission to Orders, and the status and function of clerics. I shall not deal with the prerogatives of the various degrees of the hierarchy.

---

1. At the Council of Arles (314) we find six Spanish bishops, twelve Gauls, three Britons, nine Africans, some Italians and one Dalmatian. Ninety Western bishops met at Sardica (343). They came from Gaul, Italy, Illyria and Africa. The date of the council is still disputed – 342 or 343. Like Canon Bardy, *Hist. de l'Eglise* (Fliche and Martin), vol. iii, p. 123 n. 3, I accept the second date, which has the authority of J. Zeiller.

I

In the juridical texts the term *ordinatio* itself is used to designate the choice of men for ecclesiastical functions.[1] A distinction is made between the *sacerdotium* (the priest and the bishop) and the *ministerium* (the deacon).[2] But the term 'clerk' does not seem to be used with any settled meaning either in the Constantinian constitutions[3] (which can be explained by the fact that secular society was only just beginning to make official contact with Christianity) or in the conciliar legislation at the end of the fourth century. Thus, the Council of Carthage, 397 (c. 21) thought it still expedient to state that the term *clerici* covered 'the lector, the psalmist and the door-keeper'.

Rather than labouring such points as the times for ordination (which were fixed by the decretals of St Leo and Gelasius, rather than by the councils), or the suppression of simony,[4] we ought to notice how anxious the councils were to ensure respect for the framework of the diocese. There are many decrees, varied in origin but alike in purpose, which remind the bishop that he must not ordain clerks from another church, As early as the year 300 the Council of Elvira (c. 24) prohibited the ordination of laymen from other provinces because their former manner of life was unknown. Similar measures were taken at the Council of Antioch in 332-41 (c. 13), and then at Sardica in 343 (c. 18-19), which enforced its prohibition with the sanction *non sita rata ordinatio*, and justified it by concern for avoiding discord between bishops. African discipline was similar in character,[5] and in 398

1. The compilation ascribed to the second Council of Arles speaks of *ordinatio episcopi* (canon 54). The *Statuta ecclesiae antiqua* (c. 2-10) describes the rites of 'ordination' from the bishop down to the psalmist; cf. also Leo I, *Ep. 10 ad episc. per Vienn.*, c. 4 (P.L. 54, 631-2).   2. *Stat. Eccl. Ant.*, c. 4.

3. *Theodosian Code*, lxvi, tit. 2, const. 2 (313): '*qui divino cultui ministeria religionis impendunt, id est hi, qui clerici appellantur*'.

4. e.g. Council of Chalcedon (451), c. 2 = Decretum of Gratian, C. 1, qu. 1, c. 8.

5. Carthage (348), c. 5. Carthage 397 (c. 21) = Brev. Hippo (397), c. 19 incorporated into the *Codex Ecclesiae Africanae*, c. 54. The Council of Carthage (397), however, permits clerks to be transferred from a rich to a poor diocese. The Bishop of Carthage must decide on these transfers. This provision is reproduced in the *Codex Eccl. Afr.* c. 55.

a Constitution of the Emperor Arcadius forbade clerks to be taken from the place where they had been ordained.[1] Finally, the Gallic councils in the fifth century laid down similar principles.[2] So we can, then, speak of a general discipline resulting from a multiplicity of local decisions. The frequency with which reminders had to be given is in itself proof of the difficulty in getting it observed. These encroachments have been regarded as evidence of the difficulties encountered in recruitment for the priesthood in some areas, which encouraged bishops to look beyond their own borders. But it must not be forgotten that these boundaries themselves were in many cases very uncertain, as much because of the vagueness of the civil administrative areas with which ecclesiastical districts normally coincided, as of the evangelisation of new territory bordering on two dioceses, or even as a result of the peopling of a completely new region which would follow on the clearing of fresh lands for cultivation. The motive behind this respect for territorial boundaries is twofold, and varies with the canons themselves. Sometimes it springs from the desire for examining the candidates for Orders as to their fitness, and sometimes from an anxiety to avoid contention between bishops.

Not only must recruitment be on a diocesan basis, but the clerk, whatever his Order, is ordained to fill some vacant position in his own church. We shall meet this prohibition of arbitary ordination again in connection with the organisation of the community.

Freedom to accept or to reject the priesthood is another essential point in conciliar legislation. Frequently the Fathers present the priesthood as in effect a charge, an *onus*. And while there are notable examples of bishops elevated to the episcopate against their own wishes and under the pressure of popular acclaim, the

1. *Theodosian Code* xvi, 2, 33.
2. Turin (398). c. 7; Orange (441), c. 8, require the permission of the bishop to whom the clerk was subject (reproduced in the compilation known as the Second Council of Arles, c. 35), and c. 9 forbids the ordination of laymen from another diocese; Angers (453), c. 9, in the case of preferment to a higher Order; Tours (460), which in this case justifies its prohibition by respect for diocesan boundaries and the territorial rights of the bishop; Vannes (465), c. 10, collection known as the Second Council of Arles, c. 13.

juridical texts make it clear that there were refusals of this promotion. The Council of Valencia (374), in canon 4, raises its
voice against clerks who accuse themselves of faults in order to
escape advancement. It pronounces them guilty of crime if their
admissions are true, and of lying if they are false. Gelasius himself in one of his letters remarks on the difficulty of finding
priests when the deacons refuse to proceed. The Pope does not
wish this refusal to be overruled, and recommends the bishop to
make clerks in minor Orders priests rather than prefer those who
are set against it.[1]

Conciliar legislation does not appear to be very resolute in
face of these difficulties.[2] The *Codex Ecclesiae Africanae* (c. 31)
authorises the bishop to compel his clerks to accept promotion,
but he must not force the laity to receive ordination. Perhaps the
explanation for this distinction is to be sought in the authority
possessed by the bishop over his clergy rather than in a tacit kind
of obligation accepted by the clerk when he received Orders that
he would proceed to the various degrees.

Here again secular legislation intervened in this purely ecclesiastical question of discipline. A Novella of the Emperor
Majorinus in 460 (Nov.XI) both describes the priesthood as
sanctum onus and lays down the principle of freedom on the part
of the candidate. An ordination performed under duress
would expose the archdeacon, the bishop and the candidate's
relatives to penalties, and the clerk ordained against his will was
to be restored to the lay state—*coactus non potest consecrari*. This
decision was in accordance with Church teaching, but it
was avoided in the case of a consecration to the episcopate. This
would be valid, even if it took place against the candidate's
wishes.

In 482, Pope Simplicius, à propos an episcopal consecration
which had been carried out under duress at Modena, drew the
attention of the Bishop of Ravenna to the *praeceptum paternarum
regularum*. But he upheld the status of the bishop consecrated

1. Thiel, *Epist. Pont.*, i, p. 488,.
2. This has been studied in great detail by Fr Lafontaine in his
thesis for the Doctorate of Law on *Les Conditions d'accès aux ordres
dans la première législation ecclésiastique* (MSS. Paris, 1952).

unwillingly and ruled that the Bishop of Ravenna would in future be deprived of his right to ordain if he consecrated bishops, priests and deacons against their will. It was only with Pope Gelasius that the principle of the freedom of the candidate finally triumphed.[1]

Irregular ordinations, particularly those performed by heretics, and the question of re-ordination were not often discussed by the councils. In this matter, the position of St Augustine and the decretals of Innocent I are of crucial importance but, there are some elements of a solution to be found in the councils.

With regard to Novatians returning to the Church the Council of Nicaea pronounced that 'after receiving an imposition of hands, they may continue to take their place among the clergy' (c. 8). The text is therefore concerned with Novatian clerks. Denys translates the text literally; *ut impositionem manus accipientes sic in clero permanent.*[2] But in Gratian's *Decretum* it is found in a very different form (C.1, qu. 7, c.8) derived from the *Hispana* (P.L., 84, 95): *placuit sancto synodo ut ordinentur et sic maneant in clero.*

The Council of Capua (391) likewise forbade re-ordinations, and its provisions were re-enacted by the Council of Carthage in 397 (c. 38), which makes specific reference to Capua. The Carthaginian canon recurs in the *Codex Ecclesiae Africanae* (c. 48).

Conciliar leglisation has much more to show on the subject of the qualities required in the candidate for Orders.

First of all, he must be of the male sex. The Council of Laodicaea (mid fourth century) in canon 11 forbids the appointment (καθιτασθαι) of those who are called πρεσβυτιδαι or προκαθημέναι in the Church. The meaning of this prohibition is not clear. Denys translates: *non oporteat . . . ecclesiis ordinari,* while Gratian's *Decretum*, following the Hispana version states (Dist. 32, c. 19): *in ecclesiam tanquam ordinatas constitui non debere.* The position of deaconesses in the Church will be mentioned later.

1. Thiel., *op. cit.* i, pp 201-2; P.L., lxviii, 35-7.
2. *In Mansi, Council. Ampl. Coll.*, ii, col. 680; on this point, cf. Héfélé-Leclercq, *Hist. des Conciles*, i, pp 582-3.

Defectus corporis forms the subject of some minor regulations,[1] but there is an abundance of legislation concerning 'age'. It only appears in the fourth century. The question undoubtedly drew attention to customs which perhaps varied until then with each church, but which were inspired by St Paul's: *Manus cito nemini imposueris.* The Council of Neo-Caesarea requires candidates for the priesthood to be thirty years of age, recalling that Christ was thirty when he was baptised and began his preaching. The third Council of Carthage (397), c. 4. insists that the deacon be twenty-five. In the case of the bishop, thirty is again the prescribed age, and twenty for the subdeacon. Even secular legislation concerned itself with the matter of the age for ordination but without always conforming in detail to the canonical requirements. Indeed these latter were not always consistent, and in practice they were not very carefully observed. Cases of the promotion of young men to the episcopate are numerous and famous. St Ambrose was about forty (the date of his birth is uncertain), and St Hilary of Poitiers between twenty-five and thirty-five.[2] This discrepancy between legislation and practice deprives the conciliar provisions in this sphere of much of their interest. Moreover, in the fifth century they gave way to pontifical legislation, and the councils were silent on this subject until the decisions of Agde (506) and Toledo (531).

The Council of Nicaea (c. 9) had already prescribed a preliminary examination of the candidates. But the canon itself makes it clear that it did not always take place. The African councils (Hippo, 393, c. 20; Carthage, 397, c. 22) also require it in the case of priests. The *Statuta Ecclesiae Antiqua* recall the qualities which must be shown by the bishop.

It seems, however, that popular choice by acclamation was an admitted substitute for examination by the bishop. The Council of Carthage gives the alternatives: *probatus vel episcoporum examine vel populi testimonio.*

---

1. 'Castrati' debarred (Nicaea, c. 1, and the 'Second Council of Arles', c. 7), and 'arreptitii' (Orange, 441, c. 16, followed in the 'Second Council of Arles', c. 41).

2. cf. Lafontaine, *op. cit.* pp 166–216.

The examination would deal particularly with faith and morals. Conciliar legislation scarcely mentions intellectual qualifications, though the Fathers were greatly concerned about these. The Council of Hippo in 393 (c. 1 and 2) requires in a vague and general way 'knowledge of the scriptures'.

Finally, the practice of certain professions is a bar to Orders. This was particularly in the case with those involving participation in pagan religious rites; magistrates who had organised and taken part in forbidden games were not to be admitted to the episcopate.[1] Agents, trustees and administrators of another's inheritance were not to be accepted for Orders until they retired from those offices and handed over their accounts.[2] The Church had to be protected against financial responsibility for their maladministration. Finally, canon 8 of the Council of Toledo forbids the ordination of members of the armed forces.

Various classes of people were also prevented from being ordained as a result of secular legislation. But this was not out of consideration for the interests of the Church, but to cope with a situation in which unenviable careers in the civil administration and the less interesting State services were being abandoned. Members of corporations, farmers, colonists, workers in the imperial factories, officials in the lower grades of the postal and financial services, members of municipal curiae, are all named in the numerous constitutions which directed that those who thought to escape into holy Orders were to be sent back to their professions.

II

I shall not be able to cover every aspect of the clerical status here. I shall leave out the question of celibacy and continence altogether, for this warrants a complete study in itself, and deal more particularly with questions in connection with the functions of the clergy and their role in the community.

1. Roman Council about 374, in *Epistola ad Gallos episcopos*, c. 10; Roman Synod, 402, c. 4 and 10.
2. Council of Sardica, c. 13, which implies this provision; Council of Carthage, 348-9, c. 8.

The distinction between major and minor Orders, although it does not always appear to be absolutely clear-cut, can nevertheless be detected in many decisions. The dividing line often comes at the diaconate, which marks the entry into the higher Orders. Thus the Council of Antioch (c. 10) permits *chorepiscopi* to ordain lectors, exorcists and subdeacons, but not deacons or priests. The Council of Orange in 441 (c. 22) forbids the diaconate to be conferred on married men, and this provision was re-enacted in the collection ascribed to the Second Council of Arles (c. 43). The Council of Carthage in 397 (c. 21) requires the entire families of candidates for the episcopate, priesthood and the diaconate to be Christian.

Secular law itself seems to have taken this distinction into account. A Constitution of 399 recognises that bishops, priests and deacons may not be brought before courts for having sought to avoid their civil responsibilities by taking holy Orders, whereas this would be possible in the case of lectors, subdeacons and simple clerks.[1]

Outwardly, the clerk could not be distinguished from the layman, save by the simplicity of his appearance. The *Statuta Ecclesiae Antiqua* state: *clericus nec comam nutriat nec barbam* (c. 44), and canon 45 declares that the modesty of his dress will indicate his religious profession.

As far as the organisation of the clergy is concerned, legislation in the fourth and fifth centuries remained deeply influenced by the pristine unity of the clergy around the bishop.

The bishop alone could consecrate a church,[2] mingle the chrism, reconcile penitents and consecrate virgins.[3] But in the absence of the bishop, priests were permitted to reconcile penitents *in articulo mortis*, if he had previously authorised them to do so. The Roman Council held about the year 374 made a similar provision.[4] It relates that during the paschal season priests and deacons took part in the reconciliation of penitents in the presence of the bishop. But it is made quite clear that they

1. Theodosian Code xii, 1, 163.
2. Council of Orange, 441, c. 10.
3. Councils of Carthage, 390, c. 3; 397, c. 36; *Codex Ecclesiae Africanae*, c. 6; Council of Toledo, 400, c. 20.
4. In *Epistola ad Gallos episcopos*, c. 7.

were acting in the name of the bishop. At other times of the year, by special licence, the priest could reconcile penitents in danger of death. The deacon did not possess the same authority. But the text does say that if he had done so but once out of necessity, he would be excused.

Preaching was as a rule also reserved to the bishop. Yet from the fourth century it was also undertaken by priests at Alexandria. We know that in Africa preaching by priests made its appearance in the time of St Augustine, but at Rome it was not introduced as the normal thing before the time of Gregory the Great.

The role of the bishop in the Roman cities of the later Empire cannot be described in a few lines. Secular legal texts repeatedly take it into account and patristic references are equally numerous – but there is a dearth of canonical legislation on this matter. It is a question of fact rather than of law. The part played by the bishop in civic affairs is explained by his prestige and his duty of charity. But the councils occasionally warn him against taking too much interest in cares which could become too absorbing, or even dangerous to his spiritual patrimony. Thus, the *Statuta Ecclesiae Antiqua* forbid him to undertake the *tuitio testamentorum*.[1]

Although the diocesan synod was unknown to canon law in the fourth and fifth centuries, the bishop frequently had his entourage, his *presbyterium* which was a council of priests, the composition and powers of which were not strictly defined.

But side by side with this college, the bishop made use of certain auxiliaries. The archdeacon was known to both East and West by the fourth century. His position was important. He was the bishop's right-hand man, usually selected by the bishop from among the deacons but occasionally elected by the deacons themselves. He organised the liturgical ceremonies and under episcopal supervision was responsible for the relief of the poor. He took part in the *ordinatio* of the subdeacons and the acolytes,[2] and was in charge of the diocese *sede vacante*.

The archpriest is also mentioned in the letters of Leo I[3]

---

1. On the part played by the bishop in the life of the city, cf. Moschi Onory, 'Vescovi e citta', in *Rivista di Storia del diritto italiano*, 1931.   2. *Stat. Eccl. Ant.*, c. 5 and 6.   3. *Epist.* 19.

and in the *Statuta Ecclesiae Antiqua*. He could take the bishop's place in certain of his liturgical functions, he supervised the clergy and shared with the archdeacon the protection of widows, minors and pilgrims.[1]

The submission of the κλῆροι to the bishop is strongly asserted, and this insistence was occasionally necessary. The Council of Chalcedon (c. 8 and 18) punishes clerks conspiring against their bishop with degradation. The priest, moreover, appears as the bishop's deputy, and in some cases as his substitute. But in the larger communities at least, such as Rome or Carthage, there were clerks who were, in fact, assigned to the various churches of the episcopal city.

The clerk was, actually, ordained to take over a definite office. The Council of Chalcedon forbade the ordination of candidates who had no title (c. 6). Numerous conciliar provisions re-affirm the clerk's attachment to his own church,[2] and the abundance of legislation on this point leads us to surmise that it was as well to have it frequently renewed. The absence of a clerk must be authorised by his bishop. There was much suspicion of strange clerks, and they were required to produce letters testimonial from their bishop, so that their status might be recognised.[3]

The Council of Neo-Cacsarea stipulated that there were to be seven deacons and this is what we find at Rome. In the case of the other great churches, such as Milan, the exact number is unknown but there is no reason for thinking that it did not conform to the normal rule.

At Rome the deacons were the bishop's assistants at the liturgy (baptism in particular), and in the administration of property.

A wealth of legislation reminding the deacons of the extent of their powers leads us to suppose that they had a tendency to exceed them.[4] The Council of Elvira (c. 77) actually speaks of the

1. *Stat. Eccl. Ant.*, c. 17.
2. Arles (314), c. 2; Sardica (343), c. 15 and 18; Rome (378), c. 14; Carthage (397), c. 37; Toledo (400), c. 12; Chalcedon (451), c. 5 and 20; Angers (453), 1; Tours (460), c. 11; Vannes (465), c. 5; collection ascribed to the Second Council of Arles, c. 13.
3. Laodicaea, c. 41-2; Carthage (348), c. 5; Angers (453), c. 1; Chalcedon (451), c. 13.
4. Nicaea, c. 18; Laodicaea, c. 20 and 25; Arles, c. 18; etc.

deacon as *regens plebem*. It gives him authority to baptise, but adds that the bishop must *perficere* such a baptism with a benediction. Yet if the baptised person died before this benediction, his baptism would be valid. The Council of Arles in 314 notes that in several places they were offering the sacrifice, and it forbade them to do so. The collection ascribed to the Second Council of Arles (c. 15) forbade them to sit with the priests *in secretario* or to give holy communion when priests were present, and imposed these prohibitions under the sanction of deposition. Canons 37 to 41 of the *Statuta Ecclesiae Antiqua* define their prerogatives more closely, in a manner which was restrictive but less narrow than that adopted by previous councils. Evidence that all the degrees of the minor Orders were in existence in every community is not forthcoming. At Milan, for example, there is uncertainty about door-keepers, acolytes and subdeacons. There were certainly local variations. Thomassin had shown that occasionally the minor Orders were grouped in pairs – lector and exorcist, acolyte and subdeacon – the candidate having a choice of exercising one or other of the functions in each group.[1] The complete list of the various degrees of minor Orders is therefore the result of a progressive development. For our period the *Statuta Ecclesiae Antiqua* alone present us with a complete list. They state (c. 5) that the subdeacon does not receive the imposition of hands at his ordination. Other passages note certain prohibitions laid on him. He was not allowed to touch the sacred vessels (Council of Laodicaea, c. 20, 21 and 24).

The exorcist officiated at the exorcism of the catechumens and the possessed.[2] His functions became very attenuated at Rome during the fourth and fifth centuries. The lectorate was often conferred on the very young, occasionally on children. But its importance also declined rapidly. The lector's function was to read the scriptures and to chant the psalms. The porter was not necessarily a clerk, and we might well ask whether his office was the first degree of Orders everywhere. At Rome, Siricius makes no mention of him. The *Statuta Ecclesiae Antiqua*,

1. For this, see Lafontaine, *op. cit.*, p. 528 ff.
2. *Stat. Eccl. Ant.*, c. 90 and 92.

on the other hand, speak of his *ordinatio*. We know very little about his functions. Probably he looked after the church, attended to the order of the offices, saw that the places assigned to the penitents were kept free for them, and perhaps prevented strangers from entering so that on the whole he was a kind of sacristan.

References to the obligations proper to the clerical state are less numerous in conciliar legislation. The Council of Toledo in 400 (c. 5) commands every priest, deacon and subdeacon to assist at daily Mass if there is a church in the town or village where he happens to be.

The Council of Vannes in 465 (c. 14) requires them to be present at the *matutinae hymnae* except when they are ill, on pain of being deprived of holy communion for seven days. With this same reservation, the *Statuta Ecclesiae Antiqua* require their presence at the *vigiliae* on pain of forfeiting their *stipendium* (c. 49). Finally, the Irish Council held by St Patrick about 456,[1] binds them to the *collectae* morning and evening (c. 7) and clerks who were negligent in the recitation of the psalter were not admitted into church (c. 10).[2] All these passages show that there was a tendency to demand certain pious practices of the clergy, without there being any fixed rule or particular uniformity about it.

On the other hand the councils frequently take up the subject of the proprieties which the clergy are to observe. They are forbidden to attend wedding banquets, or feasts given by Jews,[3] to frequent inns except out of necessity when travelling, and drunkenness is condemned.

The questions of work and of clerical poverty, which form the subject of so many observations on the part of the Fathers of the Church, are by no means outside the purview of conciliar decisions. The significance of these could only be fully assessed if we knew more about the social background of the clergy – and this, unfortunately is not easy to discover. Of course we know

1. There are doubts about the authenticity of the two Councils 'held by St Patrick'; cf. Héfélé-Leclercq, *Hist. des Conciles*, ii (2), 1908, p. 888, n. 3.

2. Laodicaea, c. 27 and 55; Vannes (465), c. 111.

3. Vannes, c. 12.

the origin of certain bishops who came from the noble families, from the senatorial class and the rich, landed proprietors. But this is only because we know more about the great and the famous, and very little about the rest. Yet not all bishops were of noble descent, still less the clergy as a whole. Undoubtedly many of them were of middle class, and even poor, origin, but here we are as a rule reduced to supposition, and it is impossible to establish proportions. Some of them were smallholders, who, after their elevation to sacred Orders were able to continue their farming, but others were tradesmen who were usually obliged to give up their business. Both lived on their own means, but in cases of need – though the canons are rather silent about this – the bishop granted a stipend from the revenues of the Church's property to augment it.

Here again secular legislation sought to control recruitment to the priesthood, with a view to preventing the rich and their wealth from passing to the Church and thus impoverishing the curiae.[1] Provisions of this kind could not but hasten the recruitment of men from less fortunate classes.

Like the Fathers, the councils forbade clerks to use their office as a means of making a fortune. The Council of Chalcedon (c. 3) denounced clerks who took leases of land to make money, and as a result neglected their religious obligations. It forbade clerks and monks to take such leases or to manage the property of others, but they were allowed to act as guardians, trustees and administrators of property belonging to widows and orphans. It was, therefore, the motive of gain much more than the time which had to be spent on these profane tasks which evoked the censures of the Fathers.

Yet clerks could possess property. The Council of Orange in 441 (c. 6) notes that some of them owned slaves. Secular law recognised the clerk's rights of disposition over his own emoluments, even if he were still subject to his father's control and so legally incapable of possessing a personal patrimony. Any material advantages gained by the clergy were, in fact, regarded as their personal estate and as such remained their own personal

---

1. *Theodosian Code*, xvi, 2, 17 (Valentinian i, 364) and 19 (Valens, 370).

property. Indeed, the law for clerical property was more favourable than it was to the ordinary layman, and it included all property belonging to bishops, priests and deacons. These churchmen had absolute rights, even of testamentary disposition, over it, whereas before Justinian laymen were not allowed to dispose of their *quasi-castrense* estate by will.[1]

However, for reasons of morality rather than out of concern for poverty, the Emperor Valentinian I, in a Constitution addressed to Pope Damasus, forbids women to make clerks beneficiaries under their wills.[2]

Canonical legislation too, while condemning clerks who profited financially from the priesthood, allows them to dispose quite freely of their property,[3] and to make collections to enable them to obtain the necessities of life.[4] But no Council made any ruling on the practice of the *stipendium* which was levied on the endowments of the Church by the bishop for the benefit of his clergy.

An important and distinctive legislation deals with the subject of work. To obtain a livelihood the clerk could be an artisan or a farmer.[5] Indeed the *Statuta Ecclesiae Antiqua* actually insist that he should learn a trade, and so manual labour is made a duty (c. 53). What is forbidden is excessive agricultural activity for purposes of gain,[6] and the lending of money at interest.[7]

Commerce continued to be permitted but it was not to entail such travelling as would interfere with the performance of religious functions. The Council of Elvira permitted the relatives, friends or servants of bishops, priests and deacons to undertake business journeys of their behalf (c. 19).

Secular legislation returns to this topic repeatedly. Several

---

1. *Code of Justinian*, i, 3, 33 (Leon); on this question, cf. La Rosa *I peculii speciali in diritto romano*, 1953.
2. *Theodosian Code*, xvi, 2, 20 (370).
3. Council of Carthage, 397, c. 49; *Codex Eccl. Afr.*, c. 32.
4. St Patrick's Irish Council about 456, c. 4 and 5.
5. *Stat. Eccl. Ant.*, c. 51 and 52.
6. cf. Council of Chalcedon, c. 3; Carthage 397, c. 15; collection ascribed to Second Council of Arles, c. 14.
7. Arles, c. 12; Nicaea, c. 17; Carthage (348), c. 13 and (397), c. 16; Tours (461), c. 13, which adduces the Psalms; collection ascribed to Second Council of Arles, c. 14.

constitutions recognise the clerk's right to engage in commerce[1] and clerks actually profited by exemption from the special tax levied on traders, the *chrysargyron* or the *collatio lustralis*. The Theodosian Code has preserved ten texts covering the period 343–452 on this subject. This exemption, in fact, had been very generously granted at first by Constantine and Constantius; it applied to all commerce and to all taxes on commerce, and even benefited those employed by clerks as agents for their enterprises. The idea was that commerce should provide an adequate means of support for the clerk, so that his pious works could be maintained, and consequently the concession had to be kept within certain bounds. In 360 the immunity was restricted to cover only that trade which was necessary to ensure food and clothing.[2] A curious constitution in 379 (Gratian) limited the exemption to commerce which did not exceed a certain importance.[3] In the East, Arcadius caused justice to be done in 399 as a result of a protest by the merchants' corporation, for the tax was levied on this body as a whole, and consequently it had to carry the burden of the relief granted to some of its members. The Emperor also compelled men to opt either for trade or the clerical state.[4] Finally, in the West in 452 Valentinian III withdrew all exemption from taxation in the case of clerks professionally engaged in trade.[5]

We must note finally that holy Orders were declared to be irrevocable by various councils, which forbade clerks to return to lay life.[6] But here again it is Augustinian theology rather than conciliar legislation that must be regarded as responsible for the progress made in defining the clerical character and state.

This picture of the hierarchical organisation of the Christian community would not be complete without some remarks about the place and the role of the laity, which the councils make it possible for us to make. Preaching by laymen was still practised in the third century. A letter of St Leo (Ep. 153) forbids it, but this measure did not affect all the churches. The *Statuta Eccle-*

1. *Theodosian Code*, xvi, 2, 8 (343); 14 (357); 15 (360); 36 (401).
2. *ibid.*, xvi, 2, 15.   3. *ibid.*, xiii, 1, 11.
4. *ibid.*, xiii, 1, 16.   5. *Novella*, XXXV, 4.
6. Council of Saragossa (381), c. 6; Chalcedon (451), c. 7; Angers (453), c. 7; Tours (461), c. 5.

siae Antiqua give this attenuated formula: *Laicus, praesentibus clericis, nisi ipsis jubentibus, docere non audeant* (c. 98).

The Council of Elvira (c. 58) permits a layman – if he is not a bigamist – to baptise in cases of emergency, then, if the baptised person survived, the bishop was to add an imposition of hands.

The first Council of Saragossa (381) directs that men and women should be separated at readings and meetings, and the *Statuta Ecclesiae Antiqua* (c. 99 and 100) forbid women to baptise or teach (*docere*). Yet widows who receive a *stipendium* from the Church should give their assistance *meritis et orationibus* (c. 103). At the end of the fifth century Pope Gelasius again denounced women who performed at the altar functions which were reserved to men, and once more condemned this practice.

The *Statuta Ecclesiae Antiqua* (c. 12), however, admit that widows or virgins could be chosen to assist at the baptism of women. This was not purely practical help, for the canon requires of them sufficient knowledge to prepare country women to answer the questions which would be put to them at their baptism, and afterwards to guide them in the Christian life.

A special place must be given to the deaconesses who fell within the purview of secular, as much as canonical, legislation. There is an abundance of the former, and it is restrictive in character. First of all it deals with admission to the office. Theodosius, in 390, required candidates to have borne children and to have attained the age of sixty.[1] The Council of Chalcedon was satisfied with forty years and a strict inquiry, (c. 15). The same Constitution of Theodosius – 21st July, 390 – forbids deaconesses to make testamentary dispositions of their real or personal property in favour of clerks, the Church or the poor at the expense of their natural heirs.[2] This strict protection of family interests was subsequently relaxed. Theodosius specified that, as from 23rd August, 390, widows and virgins were to be allowed to make gifts of personal property *inter vivos* in favour of churches and the clergy,[3] and in 455, Novella V of Marcian permitted widows, deaconesses and virgins to make bequests by

1. *Theodosian Code*, xvi, 2, 27.
2. *ibid.*   3. *ibid.*, xvi, 2, 28.

will, and to give donations and legacies for the benefit of the clergy, the Church and the poor.

The actual religious status of the deaconess is not very clear from the few conciliar provisions dealing with the point. The Council of Chalcedon (c. 15) declares that they receive an imposition of hands (χειροτονεῖσθαι) like the clergy. But this rite is only attested in the East. The Council of Orange (c. 26) forbids them to be 'ordained'. Moreover, deaconesses did not exercise 'sacred functions', except among the Monophysites and the Nestorians,[1] and were essentially devoted to works of charity. Our period marks their decline. At Rome they did not perform any functions after the third century, but survived until the beginning of the fifth. At Constantinople, Novella III (ch. 1) of Justinian still takes note of them, if only to determine their number.

The information given by the councils on the participation of the laity in the life and worship of the Church is very meagre. The Council of Gangra (c. 6) forbids the faithful to meet privately outside the church, unless a priest approved by the bishop be present. But the admission of non-christians to the Mass of the catechumens was ratified by the *Statuta Ecclesiae Antiqua*. They also mention, incidentally, the oblations of the faithful, both to refuse those of the *dissidentes fratres* (c. 93), and to accept those of penitents who had died suddenly (c. 79).[2]

The Council of Laodicaea (c. 59) forbids psalms written by individuals and uncanonical books to be read in church. There is appended what is perhaps a list of the canonical writings.[3] The Council of Carthage in 397 (c. 47) gives this list of canonical writings as the only ones permitted to be read in church. The *Codex Ecclesiae Africanae* (c. 103), re-enacting one of the provisions of the Council of Carthage in 407, refers to the rule that prayers, prefaces and impositions of hands must conform to the requirements of the councils and to the principles laid down by the *prudentiores*.

1. cf. Lafontaine, *op. cit.*, pp 38–9.
2. This provision was made by the Council of Vaison, 412 (c. 2).
3. This is given in canon 60, but its attribution to the Council of Laodicaea is contested (cf. Héfélé-Leclercq, *Hist. des Conciles*, I (2), pp 1026–8).

The Council of Elvira, in its reference to baptism, draws attention to the rule that there must be no payment for the sacraments, and by insisting on this reveals a contrary practice.[1]

This analysis of the data provided by the councils shows how inadequate a source they are for a complete understanding of the conception of Orders prevalent during the later Empire. But from this fragmentary evidence we can, nevertheless, detect the principal points with which Christian legislators were concerned – to organise the community by defining the functions of the various Orders in greater detail, to mark the division between clergy and laity more clearly in order to counteract certain dangerous and mistaken practices, and steadfastly to uphold the unity of the community around its head, the bishop. Although the first signs of the parochial system are making their appearance in the larger towns, it still remains quite unknown in country districts where evangelisation had only just begun.

1. c. 48: '*Emendari placuit ut hi qui baptizantur, ut fieri solebat, nummos in concha non mittant, ne sacerdos, quod gratis accepit, pretio distrahere videatur*'.

CHAPTER X

THE TRADITION IN MEDIEVAL CANON LAW

G. FRANSEN

HAVE the medieval canon lawyers anything to teach us about the sacrament of Orders?

If we look to them for a really formal and systematic treatise the answer is in the negative. But if we are concerned with their evaluation of those sections of Gratian's Decretum (1140) or the Decretals of Gregory IX (1234) which are devoted to priesthood, then the harvest is superabundant; there are about two thousand texts, pontifical pronouncements or *auctoritates* which call for attention. It has even been claimed that canon law in the twelfth century was simply sacramental theology, and especially the theology of the sacrament of Orders.

This is not the place to go into all the problems which were debated, nor the devices which canonical scholarship employed to resolve them. I shall pick out a few of them, and show what canon lawyers were thinking on these matters at the end of the twelfth and the beginning of the thirteenth centuries.

Theologians and canonists have everything to gain by contacts and comparisons. If the canonist of today is all too often a legal technician, the writers we are going to examine preserved a very lively sense of theological realities. Unfortunately their language and method assume a technical initiation, and it is difficult, without the help of a professional, to feel at home in the maze of canons, distinctions, topics and questions which occur in Gratian's Decretum, and in the chapters and headings of the Decretals.

Before beginning this survey, which owes much to the works of Mgr Gillmann and Mgr Saltet, as well as to those of S. Kuttner, I should like to make some remarks which may make it easier to understand and appreciate what follows.

The first deals with the method followed by the writers in question. As a rule, they were concerned with harmonising the various *auctoritates* – conciliar canons, pontifical letters, patristic writings. They rarely thought out a synthesis theoretically for its own sake; they rather attempted a particular solution. A given principle, stated without any reservations, cannot, it seems, be applied immediately to other cases which appear to us to be very similar. So we must be careful not to make sweeping generalisations, and we shall be false to their thought if we carry our conclusions further than the writers themselves intended.

My two other remarks deal with the subject itself. At first, the distinction between the power of Orders and the power of jurisdiction was indefinite, and emerged only slowly. Then, the conceptions of 'validity' and 'regularity' had not yet come to be designated by unambiguous terms, and we have to look to the context to enable us to distinguish them.[1] For example, in their *Summae* on Gratian's Decretum, Rufinus (1157–9) and Stephen of Tournai (1160–70) distinguish three cases in which ordination can be said to be *irrita*:[2]

quantum ad sacramenti veritatem: if it were performed by one who had been deprived of his powers, or who did not observe the prescribed form.

quantum ad officii executionem: if one were ordained *ab episcopo non proprio* without the necessary qualifications.

quantum ad beneficii perceptionem: if one were ordained without canonical title; in this case no church was responsible for one's support.

We discover, then, three aspects, three degrees of nullity. Today we should not relate them to ordination. We should say that in the first case the ordination would be null and void, in the second it would be vaild, but the powers received might not be exercised, and in the third there would be simply no right to receive the revenues of a benefice.

Medieval canonists, while distinguishing these aspects did

1. The reason for this uncertainty is often exegetical in character, as in the example quoted: what are we to understand by *irritus*, and to which aspect of ordination or its effects does it apply?
2. *ad dist.*, 70.

not define them as systematically as we do. For them *ordinare* and *ordinatio* did not bear a sacramental reference. The election of the Pope,[1] the nomination of archdeacon,[2] canonical institution given to a monk to enable him to take charge of a parish,[3] are all described as *ordinatio*. The following passage, which we owe to Gratian himself, is worth quoting in full: 'Monachi autem, si in dedicatione sui presbyteratus, sicut ceteri sacerdotes, predicandi, baptizandi, penitentiam dandi, peccata remittendi, beneficiis ecclesiasticis perfruendi rite potestatem accipiant ... tamen executionem sue potestatis non habent nisi a populo fuerint electi et ab episcopo, cum consensu abbatis, ordinati.'

Yet the term *ordo* is used with special reference to the sacrament, at least in the context with which we are concerned. For Rufinus, Order is the '*signaculum, id est quoddam secretum quo spiritualis potestas et officium traditur ei qui ordinatur*'.[4] For Henry of Suso (ca 1271) it is a sacrament of the Church instituted by the apostles. It confers character, through the imposition of the bishop's hands (in the form prescribed by the Church) and the co-operation of the Holy Spirit, to enable those who received it to perform certain functions.[5]

It is a *sacramentum dignitatis*, as opposed to the *sacramenta necessitatis*, since it must be conferred by *digniores* (the bishops) on subjects worthy to receive it, who are thus preferred to *dignities* in the Church. This hierarchy of dignities, we are told,[6] depends on Order alone; it is determined:

> *ex dignitate consecrationis, qua episcopus ceteris sacerdotibus preeminet;*
> *ex dignitate ordinis, qua prefertur subdiacono diaconus;*
> *ex dignitate dispensationis seu amministrationis.*

1. Paucapalea, *ad dist.*, 23.
2. Stephen of Tournai, *ad dist.*, 60.
3. Gratian's Decretum, dictum post, c. 19, c. XVI, q. 1.
4. Rufinus, *ad dist.*, 21.
5. Hostiensis, *Summa aurea, De tempore ordin. et qual. ordinandorum*, n. 1.
6. Gratian's Decretum, dictum post, c. 3, C. I, q. 1. cf. F. Gillmann *Einteilung und System des Gratianischen Dekrets*, Mainz 1926, p. 51.

Hec autem alia est spiritualium (in this the archpriest has precedence over the archdeacon), *alia est secularium rerum* (but here the archdeacon has precedence over the archpriest).[1]

Although we may have digressed a little with these reflections, they at least serve to show that where we tend to separate as a means of distinguishing, the older writers did not lose sight of the wholeness of 'priesthood – mission – functions', and the exercise of these functions. Yet they did distinguish these different aspects, and in this way they went further than their predecessors. I am going to try to show this by examining two points, first the influence of the feudal system on ordination, and second the actual position of the candidate for the priesthood.

When parishes first came into existence they were frequently as extensive as our own deaneries, and apart from the exceptional case, clerks would spend their whole lives in the same parish (c. 15, Nicaea). No one would be ordained unless he had a *titulus* from some church which would both be school and seminary. The candidate for the priesthood was a member of the clergy, *intitulatus*, and often spent many years training for the ministry, during which he exercised the Orders he had already received and assisted at the divine office. We find that there were varying numbers of such clerks everywhere. They were ordained to the title of a particular church, and served under its parish priest who was often called an archpriest; they represented every degree of the hierarchy, from the Order of psalmist (tonsure) to the priesthood.[2]

This unity and stability broke down under the feudal system. Ordination without title was introduced, and not a few 'wandering clerks' began to make their appearance. Innocent III attempted to improve matters by making a candidate's patrimony sufficient 'title' for ordination. Later, the *titulus beneficii* was developed. These new titles seem to have been quite unconnected with ordination, while the traditional *intitulatio* was, as it were, incorporated into them.

1. Rufinus, *ad dist.*, 21.
2. cf. S. Kuttner, 'Cardinalis: The History of a Canonical Concept', in *Traditio*, 1945, vol. III, pp 129–214, and D. Linder, *Die Anstellung der Hilfspriester*, Kempten, 1922, pp 1–43.

What was the result? It has been described as the 'regime of the private chapel'. A person would decide that the church was too far away, (or there would be some quite different reason) and so he would build one himself and endow it. Church and endowment were then granted like a fief, occasionally only for a term of years, to some clerk who had been, or would be, ordained by the bishop. If the office did not seem to befit his station, he would try to find another lord, and another church, the revenues of which would be more substantial. Similarly, the lord would be easily tempted by offers of money from applicants for a 'good' church. We also note cases where the lord was satisfied with setting one of his serfs free, and getting him ordained, while maintaining his rights to 'spiritual services'.[1] Lay investiture (for induction to the endowments of a church) had developed into the conferring of the spiritual charge itself; simony, lack of preparation for the priesthood, led to a crisis which the Gregorian reform had to overcome.

The reaction lasted for several decades. The reforming Popes succeeded in suppressing lay investiture and in distinguishing it from canonical institution. They transformed feudal investiture into a right of patronage belonging to individuals or corporations, and, as in the case of canonical elections, the patron's nomination had to be confirmed by the bishop.

So in place of the simple ordination (with *intitulatio*) that we find in the early Middle Ages, we can distinguish three stages in the advancement of a clerk to a given charge – nomination (either by canonical election or application, or by presentation by the patron), confirmation and canonical institution (the granting of the right to exercise defined sacred functions, and to receive the revenues of the benefice), ordination proper (the conferring of what is called the power of Orders).

1. St Raymond of Penaforte, *Summa Juris* (1222) (ed. J. Rius Serra, Barcelona, 1945), tit. de servis ordinandis vel non, p. 88. 'Sed numquid potest patronus retinere in liberto quem petit ordinari saltem operas spirituales, puta ut in sua capella ministret ei divina, vel similes? Dicit Alanus quod sic consensu episcopi, alias non . . . Ita etiam dicit Johannes, et michi videtur probabile. Videtur tamen sentire Tancredus quod potest simpliciter tales operas retinere, non distincto consentiat episcopus vel non.'

This reform enabled a fresh division of parishes to be made. They became smaller and their boundaries were fixed, and this made it possible for many uncertainties about parochial rights, such as tithe, to be cleared up. Until the beginning of the thirteenth century the parish priest had a body of clerks around him, responsible for singing the office (*ecclesiam officiare*), and the *cura animarum*. But this system was soon to be disturbed by the multiplication of simple benefices able to support the clergy independently of the life of the parish.

Before broaching the subject of *executio*, I will deal with the position of the candidate for the priesthood. He was presented to the bishop, as formerly, for examination (*scrutinium*). This was a strict obligation and was generally entrusted to the archdeacon or someone deputed by the bishop. Its purpose was to discover whether the candidate were *ydoneus* or not. The chief points of the examination which are put forward in distinctions 24–58 and 80–9 of the first part of Gratian's Decretum, as well as in certain chapters of the first book of the Decretals can be summed up in St Paul's well-known text: *Oportet episcopum sine crimine esse, unius uxoris virum, non vinolentum, prudentem, ornatum, hospitalem, pudicum, doctorem, non percussorem, non litigiosum, non cupidum, domui suae bene praepositum, non neophitum*' (1 Tim. 3, 2–6).

The commentaries give us, incidentally, many vivid details of the habits of both clergy and laity. They also provide a striking example of the ingenuity shown by the erudite in accommodating to the classical rubric requirements which were frequently far removed from the obvious sense of the text.

It is à propos *unius uxoris virum* that they deal with the prohibition against ordaining anyone who had been married twice, as well as anyone who had married a widow. The latter is a bigamist only 'interpretatively' – the prohibition springs not from any crime actually committed by him, but from *defectus sacramenti*, for he cannot claim that his marriage fully reflects the union of Christ with his Church.[1] The exposition on priestly prudence is the equivalent of a treatise on the lawfulness and expediency of the study of pagan authors. The commentary

1. St Raymond, *tit. de bigamis*, pp 56–9.

de ornatum is an exposition of clerical decorum and *de non percussorem* a study of the freedom of the act of faith.[1] And there were also the long treatises *de lapsis, de servis non ordinandis*, etc.

The clerk was allowed to marry so long as he remained in minor Orders. He would not necessarily lose clerical status on marriage, provided that he wore the habit and the tonsure, and took part in the divine office. If his income were not sufficient to maintain him the bishop could even give him a benefice.[2]

The obligation of the divine office, sung or recited in common, is referred to and upheld. The clerk, and sometimes the priest, who had to work with his hands to make a living was permitted to do so on condition that he did not omit the office.[3] All the clerks, even those in minor Orders, met together at a fixed hour for this. During the thirteenth century this obligation was restricted to beneficed clerks; they could, however, fulfil it by proxy, but, as Peter de Tarentaise notes, clerks in major Orders must say their office notwithstanding, for even if the presence of a substitute enabled them to discharge their duty so far as their church was concerned, it did not absolve them from the personal obligation of divine worship which they had accepted on receiving the subdiaconate. This obligation, however, continued to be subordinate and the principal obligation was the public office. This point of view persisted even after the obligation of the public office was restricted to collegiate churches and cathedrals. It was not until the sixteenth century that the standpoint changed completely – it was then stated that all clerks were bound to the private recitation of the office, but some only had the added duty of celebrating it in public.[4]

Having given this short account we must now ask how the canonists at the end of the twelfth and the beginning of the

---

1. As in the *Summa Coloniensis* (1169), of which I am preparing an edition.   2. St Raymond, *op. cit.*, p. 63.

3. St Raymond, *op. cit.*, p. 80, cf. c. 1, X, *de celebr. miss.*, III, 41.

4. cf. G. Fransen, 'L'obligation du Breviaire en Occident' in *Quest. Litt. et Par.*, 1951, vol. XXXII, pp 200–4 and M. Van der Drift, 'Het gemeenschappelijk en privaat officie in de XIII en XIV ecuwen', in *Sylloge* (a collection of theses for the doctorate in theology and canon law of the Catholic University of Louvain), vol. XXVI, fasc. 3. The text of Peter of Tarentaise has been published by Fr Glorieux in *Rev. Sc. Phil. et Théol.*, 1930, vol. XIX, p. 474.

thirteenth century 'arranged' the powers of the clergy. What are the respective places in their synthesis of what we call sacramental reality, and of the conditions under which the powers received at ordination could be exercised lawfully? The question arose in connection with the pastoral activity of the monks or with the validity of ordinations effected by simoniacs, or by a bishop who had relinquished the episcopal dignity, etc. The answer was found in a conception which we have lost: which was, in fact, swallowed up in the two notions of *cura animarum* and of jurisdiction in *fore interno* – the conception of *executio*. By way of illustration, here are some cases in which the doctrine is invoked.

The first concerns monks who were also priests. Could they *celebrare divina officia populo*? No, said Gratian, unless they had been chosen by the people, with the consent of the abbot and the approval of the bishop. And he goes on to say that this was so in the case of the secular priest as well. To exercise the powers received at ordination the approval of the bishop (*executio*) must be obtained.[1]

Nevertheless, even without this *executio* priest-monks could give absolution *in articulo mortis*, celebrate private Masses in their convent, etc.[2] Rufinus and Stephen of Tournai distinguish two types of *executio* – one *que populo a suo sacerdote debeter*, the same as the (holding of) a *cura animarum*, which infers a *populum sibi subjectum* or *commissum*, the other *que circa confectionem ipsius sacramenti respicitur*.[3] This latter is general in character and, fundamentally, ineffective. Stephen compares it to the jurisdiction granted by the Emperor to a judge. So long as the Emperor refrains from assigning him to a district in which he must – and is able to – exercise his power, he possesses merely the title and not the administration.[4]

Before their time, Roland Bandinelli (before 1148) had formulated the theory in a more general way; to exercise the *dignitas sacerdotalis* two things are necessary, *ordo* and *licentia ordinis*

---

1. See the text cited above, p. 2.
2. Rufinus, *ad CXVI*, q. 1.
3. Rufinus and Stephen of Tournai, *ad dist.*, 70.
4. Stephen of Tournai, *ad dist.*, post c. 25, C. XVI, q. 1.

exequendi. And as *licentia* without *ordo* confers nothing, so *ordo* without *licentia, nichil, quoad hoc spectat, conferre videtur.*[1]

So, then, if it is to be fully exercised, priesthood requires *executio*, which goes hand in hand with *populum sibi subiectum*, or at any rate *conventum habere*, i.e. *populum convenientem ad sacramenta recipienda.*[2] Priests and bishops who have been degraded retain only the 'character' and lose *executio: potestatem acceptam sacramento tenus retinent, effectus suae potestatis prorsus privantur.*[3] This explains why priests ordained by simoniacs do not receive *executio*. He who ordains them can only give what he possesses – he retains the *sacramentum ordinis*, but has lost *executio ordinis* and the *virtus sacramenti*. Such priests, then, are true priests, but may not exercise the Orders they have received. Does this mean merely that they are forbidden to exercise their Orders, or does it imply that their sacramental actions are invalid? I believe the former opinion is that consistent with the texts.[4]

At this point we have to state clearly what *executio* actually is:

1. It is normally received at the time of ordination: *officium et executionem sui officii ex consecratione adipiscuntur.*[5]

2. It is given by the ordaining bishop; if this bishop does not himself possess it (if he is suspended, or has relinquished the episcopate), he can confer nothing: *nemo dat quod non habet.*

3. It is signified at the time of ordination by the tradition of the instruments and the vestments.[6]

4. Although included in the *cura animarum* it seems to be distinct from it.

1. Roland, *ad c.* 40, C. XVI, q. 1.
2. Roland and Stephen of Tournai, ad C. XVI, q. 3, cf. 'Quaestiones', at the end of the edition of Roland, p. 279.
3. Gratian's Decretum, *dictum post*, c. 97, C. I, q. 1, § 3 conclusion.
4. Rufinus, *ad c.* 17, C. I, q. 1. cf. L. Saltet, *Les Réordinations*, 1907, p. 312. I cannot agree with the writer (p. 305) and cannot understand how he can make the absence of *executio* the reason for the invalidity of the Orders conferred by heretics ordained outside the Church.   5. Gratian's Decretum, *dist.* 97, § 3.
6. Innocent IV, *ad c.* Fraternitatem, 4, X, de hereticis, V, 7, V. Capitula: 'executionem autem ordinis nullus suspensus dat quia quod non habet dare non potest, et ordinatur est ille qui dat executionem, quod ex eo apparet quia dat sibi que sunt signa executionis sc. planetam, stolam et consimilia'.

5. It seems to be a jurisdictional conception – the permission, the habilitation necessary for exercising the Orders which have been received. I quote Rufinus; one has to admire the way in which he distinguishes validity, juridical regularity, and moral regularity.

In officio sacerdotali duo sunt: usus (the actual exercise) *et potestas. Item potestas triplex est:*

aptitudinis qua sacerdos ex sacramento ordinis quod accepit habet aptitudinem cantandi missam (validity),

habilitatis qua ex dignitate officii, quam adhuc habet, habilis est ad cantandam missam (juridical regularity)

regularitatis qua ex vite merito, ex integritate persone, ex sufficienti eruditione dignus est missam cantare (moral regularity).[1]

I cannot here attempt to mention all the aspects of *executio*: undoubtedly numerous texts will come to mind to fill out these notes.

I will now come to the confusion which reigned for several centuries around the idea of the *cura animarum*.

Our canonists deal with this subject when describing the powers of the archdeacon, and in commenting on the famous canon *Omnis utriusque sexus* of the Fourth Council of the Lateran which provides that absolution and communion are to be received at the hands of the *sacerdos proprius*.

If we are to understand their reasoning and their difficulties we must remember that archdeacons (who nominated incumbents and conferred their *cura* upon them) and indeed the incumbents themselves, were not always priests.

Is the *cura animarum* to be linked with the power of Orders, or with the power of jurisdiction? For Innocent III, the *cura* consists in the power of absolution, and so it presumes the priesthood. Yet one who is not a priest can present this *cura* to another, provided that the recipient is a priest.[2] This opinion, because of the authority of its author, was defended for several centuries, despite its ambiguity.

Henry Suso, however, criticised it and deemed it incomprehensible. He stated that the power to absolve belonged to the

1. Rufinus, *ad c.* 30, C. I, q. 1. cf. L. Saltet *op. cit.*, p. 314.
2. Innocent IV, *ad c. Cum satis*, 4, X, *de off. archid.*, I, 23.

spiritual order – every priest possessed it, even those without *cura*, provided they have received the *executio*. But the *cura animarum* belonged to the realm of jurisdiction. To exercise it fully, the priesthood was essential. Nevertheless, anyone who possessed the *cura animarum*, even though not a priest, was able to excommunicate and to dispense. He could not lift the excommunication for although this absolution is in the sphere of jurisdiction it none the less requires confession.[1]

This last remark is revealing. In our power of absolution we must distinguish between the power to absolve from sin and the power to absolve from censures. The first is connected with the *executio* of the priesthood, the second with the *cura animarum*.[2] As I have said, this clear and logical conception did not prevail, and we have to wait for St Antoninus (1389–1459) to provide us with a new definition of *cura*. *Quaedam potestas habendi aliquos in subditos, illis conferendo sacramenta per se vel per alium, et alia faciendo qua pertinet ad salutem animarum ut corrigendo et huiusmodi.*[3]

This definition is no more than a clarification of the description which Hostiensis had previously given (in a passage in which he does not discuss the opinion of Innocent III) and which was taken up in teaching the subject. In it the *cura animarum* is simply the *onerosa et sollicita custodia animarum, commissa alicui ut curet ne pereant sed salvantur*. It is acquired by law, canonical institution, custom or prescription approved by the Holy See. The duties of the incumbent, for which he is accountable to God, are to instruct his parishioners in the faith, to teach them the practice of virtue and the performance of good works. These are carried out *visitando, corrigendo, puniendo, sacramenta ecclesiae ministrando*. His obligations will be before his eyes at all times, *ne reperiatur negligens, dormiens vel dormitans*.

1. Hostiensis, *Lectura*, ad c. *Cum satis*, 4, X, *de off. archid.*, I, 23 ad v. *animarum*.
2. E. H. Fischer, 'Büssgewalt, Pfarrzwang und Beichtvaterwahl nach dem Dekret Gratians' in *Tubinger Theologischen Quartalschrift*, 1954, vol. CXXXIV, pp 38–82, claims (p. 51, n. 47) that *juridictio ad audiendas confessiones* is inherent in ordination itself, and not in the *executio*. I cannot share this point of view, which, so far as I am aware, has no foundation in the texts.
3. St Antoninus, *Summa Theologica*, p. 3, vol. 19, c. 6, de Archidiaconatu, § 1.

Finally, he has power to invoke the aid of the secular arm against recalcitrants. He has the right to tithe, which will provide him with the necessities of life.[1]

An examination of the commentaries on this long description reveals nothing new, so I shall do no more than just mention them.

There is one further point to discuss – the relationship between the priesthood and the episcopate. As I have already observed, contrary to what the theologians of the period were prepared to admit, the canonists made the episcopate a distinct Order from the priesthood.[2]

Rufinus, however, did not share this opinion: *episcopatus enim, et huiusmodi non proprie sunt ordines, sed dignitates*.[3] Furthermore, we have seen that when he names the various types of prelacy, he distinguishes bishops from priests *ex dignitate consecrationis*, whereas he distinguishes deacons from subdeacons *ex dignitate ordinis*.[4] Other writers, while upholding the existence of the nine Orders, asserted, however, that no one could be validly consecrated bishop if he had not previously been ordained priest. This is also the sense of the customary gloss on the Decretals, and it goes on to say that if such a bishop had been ordained priest without having received the diaconate or the subdiaconate, he could not confer those two Orders, since *nemo dat quod non habet*.[5]

This latter principle, which we have already met, is invoked

1. Hostiensis, *Summa Aurea, ad tit. de poenit. et remiss.* 1. V, n. 14. See, e.g. the Commentary by Antony de Butrio, in c. *Omnis utriusque*, 12, X, de poenit. et remiss., V, 38.

2. cf. St Raymond, *op. cit.*, p. 111; F. Gillmann, *Zur Lebre der Scholastik vom Spender der Firmung und des Weihesakraments*, Paderborn, 1920 (cited subsequently: F. Gillmann, 'Spender'), p. 9, n. 1; p. 40, n. 3; p. 80, n. 2; p. 85, n. 1; Hostiensis, *Summa Aurea ad tit. de ord. ab episcopa qui renunt. episc.*, n. 1.

3. Rufinus, *ad d.* 21: he adds: *omnes Apostoli sacerdotes erant, extra quem ordinem nullus superior invenitur.*   4. cf. *supra.*

5. Customary Gloss, *ad c. Tue*, un., X, de clerico per saltum promoto, V, 29, V, ministrare: 'Vin (centius) dicit quod bene recipit quis sacrum ordinem etiam si nullum habeat de minoribus, preter episcopalem, quem nemo recipere potest nisi sit saltem sacerdos . . . Sed quid si ordinatur in episcopum pretermisso diaconatu vel subdiaconatu? Episcopus est, dum tamen fuerit sacerdos, sed illum ordinem quem non habuit, aliis conferre non potuit.'

in support of a theory which is well-nigh forgotten today in spite of the article (almost unobtainable) which Mgr Gillmann devoted to it.[1]

Can a priest confirm? Can he confer major Orders – the priest-hood? The question arises in connection with a text in Gratian's Decretum, in which St Gregory the Great allows the validity of the sacrament of confirmation administered by some Sicilian priests.[2]

Since confirmation is a *sacramentum dignitatis* like Orders, it is easy to pass from the one to the other, and an appeal is made to the text from St Jerome in which he states that at the beginning every priest was a bishop.[3] I will trace the develop-ment of this question.

Most writers, relying on a passage in the Decretum, assert that any priest can confer tonsure. Bertrand and Henry Suso alone are of the contrary opinion. What the priest confers, they state, is not ordination, but simply the *executio*.[4] Abbots who had received their abbatial benediction as well as *chorepiscopi* could confer the first three minor Orders. Most writers from the beginning of the thirteenth century, following Huguccio, admit that the Pope, by virtue of his *plenitudo potestatis*, could give the priest power to confer the Order of acolyte, major Orders, and confirmation. For, they said, anyone could give what he had received, provided he had been equipped with the necessary *habilitas* by the Pope.[5] Several of them even admit that a con-firmed layman could give confirmation.[6] The principle to which they appealed was so firmly rooted in accepted teaching, that they began to ask how a pagan or a Jew could validly baptise.[7]

1. F. Gillmann, *Spender*, cf. note 2, p. 213.
2. c. *Pervenit*, 1, dist. 95.
3. c. *Legimus*, 24, dist. 93: St Jerome, q. 146 ad Evang., 1.
4. dist. 23, c. 20. cf. Hostiensis, *Summa Aurea*, de ord. ab episcopo . . . , 1; St Raymond, *op. cit.*, p. 107.
5. F. Gillmann, *Spender*, p. 7 (Huguccio), 31 (Laurence the Spaniard), 32 (Silvester), 33–4 (Vincent the Spaniard), 39 (John the Teuton), 42 (Tancredius), 88 (Innocent IV), 97 (Guy de Baysio).
6. F. Gillmann, *Spender*, p. 33.
7. *ibid.*, p. 31, n. 1 (ex *Summa Monacensis*, ad c. 1, C. I, v. si non habent; the same text is found in *Summa Quid sit symonia*, Sem Liège, 6N15, f 137v ad C. I, q. 1).

Basically, the reasoning was as follows: once the fact that priests have administered valid confirmation is admitted, how can this extension of power bestowed by the Pope be justified, and why should it be restricted to confirmation? It was therefore necessary to infer that the Pope could act in such a way that there would be a true sacrament thereafter and within defined limits, where previously there would have been no sacrament at all without his intervention. This inference did not go unexpressed, and there is at least one parallel case – the Pope gave permission to the English to contract marriages which were valid even when the parties were within the third degree of consanguinity. Without this permission there would have been no sacrament.[1] Ergo, this reasoning, which appears to us to be rather forced, is more easily understood if we remember the parallel traditionally drawn between marriage and the bond uniting a bishop or a priest to his church: the bishop is espoused to his church, etc.

All are agreed that a confirmation or an ordination performed by a priest without express authority would be null, while according to several writers, the Pope could not prevent a bishop who observed the prescribed rites from conferring valid confirmation or ordination. They said that the power of ordination and confirmation were inherent in the *officium* of the episcopal Orders, whereas the priest could not confer them except *ex demandatione et amminiculo ordinis*.[2] The pope alone could grant this power. The bishop himself was able to delegate what pertained to the power of jurisdiction which was conveyed *sola voluntate et verbo*; the transmission of things which fell within the power of Orders required an action – i.e. unction – as well.

1. F. Gillmann, *Spender*, p. 5, n. 1 (Huguccio, ad c. *Pervenit*, 1, dist. 95): 'Sed numquid permissio pape potuit facere ut esset sacramentum quod alias non esset sacramentum? Utique, et potuit, et potest, et fecit, et facit sicut in matrimonio Anglorum ex permissione pape contracto in tertio gradu, quod alias non esset matrimonium, ut C. XXXV, q. 3. Quedam lex . . ., similiter et in hoc sacramcnto, quod alias presbiteri non possent conferre.'
2. F. Gillmann, *Spender*, pp 32–3 and p. 42 n. (3): 'Nota quod ubi quis habet aliquid ex officio habiti ordinis, confert licet prohibitus; si vero ex demandatione et aminiculo ordinis, tunc prohibitus non confert'.

How then could the Pope convey it *sola voluntate et verbo*? The answer which is no answer at all, is that the Pope is above the laws.[1]

In conclusion, I should like to explain a passage which has scandalised Mgr Saltet so much. In his opinion, Innocent IV, Hostiensis, Bernard of Compostella the Younger would have extended the Pope's power over the sacraments so far that in their view the Pope had power to nullify ordinations and confirmations and all the other sacraments except baptism.[2] But if we look at their actual words, we find that they are more moderate. The Pope cannot take away (a bishop's) power to confirm, but he can regulate the exercise of this power, *ut in forma et in personis et in diebus a quibus et in quibus debeat*. He can only do this for a very grave reason, and must resort to the solemn form of the *constitutio*. He acts then by virtue of the power given him by Christ: *Quidquid ligaveris. . . .* However, if such constitution asserts the invalidity of sacraments conferred in violation of the norms thus established, it seems clear that this would have to be accepted.[3] I do not think there is anything revolutionary here, especially if we remember that this power, when exercised, seems plainly to be a vicarial power; furthermore we know that Innocent IV, dissociating himself from

---

1. Customary Gloss, *ad c. Aqua*, 9, X, de consec. eccl., III, 40, v. iurisdictionis: 'Sed que est ratio quare illa que sunt iurisdictionis possit (episcopus) committere clericis inferioris gradus et non illa que sunt ordinis demandare? Hec potest esse ratio: sola voluntate et verbo committitur, sive delegatus fuerit sive ordinarius, et revocatur; sed collatio sacramentorum non confertur sola voluntate et verbo, immo facto est opus quia necessaria est visibilis unctio et exterior, que est signum interioris unctionis in corde.' Customary Gloss, *ad c. Quanto*, 3, X, de consuet., I, 4, v. reservata: 'Arg. huius decretalis videtur quod papa non possit hoc delegare simplici sacerdoti, sed papa non subicitur legibus . . . unde potest committere simplici sacerdoti'.

2. L. Saltet, *op. cit.*, p. 340. cf. F. Gillmann, *Spender*, p. 87, n. (1). The subject is Innocent IV's commentary at c. Quanto, 3, X, de consuet., I, 4.

3. This is the text: 'Et quidem satis bene videntur dicere in eo quod dicunt quod possunt facere constitutiones Summi Pontifices super premissis et, eis factis, si constituatur quod non valeant sacramenta a talibus collata, non valebunt.'

his predecessors, admitted the validity of the sacraments conferred by heretics after their deposition and degradation.[1]

These passages raise certain questions. The solutions which
have been put forward recently do not appear to me to be the
right ones. The difference between the bishop and the priest is
in the realm of the sacred, and not merely in that of jurisdiction.
In certain clearly defined cases, the Pope can by an act of jurisdiction (personal or vicarial?) 'set free' the powers of the priest,
but this does not change their nature, or lessen the distance
separating the priest from the bishop, who alone remains the
ordinary minister of holy Orders and confirmation.[2]

Stability of doctrine about sacramental matter had not been
reached in the thirteenth century. Unction had for long been
considered an essential part of the sacrament. It was the sign
of inward anointing – i.e. character – which the apostles had
instituted as the rite conveying Orders when they anointed
James Bishop of Jerusalem.[3] The imposition of hands, taken in
the material sense of the word, was also taken to be of the
'essence' of the sacrament, but, generally speaking, the tradition of the instruments was not. Otherwise, as was observed, the
presence of the archdeacon would be essential to ordination.
But conclusions on these points, to be certain, would necessitate
numerous studies, particularly on the exact meaning, in the
terminology of the period, of the word substantial. St Raymond
complains about the casualness of the canonists.[4]

1. Customary Gloss, in c. *Si quis presbyter*, 2, X, de clerico excomm.
ministr., III, 27, v. degradatus. 'Sed pone degradatum celebrare,
numquid conficit? . . . R. dixit quod talis non conficit: potuit enim
Ecclesia ei auferre illam potestatem quam contulit quamvis non posset
caracter auferri . . . Lau (rentius) Ala (nus) and Tan (credus) dicunt
et melius quod bene conficit depositus sicut hereticus . . . nec papa
potuit auferre illam virtutem, et hoc verum credo.' Innocent IV, in
hoc c.: 'Sacerdos enim depositus conficit: in modum enim privati
suffragii potest.'

2. cf. J. Beyer, *Les instituts séculiers*, Desclée de Brouwer, 1954,
pp 152–9, 162.

3. cf. F. Gillmann, *Spender und ausseres Zeichen der Bischofs weihe
nach Huguccio*, Wurtzburg, 1922.

4. St Raymond, *op. cit.*, p. 110: '*Quidam tamen posuerunt hic
sompnia sua et nichil invenerunt.*'

These are, then, briefly, some reflections prompted by a first reading of the texts. We are still far from a comprehensive synthesis and I have done no more than erect a few signposts. But the problems raised by the state of canonical teaching at the turn of the thirteenth century seemed to me to be worthy of note.

CHAPTER XI

THE COUNCIL OF TRENT AND HOLY
ORDERS

A. DUVAL, O.P.

DURING its twenty-third session (15th July 1563), the Council
of Trent made a solemn pronouncement stating the essential
elements of the Catholic faith relative to the sacrament of Orders,[1]
ad condemnandos errores nostri temporis. But side by side with
this dogmatic decree, a decree *De Reformatione* drew attention
to a certain number of canonical provisions touching both the
actual administration of the sacrament of Orders, and the exercise of the powers conferred by it.[2] Indeed there are few of the
numerous reforming decrees issued between 1546 and 1563
which do not concern priestly activities more or less directly.

The second group of texts is not merely the practical application, the pastoral corollary, as it were, of the doctrine expounded
in the first. For these texts imply a theology which is not strictly
that expressed in the dogmatic decree. It is clearly not opposed
to it, indeed it assumes it, but it incorporates more or less

1. *Concilium Tridentinum.* Diariorum, actorum, epistularum, tracta-
tuum nova collectio. Edidit Societas Goerresiana, Freiburg, 1901 and
ff, vol. IX, pp 620–2. Throughout this article, 'CT' is used for
references to this monumental edition.

The text of the dogmatic decree of the 23rd Session is to be found
in Denzinger *Enchiridion symbolorum* 956a–68. Or, with French
translation and commentary, in A. Michel, 'Les Décrets du Concile
de Trente' (Héfélé-Leclercq, *Histoire des Conciles*, vol. X, 1st part),
Paris, 1938, pp 478–94. Failing these, reference may be made to the
same author's article 'Ordre' in the *Dict. de Théol. cath.*, vol. XI B,
col. 1354–63.

In English, *The Canons and Decrees of the Council of Trent*, tr.
J. Waterworth, Dolman, 1848; *The Canons and Decrees of the Council
of Trent*, H. J. Schroeder, Herder, 1950.

2. CT., IX, 623–30.

coherently other elements as well. It is a theology which is trying to get its bearings, which is in the process of being worked out, inspired by those pastoral efforts which were going on at the time, of which the council itself was to a certain extent a result. In fact, on the practical level, particularly as far as the administration of the sacrament of Orders and its exercise were concerned, the Council of Trent is as much a point of culmination as of departure. So many of its decisions are no more than the re-enactment, the pin-pointing and the extension to the whole Church of the West of measures taken by individual bishops (e.g. the *Constitutiones* of Matteo Giberti for his diocese of Verona in 1542), or by councils (London 1555, Cologne 1536, Sens 1528); and often these same decisions are the response to the petitions for reform which came in from very different areas. There was the famous *Consilium de Emendanda Ecclesia* presented to Paul III on 9th March 1537 by the select committee presided over by Cardinal Contarini.[1] There were the proposals put forward by the Bishop of Vienne, Jean Fabri (1536),[2] or by his successor, Frederick Nausea (1543),[3] the various memoranda by the Spaniard, John of Avila, between 1551 and 1561,[4] the petitions by the Polish bishop, Stanislaus Hosius (1559),[5] the aspirations of the French prelates assembled at Poissy (1561),[6] etc. Behind these texts are men, situations, streams of life and thought.

It is my aim to consider the doctrinal implications of these pastoral aspirations, the demands of this quickening theology, and the dogmatic definitions of the council, but this brief outline will need to be followed by further study if things are to be brought perfectly into focus.

I. THE PASTORAL PROBLEM OF THE PRIESTHOOD AT THE TIME OF THE COUNCIL OF TRENT

The Fathers at the Council of Trent quite naturally employed the gospel terminology of the Good Shepherd to describe the

1. CT. XII, 131–45.   2. *ibid.*, IV, 10–23.
3. *ibid.*, XII, 364–426.
4. Texts edited in *Miscellanea Comillas*, 3 (1945) and 13 (1950).
5. CT. XIII, 424–6.   6. *ibid.*, 501–17.

actual condition of the flock of Christ. True shepherds were not so numerous as the hirelings, and had to reckon with the wolves and the thieves as well.

1. The hirelings

There were too many priests. I ought to begin this study with some statistics, but will restrict myself to the complaints uttered before and during the Council of Trent *super effrenato sacerdotum numero, quos hodie turba contemptibiles reddit.*[1] In some dioceses the number of priests had become so great that a veritable priestly proletariat had grown up[2] which lived in material and moral destitution. The subject of this swarm of *nudos ac mendicos* priests, deplored by the Council of Sens in 1528,[3] was raised at Trent in 1547[4] and again in 1562.[5] More widespread, perhaps, was the harm caused by their moral wretchedness. The adage popular in the streets of Naples at that time is more telling than any scandalous story: '*Se vuoi andare all'inferno, fatti prete!*'[6] And in addition, there were innumerable incompetent and ignorant priests[7] and in some cases it could not even be hoped that they might one day fittingly perform the functions of the minor Orders.[8]

The causes behind this redundancy and mediocrity were manifold, but from the top to the bottom of the hierarchy the main reason was that service of Mammon denounced by Cardinal Contarini in 1537.[9] Rich or poor, too many priests had only

1. The phrase occurs in a scheme of canons proposed to the Fathers at Trent for discussion on 10th May 1563, CT. IX, 481, 1, 20. cf. CT. VI, 553-7; 595, 6-8, 29-31; 603, 45; XIII, 579, 12, etc.
2. cf. Bibliographical note in CT. VI, 553, n. 8.
3. Mansi, XXXII, 1185 C.   4. CT. VI, 594, 13-16.
5. L. Beccadelli's account, 29th January 1562. CT. XIII, 579, 12.
6. cf. Piero Chiminelli, *San Gaetano Thiene cuore della riforma cattolica*, Rome 1948, p. 374.
7. '*Tot apparent imperiti et indocti sacerdotes, ut infinitus prope sit eorum numerus*' (November 1547, CT. VI, 596, 9-10).
8. In a programme of reform laid before the council before 9th March 1562, we read: 'an interim, dum haec executioni mandantur, expediret, ut ociosorum sacerdotum multitudo, exclusis, qui adeo inepti sunt, ut nulla spes esse possit, eos unquam ecclesie profuturos, exerceret munia inferiorum ordinum' (CT. XIII, 608, 29).
9. He said it would be possible to give effect to such measures

received Orders as hirelings in search of position rather than devotion. Human frailty apart – for this is unavoidable in any system – the greatest share of responsibility lay at the door of the benefice system. This is proved by the many adjustments to which it was subjected in the course of the council. Adjustments, yes, but not a radical overhaul, despite many pious hopes.[1]

2. *True pastors*

The very same people who were realistic enough at the Council of Trent to see the lamentable state of so many priests were also aware that some were sufficiently zealous to rise to the demands of their vocation. A recent book has shown how much the sixteenth century helped to restore the ideals of the episcopate.[2] The same pastoral revival brought with it a rediscovery of Christian priesthood. A new kind of priest appeared of which John of Avila in Spain and St Gaetan of Thiene in Italy were typical examples. At all events, both of them had a following.

John of Avila[3] was neither a religious nor an incumbent. He had no immediate cure of souls. But there were many priests like him, and his grace was to arouse them all to a sense of their pastoral responsibilities. His effect upon the clergy was great,

---

concerning cardinals as he proposed 'si vellemus abjicere servitutem mammonae et Christo tantum servire' (CT. XII, 138, 22). This applied to all ranks of the hierarchy.

1. As that of the Spanish Dominican, Martin de Mendoza, Bishop of Tortosa, 4th June 1563: 'ecclesiam non posse ad veram reformationem restitui, nisi reducatur ad paucos et pauperes' (CT. IX, 563, 3–4).

2. Hubert Jedin, *Das Bischofsideal der katholischen Reformation*, Breslau, 1942. This book has been translated into French, with some additional matter, by Paul Broutin, S.J. *L'Evêque dans la tradition pastorale du XVI siècle*, Bruges-Bruxelles, 1953.

3. cf. Luis Sala Balust, *Obras completas del B. Maestro Juan de Avila*, Biblioteca de autores cristianos, 2 vol. Madrid, 1952 and 1953. A full biography will be found there, as well as the first part of a biography which gives a completely fresh angle on its subject. In French, see Bl. Jean d'Avila, *Audi, Filia*, translation, introduction and notes by Jacques Cherprenet (Collection 'Les Maîtres de la spiritualité chrétienne'), Paris, Aubier, 1954. cf. also A. Duval, 'Quelques Idées du bienheureux Jean d'Avila sur le ministère pastoral et la formation du clergé, in *Supplement de la Vie spirituelle* no. 6, 15th August 1948, pp 121–53.

not merely because he gathered a little band of preachers around him, but because of his examples and his counsels. In the Spanish dioceses in which he worked he was by way of being the specialist in retreats for priests. In Italy, the influence of Gaetan[1] obtained the same result by different methods. Although the group he established quickly found its way back into the ranks of the canonical religious orders, his purpose was none other than to promote the observance of the sacred canons in the lives of the clergy.[2] Thus, he was the precursor of the various families of regular clerks which appeared during this century, and, thanks to his example, Rome, Brescia, Venice, Verona, Vicenza, Naples, all knew what it was to have priests who were conscious of their priestly responsibilities. Others might make a show of their titles, but he knew but one – that of 'poor priest'.[3] Apart from the vows of religion and a certain style of poverty, the priestly ideals of Gaetan were those which inspired his friend Matteo Giberti in his remarkable efforts to revitalise the diocese of Verona.[4]

What were the marks of this type of priest? He saw himself committed to all those functions which had been alloted to him on the day of his ordination, *offere, baptizare, benedicere, praedicare, praeesse*; he was the minister of the sacraments and the minister of the word. He was a man of the Mass. St Gaetan celebrated daily, which at that time was still by no means commonplace, and John of Avila saw in this intimate commerce which

1. cf. R. de Maulde La Clavière, *Saint Gaetan* (Collection 'Les Saints'), Paris, 1902. The Italian translation has additional material (1911). Also Pio Paschini, *S. Gaetano Thiene, Gian Pietro Carafa e le origini dei chierici regolari teatini*, Rome, 1926; Piero Chiminelli, *San Gaetano Thiene cuore della riforma cattolica*, Rome, 1948; F. Andreu, *Le lettere di San Gaetano da Thiene* ('Studi e testi', 177), Rome, 1954.

2. 'Non fare nuova Religione, il che in verità non vogliamo ne possiamo: noi non vogliamo essere altro che chierici viventi secondo i sacri Canoni.' Letter from J. P. Carafa to M. Giberti, 1st January 1533, cited by Chiminelli, *op. cit.*, p. 416.

3. He signs his letters thus between 1520 and 1529. cf. F. Andreu, *Le lettere di San Gaetano*, pp 31, 34, 38, 51, 57, 62, 67.

4. cf. *Jo. Mattaei Giberti opera omnia*, Verona, 1733. This edition has an important introduction on the life and the reforming work of Giberti. For a modern bibliography, see *Enciclopedia cattolica*, vol. 6, p. 3, col. 384.

the priest had with God the imperious requirement of sanctity, a sanctity which was also demanded from him because he was a man of prayer.[1] Certainly these themes were often employed in the various manuals for priests which had been published since the invention of printing: *Liber sacerdotum, Enchiridion sacerdotum, De Vita et moribus sacerdotum*, etc., a literature which as yet does not seem to have been catalogued or studied systematically.[2]

But a priest of this type was equally a man of the word of God. Writing the first life of John of Avila, his contemporary and friend, Louis of Granada was well justified when he claimed to be offering to his readers 'a picture of a preacher of the gospel'. In 1525 the people of Rome cried, 'A miracle!' when they saw the first Theatines preaching, so unusual had the spectacle of a preacher dressed not in white, black or brown homespun, but in soutane and surplice, become. 'But the priest is made for preaching', thought Gaetan and his followers. To preach with the tongue, certainly, but also to carry out the work of the word by every means, in that close amity and collaboration of clergy and laity organised together under the lovely title of *Oratorio del divino amore*,[3] which he established in every city he lived in, with that care for the poor and the sick so characteristic of those days when the hospital was the acknowledged meeting-place for men of God as the printer's workshop was for men of letters. Having witnessed these things in Italy Reginald Pole did not forget them when Catholicism was restored in England.[4]

1. See nos. 1 and 2 in the *Platicas a Sacerdotes, Oberas completas*, pp 1284–1312.

2. A number are indicated in Fr Broutin, *op. cit.*

3. cf. Pio Paschini, 'Le compagnie del divino amore e la beneficenza pubblica nei primi decenni del cinquecento' in *Tre ricerche sulla storia della Chiesa nel pretridentina*, Brescia, 1948, pp 56–103, 269–95.

4. 'Huic autem praedicationis officio ita plane satisfactum erit, si non solum publice concio habeatur, sed privatim etiam pastor, quos ex grege sibi commisso a recta fide, vel a bonis moribus aberrare cognoverit, eos ad se vocatos paterne et cum omni caritatis affectu docendo, monendo, hortando, ac, si opus fuerit, deterrendo ad catholicam fidem, et rectam vivendi normam reducere conetur; qui vero et in fide et in moribus recte vivunt, in sancto eorum instituto confirmet.' (Reformatio Angliae (1556), Decretum IV. Mansi, XXXIII, col. 1021.)

The first superiors of the Theatines considered the ministry of the word of sufficient importance to justify devoting less time to the official prayer. Because of this, and the care of the sick, they obtained Papal permission (1529) to cut down the office to a minimum of seven psalms (or seven Paters and two Credos),[1] a privilege which subsequently passed to other regular clerks like the Barnabites,[2] and which the Bishop of Verona also obtained for his clergy.[3] It is also worthy of note that when he sketches an authentic outline of priestly spirituality at the beginning of his *Constitutiones* Giberti makes it clear that the performance of sacred functions demands sanctity just as much as do pastoral responsibilities,[4] and yet it is solely because of these pastoral responsibilities that the *Constitutiones* recall priests to their duty of perfection.[5]

I could quote other examples of this anxiety to link the

1. Brief of 21st January 1529. Text in Paschini *S. Gaetano Thiene*, pp 159–60.

2. The privileges mentioned in Paul III's Bull approving the Order in 1535, and in a similar Bull of Julius III in 1549. Texts in O. Premoli, *Storia dei Barnabiti nel cinquecento*, Rome 1913, pp 462–501.

3. cf. Paschini, *S. Gaetano Thiene*, p. 111.

4. 'Pia ad sacerdotes nostros ad sancte honesteque vivendum adhortatio' in *Jo. Mattaei Giberti opera omnia*, pp C–CI.

5. 'Hortatio ad honestam vitam. Quum clericorum honestas a capitis vertice usque ad plantam pedis versetur, nos omnes summa ope niti decet, ut nominis, professionisque nostrae memores agnoscamus, cum in Sanctorum loco simus, necessitatem bene vivendi, non licentiam peccandi esse assecutos, ne sic laicis ullam praebeamus ansam peccandi, aut jure male sentiant de clericali professione, vel hinc occasionem accipiant in vitiis perseverandi. Iccirco in primis a nobis elaborandum est, ut sanctorum opere exerceamus: luceant que coram hominibus opera nostra, simusque illud sal evangelicum in ministerio vigilantes, et solliciti, plantantes, evellentes, dissipantes, et cum summo studio aedificantes, quae ad pietatem proficiunt: aliter enim nobis alios corrigere volentibus facile objicietur, Medica cura teipsum . . . ' (Constitutiones, 1542, Tit. I, cap. I, *Jo. Mattaei Giberti opera*, p. 3.

'Hortamus igitur, et monemus clericos omnes, tam religiosos, quam seculares jurisdictioni nostrae suppositos, ut memores se quasi ad sagittam signum positos in primis eos, quibus praesunt, bono exemplo pascere studeant . . . ' (*ibid*., cap. XVI. *opera*, p. 8). These obligations are detailed in the chapters which follow.

ministry of the word with the whole life of the priest.[1] Far from being opposed to the administration of the sacraments, it is one of its components: the preaching activity of Gaetan is, in a sense, only one aspect of his eucharistic zeal. For him the consecrated Host holds the heart of that burning fire which Christ came to kindle on earth. 'I shall never be happy until I see Christians coming to the priest like starvelings in search of food.'[2] And in the canons of the Council of Cologne (1536) reprinted at Verona in 1543 for the benefit of Matteo Giberti's priests, they could read a formal request to preach whenever they administered the sacraments.[3]

3. *Wolves and thieves*

The work of the true pastors was rendered more difficult because the negligence of the hirelings had left the flock unprotected against the depredations of the wolves and the thieves. Thus, the council mentioned all those who, without any authority or mandate other than popular or administrative nomination, arrogated to themselves the title of ministers of the Church.[4] Heresy, which

1. 'Reformatio Angliae' (1556). Decretum V, De vita et honestate clericorum. 'Quia vero exemplum vitae magnum auctoritatem verbo affert, estque velut quoddam praedicandi genus; ob id curandum est iis, qui aliis praesunt, ut ceteris, cum mororum probitate, vitaeque sanctitate, tum ea propriam domum recte gubernandi laude, quam in Episcopis Apostolus requirit, antecellant . . .'. (Mansi, XXXIII, 1022.) cf. also the programme of Reform of the French bishops at Poissy (1561) in which 'good example' 'in omnia patientia et doctrina' is counted as one of the priest's functions (CT. XIII, 512, 7).

2. '. . . mai sero contento finche io non vedo li cristiani andar dal Sacerdote come famelici a cibarse . . .' (Letter of 1st January 1523). F. Andreu, *Le lettere di San Gaetano*, p. 56.

3. 'Quia igitur in sacramentis aliud videtur, atque aliud agitur instruendus est populus in cuiuslibet exhibitione, quod in eiuscemodi religioso arcano (id enim sacramentum sonat) agatur. Cum enim in sacramentis istis per signa quaedam sensibilia infundatur insensibilis gratia, congruens externis signis excitanda est fidelium fides et devotio in Deum, ut credentes ac divinum mysterium intelligentes ad Dei ac Salvatoris nostri Iesu Christi participandam gratiam accedant. Quod fiet, cum parochus sub administrationem cuiuslibet sacramenti, sacra concione populum breviter admonuerit quid in ea re agatur, (*Canones Concilii provincialis Coloniensis* 1536, Verona, 1543, fol. 29, v–30r).

4. See the dogmatic decree of 15th July 1563, cap. IV, CT. IX, 621, 21–5. Denzinger, n. 960.

had shattered the unity of Christ's flock was also responsible for creating confusion in the minds of priests and people alike about the nature of the sacrament of Orders and the powers conferred by it.

However little influence the lamentable moral condition of so many priests could have had on the development of Luther's spiritual crisis, it was nevertheless used by him as a powerful lever in his revolt against the Church. There were plenty of people to remind the Fathers at the Council of Trent about it. The principal cause of the havoc wrought by heresy in Germany, wrote the Emperor Ferdinand in 1560, had been the moral corruption of the clergy. 'If there is an upright priesthood, the whole Church flourishes, but if it is corrupt all faith and virtue decay.'[1] A reform of the clergy was necessary if only to avoid giving the weaker brethren a pretext for going over to the heretics.[2]

The serious thing about this debacle was that the whole Catholic conception of priesthood was thrown into the melting-pot. Undoubtedly the doctrine of justification was at the heart of Lutheran thought, but as the Lutheran movement developed and spread, propaganda and controversy were quickly concentrated on the Mass and the cultus of the eucharist – everything hinged on that, as the Bishop of Vienne declared on the eve of the Council of Trent.[3] The sacrificial character of the Mass was denied, and so there could be no priesthood. There was only one sacrifice, that of Calvary, and there was no priesthood save the

1. 'Cum inde sit incipienda medicatio, unde primum ortus est morbus, constet autem, morum in clero corruptionem primam causam mali hujus fuisse: consequens est, eorundem correctionem primam causam boni esse oportere. Si enim sacerdotium integrum fuerit, tota floret ecclesia; si autem corruptum sit, omnium fides et virtus marcida est. Si enim sacerdos, qui est unctus, peccaverit, faciet et populum delinquere. Vix etenim malevoli seu schismatici in ordinem redigi poterunt, nisi signis virtutum manifestis per clerum ad hoc inviténtur cessentque signa, quae hactenus fuerunt et adhuc sunt causa schismatis, et notabilis denique sequatur morum reformatio.' (CT. VIII, 45–6.)

2. 'ne infirmioribus occasio detur ad haereticos transfugiendi' (Stanislaus Hosius, 1559. CT. XIII, 425, 11).

3. 'ibi enim cardo rerum vertitur' (to the nuncio Morone, December 1536. CT. IV, 57, 14).

purely spiritual power by which every man united himself with that sacrifice and offered it to God. This power was possessed by every Christian. The only 'ministers' to be recognised were the ministers of the word of God, who had no need of any ordination or commission for their preaching.

The re-appraisal of preaching as one of the functions proper to the priest was the anxious concern of all the reformers, whether faithful to the Church or dissident. But the unacceptable excesses of the heretics in this rehabilitation of the word called for a vigorous reaction on the part of the Church in the name of the integrity of that message entrusted to her care by the Lord.

Itself a result of that pastoral awakening which stirred the Church during the sixteenth century, the Council of Trent showed how important and serious the question was by devoting long months to the elaboration of a weighty dogmatic work. The flock was entitled to pure nourishment. With its keen sense of responsibility to the flock, its realistic understanding of the clergy, the vast majority of whom were far from being leavened by the new ferment, how was the council going to approach all the theoretical and practical, dogmatic and canonical problems of the sacrament of Orders?

2. TRENT, THE SACRAMENT OF HOLY ORDERS, AND THE MINISTRY OF THE WORD

The two decrees of 15th July 1563 were the culmination of work begun in September 1562.[1] In fact, this is the third occasion on

1. On 18th September 1562, seven articles or propositions taken from Protestant theologians (CT. IX, n. 2, p. 5) were apportioned out to three groups of theologians for examination (*ibid.*, p. 6). This examination took place between 23rd September and 2nd October (*ibid.*, pp 7–36); after this, a commission of eight Fathers was nominated to draw up a draft of doctrinal exposition and of canons (*ibid.*, n. 19, pp 37–8).

This draft was presented on 13th October (n. 20, pp 38–41) and examined in the full session from 13th to 20th October (n. 22–3, pp 43–101).

A new draft (the previous one amended) was put forward on 3rd November (n. 25, pp 105–7), and examined from 3rd November to 9th December (n. 48–70, pp 169–226). Further texts or notes drawn

which the sacrament of Orders had been on the agenda. In December 1551 to January 1552, under Julius III, a scheme of eight canons had been worked out.[1] The various causes which shortly led to the adjournment of the council prevented its reaching a final decision about them or giving them its approbation. Previously, under Paul III, similar work had been done between April and November 1547;[2] but how could it be brought to a successful conclusion when the council was practically reduced to its Italian members only, after it had been transferred to Bologna? The reports of the various committees or study sessions make it possible to follow the continuity of the proceedings throughout the three periods of the council.

1. *The inquiry*

Concern that the office of preaching should be rehabilitated in the priesthood appears both in the decrees themselves and in the process which led up to their promulgation.

---

up in December and January called for fresh modifications. The full session of 9th July 1563 (n. 218, pp 601–2) decided on the final form of the decree, which was solemnly promulgated in the 23rd session on 15th July 1563 (n. 224, pp 621–2).

Canons dealing with abuses in the administration of the sacrament of Orders were detailed in a scheme of seventeen chapters put forward 10th May 1563 (CT. IX, n. 165, pp 477–85) and discussed from 12th May to 16th June (n. 167–78, 181–96, 200–14, pp 487–511, 522–48, 553–90). This text, amended once (n. 217, pp 592–601) was subjected to a final examination from 10th to 12th July (n. 219–21, pp 603–16) before being solemnly promulgated 15th July (n. 224, pp 623–32).

1. cf. A. Theiner, *Acta Genuina concilii tridentini*, Agram, 1874, vol. I, p. 603.

2. According to a work by the General of the Augustinians, Seripando (CT. VI, pp 90–2), four propositions taken from Protestant writers were discussed by the theologians between 29th April and 7th May (*ibid.*, pp 99–121).

As a result of this work and of two drafts, one of which was introduced by Ambrosius Pelargus (pp 128–9), and the other by Bishop Cornelio Musso (pp 309–10), a text of five canons was presented to the Fathers on 21st July (pp 308–9). Discussed from 27th to 29th July in general session (pp 311–20), then from 17th to 26th August by the bishops theologian alone (pp 371–4, 378–80, 384–6, 391–400), this draft received a new form (pp 400–1). But it was pigeon-holed. From 15th to 28th November of the same year, 1547, several working sessions were also devoted to an investigation into the abuses connected with the administration of the sacrament of Orders (pp 594–615).

(*a*) The first reforming decree (17th June 1546) dealt with preaching.[1] It envisaged not only bishops, for whom that was their principal function, *praecipuum episcoporum munus*, but all those who had cure of souls, so that the cry of *Lamentations* should be heard no longer: '*Parvuli petierunt panem, et non erat qui frangeret eis*' (Lam. 4, 4). In November 1563 it was considered opportune in the penultimate group of reforming decrees to draw attention to the measures taken in June 1546, and to stress their importance afresh.[2]

Prompted perhaps by a decision of the Council of Sens (1528),[3] the council authorised bishops to compel unlearned rectors, even at their own expense, to take vicars sufficiently instructed to impart to the faithful in their place the food of the divine word to which they were entitled.[4]

Were all pastors obliged to reside in their diocese or their parish? If they did not, then, according to the decree of 13th January 1547, they would not be able to watch over and govern their flocks aright.[5] But when the question came up again in 1563, the duty of residence was broadly linked with all the pastoral functions – to know the flock, to offer the sacrifice on its behalf, to feed it by preaching the divine word, by administering the sacraments and by the example of good works (the three activities included in the command *pascere*) and paternally to look after the poor.[6]

(*b*) In the opinion of the council one of the normal times for exercising his indispensable ministry was during the administration of the sacraments. What had already been said with reference to the Mass[7] was repeated and specified for all the sacraments:

1. CT. V, 241–3.
2. Session 24, 11th November 1563. *Canones reformationis generalis, canon quartus.* CT. IX, 981.
3. cf. Mansi XXXII, 1187A.
4. Session 21, 16th July 1562, decree *De Reformatione*, canon 6. CT. IX, 702, 38.
5. Session 6. *Decretum de residentia episcoporum et aliorum inferiorum*, cap. 1. CT. V, 802–3.
6. Session 23, 15th July 1563. *Decreta super reformatione*, canon 1. CT. IX, p. 623.
7. A propos the Mass in the vulgar tongue, decree of 17th

In order that the faithful people may approach to the reception of
the sacraments with greater reverence and devotion of mind, the holy
Synod enjoins on all bishops, that, not only when they are themselves
about to administer to the people, they shall first explain, in a manner
suited to the capacity of those who receive them, the efficacy and use
of the sacraments, but shall endeavour that the same be done piously
and prudently by every parish priest; and this even in the vulgar
tongue, if need be, and it can be conveniently done; and in accordance with the form which will be prescribed for each of the sacraments, by the holy Synod, in a catechism which the bishops shall
take care to have faithfully translated into the vulgar tongue, and to
have expounded to the people by all parish priests.[1]

(c) So we see that the council referred in advance to a catechism which would be published by its authority. It is very
noticeable that those who made great efforts towards clerical
reform in the sixteenth century were careful to round off their
work by publishing a catechism which enabled pastors to discharge their duty of teaching fittingly. John Gropper drew up
his *Enchiridion christianae institutionis* to meet the wishes of the
Council of Cologne (1536),[2] and Matteo Giberti recommended
it to his priests.[3] The Spanish Dominican Bartholomew Carranza, who assisted Reginald Pole at the Council of London in
1556, was inspired by its decrees[4] to compile the catechism
whose publication in his own country was so inauspicious for
him.[5] At Trent, this preoccupation with the catechism was

September 1562 (Session 22) on the sacrifice of the Mass, cap. 8,
CT. VIII, 961, 24. Denzinger, n. 946. On this point cf. H. Schmidt,
'Liturgie et Langue vulgaire: Le problème de la langue liturgique
chez les premiers Réformateurs et au Concile de Trente', *Analecta
gregoriana*, 53, Rome, 1950.

1. Session 24, 11th November 1563. *Decretum de reformatione*,
canon 7. CT. IX, 981–2. Compare this text with that of the Council of
Cologne previously quoted.

2. The Verona Edition of 1541 is entitled: *Institutio compendiaria
doctrinae christianae, ex concilio provinciali coloniensi*, and the work is
prefaced by a letter from the Archbishop of Cologne recommending it
to his clergy as the fulfilment of the promise made at the time of the
council.   3. cf. Jo. Mattaei Giberti, *opera*, pp xxxviii–xxxix.

4. *Reformatio Angliae*, Decretum, IV. Mansi, XXXIII, 1022B.

5. cf. *Comentarios sobre el catechismo christiano*, Anvers, 1558,
fol. III v. In at least two private letters, the future Archbishop of
Toledo makes explicit mention of the connection between his catechism
and the English council. On Carranza, cf. *Catholicisme*, II, 592–4.

shown on many occasions, and in March 1563 a commission was set up to go into the matter.[1] The catechism *ad parochos* published in 1566, was also characterised by this concern for not separating the preaching of the word of God from the frequenting of the sacraments, both of them being necessary supports for the Christian edifice of which Christ is the corner-stone.[2] According to this catechism, it is precisely in connection with the sacraments that pastors should do their utmost to bring all their knowledge and talents to bear in presenting to their flocks the different elements of Christian doctrine.[3] Among the times suitable for an explanation of baptism, for instance, the catechism particularly recommends the occasion of its actual administration when there is a sufficient number of the faithful present:

It will then be much easier to explain if not all, then at least one or other of the different aspects of the sacrament; and the faithful, on hearing the teaching, will see it expressed in the actual ceremonies of the baptism, which they will observe with piety and attention.[4]

(*d*) Finally, if here and there we find a very discreet allusion to the *Dominus pars hereditatis meae* to justify the claims of holiness in the lives of the clergy,[5] it is with the function of preaching that these claims are directly linked, for 'there is nothing that continually instructs others unto piety, and the service of God, more than the life and example of those who have dedicated themselves to the divine ministry'.[6] The

1. cf. the article 'Catechisme romain' in *Catholicisme*, II, 655–6.
2. Pastores . . . 'ostendent, totum christianum aedificium firmissimo quidem lapidis angularis fundamento inniti: verum, nisi verbi Dei praedicatione et sacramentorum usu undique fulciatur, magnopere verendum esse, ne, magna ex parte labefactum concidat; ut enim per sacramenta in vitam suscipimur, ita hoc veluti pabulo alimur, conservamur, augemur'. *Catechismi romani*, Pars 2a, de sacramentis in genere, n. 32. The original edition of 1556 had neither subdivisions nor headings. We are using Marietti's edition here. The passage quoted occurs on pp 143–4.
3. 'Quum omnis christianae doctrinae pars pastoris scientiam diligentiamque desiderat, tum sacramentorum disciplina, quae et Dei jussu necessaria, et utilitate uberrima est, parochi facultatem et industriam postulat singularem. . . .' (*ibid.*, n. 1, p. 125.)
4. *ibid.*, cap II, n. 2, pp 144–5.
5. e.g. the decree *De Reformatione* of 17th September 1562, CT. VIII, 965, 19–20.   6. *idem*, canon 1, CT. VIII, 965, 16–17.

example of good works is, with the preaching of the word and
the administration of the sacraments, one of the necessary elements in the pastoral task of those who have cure of souls;[1] but,
in the opinion of the council it is the life of every priest which
must be a preaching in itself.[2]

In documents which were subjected to so much scrutiny, so
many allusions to the ministry of the word do not occur by
chance. This preoccupation for linking priesthood and pastorate
together in practice is still more obvious in the conditions which
were laid down for admission to holy Orders in the canons – but
this 'liaison' was far from being imposed on all candidates:

(i) In the decree *De Reformatione* of 15th July, 1563, canon 13
lays down the conditions for the reception of the Orders of subdeacon and deacon. There must have been some instruction
relating to the exercise of the Order to be received, *'litteris, et iis,
quae ad ordinem exercendum pertinet, instructi'*.[3] Some of the
Fathers must have wished it to be more precise. The draft submitted for examination on 10th May, after stating this general
condition, reminded the deacons that they would not be ordained
priest until they had been deemed fit to preach the word of
God to the people.[4] There was plenty of reaction. It was alleged
that the measure was too strict,[5] that it was all very well for
those who would have cure of souls, but would it not exclude
men like those 'simple priests who, even if they understood
what they were saying when celebrating, were almost incapable
of speaking?' The future Urban VIII, then Archdeacon of
Bassano, continued: 'I have known such men, who celebrated
with such devotion that their prayers were undoubtedly more
acceptable to God than those of many fine preachers.'[6] Perhaps
it was the word *praedicatio* which put them off, suggestive as it

1. 'Cum praecepto divino mandatum sit omnibus, quibus
animarum cura commissa est, oves suas agnoscere, pro his sacrificium
offere, verbique divini praedicatione, sacramentorum administratione
ac bonorum operum omnium exemplo pascere. . . .' Decree of 15th
July 1563, canon 1. CT. IX, 623, 24–6.
2. *ibid.*, canon 14, CT. IX, 627, 18–19.
3. CT. IX, 627, 6.   4. CT. IX, 482, 15–21.
5. cf. CT. IX, 491, 31; 502, 5; 500, 45.
6. CT. IX, 500, 45 – 501, 4.

was of the learned and the intricate,[1] where other terms would actually have sufficed – *instruere, proponere, interpretari*.[2] After all the important thing was to declare that no one would be ordained priest who could not teach the people *inter missarum solemnia*.[3] But the supporters of its complete suppression carried the day.[4] When, on the 6th July a new version of the decree,[5] which did not contain the disputed passage, was proposed, the Bishop of Chioggia, James Nacchianti, was the only one to demand once more that every candidate for the priesthood should be able to propound the word of God.[6]

(ii) In fact, canon 14 of the same decree did include what had been left out of canon 13, by making admission to the priesthood dependent on the possession of a certain amount of pastoral science.

If there were objections to the draft of 10th May, which insisted that candidates for the priesthood would be recognisd by examination as being apt '*ad populum docendum ac ministranda sacramenta*',[7] they arose out of consideration for the existing emergency and the actual situation in the dioceses. If it was to be effective, the council must require no more than the possible. In wanting excellent priests there was a danger that none at all would be found.[8] And if there were men who came up to the standard required by the draft, would they be prepared to take on such a miserable charge for instance as one of

1. On 16th May 1563, for example, the Archbishop of Braga, Bartholomew of the Martyrs, explains that the preaching required of bishops is not the metaphysical and adulatory preaching in vogue in Italy. 'Longaque oratione comprobavit,' notes the secretary, 'maxime conveniri episcopis praedicationem verbi Dei, non metaphysice ut fit (ait) in Italia et adulatorie, sed vitia increpando' (CT. IX, 502, 18). The Italian style is defended and justified by another Dominican, Thomas Stella, *ibid.*, 511, 15. cf. also CT. III, 625. cf. also Matteo Giberti's directions: 'Cessent in sanctis illis concionibus profanarum legum minime necessariarum citationes, poetarum auctoritates supervacuae, subtilium quaestionum, et plerumque futilium inanes allegationes' (Constitutiones, Tit, III, cap. 2. *Jo. Mattaei Giberti opera omnia*, p. 50).   2. cf. CT. IX, 504, 10; 508, 25; 526, 6.
3. CT. IX, 577, 7.
4. e.g. CT. IX, 503, 14; 508, 7; 509, 22; 510, 3; 540, 6; 544, 46; 578, 39.
5. CT. IX, 595–6.   6. CT. IX, 608, 41.
7. CT. IX, 482, 31.   8. CT. IX, 654, 14.

the four hundred country parishes in the diocese of Citta di Castello?[1] Would it not be possible to require these aptitudes only of those who would subsequently claim a cure of souls?[2]

These objections explain the new emphasis in the final redaction in which it was stated that the knowledge required for the priesthood was of a strictly pastoral kind as opposed to a purely academic knowledge '*ad populum docendum ea quae scire omnibus necessarium est ad salutem, ac administranda sacramenta*'.[3] This formula is not without point if we remember that the knowledge required for the administration of the sacraments is not merely concerned with the exact conditions for their valid administration, but with the doctrinal significance behind the rites, which priests should explain to the faithful at the time of their actual administration.[4]

What are we to make of these manifestations of resistance? Merely tactical opportunism? Legislation in matters of sacramental discipline always causes a certain sacramental theology to pass into the actions and the daily life of the Church whether it is consciously intended or not. Were all the theologians and Fathers at Trent in complete agreement about the sacrament of Orders, and especially about the way in which pastoral tasks in general and the ministry of the word in particular were to be integrated within it? We must now look at the council's work in the specifically doctrinal sphere.

2. *The shaping of the doctrinal definitions*

A really scientific study of the doctrinal work of the Council of Trent on the subject of the sacrament of Orders, if it is to see this work in its true perspective in relation to the historical development of the theology of Christian priesthood, should have as its basis an accurate schedule of the documentary material used, both in the preparation and discussion of the drafts, and in the treatises of contemporary theologians. It must have a complete picture first of all of the scriptural background, making a careful examination of the way in which passages relevant to the priesthood in the ancient law are used and

1. CT. III, 649, 26–31.   2. CT. IX, 604, 34.
3. CT. IX, 627, 16.   4. cf. *supra*, p. 231.

regarded, and of the angle from which allusions to the Christian ministry in the new testament are seen. It must measure the extent of patristic research, and check the sources, either from a first-hand reading or from a consultation of the commentaries of Lombard or the Decretum. It must discover what place is given to the Pontifical – is it, or is it not, to be considered the normal theological standard in this matter?

So far as I know no such investigation has yet been made, for this account can claim to be no more than a rapid outline of the salient points.

To enable us to see more clearly how far the discussions of the council reveal a 'theology' in process of elaboration, it will not be out of place to distinguish the points which were unanimously agreed from those which were still at issue.

(i) *Unanimous affirmations*

As against the errors of the day, the doctrines of Luther, Bucer, Melanchton and Calvin, in which all priesthood was reduced to the preaching of the gospel, the council was unanimous in affirming a certain number of points as expressing the actual faith of the Church:

a. Although there is an inferior priesthood common to all Christians, there is, nevertheless, in the new law, an external, visible priesthood pertaining only to some.

This priesthood cannot be reduced to the single activity of preaching the word of God.[1] Inalienable powers[2] are inherent in it, the power of consecrating and offering the body and blood

---

1. 'Si quis dixerit, non esse in Novo Testamento sacerdotium visibile et externum, vel non esse potestatem aliquam consecrandi et offerendi verum corpus et sanguinem Domini, et peccata remittendi et retinendi, sed officium tantum et nudum ministerium praedicandi Evangelium, vel eos, qui non praedicant, prorsus non esse sacerdotes, anathema sit' (Dogmatic Decree of the 23rd Session, canon 1. CT. IX, 621, 30–3. Denzinger, 961).

2. 'Si quis dixerit, per sacram ordinationem non dari Spiritum Sanctum, ac proinde frustra episcopos dicere: Accipe Spiritum sanctum; aut per eam non imprimi characterem; vel eum, qui sacerdos semel fuit, laicum rursus fieri posse, A.S.' (CT. IX, 622, 1–3. Denzinger, 964).

of Christ (for there is a divinely-willed link between priesthood and sacrifice) and the power to absolve sin.[1]

b. The divine character of the priestly ministry is enhanced by a series of major and minor Orders, which are subordinate to it and designed to serve it.[2]

c. The priesthood is transmitted by that combination of rites and ceremonies instituted by Christ and productive of grace, which the Church calls a sacrament. Holy Orders is one of the seven sacraments.[3]

1. 'Sacrificium et sacerdotium ita Dei ordinatione coniuncta sunt, ut utrumque in omne lege existerit. Cum igitur in Novo Testamento sanctum Eucharistiae sacrificium visibile ex Domini institutione catholica Ecclesia acceperit: fateri etiam oportet, in ea novum esse visibile et externum sacerdotium, in quod vetus translatum est. Hoc autem ab eodem Domino Salvatore nostro institutum esse, atque apostolis eorumque successoribus in sacerdotio potestatem traditam consecrandi, offerendi et ministrandi corpus et sanguinem eius, nec non et peccata dimittendi et retinendi, sacrae Litterae ostendunt, et catholicae ecclesiae traditio semper docuit' (Caput I. CT. IX, 620, 18–25. Denzinger, 957). cf. canon 1, cited supra, and the decree of the 22nd Session, canon 2: 'Si quis dixerit, illis verbis **hoc facite in meam commemorationem** Christum non instituisse Apostolos sacerdotes, aut non ordinasse, ut ipsi aliique sacerdotes offerent corpus et sanguinem suum, A.S.' (CT. VIII, 962, 1–3. Denzinger 949). On the power of remitting sins, see also canon 3 on the sacrament of penance (Session 14, 25th November 1551). Denzinger, 913.

2. 'Cum autem divina res sit tam sancti sacerdotii ministerium, consentaneum fuit, quo dignius et maiore cum veneratione exerceri posset, ut in ecclesiae ordinatissima dispositione plures et diversi essent ministrorum ordines, qui sacerdotio ex officio deservirent, ita distributi, ut, qui iam clericali tonsura insigniti essent, per minores ad majores ascenderent' (Cap. 2. CT. IX, 620, 26–30; Denzinger, 958). 'Si quis dixerit, praeter sacerdotium non esse in ecclesia catholica alios ordines, et maiores et minores, per quos velut per gradus quosdam in sacerdotium tendatur, A.S.' (Canon 2. CT. IX, 621, 34–6. Denzinger, 962).

3. '. . . dubitare nemo debet, ordinem esse vere et proprie unum ex septem sanctae ecclesiae sacramentis . . .' (Cap. 3. CT. IX, 621, 1). 'Si quis dixerit, ordinem sive sacram ordinationem non esse vere et proprie sacramentum, a Christo Domino institutum, vel esse figmentum quoddam humanum, excogitatum a viris rerum ecclesiasticarum imperitis, aut esse tantum ritum quendam eligendi ministros verbi Dei et sacramentorum, A.S.' (Canon 3. CT. IX, 621, 37–40. Denzinger, 963.) cf. also Chap. 1 and Session 22, canon 2, cited supra. Canon 5, Denzinger 965, states that the various rites in the ceremonies of ordination, and particularly that of unction, are neither contemptible nor harmful.

d. The priesthood is essential to the hierarchical structure of the Church. Above the faithful are ministers, priests and bishops.[1] Priests are higher than the faithful through the character and powers of the priesthood; bishops are higher than priests both as a result of certain powers, i.e. of ordaining and confirming which pertain to them in a way quite different from the priests,[2] and also because of their authority to govern the Church of God as successors of the apostles.[3]

All these powers come from above, from Christ, through the channel of sacramental succession, not from below, as a result of the choice of the Christian people alone.[4] Therefore, election by the clergy and people is not essential for the bishop's elevation to the episcopate.[5]

1. 'Si quis dixerit, in ecclesia catholica non esse hierarchiam, divina ordinatione institutam, quae constat ex episcopis, presbyteris et ministris, A.S.' (Canon 6. CT. IX, 622, 7–8. Denzinger, 966).

2. 'Si quis dixerit, episcopos non esse presbyteris superiores; vel non habere potestatem confirmandi et ordinandi, vel eam quam habent, illis esse cum presbyteris communem . . .' (Canon 7. CT. IX, 622, 9–10. Denzinger, 967).

3. '. . . Quodsi quis omnes Christianos promiscue Novi Testamenti sacerdotes esse, aut omnes pari inter se potestati spirituali praeditos affirmet: nihil aliud facere videtur quam ecclesiasticam hierarchiam . . . confundere . . . Proinde sancta synodus declarat, praeter ceteros ecclesiasticos gradus episcopos, qui in apostolorum locum successerunt, ad hunc hierarchicum ordinem praecipue pertinere, et **positos** (sicut idem Apostolus ait) **a spiritu sancto regere ecclesiam dei,** eosque presbyteris superiores esse, ac sacramentum confirmationis conferre, ministros ecclesiae ordinare, atque alia pleraque peragere ipsos posse, quarum functionum potestatem reliqui inferioris ordinis nullam habent' (Cap. 4, CT. IX, 621, 9–18. Denzinger, 960).

4. 'Docet insuper sancta synodus, in ordinatione episcoporum, sacerdotum et ceterorum ordinum nec populi nec cuiusvis saecularis potestatis et magistratus consensum sive vocationem sive auctoritatem ita requiri, ut sine ea irrita sit ordinatio; quin potius decernit, eos, qui tantummodo a populo aut saeculari potestate ac magistratu vocati et instituti ad haec ministeria exercenda ascendunt, et qui ea propria temeritate sibi sumunt, omnes non ecclesiae ministros, sed **fures et, latrones, per ostium non ingressos** habendos esse' (Cap. 4, CT. IX, 621, 19–25. cf. also canon 7, *ibid.*, 622, 11–12. Denzinger, 967).

5. 'Si quis dixerit, episcopos, qui auctoritate Romani Pontificis assumuntur, non esse legitimos et veros episcopos, sed figmentum humanum, A.S.' (Canon 8. CT. IX, 622, 14–15. Denzinger, 968).

(ii) *Points at issue*

The preparation of these dogmatic texts entailed some discussion, in order that they should include only what was accepted unanimously, and only those things which needed to be solemnly affirmed to preserve the integrity of the Catholic faith.

As they appear in the reports of the deliberations, some of these discussions seem to have reference only to the divergencies between the various theological schools. Is the essential rite of the sacrament the imposition of hands or the tradition of the instruments? Are the minor Orders included in the sacrament? Is 'tonsure' a minor Order?

In point of fact these discussions are not unrelated to the problem which was raised not so much by the theologians as by the bishops – the link between the sacrament of Orders and the source, nature and claims of pastoral functions in the Church.

a. Priesthood and the ministry of the word

Once it has been admitted as one of the verities of the faith that the functions of priesthood are not confined to preaching the gospel, does it not follow that the power of preaching should be mentioned in the dogmatic decrees as one of the powers of the priest?

Before it came up at the Council of Trent a similar question had engaged the attention of the theologians at the Council of Cologne (1536), for whom the propagation of the Lutheran heresy was certainly no remote danger. In an official exposition of Christian doctrine compiled with the ever-present preoccupation with those points raised by the new errors, John Gropper did not hesitate, in explaining both the hierarchical structure of the Church[1] and the sacrament of Orders,[2] to name the

1. Explaining the words *Ecclesiam sanctam* in the Creed '. . . Officia ergo Christus in ecclesia discrevit, non parem membris omnibus tribuens potestatem, sacerdotalem instituens functionem, cui annexuit non humanam sed plane divinam potestatem, nempe praedicandi Evangelii, remittendi et retinendi peccata, dandi Spiritum Sanctum, claudendi et aperiendi regnum caelorum, conficiendi corpus et sanguinem dominicum, ac caetera sacramenta ecclesiae ministrandi . . .' (John Gropper, *Institutio compendiaria doctrinae christianae*, Verona Edition, 1541, fol. 68 r). Lutheran ecclesiology is envisaged in his development of this theme.

2. 'Presbyterorum officium, in primis in praedicatione verbi, dein

preaching of the word among the powers of the priest together
with the powers of absolving and consecrating. At the Council
of Trent more reserve was shown, since a solemn statement of
the faith was at issue, but the matter was discussed.

The question had been raised previously at Bologna in 1547.
Faced with a Lutheran proposition reducing priesthood to
preaching,[1] the theologians had been unanimous in condemning
it entirely, but they did not deny that the envoy had a *potestas
praedicandi*,[2] so that when the resulting draft canon in condemnation of the Lutheran doctrine made its appearance, it contained
this important qualification: '*tametsi sacerdotes ipsi populis sibi
commissis verbum Dei praedicare et sanae ac salutaris doctrinae
cibum exhibere accurate debeant.*'[3]

But this redaction was not to be retained. In vain did Lippomani, Matteo Giberti's successor at Verona, and Catharinus[4]
draw attention to the fact that by including the phrase *populis
sibi commissis*, the text was quite fair to those who would rather
not speak of 'preaching' without reference to 'mission'.[5] Those
who were purely and simply opposed[6] to it were successful in
getting it dropped.[7]

A similar vacillation is to be observed in connection with the
drafting of the decree of 15th July, 1563.

A first draft was prepared in October 1562 by a commission
of eight Fathers, comprising six bishops (three Italians, a
Spaniard, a Portuguese and a Hungarian), the General of the
Servites (Italian) and the General of the Jesuits, Laynez.
Desirous as they were of asserting against Luther that a non-

---

in conficiendo corpore et sanguine dominico et caeteris sacramentis
administrandis (confirmationis tamen et ordinis, quae solus Episcopus
ob ecclesiae unitatem retinendam administrat, exceptis) denique in
orando Deum pro totius ecclesiae et populi christiani prosperitate
situm est . . .' (*ibid.*, fol. 189 v).

1. 'Ordinem potestatem esse praedicandi, non offerendi, ideoque
eos, qui verbum Dei non praedicant non esse sacerdotes' (Proposition
submitted for examination on 26th April 1547, CT. VI, 97, 9).

2. cf. CT. VI, 104, 18; 106, 6; 110, 14; 111, 13; 116, 19.

3. CT. VI, 308, 11–14.   4. CT. VI, 314, 31; 318, 10.

5. CT. VI, 312, 33.

6. CT. VI, 311, 13; 312, 8; 313, 6; 315, 22; 316, 17, 38; 317, 16.

7. CT. VI, 373, 37.

preaching priest is no less authentically a priest, they were careful to say explicitly that preaching was one of the priestly functions: '*et quamvis negandum non sit, ministerium etiam verbi
sacerdotibus convenire, sacerdotes tamen esse non desinunt tametsi
munus hoc non exerceant*'.[1]

The Legate, Seripando, in amending this text several days
later was still more positive: '*et quamvis certum semper et indubi-
tandum fuerit, ministerium quoque verbi sacerdotibus convenire:
sacerdotes tamen esse non desinunt, tametsi munus hoc iusto aliquo
impedimento non exerceant.*[2]

Why, then, was the entire clause abandoned in the text put
forward on 3rd November,[3] and which, in the case of this canon
at any rate, would be practically final? Perhaps simply for reasons
of brevity and clarity.[4] Solicitude for refreshing the deep roots of
pastoral duty had to give way to a more clear-cut condemnation
of error.

b. The theology of the apostolic function

The difficulty in fitting the power of preaching into the scheme
of sacerdotal powers as a whole would have been less great if the
standpoint adopted by the redactors – the refutation of heresy –
had not led them to base their exposition on the necessary connection between priesthood and sacrifice.

In the course of the discussions some bishops did not fail to
suggest an alternative method of exposition.

(1) In October 1562 the Archbishop of Nicosia (Cyprus)
regretted that the various Orders had been presented as centring
around the eucharist, since this failed to show *vere et proprie*
what the ecclesiastical hierarchy really was, and that its perfection and consummation was to be found in the person of the
Roman Pontiff. So he proposed the following ordinance:

Jesus Christ our Lord, founder (*initium*) and substance of all
hierarchy, bequeathed to us the sacred words, to which are linked
the sacred traditions, and the sacraments. But the scriptures are
profitable neither for instruction nor morals unless they are explained,
and what would the sacraments be if there was no one to perform

1. CT. IX, 39, 12.   2. CT. IX, 41, 18.
3. CT. IX, 105.   4. cf. CT. IX, 85, 20.

and administer (*tradere*) them? Moreover, holy things ought not to be committed to any but holy people. It was therefore necessary for Christ to leave us a sacred order of ministers (*sacer ordo ministrorum*).

Scriptures, sacraments, ministers, all imply a sending-forth of labourers into the harvest. Another authority was therefore required to rule all the ministers, an authority to which all would be subject by divine law (*cui omnes divino jure parerent*).

The sacred hierarchy, then (*sacer omnis principatus*), is related to the sacraments, to the divine words (and also to the traditions), and to the ministers of holy things. Since there is an *oblatio* in every sacrament, and since the eucharist contains the *oblatio perfectissima* of Christ at the supper, the eucharist exhausts both the idea of sacrifice and that of priesthood, but not that of ecclesiastical hierarchy. There still remains a ministry relative to the words and sacred traditions, and to the government of the ministers themselves. This ministry, *in quo totius ecclesiae regimen vere perficitur et consummatur*, was instituted by our Lord when he said to Peter, 'Feed my lambs, feed my sheep', 'strengthen thy brethren', 'upon this rock I will build my Church', 'one flock and one shepherd'.

If all bishops are bound *pascere et docere*, functions which are related to *sacra eloquia*, and *regere*, to guide the actions of the faithful that they may be brought to the worship of God, it is no less true that *dum ipsi pascunt, pascuntur, dum docent, docentur, dum regunt, reguntur*, and all this by a single person. Where otherwise would be unity of faith, unity of law, unity of heart? Where would be the unity of the flock and the unity of the shepherd? So the Roman Pontiff is *universalis pastor, doctor et rector*. Because he is the head united to the members *vera caritate, omnes pascit, omnes docet, omnes regit, a Deo tantummodo pascendus, docendus, regendus*.

'With the supreme head thus established,' continues the Archbishop, 'we can proceed to treat of the hierarchy and then the different Orders.'[1]

(2) But Peter Danes, Bishop of Lavaur, when he intervened in the debate on 20th November 1562, said that in his opinion doctrinal exposition ought to start from the *munus regendi et pascendi* instituted by Christ. Since a small number of men would not be sufficient to govern the Church, he appointed not only the apostles, but through them, *per eos, inferiores qui eam regerent*. And so the apostles created other Orders such as the diaconate.

He goes on to reveal by his words that his standpoint was quite

1. cf. CT. IX, 61–2.

different from that of the Archbishop of Cyprus: of course the
Pope is Peter's successor, but according to St Cyprian, the
apostles had the same authority as Peter. Peter is the *pastor
pastorum*, but not *episcopus universalis ecclesiae*. Within his diocese the bishop possesses the *cura principalis*; that of the Pope is
additional; it is the responsibility of the Pope to give guidance to
his government of the diocese, with the metropolitan as intermediary. If this were not so, there would only be a single bishop
in the Church of God. No longer would there be any 'bishops',
but 'vicars' of this universal bishop.[1]

These two examples, chosen for the relative brevity of their
statements rather than because they were well-known figures, or
because of their influence on the discussions, will be sufficient
to indicate what the major question before the council really
was – a theology of the Church, a theology of the apostolic function (in the strongest possible sense of the word 'apostolic') in
the Church, its transmission and its *differentia*. They also explain
why this inquiry could not at that moment be brought to a
successful outcome, when bishops and theologians remained
deeply divided on some particularly important points.

Is the episcopate of divine institution or not? Is episcopal jurisdiction derived directly from Christ? What is the role of the Pope
in its transmission? How is the superiority of the episcopate over
the priesthood to be defined? Is the episcopate a *verus et proprius
ordo*, conferred by a *verum sacramentum*[2] or not? Is it in the simple
priest or in the bishop that the true conception of the *sacerdos
ecclesiae sanctae catholicae* is realised,[3] a conception in which the
sacerdotes minores would be but collaborators, according to the
actual words of the Pontifical: *sint cooperatores ordinis nostri*? All
these questions were disputed in the learned and impassioned discussions which took place between October 1562 and July 1563.[4]

---

1. cf. CT. IX, 158. See, in the same sense, a brief line in the
Bishop of Orense's résumé, CT. IX, 87, 37.

2. CT. IX, 71, 44.   3. CT. IX, 72, 30.

4. We cannot even give a résumé of this extremely complicated
story here. See 'Trente (Concile)', in *Dict. de Théol. Cath.*, col.
1463–73; Broutin, *L'évêque dans la tradition pastorale du XVI siècle*,
pp 52–62; H. Jedin, *Krisis und Wendepunkt des Trienter Konzils
(1562–63)*, Würzburg, 1941.

As a matter of fact the question had been aired at the beginning of the council specifically on the 'pastoral' issue. Indeed, at the end of 1546, when there was some possibility that various measures might be introduced into canon law – to all intents and purposes these were economic sanctions – to compel bishops and others having cure of souls to reside among their flocks (measures which were in danger of being no more effective than so many previous enactments, as events would show), several Spanish bishops had demanded that this duty of residence should be delared to be of divine obligation, and as such it would escape the dispensations of Rome, which were destructive of all attempts at reform. Several publications by Spanish theologians, B. Carranza, D. Soto, B. Torres, appeared at the opportune moment to support these propositions which had already been defended in 1517 by Cardinal Cajetan in his commentary on the *Secunda Secundae*.

Fifteen years later, this decree of Session VI having in fact been ineffective, the practical question of residence was referred back for fresh consideration in March 1562. Once again the Spanish bishops argued the question on the basis of principles. A special vote was necessitated on 20th April, and as a result of this, by a majority of eleven (seventy-one against sixty) the proposition that residence was of divine obligation did not figure in the decree *De Reformatione*, then in process of preparation.[1]

The whole question was reopened in October 1562, when the doctrinal decree on the sacrament of Orders appeared on the agenda. The discussion could not have come to anything when Spaniards and Italians, theologians and canonists, and the various theological schools were still disputing so many points. In view of the violence displayed by the Spaniards and the French, the Roman Curia was the whole time anxious to keep the discussion within bounds, and desirous of seeing the council despatched as soon as possible, and continually afraid that the old doctrines of Constance and Basle regarding the superiority of the episcopate assembled in council over the Pope might raise their heads again.

Writing to the pontifical legates presiding over the council,

1. CT. VIII, 463–5.

Cardinal Borromeo, the Pope's nephew and right-hand man, asked them to see that the dogmatic canons on holy Orders were as brief and simple as possible. There was no point in prefacing them with long doctrinal exposition. This had been done – and with what fulness – in the case of justification and the sacrifice of the Mass. A short introduction would suffice, and let them confine themselves strictly to the sacrament of Orders not touching the question of the institution of bishops, their jurisdiction or the primacy of the Pontiff.[1]

In fact, the doctrinal decree of 15th July 1563, went slightly beyond this minimum programme in chapter IV, by broaching the doctrine of ecclesiastical hierarchy, that hierarchical ordinance to which the bishops principally as successors of the apostles belonged, placed there as they were by the Holy Spirit to rule the Church of God.

But it avoided the burning question. It is significant that on the day when the text was solemnly promulgated, several Spanish bishops thought it necessary to give a particular nuance to their *placet* to this chapter and to the corresponding canons numbered 6 and 7.[2] These reservations indicate that the decree of 15th July 1563, which was decisive with regard to Protestant heresies, its avowed object, still left a vast field open for further doctrinal elaboration on the priesthood, which would bring together in a broader synthesis all the points at issue.

3. SOME PRACTICAL POINTS

In the various decisions and directives of the council, we have evidence of the competing claims of pastoral zeal and of the

---

1. 'quanto a l'ordine si habbino à formar i canoni più succinti et più brevi che sia possible, lasciando da canto, senza farne una mentione al mondo, tutto quello che possa spettare al primato di San Pietro et conseguentemente a l'auttorita di N. Sre, a la institution de vescovi et a la giurisdittion loro et toccando puramente simplicemente quel che appartiene al sacramento de l'ordine, et che si lasci totalmente la dottrina come non necessaria, facendo in cambio (se a lor pare) una breve prefatione, la quala non innuisca altro che il puro sacramento de l'ordine' (26th June 1563). J. Susta, *Die römische Kurie und das Konzil von Trient unter Pius IV*, IV, Vienna 1914, p. 100. cf. also the letter of 5th July, *ibid.*, p. 108.   2. CT. IX, 622–3.

faith; they make it clear, too, that the theology of Orders was still in its investigatory and inconclusive stage.

1. *The question of the minor Orders*

The position reached at the time of the council on the question of the minor Orders appears quite clearly in Peter de Soto's *Institutio Sacerdotum*, which was an edition of the prescribed course at the university of Dillingen.

After a short description of each of the four minor Orders, P. de Soto defends, as against the negations of the Lutherans, their reality and usefulness. His reasoning, based on texts and facts, is such as can be found in any contemporary anti-Protestant writing.[1] But this theologian adds these remarks:

> Certain of these functions, though necessary in the Church in former days, are no longer so today. Door-keepers and exorcists have lost that usefulness which lectors and acolytes still possess. It is not unlikely that at a General Council the Church might abandon those Orders which are apparently no longer necessary. Is it really expedient that an Order, a sacrament, should be conferred uselessly (*inaniter*)? Yet on the contrary it is desirable that those ecclesiastical activities which are of a permanent character should not be performed except by those who have received the Order which qualifies them for it.

While protesting his submission to the judgment of the Church, he actually repeats his predictions, but confesses that in his opinion:

> it would be much better not to abandon anything with such a long tradition behind it; would it not be possible to consider giving back to the door-keepers and the exorcists their proper functions in the Church? There is no lack of useful and serious work which could be attached to these functions. This is our ardent hope, for in this way especially, the derision in which the heretics hold these Orders can be silenced. Undoubtedly there are those who will say that, even if they serve no useful purpose, it is only right that they should be retained as vestiges of the past – which is something. Without disputing this point of view, we would merely like to add that it would be better to preserve these powers in activity than in idleness. In fact, to preserve anything at all, it is not sufficient merely to go on uttering its name, but the reality behind the name must be understood and preserved too.

1. cf. e.g. Gropper, *Institutio compendiaria doctrinae christianae*, Verona, 1541, fol. 183 v and ff.

The Spanish theologian was not mistaken in predicting that a General Council would concern itself very closely with this question.

In 1547 it needed the intervention of a pastor, Lippomani,[1] the successor of that Matteo Giberti whose efforts to rehabilitate the exercise of the various clerical functions in the diocese of Verona are well known, and that of a theologian, the Dominican Thomas Caselli, bishop of Bertinoro,[2] to see that explicit mention of the minor Orders was made – against Wyclif – in one of the proposed dogmatic canons.[3] The same association of dogmatic and pastoral points of view is found again in the work which was effected during 1562–3.

The doctrinal decree of 15th July 1563, enumerates the minor Orders and contains a whole chapter on them.[4] It is worth noting that, in the preparation of the text, the way in which the inferior Orders were presented as being grouped around the priest as consecrator of the eucharist rather than around the bishop, came in for some criticism. This presentation really seemed to put the bishop outside the sacrament of Orders.[5] 'The theologians, or rather the Thomists, who alone support this point of view, would do better to be silent on this matter', declared the Bishop of Viviers.[6]

1. CT. VI, 315, 4.   2. CT. VI, 316, 22.
3. For the text of this canon before this addition, cf. CT. VI, 308–9.
4. Chap. II, CT. IX, 620, 26–36. Denzinger 958. This list is to be found previously in the draft of the decree presented on 13th October 1562. CT. IX, 39, 21.
5. 'Est et aliud in constitutione hierarchiae attendendum, quam doctrina (i.c. the draft) constituit, quod omnes ordines et gradus eorum sumit respective ad Eucharistiam conficiendam, ita ut, secundum quod ad ipsam ordinanatur, ordines dici debeant (sicut dicit Thomas); quod praeter hoc quod valde dubium et infirmum est fundamentum, quia per hoc intendunt auctores hujus doctrinae excludere episcopatum ab ordine, non videtur tolerandum.' (Martin Perez de Ayala, Bishop of Segovia, October 1562. CT. IX, 76, 4–8.)
6. 'Deest etiam in doctrina ultimus gradus episcopatus, de quo nullum fit verbum, immo potius videtur ab ordine excludi, dum in ea dicitur ut minores in majores ascendant, donec in sacerdotio consummantur, quod mihi durissimum videtur, cum episcopatus ipse sit ordo. Si enim ostiarius, ad quem pertinet observare januas, si exorcista, qui nullum habent certum ministerium circa confectionem sanctissimae Eucharistiae, a theologis inter ordines connumerantur, quanto

It would have been possible to put before the eyes of this bishop some lines by a Dominican in a book actually submitted to the council for examination as to its orthodoxy:

The fact that there are seven distinct Orders in the Church is as a rule substantiated by relating them to the one sacrifice of the eucharist. But as a holy bishop of the last century noted quite rightly, in ancient times the seven Orders were, generally speaking, related to the bishop, i.e. not only to assist him at the sacrifice but also in the preaching of the word of God, as the two functions which were proper to him.[1]

And in point of fact it was in terms of the second conception that the bishops at Trent were thinking when they gave particular consideration to the attempts to be made to revivify the minor Orders.

The programme of reform, drawn up in February or at the beginning of March 1562, by five Italian bishops at the request of the Legate, Seripando, expresses the hope that the least capable of the many idle priests should at any rate be detailed to perform the functions of the minor Orders, and also that these functions should be carefully specified by the council.[2]

The draft of the canonical decree presented on the 7th July 1563, fulfils the latter aspiration completely, for it contains a long description of these functions.[3] This description, inspired by the past but with an eye to the present, sought to discover what pastoral work would be suitable for each minor Order at that juncture. The redactors proceeded further to assign to each of them two kinds of function, one of which related to the celebration of the eucharist, and the other to some kind of evangelistic

---

magis episcopatum ordinem esse dicendum est, cui tot alia sunt reservata, quae presbyteris competere nullo modo possunt? Taceant igitur iudicio meo theologi vel soli thomistae.' (CT. IX, 84, 1–7.)

1. B. Carranza, *Comentarios sobre el cathechismo christiano*, Anvers, 1558, fol. 347 v.

2. 'Describenda essent a sancto synodo munia cuiuscunque ordinis aliquanto diligentius, quam hactenus factum ab Isidoro et Gratiano'. . . 'An interim, dum haec (this programme of reform) executioni mandantur, expediret, ut ociosorum sacerdotum multitudo, exclusis, qui adeo inepti sunt, ut nulla spes esse possit, eos unquam ecclesiae profuturos, exerceret munia inferiorum ordinum.' (CT. XIII, 608, 12, 29.)   3. CT. IX, 598–601.

or administrative activity. Thus, it was suggested that the door-keeper should have the custody of the *liber animarum* and the overseeing of the cemeteries, that exorcists should seek out the sick and dying under the direction of the parish priest, that acolytes should take charge of the baptism, confirmation and marriage registers, that the subdeacon should be responsible for the distribution of alms and for teaching the catechism, and finally, it looked forward to the restoration to the deacons of their old position as the bishop's assistants and stewards.

In spite of a somewhat negative attitude this long draft aroused a certain interest.[1] But the solemn session was due to take place in a matter of eight days. So fifteen or so bishops suggested that this question should be adjourned to a later session,[2] or left to the future catechism of the council.[3] Others replied that it must be dealt with in the decree which was being prepared, but in a shorter,[4] perhaps even better, form,[5] while the Bishop of Leon declared that he was in favour of adhering to what was evident, and especially to what the Pontifical stated.[6]

The Bishop of Huesca thought the question important enough to warrant discussion even if the session had to be postponed to a later date.[7] Would not the effective restoration to life of the various Orders be the most telling answer to the heretics, who made fun of the inanity of their functions? The Bishop of Segovia,[8] in making these remarks, was supported afterwards by seven of his brethren.[9] But the preoccupation with dogma managed to carry the day and canon 17 of the decree *De Refor-matione* (15th July 1563), extolled the effective restoration of the minor Orders to prevent the heretics' declaring them *otiosa*, but without giving a detailed account of their functions.[10] The

1. CT. IX, 609, 26, 29.
2. CT. IX, 604, 23; 605, 5, 10–11; 606, 8, 35; 607, 17, 27, 40; 609, 35; 610, 24; 612, 6, 13; 613, 41, 45; 614, 20; 615, 19, 32, 37.
3. CT. IX, 604, 12; 610, 27; 612, 31.
4. CT. IX, 604, 37; 606, 18, 17, 19; 609, 16; 611, 16; 612, 15; 613, 45; 614, 13, 45; 615, 10, 21.
5. CT. IX, 607, 14; 612, 4, 11, 25.   6. CT. IX, 613, 32.
7. CT. IX, 608, 37.   8. CT. IX, 610, 8.
9. CT. IX, 610, 12, 48; 611, 24; 612, 42; 613, 10; 614, 23; 615, 3.
10. 'Ut sanctorum ordinum a diaconatu ad ostiariatum functiones, ab apostolorum temporibus in ecclesia laudabiliter receptae, et

Catechism of Trent did this later, but adhered to the strictly traditional list.[1]

In its anxiety to counter heretical propaganda with facts, the council, while rejecting the suggestion that redundant and unsuitable priests should take on the duties of the minor Orders, did however consider entrusting these duties to married clerks, who would be bound to tonsure, the wearing of the soutane in church only and who would be provided with a suitable benefice.[2] In doing this the Fathers had certainly no intention of going back on the conditions which they themselves had laid down (c. 11) for admission to minor Orders in normal cases – i.e. a certain amount of Latin and an aptitude for the major Orders for which they were a preparation,[3] nor were they unmindful of the traditional discipline concerning married clerks.[4] Canon 17 as it stands does not look at the matter from the point of view of the recruitment and the progressive training of priests, but from the standpoint of the worship of the Church, so that the faithful would have before their eyes the whole sacred hierarchy performing the service of the altar. So failing clerks to perform these sacred functions as of right in the course of their preparation for the priesthood, why not confer these minor Orders even on married laymen, sacristans, singing-men or bell-ringers, who

---

pluribus in locis aliquamdiu intermissae, in usum juxta sacros canones revocentur, nec ab haereticis tanquam otiosae traducantur: illius prisci moris restituendi desiderio flagrans, sancta synodus decernit . . .' (CT. IX, 627, 36 – 628, 2.)

1. Pars II, Cap. 7, n. 15–18, pp 294–6.

2. 'Quodsi ministeriis quatuor minorum ordinum exercendis clerici coelibes praesto non erunt, suffici etiam conjugati vitae probatae, dummodo non bigami, ad ea munia obeunda idonei, et qui tonsuram et habitum clericalem in ecclesia gestent.' (CT. IX, 628, 10–13.)

3. 'Minores ordines iis, qui saltem latinam linguam intelligant . . . conferantur . . . Cumque hinc ad altiores gradus et sacratissima mysteria sit ingressus, nemo iis initietur, quem non scientiae spes maioribus ordinis dignum ostendat . . .' (CT. IX, 626, 26, 33.)

4. This is referred to in canon 6 of the same decree. 'In cleris vero conjugatis servetur constitutio Bonifatii VIII, quae incipit: "Clerici, qui cum unicis", modi hi clerici alicuius ecclesiae servitio vel ministerio ab episcopo deputati, eidem ecclesiae serviant vel ministrent et clericali habitu et tonsura utantur: nemini quoad hoc privilegio vel consuetudine, etiam immemorabili, suffragante.' (CT. IX, 625, 30–2.)

could effectively carry them out? Since it obliged the clerk to wear ecclesiastical dress in church only, the council showed that it intended to create a new class quite distinct from that of the married clerks who were employed as administrative officials by the Church, or who were content merely to live on the revenues of some benefice.

2. Preparation and admission to holy Orders

In 1537 the eminent persons who signed the *Consilium* addresses to Paul III denounced, among other abuses in the recruitment of the clergy, the conferring of the priesthood on youths.[1] This complaint was frequently heard at that time. It raised the question of the canonical age for ordination, and particularly the religious and moral question of the age at which vocation could be discerned. Blessed John of Avila, writing for the council in 1551, is extremely forthright on this subject. The older candidates for the priesthood were:

the more sure the choice would be; and the younger, the less sure. In youth, nature has not yet borne its fruit, nor even revealed what it is going to be, in spite of the promise of flowers. Experience teaches us that many children seem to be angels, but turn into something very different afterwards. Young shoots do not guarantee the harvest until they have grown and developed, and the ripening grain has appeared. Experience teaches us this in the religious orders. We can be more sure about a mature man who takes the habit than about one who does so while still of tender years.[2]

The normal age for ordination, in his opinion, should be twenty-five for the subdiaconate, twenty-seven for the diaconate and thirty for the priesthood.[3]

1. 'Primus ˹abusus in hac parte est ordinatio clericorum et praesertim presbyterorum, in qua nulla adhibetur cura, nulla adhibetur diligentia, quod passim quicumque sint imperitissimi, sint vilissimo genere orti, sint malis moribus ornati, sint adolescentes, admittantur ad ordines sacras et maxime ad presbyteratum ad characterem, inquam, Christum maxime exprimentem.' (CT. XII, 136, 4.) On this subject, cf. G. Pellicia, ' La preparazione ed ammissione dei chierici ai santi ordini nella Roma del secolo XVI '. *Studio Storico con fonte inedite*, Roma, 1946. Important account in H. Jedin, *Rivista di storia della Chiesa in Italia*, I (1947), 302–5.
2. Text in *Miscellanea Comillas*, 3 (1945), p. 16.
3. *ibid.*, p. 30.

When the question came up at Trent these ages were in fact proposed by a certain number of bishops, amongst whom were several personal friends of John of Avila from Spain. But evidently everyone did not share in this view, and it was because conflicting interests were at stake that such different positions were taken up. There were, in fact, two questions. The first was: at what age could a person begin to appear on the Church's list of officials? Any bishop might quote *Sinite parvulos venire ad me*,[1] but no one was deceived by arguments which would make it possible for tonsure to be received at the age of ten, eight or even seven. The council confined itself to declaring that no benefice could be validly held by anyone under fourteen years of age.[2] We must not be too ready to assume that the pastoral point of view was totally lacking in this ruling, for the possession of a benefice would be at least a partial solution to the problem of maintaining the youthful candidate for the priesthood during his training. This leads us to think that the majority of the Fathers at the council were very favourably inclined towards an early discernment of vocations to the priesthood. Which brings us to the second question, which is decidedly pastoral in tone: if we are to have good priests, should training begin in adolescence or in manhood?

But first what is meant by 'good priests'? Men who are wholly wrapped up in their pastoral responsibilities? This seems to have been the motive behind John of Avila's demands. If the life of the priest is to be a sermon in itself, then one thing is of supreme importance – he must be faithful to his vow of celibacy. 'There is no need of long speeches to prove what a scandal the dissolute life of clergy has become. It is before our very eyes', said George Dracovitsch, Bishop of Pecs. 'Clearly it is because of ourselves and our lives that the word of God and the sacraments are unwelcome.' Celibacy was in bad odour. Was not this just what might have been expected when 'young men' were accepted and ordained 'elders', *presbyteri*? If celibacy was to be retained, then there must be no more subdeacons under thirty years of age.[3]

'Sophistry!' replied his opponents. Continence was not a

1. CT. IX, 580, 9–10.
2. Canon 6. CT. IX, 625, 24.   3. CT. IX, 544.

question of age, but of the will, and therefore of training. The devil was trying to trick us, to destroy the priesthood. Too many requirements, and we should find ourselves with no candidates at all. Furthermore, reform did not consist in making new laws, but in getting the old ones observed. If we trained young people in chastity we should have chaste priests.[1]

This was the view of one who had experience of the early Jesuit colleges, Diego Laynez, St Ignatius's successor as head of the Company. And the problem raised here was the problem of the seminaries.

Had the Council of Trent taken no other measures save that on seminaries, contained in canon 18 (15th July 1563),[2] it would have done enough to justify all the hopes of renewal in the Christian Church. This was how the Fathers themselves felt about it. It was noted by witnesses who were themselves present,[3] and it subsequently became one of the most cherished themes of historians and apologists of the council. The story of this decree on seminaries has already formed the subject of

1. 'Quoad aetatem ordinandorum nil immutandum esse de his, quae loquuntur iura posteriora, quia post statuta posteriorum conciliorum non successit aliqua causa mutandi decreta ab eis facta. Incontinentiam clericorum non esse ex defectu aetatis, sed ex defectu educationis. Educentur igitur juvenes in castitate, et habebimus castos sacerdotes. Dixitque, quod videtur esse instigatio daemonis ad destruendum sacerdotium, dum sub praetextu castitatis inducit, ut presbyteri fiant senes, ad hoc scilicet, ut nullus fiat presbyter . . . Reformatio non consistit in legibus condendis, sed in observantia legum' (CT. IX, 589, 1–9).

cf. also what a Spanish Benedictine abbot said: 'De aetate ordinandorum dixit, continentiam potius causari a firmo proposito quam ab aetate. Id probavit exemplo senum Susannae et aliorum, ex quibus conclusit, non esse attendendum ad aetatem ordinandorum nec mutandos canones antiquos, ne forte, dum quaerimus tam longam aetatem, nullos sacerdotes habeamus' (CT. IX, 582, 7–11).

2. CT. IX, 628–30.

3. 'Praecipue id extremum quo clericorum seminarium instituitur ita unanimes omnes amplexi fuerunt ut dicerent aliqui, etsi alius nullus ex hac synodi fructus proficisceretur, hunc tamen, qui ab hoc decreto jure expectandus erat, uberrimum futurum. Affirmabant alii hoc institutum de erigendis seminariis aut unicum aut nullum aliud collapsis et pene desperatis christianae reipublicae moribus reducendis atque instaurandis remedium superesse idque non tantum a patribus omnibus, sed principium quoque judicio maxime comprobari.' Paleotti, in A. Theiner, *Acta genuina concilii tridentini*, vol. ii, p. 661.

several works,[1] so I shall confine myself here to a few remarks.

The actual idea of the seminary was not new; it had been under discussion for some time and the Protestants had already put it into operation.[2] Cajetan seems to suggest it in 1552,[3] the Council of Cologne in 1536;[4] it was taken up the following year by Contarini in the *Consilium de emendenda ecclesia*,[5] and by John Nausea in 1543;[6] it appears several times in John of Avila;[7] the Portuguese bishop, John de Melo, extols it in 1552;[8] so does Cardinal Otto Truchsess in his preface to Peter de Soto's *De Institutione Sacerdotum*, and the Polish bishop, Stanislaus Hosius in 1559.[9] In 1556, Reginald Pole saw in the seminary the means of supplying the clergy needed as a result of the restoration of catholicism in England, and the decree which he issued[10] furnished the exact text of the draft canon presented at Trent on 10th May 1563.

In this draft, the penury of the clergy was put forward as the first reason justifying the setting up of seminaries. '*Cum magna sit hoc tempore ecclesiasticorum penuria, praesertim idoneorum.*'[11] Nothing could be more true after years of schism and persecution in the case of England and the same considerations were undoubtedly valid for the German dioceses also ravaged by heresy. But the clerical problem in Spain and in Italy particularly was exclusively one of quality and the same draft of 10th May 1563, also asked the council to do something about the ungovernable number of priests.[12] Opposition to both passages was readily forthcoming.[13]

The text was consequently amended, and the preamble concerning numbers was displaced by a preface which dealt purely

1. cf. A. Degert, *Histoire des Séminaires francais jusqu'à la révolution*, Paris 1912, vol. 1, pp 1–29. A. Laurent, 'L'influence du protestantisme sur l'origine des séminaires', taken from his thesis for a doctorate, Angers, *La pensée catholique*, 1950, pp 26–41.

2. cf. Laurent, *op. cit.*   3. CT. XII, 35–6.

4. 'Canones concilii provincialis coloniensis', Verona, 1543, fol. 11 v.

5. CT. XII, 136.   6. CT. XII, 425.

7. cf. A. Duval, *Suppl., Vie Sp., art. cit.*, passim.

8. CT. XIII, 125.   9. CT. XIII, 425, 11–19.

10. Decretum XI. Mansi, XXXIII, 1029–31.

11. CT. IX, 483, 67.   12. CT. IX, 481, 18–22.

13. CT. IX, 500, 31–5.

with training, in which it is easy to trace the themes developed by Laynez.[1] So in the minds of the Fathers who voted canon 18, the founding of seminaries was the answer not so much to the problem of recruitment, for there were too many priests, as to the problem of training.

We must not lose sight of the actual situation in many dioceses, especially in Italy, and of the frequently lamentable character of their clerical proletariat, if we are to realise that the purpose of canon 18 is not to prescribe in detail the standards required in the ideal seminary, but to ensure a minimum.

Although the council puts every bishop under an obligation to establish a seminary in his diocese, it does not compel candidates for the priesthood to pass through it. The draft of 10th May is satisfied with the aspiration: *ut, quantum fieri poterit, omnes qui futures sunt sacerdotes in ea (schola) educentur et instituantur.*[2] But nothing of this was retained in the final text.

Compared with the first draft, canon 18 as it stands is more precise, more definite as to the programme of studies. But it falls short not only of the arrangements extolled by John of Avila in Spain, but also of the suggestions made at the council itself by several Fathers including Laynez.[3] The discussions on the degree of learning required for ordination, which we noted above, are reflected here. A fairly high minimum was stipulated: holy scripture, ecclesiastical books, the homilies of the saints, a sufficient knowledge for the administration of the sacraments (which, let us not forget, implies some preaching) and particularly of penance, and, finally, the rubrics. One may well conclude that the inspiration behind this programme lay in what had already been effected in some places, for example, at Verona.

The greater part of the canon, and it was the subject of lengthy discussion, dealt with financial matters. Various measures were taken to make it possible for bishops to ensure the

1. 'Cum adolescentium aetas, nisi recte instituatur, prona sit ad mundi voluptates sequendas, et, nisi a teneris annis ad pietatem at religionem informetur, antequam vitiorum habitus totos homines possideat, numquam perfecte ac sine maximo ac singulari propemodum Dei omnipotentis auxilio in disciplina ecclesiastica perserveret: sancta synodus statuit, ut . . .' (CT. IX, 628, 14–18.)

2. CT. IX, 483, 31.   3. cf. CT. IX, 589, 18ff.

maintenance of the seminarists and their professors. The interesting thing about these measures is that they made the seminary a diocesan responsibility, and the leading benefices in the diocese had to send their quota to support it.

The Council of Trent, by its canon on seminaries, provided zealous bishops with the necessary juridical support for undertaking the training of a new clergy who would be better equipped for their pastoral responsibilities. What would their way of life be like?

3. The pattern of clerical life

It is said that 'the Council of Trent made the kind of clergy we know'. Yes, but was the pattern of clerical life the same in Italy, France, Spain, Germany? Do we not frequently attribute to the council as such, those orientations resulting from the personality of the various reforming priests and bishops, from the actual environment in which they worked or from the particular circumstances of each country?

If we look through the very important collection of decrees *De Reformatione* promulgated by the council between 1546 and 1563, we see that the texts which actually deal with the priest's manner of life are very few indeed. The ministry of preaching, the administration of the different sacraments, the rule of worship, ecclesiastical procedure, the complicated system of benefices – these things almost exhaust the subject matter of the canons. But as we have seen, they do more than once refer to the holiness which the pastoral ministry demands. But what measures must the priest take to submit to these claims of holiness? What 'exercises' are enjoined on him? How is he to order his relations with that world of men which is in his care?

On all these points the council contents itself with a vigorous reinforcement of the ancient canons 'relative to the life, propriety of conduct, dress, and learning of clerics, and also touching the luxuriousness, feastings, dances, gambling, sports, and all sorts of crime whatever, as also the secular employments, to be by them shunned'.[1] Particular blame was laid on those who

1. Session 22 (17th September 1562). Decree *De Reformatione*, canon 1. CT. VIII, 965.

habitually wore lay dress, 'setting their feet in different paths, one of God, and the other of the flesh'.[1]

There is nothing new in any of this. If they had wished, the Fathers could have gone much further at the council and could have at least suggested more even without actually imposing. A certain number of them must in fact, have been aware, through personal acquaintance or through reading his *Constitutiones*, of what Matteo Giberti, for example, had tried to do for the pattern of clerical life in Verona – detailed rules about dress from the hat to the shirt; about the wearing of jewellery and the harnessing of horses; no nocturnal perambulations, no serenading, no aubades; directions as to deportment, conversation and company; a kind of special hostel to be started in town for the benefit of country priests; regular visits to the bishop of obligation, etc.[2]

It is certain that the pastoral situation in the West in the sixteenth century called for an attitude of retreat, of separation on the part of the clergy. Why, then, was there this preoccupation with 'contact' between pastors and their flocks? The contact was there but often in the wrong way. The clergy allowed themselves to be drawn into what was less good in the lives of the laity and did not seek to lead men to God. At a time when unbelief was rare, if actually conceivable at all, the faithful needed priests who would show themselves to be priests, and bishops who would be bishops. The council gave a very severe reminder to bishops that they must not permit their dignity to be despised.[3]

1. Session 14 (25th November 1551). Decree *De Reformatione*, canon 6.

2. 'Constitutiones gibertinae', tit, 1. De Vita, habitu, conversatione et honestate clericorum. *Jo. Mattaei Giberti opera omnia*, pp 3–15.

3. Session 25 (3–4 December 1563). Decree *De Reformatione*, canon 17: 'The holy Synod cannot but sorely grieve at hearing that certain bishops, forgetful of their own estate, do in no slight manner disgrace the pontifical dignity; comporting themselves with an unseemly kind of servility, both in church and out of it, before the ministers of kings, nobles, and barons; and, as if they were inferior ministers of the altar, not only most unworthily give them place, but even serve them in person. Wherefore, the holy Synod . . . (charges) . . . them that . . . having before their eyes their own rank and order, they everywhere bear in mind that they are fathers and pastors.' (CT. IX, 1093, 12–20.)

Probably some bishops and clerks understood only too well what was meant.

At a time when heresies which denied all priesthood were spreading, heresies which believed only in ministries and not in the ministers instituted by Jesus Christ, and which insisted that these preachers should be indistinguishable from their co-religionists in their way of life, the maintenance of external marks of separation by the Catholic clergy was a kind of outward proclamation of the permanent reality of priesthood, as the use of Latin at Mass served to affirm its sacrificial character, and processions of the blessed sacrament the Real Presence.

From this point of view what is particularly noteworthy is the reserve of the council, which is maintained even on the delicate question of the celibacy of the clergy.[1] Considerable pressure was brought to bear on the council by the imperial representatives to grant the German clergy permission to marry; this, it was said, was the only way to end the scandal of so much notorious concubinage, and to restore the moral standing essential in the dispensers of the word of God and the sacraments of the Church. But the council contented itself with affirming the invalidity of marriages contracted by any who had taken solemn vows or who were in major Orders,[2] and did not touch the question of the theological and canonical functions of the obligation of celibacy.

The decrees of the Council of Trent did not exhaust the riches of that renewal of the priestly spirit of which they were the fruit, but they did provide a norm for the most pressing and urgent tasks.

1. G. Constant, *Concession à l'Allemagne de la communion sous les deux espèces*, Paris 1923, pp 546–612, 1013–23.
2. Session 24 (11th November 1563). Dogmatic decree, canon 9. CT. IX, 968. Denzinger, 979.

CHAPTER XII

THE PRIEST, PAGAN AND CHRISTIAN

P. IDIART

To begin with we can state categorically:

1. Many Protestants consider a non-universal priesthood to be a survival of paganism.

2. Those Catholics who regard their priests as 'druids' give the impression that they share this opinion.

All the positive efficacious reality that Catholics attribute to presbyteral priesthood appears to Protestants to be an affront to the unique and all-sufficing priesthood of Christ. They regard it as a pagan corruption of the pure primitive idea of salvation through Jesus Christ alone.

Catholic priests, who have experienced their own unworthiness as ministers in the holiness of their ministry, know that they can convey, and even transform, without adding anything, that they can be indispensable yet unprofitable servants. Protestant mistrust, however legitimate it may appear to them in the abstract, will have difficulty in taking root in their priestly conscience. On the other hand the tendency of some of the faithful to slip into a magical attitude can cause them grave disquiet; and this disquiet, which marks the pastor who is anxious that the reception accorded to his ministry should be authentic, can and even must become the disquiet of a minister who is careful not to make himself a screen, not to intercept for his own advantage that which passes through him, that it may not be halted there, that his own darkness may not obscure the light which he proclaims, but is not. And if the temptation to a magical attitude on the part of the faithful has a very long ancestry in the religious history of humanity, long before the beginnings of Christianity, is not the same equally true for the temptations, if not the disquiet, of the minister?

But the mere fact of comparing the pagan and the Christian priest, while evoking both Protestant objections and Catholic temptations, will show how far our interest in this sort of comparison has changed since Reinach and Loisy. The pagan is no longer a legendary figure, mysteriously involved in early controversies or in missionary expansion. We come into contact with him afresh every day; we recognise him in doubt and atheism and suspect him in the lukewarm and the lapsed; we are apprehensive of him in sheer habit or extravagance. Once we thought that the pagan was an enigma diminished by time or distance, a fit subject for the patience of the historian or the taste of the follower of what is strange. But now we find that he has sprung to life again before our eyes, the same in some ways and different in others, so that we cannot say whether his appearance has actually changed, or whether it merely seems to have changed because he is nearer to us. Yesterday the comparison of Christianity and paganism was a matter for the scholar or the specialist, but from now on it must figure in the programme of all pastoral thought. Yesterday the history of religions presented contemporary 'primitive' man as an anachronism, but today sociology and the study of religious phenomena have led us to recognise other 'primitive' men for ourselves in every latitude and in every age. Yesterday the term 'pagan' had an ancient, barbarous, savage and backward ring; today 'pagan' seems to refer to the invincible 'old man' rather than to the misguided and floundering 'pre-Christian'. And many questions which seemed to be completely forgotten are being asked again in new terms.

But if we pause a little the questions change. For where the apologist endeavoured to construct a hierarchy in which Christianity takes chief place, we tend to look for the characteristic, original and specifically Christian note. Where the historian isolated in order to analyse and compare term by term, we immediately look for the permanent underlying structure. Where certain rationalists still persist in seeking indisputable evidence that Christianity existed before Christ, we like to think, with St Justin, that we can recognise the economy of revelation, the encounter with the uttered word, in the divine covenants, and the encounter with the scattered word, in human restlessness. Where the Protestant trembles and mistrusts, and where the pastor, anxious about authenticity, questions himself in his desire to answer objections and enlighten doubt we can substitute the attitude which seeks to uncover historical influences and sociological laws, the manifold ways in which God has so frequently made use of our words to teach us of his love.

Formerly men tried to understand pagan priesthood on the one hand, and Christian priesthood on the other, in order to compare them, to appraise resemblances and differences, to distinguish historical connections from fortuitous parallelisms. But they quickly discovered that this kind of comparison runs into insurmountable difficulties.[1] If we attempt to explain the Christian institution of presbyteral priesthood historically by reference to its biblical or extra-biblical associations, we find that in order to place the various contributions, to define and date the strata, we are led into a form of analysis which is largely conjectural and which disintegrates the object it affects to study to the point of dissolution. If we try to define the structural originality of the Christian priesthood in terms of similar functions in other religions, we discover that every religious tradition has its own structures and each offers a completely original version of priesthood, the meaning of which is closely dependent on the religious whole which is envisaged and apprehended, both in the universal and in the particular. It is only from within that a constant religious reality, attitude or institution can be understood. In this field, no near type or specific difference exists to make an objective classification possible. The only universal is the relationship of man with the Wholly Other, and in this relationship certain concrete and historical forms are developed. The same universal religious purpose can be found more or less happily embodied in the infinite variety of religious manifestations practised by men. Each religion is like a language, or more accurately a tongue, codifying the methods of exchange in a

1. The *Revue d'Histoire des Religions* mentions no complete scientific study on priesthood after 1910, the date of Hastings' Encyclopedia, which itself refers us to the particular articles on each religion.

particular historico-cultural pattern. We cannot understand and compare religious phenomena from the outside, as objects, by reference to their historical environment, or to their place in a given structure, without seriously misreading them and distorting their meaning, if we do not bear in mind that they express a purpose, that they are not objects but signs, referable to a signified before being capable of correlation. Strictly, a valid comparison between the pagan and the Christian priest ought to take into account at one and the same time the historical affinities which have given the Christian priesthood its morphology, the structural norms which have given the priesthood its place in the syntax of Christian attitudes, and the religious implications behind the ministry of the Christian priest; at one and the same time, not successively, for the phenomenon of priesthood is not to be identified with modes, nor with a structure, nor yet with significations, nor even with all these things, but with all these things in their relationship one with another.

The science of comparative religion is still some way from being in a position to undertake such a study, but meanwhile we will begin with an epitome of the theology of Christian priesthood, and follow this with an attempt to reconstruct its pagan context, having in mind significations rather than structures, and structures rather than forms. This method, the very opposite of that adopted in 'positive research', will leave in the shade many important historical and sociological aspects, but it will lead us directly to enquire into the divine intention which nursed the birth of the Christian priesthood. And, finally, for the Christian, be he Protestant or Catholic, can the comparing of his faith with other religions have any purpose other than to teach him more about his own faith?

I. PRIESTHOOD AND CLERGY

'And every priest, indeed, standeth daily ministering, and often offering the same sacrifices, which can never take away sins: But he, offering one sacrifice for sins, for ever sitteth on the right hand of God . . . For by one oblation he hath perfected for ever them that are sanctified . . . Now where there is a remission (of sins), there is no more an oblation for sin.' (Heb. 10, 11–18). 'There is verily an abrogation of the former commandments, for the weakness and unprofitableness thereof . . . (and) an introduction of a better hope, by which we approach to God.' (Heb. 7, 18–19). 'For if that first (testament) had been faultless, there should not, indeed, a place have been sought for a second . . . Now in saying a new, he hath made the former old. And that which decayeth and groweth old is near its end.' (Heb. 8, 7, 13).

If the epistle to the Hebrews had not described Christ as High Priest which implies the concomitant existence of an inferior priesthood, its teaching might have been held to infer the decisive avoidance of all humanly-organised priesthood both before and after Christ. Does not the one, eternal, supremely efficacious and final sacrifice of Christ, which is alone acceptable, render all other sacrificial actions superfluous and unprofitable? Are the Protestants not right in seeing a fundamental betrayal, a sacrilegious and pagan corruption, in a human priesthood permanently constituted to celebrate the renewing of the 'memorial of the Lord'? Ought not Catholics to be disturbed by the comparisons made by historians between the organisation of the Christian priesthood and the 'patterns' provided by the contemporary mystery religions or the Essenes?

Before coming to the heart of the discussion, the relationship between the priesthood of Christ and the presbyteral priesthood, it will be as well to dispel one basic ambiguity underlying the term 'priest', by investigating its use in comparable religions. In our minds the ideas of the priest as a consecrated man who exercises a priesthood, and as one who belongs to a juridically defined and organised body known as the clergy, are inseparable. But it is important to bear in mind that there are two functions here, two distinct significations, and that it is profitable and even indispensable to distinguish them, especially if their coalescence is to be understood and justified.

Whether the priesthood is seen as an instrument of mediation between men and the divinity, or whether it is closely linked with the ritual function of sacrifice, its existence does not inevitably involve the existence of a clergy, nor even of priests as official mediators or permanently appointed professionals of the holy, nor yet of the specially detailed or qualified mediator or sacrificer. In the most elementary forms of sacrifice the sacerdotal role seems to pertain to the victim rather than to the sacrificer.[1] Religions without priests are far from being exceptional. Numerous examples may be found in the Totemism of the American Indians or of the Oceanians, in the familiar cults developed in ancient Rome or south-east Asia, and even in the higher forms of religion which are of para-biblical orgin, such as Islam. It is even more usual to meet a familiar or charismatic priesthood alongside a clerical priesthood, to say nothing of the sorcerer who is sometimes an official and sometimes quite unknown.

It would be possible to go further, and question whether priesthood – or, for that matter, the presbyterate, or even sacrifice (though this would be more difficult) – were universal phenomena. But it would be equally possible – why close our eyes to it? – to describe as priests the bonze and the shaman, the Hogon of Bandiagara, the metal-worker of the Soudan, the Balian of Borneo, the charm-bearer, the dissector or the drummer. Rather than split hairs about the use of the word priest (which is really not a concept, but a word, except in the case of the priesthood of Christ alone), it would be preferable to concern ourselves with the significance of the clergy, and the appearance, or disappearance, in some societies, of a class, a caste or a group with priestly functions.

It is frequently said that the priest succeeded the kings and the sorcerers, but we must be careful not to take this statement too literally. The bible itself gives us a very clear example of a priestly organisation preceding the institution of the monarchy. We can only say that in the vast majority of cases, societies, which in the course of their organisation began to distinguish and specify the various functions found the need to equip themselves with priests less pressing than the appointment of their chiefs and the accrediting of their sorcerers. Priests forming a distinct social group and having a more or less officially defined role and status, are not normally found except in societies already

---

1. cf. Hubert et Mauss, 'Essai sur la nature et la fonction du sacrifice', *Année Sociologique*, v. ii, 1899, pp 29–138.

shaped in the hierarchal pattern, or, as some might prefer to say
societies in which the 'division of labour' has already become
highly organised. The existence of the clergy as a group seems to
be the mark of a certain state of social development much more
than of a definite type of religious attitude. Islam and China
show us, moreover, that the state of a society which makes it
possible for the priesthood to be organised as a clergy, presumes
a very high degree of social evolution, but without as a result
providing the necessary conditions for a high degree of culture.[1]

The existence of an organised clergy in functional co-relation-
ship with a type of social structure is not without its resulting
influence, which is of a very consistent pattern even in extremely
different religious attitudes. Under various forms, the clergy are
organised hierarchically around a priesthood which is exercised
both collectively and in various orders, so that one belonging to
the first degree of the priestly caste possesses less sacrificial power
than one having no priestly status at all in the same society. This
is so in the case of the young levite, for example, who is certainly
less of a priest in Israel than the simple father of a family. For it
is the actual organisation of the priesthood into a clergy that best
shows the distinction between priestly power and clerical status.
Furthermore, when it is associated with a restricted group, class,
order or caste, clerical professionalism inevitably carries with it
a competence to come into contact with the sacred, and a knowledge which is more or less esoteric in character. Specialisation
and esoterism go hand in hand with more complicated customs
and rituals, but not necessarily with a higher form of theology or
mysticism. But beneath these different aspects the fundamental
mark of the organised clergy appears to be the classification and
segregation of a social group, insulated by a collection of taboos
and prohibitions. Also, it seems that the religious category most
closely bound up with the presence of an organised clergy is the
distinction between the sacred and profane, the order of nature
and the supernatural order.

It may appear strange to us that the sense of the holy does not
necessarily imply the sense of the profane. Everything that we

1. cf. G. Van der Leeuw, *La religion dans son essence et ses manifestations*, paras. 26 and 50, Payot, Paris, 1948.

have been able to classify under the head of primitive mentality reveals the picture of a world which is seen as both sacred and profane, but these characteristics are not thereby regarded as ordained, much less as separable. And, whatever we might think of it, it seems that the organised priesthood appears when the sense of the profane has assumed extent and solidity. The consecration of a priest is as significant for the neutralising of the power of the numinous surrounding him as for attracting an additional immanence of the sacred. Priests would be professed as much to dispense the rest from priestly functions and from the taboos connected with them, as to provide society with competent sacrificers and mediators. It can even be stated, in the case of the Egyptian priesthood, for example, that its essential function was not to fill the cosmos with the sacred but to render its awful pervasiveness ineffective.[1]

The Christian priesthood, also organised as a clergy, appears in strong contrast to all this and we might well ask what light upon it we can expect from such a remote reference. But this rapid survey of the ambiguities underlying the term priest may help us to clarify some obscurities and perhaps to avoid some confusion, such as, for example, the frequent confusion between the function of the priest and the canonical status of the clerk, between the transmission of the power of orders and the juridical organisation of the sacerdotal body, between the social role and the sacramental role. But, at any rate, we can begin to answer the twofold question which led us along these lines.

First of all, to the Protestants we can allow, if not concede, the point that the actual organisation of the Catholic priesthood has been subjected to many influences which are unknown to pure evangelicalism, not only in the beginning but throughout the centuries. But the Church, which has regulated and adapted the organisation of the priesthood as a clergy, has never pretended that the details were instituted by Christ. The Church even professes to recognise her good in the forms of religious life best adapted to the various cultures, on condition that, when purified, they provide the best vehicles for her message. There are no

1. cf. G. Gurvitch, 'Les Théocraties charismatiques' in *Déterminismes Sociaux et liberté humaine*, P.U.F., Paris, 1954.

survivals of paganism in the Catholic priesthood, but deliberate and fruitful borrowings which have ripened within varied sacerdotal organisations, each one a polypary of customs organically developed on the same tradition. But there is not one of these borrowed forms which gives grounds for declaring the very principle of priesthood derived from Christ to be pagan. On the other hand, the existence of an organised Protestant clergy with no specifically priestly powers is rather a paradox, and while it could not be described as pagan in the classical sense of the word, a religious institution of this kind would have great difficulty in vindicating any claim to antiquity beyond the sixteenth century.

Catholics ought to be aware of the permanent sociological temptation presented by a highly developed organisation of the priesthood in clergy. Sacerdotal professionalism and the social segregation of a separate priestly body strengthens the natural inclination to insure against the embarrassments of the sacred, to escape them, to lay the burden upon a professional who makes that his business. It is in danger of leading to a corresponding separation of the profane, so that the layman may come to divide his life into two compartments, if not to feel that he is somehow different from the Church which has become concentrated into the hierarchy. It is under cover of this very temptation that the magical attitude has returned, for it is related less to superstitious beliefs than to a Promethean desire to tame the divine, to deflect it when it becomes troublesome, to make use of it rather than submit to it, to bargain for its help at the least cost. There is no need for the magical attitude to survive because it is so easily reborn from its own ashes; our contemporaries do not really need to remember the druids, nor our priests to be their lineal heirs, to make the effortless discovery of a kind of relationship which is just as much instinctive as religious. For religion and magic form a dynamic pair, assigned to the attention of professionals, and perhaps as universal and as fundamental as nature and culture.

And there is the other temptation, less universal but constantly present with the organised clergy, the temptation to clericalism. This would appear to be the right moment to state that this temptation incidental to the profession is not the clericalism of political intervention denounced by those who advocate the separation of powers, for the contingencies here are too recent for historical comparisons to be able to support a judgment. It would seem to be rather that spiritual clericalism which is just as active in simony, in coercion of conscience, in pride of caste. Do not let us be too ready to think that these temptations have now been overcome.

Despite the dangers involved, and many further examples could easily be given, the actual principle of the organisation of the priesthood is none the less found at the very beginning to be bound up with the institution of Christian priesthood. It is difficult not to see in this something more than a mere coincidence due to social conditions prevalent at the time of Christ and the apostles. Undoubtedly we ought to emphasise the fact that the whole people are clothed with royal priesthood, and that, consequently, the business of organisation begins at baptism, which separates the priestly people from the profane, sinful world, and which gives meat and drink in the name of our Lord Jesus Christ. But within the priestly community the transmission of apostolic powers names and separates those who receive the imposition of hands; yet before this additional distinction is made they have already been set apart by their place and their role in the assembly.

This place and role can only be explained within the authentic tradition. The pagan context cannot explain or justify what justifies itself and explains itself. But the types and shadows which prepared mankind to receive the gift of God can still help us to understand it when we are dazzled by the brightness of the direct light.

2. CHRIST THE PRIEST, SOLE ARCHETYPE OF ALL RITUAL PRIESTHOOD

'So also Christ did not glorify himself to be made a high priest; but he that said to him: Thou art my Son, this day have I begotten thee ... Thou art a priest for ever according to the order of Melchisedech ... and being consummated, he became the cause of eternal salvation to all that obey him ...' (Heb. 5, 5-9).

'But this, for that he continueth for ever, hath an everlasting priesthood. Whereby he is able also to save for ever them that come unto God by himself, always living to make intercession for us ... this he did once, by offering up himself' (Heb. 7, 24-7).

The epistle to the Hebrews claims that the priesthood of Christ is absolutely and completely unique, and this claim rests on two explicit rights which Christ the Priest alone can possess. On the one hand, his sacrifice as mediator is perfect, eternal, supremely efficacious, wrought once for all for the benefit of the whole world; on the other hand, his vocation and ordination to the priesthood after the order of Melchisedech king of justice and peace, are 'without father, without mother, without genealogy, having neither beginning of days nor end of life'. (Heb. 7, 16).

The priestly mediation of Christ is utterly unique and cannot possibly be compared with any other because his position as priest cannot be dissociated from his character of Son of God, 'perfected for evermore', appointed by 'the word of the oath' without repentance (Heb. 7, 28; cf. 7, 20 sq.).

By making a radical distinction between priesthood 'after the order of Melchisedech' and the priesthood of Aaron 'after the law', the epistle to the Hebrews dispenses us from any necessity for looking at any other priesthood whatever to understand the priesthood of Christ. We have already seen the ambiguity in the word priest, which is a convenient label to attach to very different realities. We have already learnt to make the distinction between priesthood and clergy. The epistle to the Hebrews reminds us that if the word priest were relevant to Aaron then it could not be applied to Christ. It tells us that the priesthood of Christ is the least clerical of priesthoods, the most foreign to all organisation, since 'it is evident that our Lord sprang out of Juda; in which tribe Moses spoke nothing concerning priests' (Heb. 7, 14). The utter originality of the priesthood of Christ in relation to these types and shadows prevents us from seeking enlightenment as to its meaning, except by way of contrast, in any other sacerdotal context, either pagan or Aaronic. To understand what 'priesthood after the order of Melchisedech' might be, it is no use trying to find out what priesthood in general is; it may even be good method to forget what we thought we knew about it. And as the Christian priest himself is the inheritor of the priesthood of Christ, after the order of Melchisedech and not Aaron, the epistle to the Hebrews itself compels our comparisons to follow unexpected lines which will adhere more closely to inner meanings than to outward forms.

Jesus is priest not by office but by nature; the unction annointing him is the incarnation of the Word, and not a rite. And as his priesthood is not something added to his essence as Son of Man and Son of God, so his function as mediator is not distinct from his royal or prophetic functions. He is pre-eminently king, prophet and priest all together and all in one, integrally, in his nature and in his person.

Nothing could be more alien to the priesthood of Christ than the ritual priesthood conspicuous in a society in which the functions of king, sorcerer and priest have become distinct. We see how the epistle to the Hebrews loves to oppose the priesthood of Christ to the priesthood of Aaron instituted by Moses— himself disqualified from accepting a plurality of offices. No official, be he haruspex, hierarch or levite, ritually consecrated and juridically appointed, exercises any priesthood which can be compared with that of Jesus Christ, save in contradistinction. The priesthood of Jesus is indissociable, like that of the patriarch, Abraham, for example, who bore 'in his loins' Aaron and Moses (cf. Heb. 7, 10).

By his vocation and election to the priesthood of his own nature, Christ is more closely allied to David, the elect of God, or to Isaias, called to the prophetic ministry. Christ, the object of divine predilection, and the instrument of God among men, does not, however, receive his power and his mission as mediator like a bolt from the blue in the form of a gratuitous *charisma*, as the spirit of the god falling upon the shaman or taking possession of the songhay, nor even as the timely revelation of his destiny, like the Indian warrior who might make the acquaintance of his totem in a mystic dream. Priest by nature, Christ is born for his function like the Brahman, the elder of Soudanese twins, or the uboa, whose particular training is recognised by the Bassoui from his birth, or even like John the Baptist, who was 'more than a prophet'.

But, as distinct from any other predestination, the election of Christ is neither fortuitous, gratuitous nor repeatable. The Father called the Son because he had no other, because he alone was capable of answering, 'Here am I' (cf. Heb. 10, 6–10). Not only is Christ born for his function, but it is for his function that he had to be born, for without his birth his function would not have been possible. He IS priesthood itself and mediation itself. Only that, and all that. Apart from him there is nothing more than an artificial, imperfect and delusive figure, an 'a-reality' of priesthood and mediation. If the term priest has any meaning, it can only be as a proper name, a synonym for Jesus Christ, the only possible priest, the only living priest, the only priest completely and totally real.

The only analogy to the role of Christ that the pagan religions can offer is in the sacrifices of the god celebrated as a death and resurrection mystery, by which the initiates are associated with the power of the invincible life of Dionysius, of the Isis-Osiris pair, or Tammuz and Ishtar, or of Prajapati, or of the ancestors or founders of esoteric societies in the so-called primitive religions. Assimilated into the fertility rites (which were rites of immortality as well), the sacrifices of the god are the focal point of a complex symbolism which is difficult to reconstruct and still more to interpret. If it were right and possible to formulate a general law to cover them all, we could perhaps put forward, as a hypothesis, the theory that the function of the sacrificed god seems to be so much wider and more fruitful, so much less added to his personality, in a word, so much closer to the role of Christ, when the god in question is primordial, more closely connected with myths concerning origins. At any rate, the strictly fundamental characteristic common to all these cults based on the sacrifice of the god is that the sacrifice is founded on a myth. And it is this point which now claims our attention.

The only possible priesthood, the only real priesthood, the priesthood of Christ, is an archetype to which we can find an approximate equivalent in pagan religions only on the mythical level, and not at all on the institutional level. And so, if the pagan context can throw any light on the priesthood of Christ, we must approach it through a study of the function of myth.

The term myth has become devaluated partly as a result of the contempt of Christians for diabolical and crude superstitions and partly as a result of the limited and presumptuous rationalism of the age of enlightenment. In current speech myth has become synonymous with fable or fairy-tale, devoid of any foundation or probability. In the language of psychology it signifies a dream of the impossible, an emotional delusion, a symbolical projection of a psychic state, and *mythomania* is a mark of neurosis. Sociologists have listed among the myths of the twentieth century those compulsive ideas or ideals which inspire and govern action, such as progress, the race, a classless society. All these various interpretations are derived from the basic meaning of myth in the history of religions, where it appears in effect to be a tale, an imaginative literary work; it constitutes the projection of a collective psychology and the symbolic norm of the psychology of individuals. It is also the ground and motive force underlying a given culture, the principle of its activities and organisation; but it is all these things only because it is primarily the sacred narrative of origins providing an account of the beginning of creatures and happenings; a rough and ready, rather than naïve, metaphysics, giving the secret, the meaning and the normal ways of the mystery of existence.

The anthropomorphisms in the pagan mythologies are no less intentional than those in the bible. Humanity did not wait for Plato to discover that imagery speaks when logic is silent, and, like Professor Claude Levi-Strauss, we ought now to be asking if humanity was not right in concerning itself with the image before it took an interest in logic since logic, pushed to its limits, returns to imagery without any guarantee that it has ever been free from it. For

the true significance of myth is not that it gives an objective picture of the universe. . . . What it does explain is rather the way in which man sees himself in his world. Myth should not be interpreted cosmologically, but anthropologically or, rather, existentially. It speaks of a power or powers experienced by man as the 'principle', which binds alike his world and what he himself is able to do and suffer. It speaks or conceives of them as it sees them in man's known world of things and forces, in the sphere of man's human life, of the things he loves, of the things that guide him, and of the things he can do. It speaks, for example, of the egg of the world, of the tree of the world, to represent the principle and origin of the universe. Or again, it speaks of the conflicts between the gods, from which have arisen the conditions and ordinances of the world. It speaks in earthly fashion of what is not earthy, in human fashion of what is divine . . . for its authentic purpose, which is to speak of a higher power to which the world and men are subject, is hindered and concealed by the 'objectivising' character of its expression. . . .'[1]

Myth is the story of the archetypes, or rather their dramatic presentation, their living re-enactment. In the mythical narrative, events take place in a special time-sequence, preceding and transcending historical time, an age (*oeuvum*) on the threshold of time as we know it, during which the world was ordered, and passed from chaos to cosmos. Place, too, is special in the narrative: it is an environment which is known but indefinable, remote, and forbidden to the living, the mystical reverse side of a familiar landscape, and it is impossible to say whether it still exists or whether it has vanished; it remains, but as if it were no longer. The mythical narrative is the story of the gods, the great ancestors, the civilising heroes, the first men, who, at a time between the temporal and the eternal, in places which are neither earth nor heaven, but both in one, fashioned the world as we know it, ordained the decisive moments of life and death, devised techniques and customs, meted out to living creatures their privileges, role and station, and organised nature and society. In myth, beings, desires, actions and even hazards themselves possess new potency – they are the archetypes, the ancients, the precedents; they forge, found, beget, predetermine, in all power and freedom, the whole future of humanity. Myth is the archetypical conflict between the powers of order and the powers of disorder. What is at stake in the struggle is the birth of the world of history and its law, the success of a primal existence serving as a pattern for the temporal order which would follow.

1. Bultmann, *L'interpretation du Nouveau Testament*, Aubier, Paris, 1927.

The archetype is the unparalleled act, fortuitous but decisive, which lays the foundations of an eternal law, the law of all real existence begotten by it. For if the archetype is without precedent or justification, it is the pattern, the explanation and the source of everything which will reproduce it by repeating it unwearyingly. '*Nihil novi sub sole*', said the ancients – all earthly reality only exists by deriving its existence from an archetype, by symbolic reference to the symbolised. The whole cosmos is but a replica of the archetypes from which it has both existence and form. Myth provides an explanation for the normal sequence of events and the principle which governs them, because the cosmos is but the continuance of the mythical 'then' unfolding into the present, the indefinite interpretation of everything implied in the primal act. The world as we know it is but a semblance, a symbol, a devaluated replica, a contingent existence, subsisting merely by its constant reference to the mythical world of the archetypes.[1]

It is because they are placed within this mythical world that the sacrifice of Dionysius, the dismemberment of Prajapati, or the resurrection of Osiris evince so much potency, and have so much more reality and effectiveness than man's daily experience of death in which there is no refuge. Less important personages, eponymous ancestors, totems, civilising heroes, are not able to develop so much cosmic potency, but, being closer to normal realities, they offer men an easier natural cycle ensuring the harvest, good fortune in war, abundance of game, a better future in the beyond. The efficacy of the archetype, in effect, pays tribute to a two-fold claim: it has potency in direct relation to its primordial character, to its closeness to essential existence, to its being anterior even to the mythical age of the derived archetypes; and it is repeatable, accessible, frequently useful and usable, in so far as it is not too remote from ordinary man, from normal earthly realities, on the very threshold of everyday life, and, as it were, on the frontier between the cosmised and cosmising.

It would not seem that violence is done to the pre-eminent dignity of the priesthood of Christ when we see in it the response

1. cf. M. Eliade, *The Myth of Eternal Return*, Routledge, 1955.

to the anxious hopes of humanity, so crudely expressed by the myths in their wavering between the potent but remote intercessor and the familiar, but limited, benefactor. At any rate, we cannot understand the tremendous enthusiasm unleashed in the Roman world by the good news of the Unknown God if we do not appreciate how the anxiety of religious souls in paganism, confronted by such contradictory systems for their salvation, was suddenly evaporated by the irruption of the eternal Son of God who was born in the flesh to redeem his fellow men. This Son, 'upholding all things by the word of his power', who, 'in the beginning . . . founded the earth', is he whom 'it behoved . . . in all things to be made like to his brethren, that he might become a merciful and faithful high priest with God' (Heb. 1, 3, 10; 2, 17; cf. *pass.*).

The enthusiasm of the epistle to the Hebrews is ineffective unless men are successfully liberated from the trammels of habit so that they can really understand the revolution achieved by that Witness who could see and feel so much better than the myths had ever dared to promise to their dreams. Then, since the apostle's hearers could make use of their pagan classifications to understand, assimilate and pass on the Good News, may we not believe that they understood, accepted and proclaimed the priesthood of Christ simply and profoundly, as the complete realisation of the illusory and doubtful hopes expressed in their myths?

But the mythical archetype, in paving the way for an understanding of the absolutely unique and supremely efficacious priesthood of Christ, can also help us to see the point of the repetition of the One in the many in the presbyteral priesthood. For what continues to be unintelligible to the Protestant, who cannot free himself from the assumptions of a particular historical context, created no sort of difficulty at all for the Gentile converts who were accustomed to this dialectic of the archetype and its repetition.

The mythical archetype generates a repetition in time, but this has only a participated, fragile, inadequate existence. The cosmos inaugurated by the myth becomes progressively weaker as the temporal cycle uses up the force of primal energy. The world grows old. The order established in it by the forces of cosmisation languishes, and the forces of disorder, chained and muzzled, yet always threatening, put the world in increasing danger of a return to chaos. Sometimes it is the chthonian powers of chaos who really hold sway, and power and life are in their hands, and the heavenly gods can then do no more than canalise and tame them as Apollo transformed the Erinnyes into the Eumenides. When this happens, the world becomes old through sclerosis. Elsewhere a more dramatic or cynical outlook on the world, as among the African Bantu, for example, holds that the master of life, disappointed in men, retired to Empyrean, abandoning his work to irrascible spirits (genii) – at any rate, the imprudence or the weakness of men contributed towards hastening the process of decay in the temporal order of things. Taboos, traditions and customs are, as it were, the directions for use of the universe; they respect its constitution, maintain its stability, and preserve its efficiency. Infringement of the mythical norms, faithlessness of the symbol to the archetype – these are daily threats to the order of the world, be they culpable or involuntary, conscious or unconscious. Abandoned to the erosion of time and the foolish malice of human beings, those gullible accomplices of chaos, the work of cosmisation would rush rapidly to its ruin if recourse, either permanent or occasional, could not be had, to the power of the archetype against its own degeneration in order to stave off senility and infuse something of its original vigour and purity into the daily round. This refuge is the rite, or more strictly the liturgy, the ritual reactualisation of the mythical archetype.

The myth, as a re-telling, as a dramatic presentation of the archetype, is in itself a ritual element, for it is much more an image, a symbol, than a narrative. The actual rite is another form of dramatic presentation, a mimed and gestured presentation. The liturgy, the sacred celebration, is the representation of the archetype through the myth-narrative and the ritual-action combined. If we were pressed to define their respective functions, perhaps we could see in the myth-recital, vibrating in the rhythm of the sacred word and accompanied often by the voice of the spirits or the ancestors reverberating in the drum or

the bull-roarer, the reactualisation of the mythical age in our
own time sequence. The ritual action, on the other hand, represents within the sacred space, and in an ephemeral way, that
nor-earth-nor-heaven where the god-for-man and the man-for-
god were begotten.

Sacred time, sacred space, sacred action, when the actor of
the mime is specially prepared and appointed for this function,
the rite, in the broad sense of 'narrative-place-mime', revives
the potency of the normal pattern by bringing it closer to the
archetype from which it is derived and to which it refers. Is the
rite really a means of reactualising the power of the archetype? We could not say this, since the archetype remains unique
and is nevertheless inadequate. Is the enfeebled time sequence
annihilated and 'today' put back to the yesterday of the archetype? Again, we could not say this, since the past is not forgotten, although its exhaustion and the resulting inconvenience
do disappear. The enigma of how remains. But there is overwhelming certainty that the rite is a bath of rejuvenation which
gives back to the world its youth. Its potency is ruled by custom
and its calendar is adjusted to the needs of daily life – the feasts
of the spring and the first-fruits, the feast of the New Year
and mid-summer, feasts of the dead and initiations, feasts of
the harvest and purifications. But then there are unforeseen
events – and these are so much more formidable – ceremonial
occasions, evil omens, cataclysms and misfortune. While the
normal pattern only derives its existence from the archetype by
a near-symbolism which makes it more disposable than real,
the rite, on the other hand, evokes the potency of the myth by a
strict and careful symbolism, which is explosive if one does not
guard against it, but compelling when one knows how to use it.

The archetype transcends, rather than precedes, the normal
sequence of events. It creates (rather than inaugurating or renewing) it in a continuous but rhythmic fashion through the
rite. It reintroduces itself the more easily into it to revivify
and purify it, since it is already written deeply and intimately
within it. Even more than the first outburst of creative energy,
which time would effectively stem, even more than the resur-
gence of the renewing energy which, at the bidding of the liturgy,

would set the world in motion once again, the archetype of the myth and of the rite is the divine, the numinous, the transcendent and the immanent.

The effective realisation of the unique and eternal intercession of Christ for the sins of his brethren simplifies this problem of immanence and transcendence which the pagan traditions were compelled, rather laboriously, to interpret in the light of their experience of time and of the sacred. The reactualisation of the archetype or the annihilation of time are no longer the point at issue, for it is Christ actually alive and sitting on the right hand of the Father in the sanctuary not made with hands who is our high priest. Ritual repetition is concerned less with remaking than interpreting. It represents in the sense of revealing rather than reproducing. It makes present because attention to the presence must be revived, rather than to restore reality to the awaiting. And if the gospel, which bears witness, repeats its *in illo tempore*, the liturgy never sings of anything but *hodie*.

If the priesthood of the priest is related to the category of symbol and rite, if it is linked with the only real and unique priesthood in Christ, like the repetition to the archetype, it is always necessary to bear in mind that the need for the Christian, as distinct from the pagan, rite does not spring either from the feebleness of the work of salvation wrought by Christ once for all, or because time has consumed its power, since it is eternal. Fundamentally, the usefulness of the symbol is pedagogic – it is the faithful who need this re-presentation of the mystery in their own space and time, for each single one of them must be brought face to face with this mystery in the psychologically normal exercise of his freedom in the faith. It is not the work of Christ which needs to be continued, achieved or resumed. The sacrament is for man. The only thing which is new, if it really is new, is the continual growing into the pleroma of Christ, which will take into itself whatever the individual Christian, in his freedom, has made of his time. But even on this level, the sacrament remains the visible celebration of unity and is the interpreter of an efficacy which is realised in the mystery of the Spirit.

We are not detracting from the absolute and supreme uniqueness of the priesthood of Christ if we make it the archetype of a ritual priesthood with a plurality of priests. Nor do we derogate from the pre-eminent dignity and real efficacy of the presbyteral priesthood if we see in it the answer of the infinite solicitude of God to the needs of mortal men, who must see and touch if they are going to be able to accept the love which is offered to them. Why did God *want* to need men? Why has Christ our Saviour associated with the permanent efficacy of his eternal sacrifice the sporadically permanent efficacy of its ritual translation in time? His power is absolute: he could have dispensed with it. Let us not therefore deem it superfluous. His power is absolute and perhaps even the incarnation itself was not necessary. And the rite of the eternal sacrifice is indeed in the line of the incarnation of the Eternal Word. If we must have a reason, then infinite love will provide it. But it would also be possible to put forward without hesitation the compassionate desire to crown the expectations of the pagan, heavy with sin certainly, but also lifted up by the anguished indictments of Job.

But at this point do not the Protestant objection and the Catholic disquiet revive? While marvelling at the economy of revelation, at the tutorship of God which both prepares men and adapts itself to them are we not surprised that a 'good pagan' had so little trouble in entering into a mystery in which everything is done to perplex us? Undoubtedly the good pagan had the supreme advantage over us in that he had a sense of, and a taste for, mystery. But had he not a flair for syncretism as well? The pagan of our own day, at all events, seems much more disposed to remake God to suit his own requirements than to welcome the God who comes to meet him.

In assuming these types into himself Christ fulfils them, and the 'poor' recognise in him the one they had been waiting for. But in fulfilling these types, Christ transforms them, and the 'wise' may be taken by surprise, or refuse him. The 'scandal to the Jews' was also 'foolishness to the Gentiles'.

3. THE CHRISTIAN DIALECTIC OF THE ONE AND THE MANY

Both among the Gentiles and the Chosen People, the governing principle of the economy of revelation before the coming of

Christ was the crystallisation of the simple and only God in a whole host of sacred symbols. As soon as the prophets, who had finally persuaded Israel that there was but one God, were silent, and as soon as Greek religious criticism had been successful in transforming Homer through the purifications of Plotinus, God spoke in his Son and made known the unique love of three Persons. The profession of faith at Caesarea rouses men afresh to the search for God; neither the prophet nor the philosopher had lost their way, but they had only travelled half the journey and thought they had reached the end of the road.

The mystery of the Trinity opened up a new thought to men. It took the Church four centuries to get a real grip of its principles, but even when it had been grasped, it continued to demand that the conversion of the mind should be sustained, and indeed surpassed. Nothing Christian escapes the law of the real Trinity, nor even anything in existence, since man is but an image of it. The priesthood of Christ, of Jesus, and of the priest, is above philosophy and prophecy in the three dimensions of unique love.

The transcendent myth is immanent in this everyday world habitually through the symbol which fashions, so to speak, the tissue of the cosmos, and actually through the ritual, which is the revivifying of the archetype. The intercession of Christ seated at the right hand of the Father transcends time, but remains immanent in all earthly reality and happenings, habitually through the sacrament of his Church, and actually through the priest who reflects in an undefined way the active presence of Christ dwelling amongst us. The relationship between men and God is never apprehended save in this interplay of immanence and transcendence, but these words never mean the same thing – either in their reference to space or time – to the pagan, the Jew and the Christian.

In the majority of non-biblical religions, if not in all, the mythical age transcends time because it precedes it. The mythical archetype is essentially original, cosmogonic, as in the first chapters of Genesis. The source and the explanation of history precedes time. The Greek thinks of man as marching backwards into a formless and hopeless future, his face turned towards the past, which he scrutinises tirelessly in his search for wisdom. History itself, as we understand it today, does not exist; time corrodes but does not create; it produces nothing which is fundamentally new, no invention; it is the work of fate and not of freedom; it is a perpetual repetition, or at most a making explicit of what was implicitly ordained at the beginning, once for all. When historic time does take a hand, it is to disintegrate the world in spite of the cyclical renewal of the cosmos by the rites; it slowly pushes the world towards the final catastrophe, which will put the whole work of cosmisation in jeopardy either by water or fire. But even this role is contemptible, for after the flood or the conflagration the light of another Genesis will dawn, and the world will be started on its round again by the same deeds and the same words, just as the new day succeeds the old day, or as spring follows winter. The whole universe is a hell without hope: Varuna sleeps, all is calm, dazed but orderly; Varuna awakes, and everything is turned upside down; but Varuna slumbers again and life begins anew, beneath a sun which is not new but rediscovered. If they are so sad in Hades it is because they will only see the light again by experiencing the agony of life afresh. Buddha is the Saviour of mankind because he liberates it from living existence.[1]

In biblical revelation it is almost the exact opposite. History, in Genesis, appears to be made up of uncertainty, hope and liberty. Of course, the narrative of origins is not without importance, since it explains the everyday world by reference to the purpose of God and the weight of sin. But the ground of history is no longer before time but after, the history itself is punctuated with covenants, and actually inaugurated with the promise, the excited, impatient and anguished expectation of truth and life in the day of Yahweh. From the literary angle alone, this inversion of perspective is radical and patent. The pagan mythologies painted their cosmogonies in the colourful, fertile and inexhaustible symbolism of chaos, while conceiving the final catastrophe in the most prosaic imagery, scarcely distinguishable from normal reality, save by exaggeration. Genesis, on the other hand, seems reluctant to use even the most judicious symbolism,

1. cf. M. Eliade, *op. cit.*, Routledge, 1955.

cutting out popular traditions more ruthlessly even than the
Roman historians; but in contrast, the apocalypses display all
the allure of the Oriental imaginative genius, rediscovering the
fruitfulness of symbols, and an aesthetic syntax which is above
logic. The people of God are the people of the promise, the
people of faith and hope, the people who wait on history and
mould it. Israel marches in the light of the stars, straining to
the future because God is of tomorrow, rather than yesterday or
today. Israel has a destiny, but it is no fragile and deceptive
stereotype: the destiny of Israel is fulfilled each day as God sees
fit. And Israel knows that she is not merely the servant but the
spouse of the Living God. To go to meet God Abraham had to
uproot himself from the land of his fathers, from the wealth of
Egypt, from the wisdom of custom and the prudence of fore-
sight; his sons continued to be uprooted from the nations, separated and consecrated, in permanent conflict, for intercourse was
impossible – even common words did not have the same meaning, since what was called an echo by the Gentiles was interpreted as a signal by the people.

Jews and pagans would have had more opportunity to become
conscious of their differences had they been able to conceive
that the last word, the end of all prophecy and all philosophy
in the Uttered Word, instead of taking sides in their discussion,
would invite them to surmount their differences in 'making all
things new'. The Eternal Word, the Word of the beginning
and the end, the Word who laid the foundations of the world,
the Word for whom history worked and waited, rose up, in
Jesus Christ, from the very crux of events, and emerged out of
the world and history to rule them. No apocalyptic frenzy, no
cosmogonic explosion; the advent of the Wholly Other found
the universe silent, stunned like Medusa, by the supreme unex-
pectedness of his self-revelation. In the eternal, but through
history, Christ plays the same archetypical role as, before or
after time, the a-historical archetypes played in myth or apocalypse. From the literary point of view, i.e. in the sphere of the
explanation of the mystery by word and image, the revolution
is marked by the appearance of a dialectic in three dimensions,
which took the place of a simple polarisation towards either the

past or the future. Christ is dead, he lives, he comes again; the Christian is under the death of sin, the grace of salvation, and the earnest of the Spirit. Each one of the three dimensions can be situated in either general or individual history, since the mystery is kneaded into history – the date of death is the 14 Nisan, life is today, the return is tomorrow; sin is of this mortal life which is given over to death, grace is of the life of the Church vowed to eternity; the glory which is even now possessed will only be revealed on the other side of the body of death. But the transcendence of the mystery shines forth in that very event which claimed to contain it: our Lady was preserved from sin by that sacrifice for which she furnished the victim, so that she might furnish it spotless; 'in forming Adam, God was thinking of Christ', and pardoned his disobedience '*ante praevisa merita*' even if 'he did not create him, so that his Son might be his pre-existent Saviour'; our Lady is already glorified in her body, and every moment 'the Son of Man comes as a thief' to the bedsides of the dying; 'this world is already judged' and the guests seated at the wedding banquet.

The radical and absolute originality of the word brought to men in Christ is to be found in the recreation of the link between time and eternity, the one and the many, and the restoration of the natural order by grace. Whether in myth or apocalypse, the archetype was a unity, and its repetition a plurality like a mirror shattered into fragments; the mystery of the multiplication takes place in the insurmountable gulf between the divine and the earthly. Christ is amongst us, familiar yet exceptional, and he remains unique. He rediscovers the unity of the Father and, by dividing himself among the many invisibly yet intimately, palpably yet secretly, he leads men back to that unity. The archetype is henceforth in time and eternity, and although we might say that he is in them in different ways, we could not say that he can be placed in the one more than the other. And, like the archetype, repetition is a kneading together of the temporal and the eternal, though in a different way, and we could not say that it is in time rather than above time. God has bridged the gulf; the Son is increased by his brethren in the flesh, and men are gathered to him who is their recapitulation. No longer is the eternal outside time, nor the temporal without the eternal. There is a history of the eternal and an eternal of history, which the words themselves will no longer be able to separate without betrayal.

Nor has space any reason to be envious of time. The rite, in effect, makes concrete the relationship of the repetition to the archetype through a coming-together; essentially it is the assigned place of meeting signified within the space provided for the ritual action. The Church, the priest, the sacramental action present and active in the world, possess the same function in space of drawing together, and putting into relationship with the unique and eternal sacrifice in every place where Christ is being formed into a defined community. But here again the relationship of immanence and transcendence with space does not mean exactly the same thing to Jews, pagans and Christians.

Some pagan rites are scarcely more than superstitious gesticulations because the myth which inaugurated them has been lost in the memory of the community. But we rarely meet with liturgies in which the sacred space is not precisely specified and determined. Each type of rite may have its favourite space, but communities which do not function on a logical space are rare, and doubtless, before Galileo, few men had lived who did not know with exact certainty where the centre of the world was to be found. The centre of the world is that privileged place where a meeting between men, spirits and gods can be effected, often because, as tree, mountain, pillar or pyramid, it is functionally in relationship with them all.

Unique and full of dangers, remote, inaccessible or forbidden, the centre is sacred space *par excellence*, the prototype for the ritual place, for encounter with the divine seems to have been possible there without any liturgy, through the very power of the place itself. Every sacred place is derived from it or is referable to it. Frequently the sacred action is but the mime of some fortuitous action performed at the centre, and which consequently preserves or inherits its power of evocation. The mythical heroes, the shaman or the high priest alone have personal access to the centre, for to approach it requires a fabulous courage to brave the dangers, a proved ingenuity to defeat the snares, or an exceptional holiness which is proof against even the most sacred. Yet it is of the highest importance to attain the centre; it is through the centre, and through it alone, that the transition from a larval and illusory life to the life that is true can be made, that the miserable condition of humanity can be radically transformed through contact with the divine. But the essential thing is for some pioneer to reach it, for his success will benefit the whole of humanity, either because by imprisoning him, as it were, humanity will effect a passage under his guidance, or because the forerunner returns with the pledge or the secret that opens the door, or because a repeatable liturgy is born from it, which will obtain its fruits for humanity. There is only one saviour, as there is only one centre, but just as the archetype breeds repetition, so the prototype attracts a plurality of places; each altar is a high place, the tree of the world is the central pillar of the tent, ascension or emergence into true life takes place in the village square or on the initiation site. But the prototype is one place only, the unique centre of the unique encounter, but many places borrow from it its capacity for encounter, and thus what is normally the privilege of one is put within the reach of all. The whole space of the universe, without directly borrowing from it, finds itself drawn towards the centre, and every action placed within the field of its magnetism. From the simple journey to the wanderings of the soul after death, by participating in processions, pilgrimages, the stages of initiation or the mystic life, every single step taken, every walk, every voyage has some link with the centre, either prototype or local, real or symbolic. The centre itself is none other than the mystery of the divine inaccessible, which is nevertheless closer to all things than they are to themselves.[1]

Israel knew God so well as to know his Name, which was written in her books although it might not be spoken. Solomon built a temple for him so that he might dwell in the midst of his people and make his abode there after he had led them through the desert and in battle. Towards this temple each year the

1. cf. M. Eliade, 'Le symbolisme du Centre' in *Images et Symboles*, Gallimard, Paris, 1952.

people filed up in ranks to gather around their God, everyone according to his order, his tribe, his status and his age. But the high priest alone, the successor of Aaron, could penetrate within the holy of holies. Yet behind the veil hiding the majesty of the presence of God . . . there is nothing save the vestiges of that covenant which they all held much more firmly in their hearts. For Israel 'adored that which they knew' even 'in spirit and in truth', but man needs a majestic temple although he knows it is empty, a long solemn pilgrimage towards the law although he already knows every line of it, lest he should bow down before an idol which is the work of his own hands. Israel knows that she lives under the eye and in the hand of God. God is in the wind, the cloud and the fire, but not even Moses was able to see his face, although afterwards no one could bear that he look upon him, transfigured as he was by what he had seen. Since Israel knew whom she worshipped, she also knew that an approach such as sacrifice was only acceptable in obedience and faithfulness. Beyond that, Israel knew only that one did not ask God for the balance-sheet. Jerusalem is the centre of the world because God's house is there. He does not inhabit it because he is not of this world. But all the same it is at Jerusalem that one can come very near to God without dying. For to reach God is impossible, out of the question; even to live in his sight is difficult enough.

The high-place of Christianity, where the reconciliation of men with God, the passing from the illusory to the true life, is effected under the guidance of the only Saviour, is Calvary, where the Cross was planted over the skull of Adam. But no one can determine exactly where the Centre-Calvary is. However, side by side and above an approximate place, and without any trouble at all, the pilgrim finds it in the 'memorial of the Lord' celebrated according to the particular rite to which he belongs. For the God of Israel, dwelling in inaccessible light, comes near and makes himself tangible to us so that in all places, at every moment, everyone may meet him, and come closer to him than any mythical hero has ever claimed to be able to do. And yet, no longer has he a dwelling-place amongst us, as he had the temple, in which he dwelt as fully as he could anywhere; this is because we ourselves have no abiding city on this earth, but merely temporary tents on our return journey to the Father's house, where we are awaited by him whom we have already met and who actually accompanies us on the road. And our journey itself is but a meeting brought about only to be ended without ever being fulfilled.

Truly the Christian centre is no longer a place, but a person; and this person, the person of Jesus Christ, is offered to us through all the 'mediations' in which human personality can be offered, but here we meet it as God, for it is the Word. By substituting the personal character of the incarnate Word for the image of the centre, Christ is the answer both to the expectation of the pagan, who was looking for some assurance in the flesh, and to the demands of the Jew, who would avoid every idol – the person is offered and reached through the mediation of the flesh, but the meeting is no longer merely physical contact, any more than a person is flesh alone.

The radical novelty introduced by Christ on the level of tangible space is the dialogue between flesh and spirit, comparable to the marriage between the eternal and history. The Jew, with his acute sense of God, firmly enclosed the mass of humanity in a flesh stirred only by the breath of the unique Spirit, and actually went so far in his distinction between 'breath' and 'Spirit' that he could not conceive of an encounter between them. The Greek, with his Promethean sense of man, did not easily resign himself to not being a fallen god, a degradation of the One through the multiplication of flesh. 'The Word was made flesh.' A new Adam of spiritual flesh has arisen, the first-born of the dead. A new people, neither Jew nor Greek, has been born of him, a people clothed with the immortality of the Spirit while still in the flesh. The Spirit is 'poured out upon all flesh', and all flesh leads to Christ, since what is done to the least of his brethren is done to him. A part of flesh itself has become his flesh. And the Church, his body, is in the world.

In considering the priesthood of Christ against the background of the pagan dialectic of archetype and repetition, it is clear to us that, without doing violence to its uniqueness, the rite is so much better able to proclaim the multiple manifestation of the priesthood of Christ when the perfect concomitance of the action makes it possible for the act of Christ and the act of the priest to be regarded as the face and reverse side of the same operation. By resorting to the Christian dialectic of the eternal and history, it is easier for us to realise that by being identified with the present activity of Christ himself, the sacramental action, without distinguishing today and for ever, can be both memorial and proclamation. In the Christian context of the dialectic between flesh and Spirit, the relationship of the *sacramentum et res* is set up more authentically than through the images of doctrinal interpretation. But the transition from the pagan to the Christian context throws light on the cosmic role of re-creation played by redemption in Christ. At the same time, presbyteral priesthood is recognised in its subordinate but active place, in the leading function of vicarious satisfaction. Within the body of Christ and his pleroma in process of formation, which is the Church, the sacraments, centred on the priesthood, are the relaying of the humanisation of the Word for the divinisation of humanity. Presbyteral priesthood plays its part in the resuming of history into the eternal, and in the co-extension of the eternal to the particular event, not by adding its own force to the work of the Spirit, not by becoming part of the flesh of Christ which bears the total burden of centuries, but by being the connecting link which enables the Spirit to unite men to the body of Christ without doing violence to them, and to multiply himself without dividing himself, like the eucharist, which is itself figure, means and earnest. That is why, in the community – the efficacious figure both of the Church and of the pleroma – the priest is chief, not because he represents a particular and incomplete section of the social cell, but because in the cell of the local church he is the authorised and effective mediation which makes communication between persons possible, so much more authorised and so much more effective when any objective reality which might become a barrier is swallowed up in the pure function of putting into relationship.

Is it necessary to emphasise that the pagan perspective of the archetype and its repetition is so much better able to distinguish and to separate the ritual priesthood of the many from the unique priesthood of the archetype when it sets up their profound unity on their fundamental interdependence, divesting ritual priesthood of any efficacious reality – other than modal – of its own? The transition to the Christian point of view, on the other hand, in including as it does the whole of cosmic transformation in the actual ministry of Christ, far from causing the place of ritual to disappear, actually helps to restore the reality of the sacrament by restoring its function, which, although deriving from the historic flesh of Christ, is original. But there must be mutual adjustment between the two points of view, for Christ's originality is not a disowning but a ransoming, and he has preserved the form of a clergy organised for repetition for his own priesthood of recapitulation.

We realise that the Protestant would have difficulty in seeing things from the angle of cosmic redemption, when he cannot even bring himself to admit the real activity of grace in conversion or even in the state of blessedness. We also realise that the Catholic instinctively prefers a cosmic salvation into which he himself is to enter personally, actively, oblatively, a comfortable way of vicarious satisfaction, in which exactness in observing the rubrics will enable him to profit by his baptismal privileges in perfect tranquility. The hardest thing for him is to remain where grace has placed him, and to be converted either from 'Judaism' or 'Gentilism' to the scandal and folly of the faith.

Israel rejected Christ and preserved apocalypse. In those very lands where Greek wisdom had outstripped the myths, Islam rejected Christ to return to Genesis. And where Luther and Calvin did not undermine hope by destroying its supports, Promethean materialism has brought paganism back again. Yet the grain of mustard seed has not stopped growing.

But it is not given to us today serenely to contemplate the progressive stages and the advancement of revelation, as if the spread of the good news rolled forward like the crest of a surging wave. We must open our eyes to reality, shake off the stereotyped, and realise that salvation in Jesus Christ, offered today to more than two thousand million men, moves scarcely a quarter of them in the immediate care of the presbyteral and ritual priesthood. If we are neither Protestants nor paganisers we have to remember that that shedding of blood on the 14th Nisan is not the only tangible reality on which to base a legitimate hope of salvation for our two thousand million brethren. If we are neither Jews nor Marxists, we do not have to postpone the fulfilment of the promises by cheerfully sacrificing the generation that awaits it. Today Christ offers his agony for two thousand million men, and it can only be that, for those same two thousand million today, every priest offers that same agony in the Church.

Just as the archetypical priesthood of Christ is unintelligible if it is artificially severed from the whole work of salvation which is his function, so Christian ritual priesthood is unintelligible if it is improperly severed from the whole field of its application, which is contemporary humanity. This will compel us to go beyond that narrow point of view which regards the sacrament of Orders as a series of degrees, and to renew our vision of priesthood in the fulness of the dimensions in which it is lived by the Church, for the world, in Christ. The relationship of the priesthood summed up in Christ the Mediator, with the priesthood exercised by the mediating Church, is only really understood in its living existence in all Christians, from the newly baptised to the Bishop of Rome, not in diffusion but in hierarchy, in the harmony of the body of Christ and in the liberty of the gifts of the Spirit.

And it is only as seen from this real and total point of view that the pagan context and the Christian context will rediscover their convergence. Salvation in Jesus Christ has been efficaciously achieved for all men and effectively put before them whatever their personal state and place as individuals in the chronology of history, in the different rhythms of the economy of revelation, in the geography of their relationships and the sociology of their condition in life. It could not be otherwise, since Christ is dead and risen again, and everything is under grace. The efficacy of the salvation which has been achieved, and its effective application to the entire universe are manifest in the existence and activity of the Church, which is the ritual home of the hallowing of the cosmos assumed by the incarnation of the Word. But immanence is not confined within the borders of the rite. The archetype adopts the rite and focuses himself in it, in order that daily life may be re-created. It is the priesthood of Christ which determines the priesthood of the Church, but not so that its efficacy is limited to the officiant of the rite. Christian priesthood is summed up in the bishop, but is not confined to him. The priestly function is exercised by the holy people, and it is to radiate outwards. But the radiation of the Christian rite has not the same compulsive effect as magic; ritual priesthood mediates what does not need to be repeated, but only shown forth. That is why Christian priesthood rests on the rite, but is exercised through the apostolate and the kingship of a sanctified people.

Have we Christians sufficiently grasped the truth of our integration into the process which saves the world from sin? It does seem that the gravest danger which besets us is that, because of our desire to be saved, we forget that Christ made us saviours. And indeed there is more paganism in the desire to be saved without being a saviour, than in the fear of being a saviour without being saved.

DISCUSSION

M. Martimort: Thank you. I think you may first be asked to give a few explanations, for some of us will be a little perplexed by the use of a vocabulary which is your discipline, and we shall no doubt want to compare it with the vocabulary of theology which is more familiar to us.

If you like, we can begin by exchanging views on this matter of vocabulary.

Fr Bouyer: I should like particularly to note what you said about myth in Christianity and in other religions. You emphasised the fact that what is quite peculiar to the Christian myth is that it is not concerned with the beginning of history, but that it is, on the contrary, a myth about the consummation of history.

I think this is extremely pertinent, and that we have something quite definite here.

However, there is one question I should like to ask you. It is very true that the majority of myths are cosmogonic myths which explain origins, but is there not also, sometimes in co-existence with them, or in oriental religions such as Brahmanism, a type of myth which, properly speaking, does not give an account of the beginning any more than the end, an absolutely a-temporal explanation which assumes that there is neither beginning nor ending?

In many oriental religions – Brahmanism particularly, and even Buddhism – what the myth does make clear is that there was no beginning. Don't you think this is so?

M. Idiart: Well, I think we can, in fact, explain the matter like this: fundamentally, history is a peculiarly Judaeo-Christian conception; the historic event, in other systems, is only a repetition and an explanation of the myth.

The non-biblical universe can sometimes be described as a pulsatory universe oscillating between a genesis and a final catastrophe in fire, water or other cataclysm. Elsewhere this universe is purely cyclic.

The Buddhist universe, notably, is a diabolical cycle of suffering, from which one simply must escape.

Outside the Judaeo-Christian tradition there could not be, properly speaking, any history because there could not be anything really new, any progress. If time had any function at all, it was simply to disintegrate, to weaken, to disturb, to consume, and not, like history, to bring about, to create, to fight against the erosion of time, to resurrect.

Fr Bouyer: I should like to ask a second question on this point, concerning the relationship between the myth and the rite. If I have really understood what you have said, you suppose the myth to have come first, and the rite second. I think this is true in most cases, but is it true in all? I have the impression that in the only religions I know anything about – the 'Mediterranean' religions at the time of the origin of Christianity – the rite, on the contrary, seems to have come first, and the myth arose at a certain phase of historical development as an explanation of a rite which had previously existed without the myth.

There is actually the quite striking example of Roman religion before the translation of the Greek gods to Rome, which at bottom never really adjusted itself to the mythical scheme of things, and which was a rite existing absolutely on its own.

M. Idiart: Yes, Roman religion is clearly an altogether exceptional case, and very embarrassing, what is more, for the student of the history of religions; I think M. Dumezil has thrown some light on it.

The Roman case is as deviationist a phenomenon as that of Judaeo-Christianity. It is a mythology which historically has only come down to us through a historical re-presentation. It seems that the Romans had forgotten mythology.

Fr Bouyer: Yes. But had they ever had one?

M. Idiart: The works of M. Dumezil have made it clearer than ever that they had. All early Roman history is in reality a collection of historicised myths, somewhat in the same way that certain parts of Genesis present the appearance of being historicised myths.

Fr Bouyer: Perhaps. But looking further than Roman religion, what about the agricultural religions of the Mediterranean, the 'mystery religions'? When we look at them and compare them with primitive Christianity, surely we can see that these religions consisted simply of imitative magic without any definite ideas, and that explanations came afterwards.

M. Idiart: There you are raising the problem of classical religions, the whole problem of reinterpretation.

There were rites which survived the forgotten myth. Very frequently, especially in developed society, we find ourselves faced with reinterpreted ritual customs – customs which had been interpreted afresh, after the myth which had given birth to them had been lost; rites possess more stability than oral traditions. Generally speaking, these societies had lost, if I may say so, their sensitivity to myth; they no longer shared the mentality which had established the rite at the same time as it formulated the myth. This reinterpretation was often effected in an 'allegorical' and no longer in a 'mythical' way. This seems to have been the case with many rituals in the classical religions.

Fr Bouyer: Are you not approaching it in an *a priori*, systematised way?

M. Idiart: Yes, that is inevitable.

Fr Bouyer: And yet all the proved facts we have seem to show that in Roman religion certainly, and without any doubt in the mystery religions as well, the rite existed at a given moment without any evidence of any particular myth, and then at a given moment, the myth seems to have been born. Then it is possible to say: 'Yes, but that could be a development which had occurred previously'. It is not an admitted fact.

M. Idiart: This is a problem in all classical religions. We are so much better informed on them than on others, as a result of literature. We always feel that literature about religion provides the only possible source of information. Now I do not believe this, for these religions were actually born into a territory about which literature tells us nothing.

Fr Bouyer: Nevertheless, I think that behind it all there is a certain anthropology, a certain conception of man which puts the intelligence-reflex at the basis of everything – which is not so certain.

M. Idiart: It is a theory.

Fr Bouyer: And now, although I do not want to pursue the matter, there is something else which I should like to point out, which follows from what you have said, and seems to me to be very pertinent. When we look at Christianity and compare it with its early contemporaries, what seems to me to be very striking is the radical novelty of the Christian conception of ordination, in the sense that, as you said just now, the other ancient religions, far from giving a certain man a power which he did not previously possess, reserved to him a power which was supposed to belong originally to every man. This is important, for a pagan, magical conception of the sacrament, of the rite, consists in thinking that the sacrament, the rite, will operate automatically, whoever performs it. While the conception underlying ordination is that it is not enough to pronounce certain words or to perform certain actions to make the sacrament, it is necessary for Christ to be behind it, for him to send you as his own agent. Without this, it is a physical action, and no more. In the mysteries of antiquity it is very striking to see that the 'clergy', i.e. those to whom the performance of the rite was reserved, had in fact received no power to perform it. On the other hand, people were satisfied that it did not matter who performed the action and spoke the words, and so long as he did so properly the rite was effectively performed. For example, if Alcibiades and his band were condemned for having parodied the mysteries, it was by no means because the whole thing was a sham, but, on the contrary, because having performed the rites they were thought to have performed the holy mysteries correctly without being priests.

This will enable us to see the quite distinctive character of Christian ordination.

M. Martimort: May we have a little break here, please? I am putting myself in the shoes of the average parish priest. After this session we shall have to advise him of our conclusions. For his benefit, here are three which follow from M. Idiart's account. If we wish to give our people the right notion of Christian priesthood, we must always present them with a synthesis of three elements which must never be dissociated from each other.

1. There is only one priest – Jesus Christ.
2. There is a priesthood shared by all the baptised.
3. There is a priesthood in which only some participate.

Perhaps it is because we do not make enough of the uniqueness of Christ's priesthood and the priestly character of all the baptised and the direct relationship they have with the Lord, that we come across so many deviations in the conceptions which people form of priesthood in their own minds.

Keeping to the pastoral sphere, I will draw another conclusion from M. Idiart's account. Because we cherish the originality of our own priesthood which is peculiar to Christianity, we must always place our activity within that tension between an event which occurred once for all – that apex we were hearing about – and what our hope is looking for at the end of time – the myth M. Idiart referred to. This historical dialectic must always be preserved.

Then, I think we have to make an examination of conscience about our pastoral media, which have perhaps disregarded these various tensions, both between the priesthood of Christ, that of the baptised, and our own, and between the present moment in which we work, the past historical event, and the parousia which we await.

CHAPTER XIII

HOW CHRISTIANS REGARD THE PRIEST TODAY

F. BOULARD

FEARING to discuss such a question as this without a preliminary inquiry, but fearing still more to see my desk laden with all the most daring and contradictory theories on priesthood as a result of such an inquiry, I have had to tackle it in a roundabout way; i.e. by not asking for an answer to the question which had been put to me, but by attempting to determine its substance by means of objective 'outward signs', which would not demand any critical opinion on the part of my correspondents, and which would actively tend to discourage any theorising.

The basic questionnaire was intended for priests – parish priests in large and small towns, in the country, Catholic Action chaplains, home missionaries. Here is the gist of it:

(1) When people call at the presbytery, what kind of services do they ask for?

(2) When you hear a priest criticised, what is he being reproached for?

(3) When people realise that they have got (or have had) a 'good priest', what is it they appreciate in him?

Then I specified:

1. In each of the three questions, distinguish clearly between
   (a) the militant Christians
   (b) the average practising Christians
   (c) the 'occasional conformists' (those who perform only the great religious acts of life).

2. It is absolutely essential to specify the type of parish (or at any rate the type of deanery), and to note whether it has

(*a*) a practising majority
(*b*) a minority of practising Christians
(*c*) a significant proportion not even baptised or catechised.

Then I turned out a second version of this questionnaire for the use of the laity. It was less well thought out. I should similarly have asked each to reply only for his own milieu but in actual fact as things turned out this is almost what happened.

I had neither the time nor the means to undertake a systematic and scientific survey, but the fifty-two replies came from very different geographical and social backgrounds:

twenty-one from the laity:

six from the large cities (Paris, Lille, Bayonne), fifteen from small towns or rural areas [four in class (a), ten in class (b), one in (c)].

thirty-one from priests:

nine from the large cities (Paris, Lille, Arles), twenty-two from small towns and rural districts [eight in class (a), nine in (b), five in (c)].

Geographically, all areas were represented except the East, (where the sources on which I was relying failed); North, ten; Normandy, six; Brittany and the West, five; Paris and its environs, six; Centre, four; Massif Central, eight; South-West, three; Midi viticole, one; South-East, six.

While the replies from priests embraced all religious levels, those from the laity came almost exclusively from the militants – A.C.O., M.F.R., A.C.I. (these alone lend themselves easily to an inquiry of this type), which clearly reduces the value of the evidence. In only one of them, which came from a rural group closely integrated to its environment, do we hear the direct voice of the ordinary people.

Out of prudence, then, I shall keep almost exclusively to those points on which the answers show a very general agreement. For the same reason, I shall not mention geographical areas (I have too few examples from each); but I shall, where it serves some purpose, note the type of district (a, b, c, large towns, etc.), and the social environment (working-class, middle-class, student, rural, etc.).

What I have been actually asked is how Christians regard the priest. No doubt it would have been interesting to have broadened the inquiry, for Christians in many circles (I am thinking especially of those circles where the working-class movement – or indeed the world of international capitalism – is a living reality) cannot but absorb, in their idea of the priest, the reflections of their surroundings and of current literature, in which the priest no longer has much significance at all.

So the problem was to ascertain the elements of a popular typology of the priest. With this in mind there were the three points in the questionnaire:

1. What kind of services are asked of the priest? From the things people usually ask of him I have tried to discover what their idea of his mission is.

2–3. What is the priest reproached for, and what qualities are appreciated in him? From these contrasting tests I tried to find out what the ideal of the 'good' priest was for Christians as a whole. The replies I received lead me to deal with these aspects together.

When we try to discover what kind of services Christians, practising or non-practising, expect from their priests, the first (and very important) fact which emerges is that the replies are almost completely unanimous for all districts and for all social levels. This unexpected harmony enables us to draw some very definite conclusions about the state of the popular mind on this question.

The second fact to emerge is that there is no ascertainable difference between the average practising Christian and the occasional conformist in what they expect of the priest. There is a little more confident tone about the practising, but that is all. But there is an obvious, almost essential, difference between the requests of this first group and those of the militants. I shall therefore divide my statement into two parts, each of which will contain the reactions of one of these two groups.

I. THE ORDINARY PRACTISING CHRISTIAN AND THE OCCASIONAL CONFORMIST

1. First set of calls on the priest: the great religious acts of life.

(a) Contacts

I should like to speak of these great religious acts of life, which are made many and various because of the different ages of the members of a family – baptism, catechism, first communion, marriage and burial. People come to fix the time, make arrangements for the ceremony and pay the fee; and also to obtain permission to marry elsewhere, or to lessen the number of years in catechism, or to ask for a dispensation on account of age. They call to ask the priest to visit a sick person (with marked differences in the various regions and milieux): in one place they will be anxious to see that all the sick receive the last sacraments; in another they will keep the priest in the dark, and he will only hear about the sick person in his last extremity, if not after death; in one place the family will inform the priest and ask for a visit even when there is no immediate danger; in another place it will be a neighbour ('Above all, don't say I told you . . .'). They will come to ask for a Mass for their dead (and, in the case of many of the non-practising, to be excused from attending it). 'They also request', says a priest from Provence, 'the ministry of prayer for an assortment often of the most odd intentions, with the idea of paying for this service (of prayer) in money'. They also come to pay their religious dues.

These things sum up most of the contacts which exist between priest and people – contacts which are more real and personal in the country, more 'administrative' in town, but everywhere are a valuable opportunity for priestly work among the parishioners for whom these great acts frequently represent the whole of religion. But this is not the place to discuss this educative aspect.

(b) The typology of the priest which emerges

But this is the place to note that all this necessarily implies that the occasional conformist and even the ordinary Christian has his ideal of the 'good' priest. I want to stress that for many these great acts are the whole of religion. The 'good' priest is the religious functionary who performs beautiful ceremonies correctly, who is brief and to the point, not expensive, who does not make changes by introducing such novelties as C.P.L., and who respects, as a gentleman should, the good customs of the place in which he is temporarily resident; he is the understanding man, accommodating, obliging about the regulations, who doesn't make a fuss about nothing; he is able to 'de-condition' the faith – as a young student replied to me. But also – and this is a logical consequence – he is the priest who is not always out, off who knows where; he is one we can be sure to find at home when he is wanted.

An obstinate desire to have the priest living on the spot is associated with this outlook: it is actually more obstinate among the non-practising than among the practising. (I have not conducted an inquiry among bishops, although this would have been very revealing: what reasons are advanced for wanting a resident priest? Are they always priestly reasons? They would undoubtedly throw sad light on the stifling of priesthood which occurs where its true purpose is not understood.)

2. Second set of contacts and calls

(a) Contacts

I must say how surprised I was to find such virtual unanimity in the fifty-two replies on this point. In all areas and at all social levels we note the same general calls on the priest for material services or for advice of a moral character (I have attempted to include both these things in the one word – help).

(i) Material services: in all milieux – to find rooms, to get an introduction in connection with some job or position, or a little financial assistance; in working-class districts – to intervene if there has been trouble with the police or with the customs (in frontier towns); in the country the priest is called in to doctor sick animals, or to run a sick person to hospital in his car.

Doubtless because of the isolation of the villages, and perhaps because of the state of de-Christianisation which has become normal, these calls on the priest for material services seem to be more natural in remote areas than elsewhere.

'Most frequently I am asked to make purchases for them in town', writes a priest. 'They know I get around a good deal. Almost every Sunday I call at the chemist's after the first Mass, so that I can take the medicines to my other parishes.'

'Often they ask if I have room in my car. A neighbour finds it quite natural to get a lift to town on Sunday morning; he goes to the hairdresser's while I say the first Mass, and I take him back home where I say the second Mass, but where there is no hairdresser's. (At the present time not a single man on the land comes regularly to Mass in any of my six parishes.)'

'Very frequently they ask for advice on how to cure people, and even more frequently, animals. They are actually surprised when we give an evasive reply – it seems that in the old days priests were as good at this as the doctors and veterinary surgeons are today . . .'

'They all appreciate it when a priest is ready to do a service quickly and well, night and day, both for those who are for and those against the Church. The majority of priests have been and still are admirable from this point of view.'

But there were similar echoes from Christian districts. 'In some cases they ask for particular services, according to individual abilities; several priests are water diviners, one is a specialist at timber felling, two bee-keepers, and several curate-electricians.'

My correspondent continues, passing on to education:

'Seventy curate-teachers: they are expected to give more and better references than the school over the road. Similarly, many priests are local secretaries to the country savings banks: they are expected to be brilliant financiers! The same goes for those who are trustees of local mutual benefit societies.'

Throughout the whole of the rural part of the diocese, curates especially are all expected to be producers, organisers of fêtes, supporters of the football team.

(ii) The last observation leads me from material services to educational functions – requests for private tuition, particularly with holiday homework; applications for places in schools for difficult children; above all, the organisation of groups for minding children (is it necessary to say that the reason given in many replies was to relieve the parents of their children on early closing days and Sundays?).

(iii) Going a little further up the scale we come to moral counsels, which also figure almost everywhere; inquiries about the morality or religious practice of a servant to be hired, or about a proposal of marriage; problems in connection with the education of children, or about their future; advice and comfort in difficult family situations – estrangements, marriages to patch up, questions of inheritance, etc.

Let us make it clear that all this is as true for the non-practising as for the practising. 'All priests who understand us,' writes a group of militants very close to the people, à propos the non-practising, 'all priests who are known to be really devoted, generous and discreet, who do not force your hand about religious practice, will be asked to give a great deal of advice on moral questions'.

This is equally true for paganised zones (category c), even on the part of unbelievers, provided that the priest has been among them long enough for confidence in him to be established.

And I am able to state that in North Africa this is even true of the Moslems, who go to their parish priest far more often than one would have thought, for moral advice, and even to patch up family quarrels provided they know that he is a just and prudent man.

(iv) We come now, still in connection with ordinary Christians and occasional conformists, to advice about one's personal life. But my correspondents note that this occurs much more rarely: 'They must have had a very hard blow, before . . .', says one; 'Very infrequently', says another. The personal attraction of the priest counts for even more than the customs of their milieu in this matter. A Catholic Action chaplain in the North says, 'Speaking to people about their lives has to be really *willed*. They are at first taken by surprise, but they are glad in the end.'

Of course these calls are not all disinterested, particularly where references for a job at the factory are concerned. A town priest writes: '. . . a kind of association between clergy and management. Frequently, expressions of this sort will be used to persuade the priest to use his influence ... "Don't worry, I'm a quiet chap; I'm not one of those who go joining unions, stirring up strikes and making trouble for the management . . . I shan't start a riot".'

But the massive fact of these manifold calls, in an age when it is so easy to do without the priest (think of all the officials at the Town Hall, the social workers and social security), attested as it is with the impressive unanimity of both town and country, and at all social levels, cannot be lightly dismissed. The only explanation given by those of my correspondents who were rather surprised to discover it, was furnished also by priests and laity, from Lille as well as Limousin, from the Somme or Les Charentes as well as Nantes: 'They trust the priest . . . they have confidence in his discretion.'

(b) *The typology of the priest which emerges*

And through the unconscious homage of these utilitarian calls we discover a second mark of the ideal priest: he is not arrogant, he lives very close to his people, he belongs to them all, he has not his favourite houses, or, as a lay missionary said: 'he is affected by a sort of law of gravity which draws him instinctively towards the humble and poor . . .'; the priest who gives you a friendly welcome, who is even-tempered; who has been in the parish so long that he knows everybody, who never seems to be in a hurry, who always has time for you, who puts you at your ease; who can listen to you and understand you, who is interested in your family, in the difficulties of your life – even the material ones – who, to use a common expression, 'does things for you'. 'If you give them a pleasant welcome,' wrote a priest from the diocese of Nantes, 'people will come to you for anything'. Undoubtedly the source of the frequent dissatisfaction with the large town parish is to be found in the 'gulf of silence' which exists there, where the priest can so easily become distant and anonymous.

The good priest is the discreet priest: 'He is as deep as a well; you can tell him anything . . .' 'I must allow myself to enlarge somewhat on this,' writes an A.C.I. militant, 'because I am

very struck by the ease with which the clergy divulge and discuss secrets confided to them outside confession'. But discretion
also means respecting people's freedom, not putting pressure on
them to practise religion; the priest who doesn't nag you, who
is no narrow party man.

The good priest is the human priest, free from pious talk and
the common-place, in whom human life and divine life are not
submerged by a third – Church life. 'A very faithful young
woman,' writes an A.C.I. militant in a large town, 'lost her
month-old baby. The parish priest rang her up to convey his
"deepest sympathy", the curate said some words to her about
the little angel in heaven, and the chaplain to her husband's
group did not mention it at all.'

On the other side of the picture the good priest is good at
organising parochial entertainments – plays, outings, fêtes; who
can hold the children, who is popular with the boys and takes
them off your hands very nicely. Is this thought at the back of
their minds: 'Priests don't work, so they have time for all this
sort of thing'?

3. The good religious official; the good pastor always ready
   to help you.

We shall soon be able to portray the good priest as he appears
to the ordinary Christian and the occasional conformist. Two
further characteristics are clearly detectable in the replies as a
whole:

(*a*) detachment from money.
(*b*) piety.

(*a*) When people say that a priest is a man for the money (I
am speaking of the individual priest, not priests in general, for
everybody knows that they all answer to this description!), his
influence is greatly compromised. On the other hand, the example of the priest who gives everything away, who takes the
bread out of his own mouth is cited with real feeling everywhere:
'He would have given everything he had away'; this is the mark
which makes most impression on those of our parishioners who
are attached to this world's goods. Even though, in a pagan

district, they never manage to understand it: 'It is his temperament', they say, or rather, 'It is his religion . . .'

But being a man for the money can mean two very different
things: one who talks about money too much, who asks for too
much; or one whose standard of living is too bourgeois, too
comfortable. The man who gets on without too much effort,
the shrewd man who has acquired a good position that enables
him to run a car (this criticism crops up frequently in the inquiry, and comes not only from populous districts or elderly
people – I mean, of course, a car which is too luxurious or not
obviously necessary), and to afford a holiday.

(b) Then, except perhaps in pagan areas, the ideal of the good
priest includes piety. A holy priest, one who has habits of
prayer is respected. People are impressed when he believes in
it, provided that his faith is robust and tranquil, not strained
and tense. When it is said of the priest that he doesn't believe
in it, he has been rejected.

A single reply, quoting one impression only, says that the
priest's private prayer in church is appreciated even by the
non-practising. Although there is only this solitary witness to
it, I am ready to believe that it is true.

(c) In this picture of the popular idea of the good priest, I
hesitate to mention the question of his chastity. In all milieux,
in town as well as in the country, in pagan, indifferent or
strongly practising areas (and here, often, more strongly than
elsewhere), the unhappy words continually recur: We don't
believe it.

'Rumours concerning women no longer cause any scandal
because continence is deemed to be "physically" impossible,
and so nobody believes that the priest is chaste' – this comes
from a large town.

'Because he wants to remain a bachelor he is not in a position
to bring up a family, but that is not to say that he stays chaste' –
this from an indifferent rural area.

A missionary from a largely practising area writes (surely a
little pessimistically?): 'If there is criticism, it always starts with
some rumour about a woman or a girl. Very rarely do the priest,
the lady organist, the more zealous girls in the catechism, or the

militants of Catholic Action escape suspicion. "They are well in with the priest" – these words cover a good deal of mischievous insinuation. And the Catholic Action chaplain who gives the female members a lift in his car is not above suspicion either.'[1]

(d) This picture of the priest as he appears to the ordinary Christian and to the occasional conformist is now essentially complete. But we have still to note a difference between the densely populated towns and the countryside. In the working-class parish the popular priest is the type who can laugh with you and make you laugh too, the good fellow who is 'one of the people'. They will remember a priest by little anecdotes such as these: 'Father X, he once threw off his cassock to administer a little correction to the anti-clerical mayor . . . He was a character, he was', or, 'Father Y, he played football, you ought to have seen him . . . He actually trained Machin, the international player'.

In small towns and rural areas, they do not care for the popular priest who is too free in his manners and conversations, who is not well-behaved. They have unhappy memories of him if he was sarcastic or if he laughed at them or indulged in banter; they naturally assume that he really was contemptuous of them.

Basically, for the great majority of ordinary Christians and occasional conformists, the ideal of the good priest is certainly not Bernanos's country priest, but the kind of gentleman who does what he has to do properly, and at the same time is not too demanding, who gives you comfort inexpensively, who doesn't upset people, or bring up tiresome questions.

If he makes changes in religion, or meddles with things that

1. The discussion which followed this account led to some modification of the harsh verdict resulting from the inquiry.

First, we must distinguish the two types of reaction: the priest 'ought' to be chaste, but people don't believe he really is; it is 'impossible' to be chaste, so the question doesn't even arise.

In a really Christian area, where vocations to the priesthood are still very frequent in families and are held in honour, we can readily conclude that people do believe that priests are normally chaste (the contrary would imply a general hypocrisy, which no one would admit). And surely we can say about the chastity of priests in general, and of a particular priest, what we said on the subject of money.

don't concern him, or indulges in politics (i.e. applies his religion to social questions), he will not be very well spoken of. 'They easily suspect the orthodoxy of the priest who wants to make changes, or who proclaims the gospel in its purity', writes the priest of a small town.

It is hardly necessary to make much distinction between the average Christian and the non-practising, except the latter are more definite in seeking to bring the priest down to their own level.

Do we give sufficient consideration to the fearful burden of this general opinion of the priest, this leaden cloak which silently smothers his spiritual drive – especially if he is isolated?

Because they do not ask the priest to do the things he is there to do, they end by making him into something he ought not to be.

It is not at all surprising that a people unconsciously dominated by this mental picture should no longer, save through exceptional grace, be 'capable of priesthood'. How can such a picture, which is in all their minds, fire their sons with enthusiasm?

2. THE MILITANTS

(a) The facts

I have left the militants till last for in their case the whole outlook is different. Here again, the virtual unanimity of their replies is impressive. They make it quite clear that they alone (or almost) possess an exacting conception of priesthood, and furthermore they are agreed in detail as to what can be demanded of the priesthood.

Mention is made of the type of militant (militante, especially) who scarcely asks of the priest more than that he should support the recruitment of members for the group and see that there is someone (often a priest) to preside at the meetings, or who canvasses him on behalf of the apostolic school of the Fathers of St Joseph, or the orphanage of Sister So-and-so. This happens naturally in a middle-class parish.

But a variety of it exists even in working-class parishes. 'If by "militants" you mean those who shoulder some responsibility on the parochial level (as scout and guide captains, group leaders), they expect me to be an expert in their own particular field of activity. As to services of a spiritual kind, I feel that their real needs are not keeping pace with their active work. A scout leader who is a turner at the factory asked my advice about the way in which the training of his scouts should be planned: that is all very good – but not once has he asked how he should think of his responsibilities at work. Moreover, I should find it impossible to offer him concrete advice on that point, because I am unfamiliar with that side of his life.'

Real militants, too, often ask the priest for advice about their children, or to do something for them, but their visits to the presbytery go further than this, and are more demanding. What they are looking for more than anything else is spiritual support. They come to talk about their apostolic work, the struggles they have in their own particular environment. They seek help to hold on, and guidance for their activity. They come about their personal life too, seeking comfort and courage when they feel they are slipping.

Can we say that what a country priest wrote is generally true: 'Militants ask for nourishment and spiritual direction, but they quickly tire because they expect immediate and tangible results. Teaching on the subject of theological hope is perhaps the most important of the priest's duties, so far as the militants are concerned.'?

(b) *The type of priest which is indicated*

What do the militants, in their various classes, expect of the priest? What is their idea of the good priest? I have collected a few details:

The discreet priest, who does not exploit the zeal of the militants, but channels it into their own particular vocation; the priest who is able to discern the relative importance of one's various commitments. 'I am thinking of a young mother of nine children (aged eleven to one),' writes a responsible official of A.C.I., 'with very little help, an A.C.I. militant, secretary of the parents' committee for schools and colleges, and involved in work for destitute children as well, who was approached about taking on the "Friendly Hour" in the parish, which was thought to be more important . . .'

The priest who does not hold forth on things he knows nothing about, but who is thoughtful and aware of the problems of adult life; the priest who has time for a chat, time to listen to you; the reliable friend who is never blasé or sceptical, but is able to give consistent support to the militants, and who can be relied on to show his solidarity with them in face of public opinion. (I notice also that this is mentioned twice – the priest who does not criticise his colleagues; no confidence is felt in such a man, because people naturally expect to be criticised in turn behind their backs.)

Above all, he must be a man of faith (and they are very demanding about sermons as well as confessions, and a conscientious, real worship), the profound priest, the man of God, who can enlighten their lives and their mission because his own personal life is one of generosity, effort and prayer.

They want their priest to be occupied with priestly work, and not absorbed by the secondary and factitious.

Their demands go further and become more and more explicit; they ask for a climate of truth between priests and militants, which will bring out their common responsibilities and worries. A priest in a working-class parish notes the criticisms he has heard; '. . . he hasn't really entered into our way of living; isn't really interested in the responsibilities which burden our lives . . . keeps us on the spiritual level, in the worst sense of the word ("do not let yourselves be corrupted") . . . hasn't the spirit to put us in the right disposition for sharing people's troubles, save through a kind of prayer which is fundamentally nothing but an easy way out, if it is not transformed into action.'

But the real militants do make it possible for the priest to deploy the full potentialities of his priesthood.

You will have noticed how different this ideal of the priest is from that held by your average Christian. 'This is a parish of some six hundred souls; an active and very zealous young priest a chaplain to J.A.C.F. and M.F.R. has really shaken this practising but dormant parish; we value him very much. But the merely practising find him tiresome and unreasonable. And the non-practising are pleasant to him, but that is as far as they go . . .'

How are we going to cope with it all? With all consideration, tact and respect for the consciences of others, and without surrendering anything that is authentic in the universal appeal of the good pastor who is obliging and oblivious of himself, quite frankly, we have got to gravitate towards the priestly ideals of the militants.

For human psychology, and particularly popular psychology, is undoubtedly more complex than it appears to be at first sight, and perhaps in actual fact many of the non-practising call for sanctity in their priests far more often than our analyses and inquiries would lead us to think.

A Christian veterinary surgeon concluded his reply with these words: 'Spiritually, this district is languishing, simply for want of a priest, and we know it, to our cost' – words which find an echo in this reflection which came from a hard and materialistic area: 'He was a good priest . . . we can see, now that he has gone, all we are missing – it is worse than a place without a doctor'.

Beneath the blanket of mere conformity or the inability to express themselves – at any rate when this is not the result of shyness – we can undoubtedly hear the call for a true priesthood. This rural attitude is so much a part of its environment that its reply is a mere tissue of quotations, puts it beyond question.

The ordinary Christian:

One farmer to another: 'Our new parish priest looks like being good. He has already got the young people together, and talks to them very nicely. But do you know what his opinions are about the social order? Does he really believe, in his heart, that God came to this earth to be a working man, that he toiled just like ourselves? Now, it is an extraordinary thing, but there are very few priests who really do believe it. They say so, yes; but they haven't worked with their hands; they don't know what that is. I'm going to see our priest. I am going to make him talk about work, the land . . . I can't put into words any more than that. But if he doesn't believe it, I shall soon know; I shan't let Henry go – a priest who has no social gospel does a great deal of harm to young people and puts them off religion.' (Jan. 1955.)

The militants:

If they are not encouraged by their priest, and *a fortiori* if they are frustrated by him, most of the militants will lose heart, will give up all their activities, and will fall like a shooting star, from the spiritual point of view. But those who have really caught on will hold on, with the help of their movement, their chaplain or a neighbouring priest.

All this is difficult to put into words, especially for country-men, so the priest must take them into his confidence, read between the lines, as it were, and let them know that he too has his problems; they must feel that he has an intense supernatural life. Even the non-practising, even those whose minds are riddled with Marxism, know if the priest has a supernatural life or not. 'I am going to ask the priest for a lettuce. I need to sense the presence of God when I talk to him.' (1947.)

The occasional conformists:

'We know quite well that the fête the priest is preparing isn't for the sake of the money – he's not interested. It is to spread joy and fellowship around, as he said with his own lips. So we gathered that he was asking us to help him too, just like the others; he is not going to leave us workers out because we don't go to Mass. He has only to name the day when he wants us to get together, and tell us what he wants us to do, and we shall all be there.' When this fête came off, it was the talk of the whole countryside and brought about a harmony which has lasted several years, because it went hand in hand with many other things: a presbytery which was open to all, and where all were welcome, living religious ceremonies, the use of a clear and simple French, the gradual establishment of a single group for religious work, a lively catechism in which parents were invited to co-operate, sermons which started off from our everyday con-cerns, but lifted us up to God. Some words which the priest often used to say to those working for the fête were repeated again and again: 'I ask all those who will, to pray very hard that because of this fête we may all love one another more'. 'Our priest isn't like the others. He doesn't abuse us because we don't go to Mass. He is not overbearing – he says, "If I lived like a saint everybody in the commune would begin to think that there was a God, and they would go to Mass. It is my fault that they are not there". You ought to hear him talking about the saints: "men like ourselves, with faults like ours; most of them were ordinary people whom God loved so much because they put so much faith in him, and because they did their everyday work conscientiously to please him".' (Summer 1954.)

The ordinary Christian:

'Since he came here, we have come to understand so many things we didn't even give a thought to before. We must admit that we went to Mass really out of habit and routine. Now I dare no longer speak evil of my neighbour having hardly got out of Mass – I used to do this without thinking, "like drinking water", as he says. I know now that I was sinning against charity, against women for whom Jesus willed to die because he loved them so much.' (Reflections of this kind are frequent.)

'The parish and the whole countryside as well seem to belong to another world. Without our priest it would never have dawned on us that we can't save our own souls without saving others, that we belong to a community, and that we must give an example to the parish.' (1947.)

The militants:

'The priest has made us realise that up to now we were only doing our own work, even when we were helping others. We have been led to do as he does – to work for God . . . that strengthens our morale when we do not succeed, and humbles our pride when we do.

The sort of "labourers" we like are to be found, too – the young men have no desire to forsake the land, because the priest keeps them together and takes trouble over them.' (All Saints 1954.)

CHAPTER XIV

PRIESTHOOD IN THE CHRISTIAN EAST

C. J. DUMONT, O.P.

I HAVE been asked to draw attention to certain aspects of Christian tradition about the priesthood which have been maintained in the East, principally in the Orthodox churches, but which have either completely disappeared or have been seriously diminished in the West. Obviously it would be most instructive to look at this dual evolution from the angle of its historical development. But this would take us too far, and in any case, it would require more erudition than I possess. It would be also interesting to embrace all the churches of the East in our study, and not only those of the Byzantine rite. But I shall naturally limit my exposition to the latter, and more particularly to the Russian church, because that is my special subject. We must not lose sight of the fact that the field of this inquiry is thus notably restricted. Very important canonical differences between the various Churches could in fact be noted – Nestorian, Monophysite, Orthodox, and even, although to a lesser degree, between the latter themselves. It is the same from the theological standpoint. On the whole, however, I think that the principal characteristics which we shall observe in connection with priesthood in the Russian Orthodox Church are found in the other Eastern churches; they will, I think, at any rate be sufficient to give us food for thought. And in conclusion I shall speak of the problems raised by the maintenance of traditions proper to the East in the Catholic churches of the East. Actually, this exposition could more properly have been entitled 'How is priesthood understood and lived in the Russian Orthodox Church today?'. Obviously I shall not stress the points common to both Oriental and Latin traditions – I shall concentrate more on those points where they diverge.

1. BLACK AND WHITE CLERGY

In the Latin Church a distinction is made between secular and regular clergy. This distinction is also found in the Russian church, but there it is singularly more important and more obviously stressed. Two principal contributory factors emphasise this distinction:

1. The regular life (this term does not exist in Orthodox law) is not known except in its strictly monastic form.
2. The secular clergy (this expression, likewise, does not exist in the Russian language) are all, and I venture to say, almost of obligation, married.

The custom has arisen of distinguishing them by the titles 'black clergy' (monastic) and 'white clergy' (parochial, married), but this does not really correspond to any notable differences in the colour of their habit (though it is more rare to meet a monk with a coloured soutane than a member of the parochial clergy).

Monasticism in the East, as Fr Rousseau has already pointed out, has always preserved its proper character and is not linked either in law or in fact with priesthood. Only a certain number of monks in a monastery are clothed with the priesthood; some of the others receive the minor degrees of the sacrament of Orders, up to and including the diaconate, and deacons and priests together form the category known as *Hieromonks*. The others are just called monks. The number of priests is in principle determined by the needs of the monastery, which include not only the spiritual service of the community itself, but also the spiritual service of the faithful, since each monastery is normally a place of pilgrimage.[1] Admission to the priesthood,

---

1. It is customary to emphasise the purely contemplative character of monastic life in the East. It is right to note it. In fact, there is nothing in Russia and the other Orthodox countries comparable to our own active religious orders. Sanctification through prayer, monastic asceticism and work (especially, but not exclusively, manual work) remain the proper and essential end of the monastic life. It must not be forgotten, however, that the expansion of Christianity in Russia, as almost everywhere else, owes much to monasticism; monasteries were the chief means of Christian penetration in pagan regions. Furthermore, there has never been any lack of monk-priests

however, was not entirely governed by this consideration; the degree of culture and the personal aspirations of each candidate were taken into account. There was also, at least for those who had received the diaconate, promotion on account of seniority, which frequently permitted admission to the priesthood as a reward for services rendered, after long years spent in the exercise of this minor Order.

We must note the general practice of conferring a certain minor Order for its own sake, without any prospect of later promotion to the priesthood. It obtained among the parochial clergy as well, both in the case of the Orders of lector or sub-deacon (considered as a minor Order) and for the diaconate. This custom is partly dependent on a canonico-liturgical tradi-tion, which forbids a person who has been invested with a sacred Order to perform the functions of a lesser Order. This is strictly observed among the Orthodox, at least so far as the priest is concerned, for he never performs the fuctions of the deacon. The adage: 'He who can do the greater, can do the lesser' does not apply here. According to current thought, the exercise of an Order inferior to that which one has in fact received is tantamount to a forfeiture of it. The importance of the role of the deacon and of the inferior Orders in the liturgy (especially in the pontifical liturgy) largely explains this custom. In principle, the liturgy is always sung, and the role of the deacon is very prominent in it. But his role is restricted to this liturgical celebration, which takes up only a small amount of his time. So he will earn his living in another occupation, usually of the

---

personally attached to truly missionary work; they have existed down to our own times, either working among the pagan population of Siberia, or bringing back into the bosom of the Church those who had been led astray by the various sects or by the great schism of the 'Old Believers'. There was also a missionary activity, undertaken especially by the monks, which was directed towards Catholics (Uniates particularly) or Protestants. The monastery of Pocaey in Wolhynie represented the furthest outpost of orthodoxy in Eastern Europe; it had a printing press and was responsible for disseminating tracts, brochures and books of Orthodox propaganda. Moreover, publications, whether of apologetics or Christian teaching, were furnished largely by the monasteries, where the most cultivated section of the clergy was to be found.

artisan type, which can easily be interrupted to accommodate his liturgical engagements (Mass, administration of the sacraments, funerals, votive offices). There is absolutely no need for advanced intellectual attainments on the religious level for this.

The practice of concelebration and the fact that the private Mass is unknown have also contributed to the persistence of this custom. To enable several priests to take an active part in the celebration of the same liturgy there is no need to reduce one to the role of deacon and the second to subdeacon; not only several priests but several deacons and subdeacons, not to mention inferior ministers, can concelebrate the divine liturgy, each performing his proper function. We must note, however, that concelebration is always a solemn Mass with the Orthodox. Every priest does not celebrate every day in the monasteries. On ordinary days in a given church (there may be several churches in the same monastery, in which Mass is celebrated each day), the celebration of Mass and office is the responsibility of the priest for the week, the *hebdomadarius*, assisted of course by a deacon. The higher the rank of the feast, proportionately the greater is the number of concelebrants. Only on great festivals do all the available priests and deacons concelebrate. It is not customary for the priest to communicate when he is not concelebrating. In principle, the deacon should communicate at the Mass he concelebrates.

Let us say, in passing, that the practice of Mass stipends as established in the Catholic Church does not exist in the Orthodox Church, and so the economic factor does not enter into the question of the daily Mass or of its concelebration. The whole of the offerings of the single and only Mass solve the economic problem in so far as it is raised.[1]

1. This accumulation of offerings is itself bound up with a peculiarity of the Byzantine rite. The faithful, on entering the church, buy the *prosphora*, or little breads, from which during the *prothesis* the priest chooses portions representing the living and the dead for whom they desire the priest to pray and offer the holy sacrifice, and places them by the side of the fragment of bread to be consecrated and called 'the lamb'. The *prosphora* themselves are returned to them, but the portions are placed in the precious blood after the communion as a symbol of the participation of those they represent in the fruits of the sacrifice. The number of the *prosphora* is, naturally, unlimited.

More important than the survival of a proper exercise of the Orders inferior to the priesthood, the diaconate, in particular, an exercise strictly confined to actual liturgical functions, is the fact that, in principle, admission to the episcopate is a possibility only for monks. This flows quite naturally from the tradition which demands absolute continence and celibacy of the bishop. To be a bishop, one has to be a monk. This entails a certain number of important consequences which we shall examine later.

The parochial clergy are generally married. We remember, of course, that neither the priest nor, indeed, the deacon is able to marry, but a married man can be admitted into sacred Orders, diaconate and priesthood, while continuing to live the married life. Canonically there is no reason why a celibate should not be ordained for parochial work; in principle there can be unmarried priests who are not actually monks and indeed, in these days of emigration there are such cases. But in former days this was much more rare, if not quite exceptional. In the estimation of the people there was no distinction – the unmarried priest was a monk. There are, naturally, widower priests who are not monks. The custom of elevating such priests to the episcopate is becoming more and more common in Russia, but in that case they also become professed monastics. The widower priest who would like to contract a second marriage may be reduced to lay status. He then loses any right to exercise his priesthood, even if his second wife dies. It is noteworthy that important pastoral charges, especially in the large towns, were readily, but not exclusively, entrusted to widowers. The reason for this was undoubtedly because they were more 'free' to carry out the more weighty responsibilities of such charges.

The fact that the parochial clergy are almost entirely married entails various consequences.

The first is that for many years the 'white' clergy formed a sort of class or caste in the nation. Until 26th May, 1869, pastoral charges themselves were actually reserved to the families of priests or inferior clerks, so that the daughters of priests were 'attached' to them and received them as their inheritance; these charges were of course filled by their priest-husbands, who as a rule were themselves sons of priests. There were few vocations to the priesthood, apart from the monasteries, outside the families of priests. After 1869 the position was distinctly modified, but this state of affairs survived largely through custom. The families of priests are recognised by their names. Among country folk, who form the vast majority of the Russian people, the use of a family name was not generally introduced until quite recently. The children of priests arriving at the 'seminaries' (the teaching establishments where they received a more extensive education than in the simple primary parochial schools, and where the top class was known as 'theology' because the rudiments of this science were taught in it) received a 'proper name', usually derived from a liturgical term (the title of a feast, or a portion of the liturgy, or some object of *cultus*). The language of priestly families retained certain peculiarities arising from the archaisms in vocabulary or grammatical form which had survived from old Slavonic. Briefly, a whole system of social principles contributed to make the married clergy a kind of caste or class. Marriages between sons and daughters of priests were frequent and prolonged this state of affairs. What I have to say later about the role of the priest's wife, especially in the countryside, makes understandable one of the most profound reasons for this.

The second result of a married clergy is in the economic sphere. In a land where, until the revolution, customs had remained extremely patriarchal, and people were generally prolific, the priest usually had a very large family whose needs he had to provide for. The resources of his flock were naturally insufficient. Fees were meagre in sparsely populated areas. The salary guaranteed by the State was very slender (in 1893 there was a budget of 2,000,000 roubles for the whole of Russia!). There was also a collection in kind made each year the result of which naturally depended to a certain degree on the regard in which the priest was held by the people, as well as on the extent of their generosity and on the abundance or the scarcity of the harvest; finally, there was the produce of a very modest piece of land which the priest, helped by his family, could cultivate. The necessity of cultivating the soil had the advantage of giving the priest something to do, for without it time would have hung heavily on his

hands, since his parish work consisted only of the celebration of
the offices on Sundays and festivals; the administration of the
sacraments, marriages, baptisms; the performance of the funeral
rites; visiting the sick and rather numerous votive offices celebrated either at church or at home; finally, the teaching of the
catechism in the local schools, most of which had been for long
entrusted to the care of the clergy. Before the revolution in
Russia there was nothing resembling what we call charitable
organisations, especially in the country. Things are different
today among the emigrés. In the Soviet Union the pastoral
activity of the clergy, unless it is clandestine, is strictly confined
to the sphere of worship.[1] The isolation of the priests in villages
often far apart from each other and without means of rapid
communication, is certainly one of the reasons which, from the
moral point of view, militated in favour of the maintenance of
a married clergy. From the economic point of view, the priest
was greatly helped by the possibility of having his children
brought up in the diocesan establishments known as seminaries.
Of course, in principle these were only for those of his sons
who felt drawn towards the priesthood, but in practice they
were very largely open. The standard was perhaps that of a
secondary school – not always very high – but at any rate they
led on to the higher religious teaching establishments known as
'ecclesiastical academies'. This was the usual way a bishop's
career began. This was envisaged very early, so that marriage

1. The material circumstances of the emigré clergy are often very
difficult. As a result of the dispersion, numbers are small in the
parishes, and consequently the faithful are unable to support their
priests, especially if they have families. It is not unusual for these
priests to have to find work to obtain the necessities of life; they find
work in factories as artisans, where it will be possible for them to take
time off for the performance of their ministry, or they take some job
in a shop. In Soviet Russia it was this necessity for earning a living,
together with the pressure of the persecuting laws, or sheer hostility,
which compelled many priests who remained at liberty to abandon
the pastoral ministry in the years immediately preceding the war.
Here we have a form of 'priest-workman' which we have not heard
much about, but it would be interesting to study their experiences,
if that were possible. But even before all this, under the previous
régime the circumstances of the married clergy brought them much
closer to their flocks than is the case in the West.

might be avoided and the first commitments of the monastic life entered into. The choice of bishops was often made from the ranks of the professors, without being restricted to them (superiors of monasteries – *higoumenoi* or *archimandrites* – were frequently chosen directly); they were successively professors, directors, inspectors of seminaries, occasionally of ecclesiastical academies, then finally they were made bishops, very often receiving the position of auxiliary bishop at first. Monastic tonsure was usually taken about the time when the 'master's dissertation' was delivered and defended. Promotion then followed very quickly, according to the candidate's dispositions, and men were admitted to the episcopate at a very early age. As we have seen, in these cases the obligations of the monastic life scarcely extended beyond that of celibacy, and the new bishop had hardly lived in the monastery to which he was canonically attached, if he had lived there at all. He might not even be personally attracted to the ascetic exercises connected with his profession of the monastic life. Once bishop, however, he lived in a monastic atmosphere, for, except for a layman employed for administrative purposes, he was then surrounded largely by monks; the pontifical offices were always performed according to monastic ritual. Generally (there were, naturally, exceptions) the bishop's living standards were monastic in character; simplicity of life and furnishings, frugality at table, etc. Perhaps it is not pointless to observe that the liturgical rite itself helped to show the bishop as the father of his people, and thus facilitated confident relations between the faithful and their bishop.

On the other hand the fact that the bishop was a monk, and that bishops were chosen almost exclusively from the monks, created an undeniable state of tension between the black and the white clergy. The latter knew that they were doomed to find the higher charges, particularly the episcopate, barred to them, unless their wives died (and this concession was of quite recent origin). This fact, together with that touch of class or caste about the clergy which we noted in passing, was at the root of one of the most serious difficulties which confronted the Russian Church. The social aspirations secretly stirring the hearts of the masses at the beginning of the century, which flared up into the first revolutionary movement in 1905, found in the married clergy as a whole, and especially perhaps in their families a particularly fruitful field. The 'seminarists', i.e. the sons of priests who were receiving a more advanced education in the seminaries, formed an important section of the Russian intelligentsia. Violent demonstrations took place in several seminaries in 1905. Those who came out, either because they themselves had abandoned their priestly career, or because they had been expelled by ecclesiastical authority, went to swell the ranks of the revolutionary movements. It was a section of the clergy themselves, roused by their own social aspirations, but without going to the extremes which marked the beginning of the 1917 revolution, who supported the establishment of a new régime from which they hoped to gain for themselves liberation and promotion. Schisms in the Church attended the advent of the Soviet régime. Their programme consisted not only of supporting in a general way the social reforms implemented by this régime, but of eliminating the kind of class opposition existing between the monastic and the married clergy; they demanded and instituted, in the dissident groups, the remarriage of widower priests and the admission of married priests to the episcopate (the living Church, the Church of the Renovation, etc.). It is very curious to note that, although it had been the most violently opposed by the civil power at first, it was the traditional Church which triumphed in the end, after vicissitudes which we cannot describe here; the various schisms disappeared and their pretensions were abandoned. But large numbers of their erstwhile supporters, after returning to the traditional Church one by one, came to occupy the principal positions in it. Perhaps we must regard as a compromise designed to narrow the gap separating the sections of the clergy the fact that a high proportion of widowers have recently been nominated bishops.

However we must not make too much of this opposition between the two sections of the clergy. Even if the 'episcopal house(hold)' is largely composed of monks, the married clergy frequently have a large share of the administrative posts. Laymen, moreover, play a greater part in the administration than with ourselves. Although the bishop in his dual character of bishop and monk is the head of the whole monastic organisation of his diocese (the bishop frequently reserves to himself the office of superior of the most important monastery in his diocese, but nominates a vicar, *higoumenos* or *archimandrite* for the day-to-day government of the house), he is at the same time the head of the whole parochial organisation, and by the virtue of this he is assisted by a council in which not only the parochial clergy, of course, but even the laity are canonically represented, as is also the case on the parochial council. Their role is not restricted to material questions. They have, in principle at least, a voice in the administration, in nomination to offices, etc. This participation of the laity in the responsibilities of government is a very constant tradition in the Orthodox Church, and it extends to the actual councils themselves. This subject deserves more attention than it has yet received. As the theology of the sacraments was formerly built on the practice of the Latin Church alone (it has taken several centuries to rediscover, thanks largely to the liturgical movement, a broader and more satisfactory outlook), so today we perhaps tend rather to build a theology of the laity (in itself and in its relations with the priesthood) on a practice which is also purely Latin and Western, without taking into account the contributions furnished by an Eastern tradition which, a few details excepted, has not ceased to be legitimate even if it has not received the sanction of current Catholic canon law.

An allied subject is the part played by lay professors in higher religious teaching. This is particularly obvious in Greece, where in the two existing faculties of theology (Athens and Salonika) only one of the professors is a priest, and even then he teaches a subject which is not properly theological – Church history. All religious teaching can be said to be in the hands of laymen, since the faculties train the professors of religion, themselves laymen, for all teaching establishments of whatever standard. In Russia, where, as we have seen, ecclesiastics occupied and still occupy an important place in the higher teaching of the sacred sciences, numerous chairs were given to laymen. It is the same among the emigrés. That this state of affairs is not an unmixed blessing is particularly obvious in Greece, where the laity have assumed a monopoly. The bishops realise that their principal responsibility is the maintenance of the true faith, but they are unable to take any effective measures in this sphere, less perhaps from lack of competence (there are, of course, some learned bishops and clergy) as from the impossibility of making themselves heard and obeyed. But if this state of affairs is not wholly admirable, neither are its disadvantages absolutely overwhelming. Here again, then, is a question which merits study.

I do not intend to deal with the rather delicate question of the influence of married life on the spiritual level of the clergy. It is actually important to emphasise that the use of marriage is not unrestricted. The simple Christian must prepare himself to receive holy communion not only by prayer but by fasting and continence; similarly, and with greater reason, for the priest. But although this has only a limited bearing on the life of the ordinary Christian, since it is not customary for even the most pious to communicate more than four times a year, it affects the priest to a much greater degree, since his pastoral duties require him to celebrate, if not daily, at least frequently. In addition, in the case of the priest, Lenten abstinence applies equally to conjugal continence, and there are four fasts in the year: the great Lent, analogous to our own, but commencing on the Monday of the first week; the 'Lent' of the apostles, commencing on the Monday after the octave of Pentecost and lasting until the vigil of the feast of SS Peter and Paul (29th June) – its length varies, but it may be six weeks; the 'Lent' of our Lady, from the 1st to the 14th August; the 'Lent' of Christmas, corresponding to our Advent, but beginning on 14th November, the feast of the apostle St Philip. To these must be added, with some exceptions, the Wednesday and Friday of each week. It is naturally difficult for me to, say whether these precepts are always carefully observed, but I do know that as a rule the clergy attach great importance to them.

Neither the monk nor the married priest is bound to private canonical prayer so they have nothing corresponding to our breviary. The custom, however, is for them to sanctify the day by the recitation of a collection of prayers called, in Russia, the

Pravilo (the rule, or canon), in which the psalms naturally occupy a great place. A priest's prayer book will of course make it possible for him to do more than this. The text of the ordinary of the office is found there, as well as the troparies and the *Kontakia* for each day (short liturgical pieces corresponding, broadly speaking, in contents and length to the collects of our own office). It also contains some votive offices, which are portions of the long office of e.g. the Holy Angels or St Nicholas, to whom there is great private devotion.

In the monasteries, moreover, the whole community does not assist at the whole of the office, except on the great festivals. The monks who are listed for the week attend, as do the cantors. The rest are usually present only for part of Matins and for Compline. Throughout the day, during their work, they sanctify their tasks by the private recitation of the *Pravilo*.

In spite of the conjugal ascesis of the married clergy, and the spiritual exercises practised both by them and the monks, it is undeniable that the spiritual level of the clergy is not always very high. But among the causes underlying this we must remember the general lack of culture in large numbers both of the monks and especially of the rural clergy. Still, we must not judge too much by outward appearances, which, though often rather coarse, are not incompatible with true interior refinement, a real sense of justice and a profound understanding, albeit unpolished in its expression, of the Christian mystery and the claims of evangelical perfection. I have had occasion to observe this repeatedly.

I have alluded in passing to the priest's wife. As a rule she is herself the daughter of a priest, brought up in the peculiar but religious surroundings of a home where the service of God and man is the whole preoccupation of the entire household, and so she naturally considers her position as *matouchka*[1] as a true vocation; indeed, a vocation is necessary to meet the demands of such a state of life. In the country districts especially, if family cares allow her any leisure, she plays an important role in looking after the church and preparing for festivals, and

1. A familiar diminutive meaning 'little mother', corresponding to the current title 'little father' (batouchka) given to the priest.

an even greater role in the field of charitable works. She always performs all these activities with the greatest discretion, effacing herself completely during the offices, mixing with the people and taking care to treat them all alike.

I must just mention the attitude of the faithful towards the married clergy. It is a classical argument in anti-Orthodox propaganda that the faithful could not have any respect for, or confidence in, a married priest, especially in the matter of confession. I can say that this is not usually the case – the exception is always possible, of course. Actually I have never found anything resembling it at all – I would almost go so far as to say that the very opposite is true. Although so restricted, the recent experiment in Germany of ordaining to the priesthood two convert married Lutheran pastors seems to corroborate this observation.

Finally, I ought to mention that the possibility of ordaining married men greatly facilitates the re-establishment of parochial religious life in the Soviet Union, which has been made possible by the actual course of events; and so, I may say in passing, does the use of a liturgical language very similar to everyday speech. I shall say no more about this, since I am not dealing with the religious situation in the Soviet Union, but I do think it is relevant to my subject just to mention this important aspect of the problem of priesthood at the present day.

2. THE EASTERN TRADITION IN THE CATHOLIC CHURCH

It is well known that for centuries, more particularly since the Council of Florence, the lawfulness of Eastern traditions especially in liturgical matters, has been recognised by the Roman church, and that union with the Holy See may be contemplated in the certainty that these traditions will be maintained. But in fact the peculiar character of all the Eastern traditions is far from having been preserved in those Eastern churches which are in union with the Holy See. The responsibility for this cannot always be placed on the Holy See itself – far from it. Since the establishment of the congregation for the Eastern church, and since it resolved to make the pontifical directions in this

matter its own (that has not always been the case!) the Holy
See has intervened on numerous occasions in favour of the
maintenance or re-establishment of liturgical texts or customs
which, in the churches concerned, had been gradually and
spontaneously modified under the influence of the Latin tradition; these interventions, indeed, often met with very lively
resistance on the part of those concerned. But the Eastern
congregation is not all-powerful. It occasionally meets with a
lack of understanding (or simply want of experience) on the
part of other tribunals, whose members, Latin in origin, do
not always perceive the reasons militating in favour of the
maintenance of traditions which seem to them less felicitous
than those which have been adopted by the Latin church.
This latter consideration seems to have played an important
part in the codification of Eastern Catholic canon law which
has been completed, although only promulgated in part. It
must be said that this state of affairs can scarcely be attributed
to the Eastern members of the commission for codification,
for their opinions have not always been heeded and followed.
On certain points, moreover, the commission could hardly do
other than ratify the canonical provisions which had for long
been accepted in the Eastern Catholic churches concerned. We
will now examine the principal points on which Catholic discipline on the subject of priesthood differs in fact and in law from
Orthodox discipline. Although the principle of compulsory
celibacy has not been introduced where it had not already been
imposed, it is none the less clear that it is the intention of the
Church to extend the custom as far as possible. The bishop, who
in the last resort calls his subjects to sacred Orders, is always
free, if he considers it opportune, to let his choice fall only on
celibates, and thus gradually to establish a completely unmarried clergy, however possible it may be in theory for married
candidates to proceed to ordination. There are those Eastern
bishops who have adopted this line of action. This rule has also
been adopted, in fact, by the colleges of the various Eastern
rites at Rome. Another restraining influence on the custom of
a married clergy has its origin in the emigration of important
sections of the Eastern clergy into Western countries of the

Latin rite. There are countries, or whole areas of certain countries, where married Eastern Catholic priests can find no refuge unless they cease to exercise their ministry, because the local Latin ordinaries have so decided. The reason usually given for such a measure is the scandal that the presence of married priests would constitute for the Latin faithful, accustomed to considering priesthood and celibacy as going together. Undoubtedly it is also feared that their presence would, in the less fervent ecclesiastical circles, encourage hopes for a modification of the discipline of the Latin church on this point; it is precisely in those countries where the habits of the clergy leave something to be desired that these restrictive measures are most rigorously applied. There is no point in emphasising the gravity of the problem which this strictness raises in the eyes of our brethren of the Eastern Catholic rites, to whom the preservation of the legitimate traditions of the East had been solemnly promised. But this is not the place to consider this problem. We must be content with having noted it.

Another point of Eastern custom which has been almost completely abandoned among the Uniates is the 'non-exercise' of an Order below that which has been received. In the majority of the Uniate churches it has become quite normal for a priest to perform the deacon's function. Similarly, the Catholics are obviously very reluctant to ordain a man deacon if he does not show an aptitude for eventually receiving the priesthood. It is very curious to observe that whereas among us Westerns there is a movement which seems to favour, chiefly because of the shortage of priests, the restoration of an earlier discipline for the lower Orders, this discipline, which has survived in the East, threatens to disappear there although it has become or is becoming Catholic.

The custom of concelebration has been generally preserved in the Eastern Catholic church, but the devotion of the daily Mass – and, it must be said, the custom of Mass stipends (applied to the principal intention of each concelebrant) are causing it to lose its solemn character, which has been kept, as we have seen, among the Orthodox. In the communities, the daily concelebration of all the priests present is the rule; Masses are not multiplied except to meet the needs or the convenience of pastoral requirements. It must also be noted that among the Catholics each priest is careful to omit none of the prayers of the Mass, and while they are being chanted, they all recite them in a low or medium voice. In many places the custom of chanting together has been introduced, and so the words of institution are sung in a loud voice, whereas among the Orthodox the principal celebrating priest chants them, while his concelebrants simply unite themselves with him secretly or in a very low voice. It is obvious that different conceptions of concelebration and, more deeply, of the unity of sacrifice and priesthood underlie these customs.

We must now note that in that part of the new Eastern canon law which has recently been promulgated the subdiaconate has once again become a nullifying impediment to matrimony, and that it is an important modification of Eastern discipline. This restoration of a point of discipline which has completely fallen into desuetude among the Orthodox has no meaning apart from the assumption that the subdeacon will later proceed to the diaconate and priesthood. In actual fact, among Orthodox, a good number of young men wishing to take an active part in the pontifical ceremonies, but without the slightest intention of pursuing an ecclesiastical career as such, are ordained subdeacons even when they are still quite young. We can see the difficulties which can and do arise from the new Catholic discipline when the question of mixed marriages arises!

Finally, the traditional aspect of Eastern monasticism is in danger of being seriously modified by attempts to introduce into the East the great variety of Western religious orders. This is envisaged by the directives of the Holy See, to which new vigour was given by the initiative of Pope Pius XI. Today a large number of the great Western religious orders have members, and often already the equivalent of entire provinces, of the Eastern rites (e.g. Jesuits, Franciscans, Capuchins, Benedictines, Dominicans, Redemptorists, etc.). It is difficult to say how far these developments will go, but it is certain that as such developments take place the traditional relationship existing in the East between the monastic principle and priesthood will be modified.

22—TSOHO

DEBATE: ASSIMILATION OR SEPARATION

Fr Rouquette: It seems to me that we are really raising a deeper question than that of the clerical manner of life.

We are faced with a situation which has no parallel in history – the birth of a new form of loyalty which is purely sociological in character and which has no geographical or historical roots; the *patria* of the proletariat. To complicate matters one of the essential elements of this proletarian *patria* is a Marxist ideology; furthermore, it is engaged in a defensive warfare, legitimate on the whole, against the other *patriae* of the modern world. Really to belong to this new *patria*, and to work in it, you have to be assimilated into it, and this involves the acceptance of everything in it, even the things which are less good, just as Ricci or Nobiti did when faced with another civilisation in China, on condition that these things can be reconciled with Christian faith and morals.

This is a question which has not yet received sufficient attention, but it is the reason for that conflict which we have all spoken about here. We are confronted by these two *patriae* in the same parish, these two orders of civilisation, these two psychoses (we can use this term); there have been war psychoses in all the national wars, and it is as difficult for one man to be a real pastor to our own two *patriae* as it would be for him to be chaplain to both camps during a national war.

M. Martimort: Is not the phenomenon you describe so well a world-wide thing; do not missionaries find the same conflict in propaganda countries; does it not frequently break out into open warfare?

Fr Rouquette: Yes, it is the same all over the world.

M. Perrot: It creates a problem of vocation for the secular clergy. For if we are to understand that these various *patriae* really do exist and that priests are necessary to serve them, is it possible for one man to be a priest to them all?

We are often told that the priest must be every man's priest.

This call, this duty to be a source of unity is inherent in our priesthood itself. But can anyone bring about a union between men belonging to *patriae* which are at war?

If we do not go beyond the very narrow sphere of the parochial circle, which, as far as people are concerned, is somewhat indeterminate, the priest can manage to belong to all his practising parishioners, to all the people who come to the Sunday Mass.

But we look beyond this group to the non-Christians outside – we have been sent to them as well; how can one be 'everybody's man'?

I put this question to the theologians: Can our vocation as secular priests be restricted to a particular sphere?

We are told: 'The secular priest is at the disposal of the bishop for any task he may wish to entrust to him.' Since the diocese is a territorial entity and all these social loyalties and circles, both Christian and pagan, are mixed up together in it on the parochial level, ought we not to allow a certain number of specifically missionary vocations among the secular clergy within the diocese, so that some priests may belong to the working-class – or any other – *patria*?

These are extremely important questions for the direction of vocations and the training of priests.

M. Martimort: I think it ought to be stated, first, that the bishop is the centre of unity, and it is easier to find room for a diversity of tasks when the priestly body is closely united to its bishop.

Secondly, I think these different vocations have their place, but with the obvious reservation that we have got to know how such a vocation, like a *charisma*, is to be tried and discerned.

What has frequently confused the discussions we have had on this question is perhaps a failure to understand this discernment of *charismata*. No one can be certain of having such a vocation merely by claiming it. This distinction must always be borne in mind, and indeed it is only in so far as we do bear it in mind that we shall make it easier for these vocations to blossom and for them to have a chance of expressing themselves.

Fr Régamey: I hope you will forgive me for wanting to say a word or two – this really isn't my line at all – but all that has been said bears out what I have felt for many years, and for many reasons.

It does seem important to consider this word assimilation. We are usually preoccupied with adaptation. But that is not enough. I think in one sense it goes too far, and in another it does not go far enough. The more we think about it the more we shall realise that one of the most serious defects of contemporary thought on this matter is connected with this very word adaptation. We make tremendous use of it, but it is a very ambiguous term.

I woke up to this a long time ago. At the very beginning of my ministry in 1935 or 1936, I remember a young architect surprised me by saying: 'We Catholic artists have had dozens of retreats preached to us by any number of priests and religious. But there was only one who was completey successful. That was Father Janvier – because he did not treat us as artists.'

My own experience has borne this out. It is true of artists and it is true of the working classes, and, *mutatis mutandis*, in other fields as well.

We can easily imagine the preacher who has been asked to speak to artists eagerly saying to himself, 'I am going to talk to artists' and taking all his illustrations from art. It is there that he goes wrong. In the same way Englishmen will forgive a Frenchman completely for his mistakes in English, but will begin to laugh as soon as the Frenchman uses an 'anglicism'. As soon as we start adapting, it doesn't work.

The great thing, I think, is to become naturalised. For example, if you haven't got a working-class outlook which goes down into your very subconscious itself, either because you were born or have been assimilated into it, and the latter is a long and difficult process, you can't pretend to be able to speak to workers, as workers.

You must be one of them, one of the same 'race', and then you are one with them in everything. You cannot but have a coherent ministry, and occasionally it will really catch on in a big way. A coherent and specifically working-class ministry must be carried out by a man with a working-class mentality, even if he himself does not work with his hands; someone whom the workers feel is their 'blood-brother'.

Adaptation goes too far in the sense that a man who adapts himself not exclusively, of course, but especially, to what is most confined to that particular environment, whereas a man who is

naturalised (a 'co-national', as it were) can open out his environment to things beyond its own borders; he can be the man of
God, the man of the whole mankind, the man of the outsider,
the man of the enemy, because there is no doubt about his
nationality.

It is obvious, too, that adaptation does not go far enough.
When you adapt yourself, what happens in effect is that those
to whom you are adapting yourself know quite well that it is
artificial, that it is not natural, and it will get you nowhere.

All the problems we discuss must, I think, be grasped on
entering fully into one's priestly vocation, for the priest is not
the kind of intermediary who is a barrier, but a man among men,
completely human, co-naturalised, a mediator who belongs both
to God and man. A man of God, he can yet be the man of his
class. In that class he must be the man who makes it see beyond
itself, but he cannot do this if he is merely adapting himself to
it, for then he is neither fish nor fowl. He can even belong to
several milieux.

M. Boulard: The problem raised by Fr Régamey is a relatively
simple one for the working-class missionary, or for the missionary who has to be assimilated into one kind of people only. So it
is for a chaplain working among the middle classes, or with
Catholic Action in the country. But is it not rather fanciful to
hope that one day the parish priest will be assimilated into all
the classes for which he is responsible? The most he can expect
is that he may not come off too badly. To consider this problem
of penetration into all classes on the parochial level is, in my
opinion, to ensure an impasse.

It is only on the level of the diocese that we can hope to solve
the problem of how the priesthood is to be authentically represented in all classes. It is by their attachment to the bishop,
who has the plenitude of the pastoral charge, that groups of
priests can guarantee that the priesthood makes an effective penetration into every class.

Perhaps we can look for the unity of these various approaches
on a lower echelon (that is my present position in sociological
thought) on the human level itself. There it is already possible
to contrive a certain unity of the priestly presence amidst all the
complexity of the social classes.

Fr Régamey: Assimilation into the various classes can be
effected, I think, because the penetration of which Canon

Boulard is speaking can be understood in different ways. There are many degrees of this penetration. There is penetration on the sociological level, as well as on the level of habits, customs, outlook; but there is also the penetration of man in his own nature.

To speak to that which is most interior, most eternal, in man is, I think, to go very deeply indeed, and obviously it cannot be done except by language and all that is implied by language, which is of time and therefore exterior. Now the business of passing from interiority to exteriority, from the eternal to the temporal, is involved here. And in it there are many stages, and it operates on many levels. . . .

So I think that the priest, diligent though he be, will only really be able to touch certain categories of people in an entirely human way.

Dom Rousseau: It seems to me that Fr Régamey's words are directing our thoughts towards something which is, at heart, the priest's personal charismatic sanctity. Look at the Curé d'Ars: look how penetrating he was; but it is a very uncommon.

Fr Régamey: But we are striving to attain it.

Fr Liégé: I wonder if this question of assimilation is not particularly urgent in the field of the Church's specifically missionary activity. In the mission of the Church and in the sacerdotal functions, the distinction between the missionary order (the sequence of the word and of evangelisation) and the eucharistic order, to which the order of the word and of evangelisation must unfailingly lead and re-lead, must be taken more seriously.

So, in my opinion, for the priest who is more by function the pastor, the president at the eucharist, the ideal would be that he should not be obliged to be the priest of any one particular class of men, but that he should be the Catholic priest of a Catholic assembly. For there is not one eucharist for the middle classes and another for the working classes. The eucharist presumes an already united people, in a Catholicity which assumes that there will be diversities and divergencies. So, per contra, and as far as the work of evangelisation is concerned, it seems that we ought to go to the very end in assimilation, because there is a word for the middle classes and a word for the working classes. It is the same gospel, but it gives the answers to problems experienced and formulated in different ways, and it has to be proclaimed in the language and in the life of communities of men. The missionary has to make the gospel seen and heard within the particular community in which he lives and which is his own *patria*. The liturgy of evangelisation can be a specialised thing adjusted to a particular group. But the eucharistic liturgy must seek to avoid this.

Why not admit that the advantage of a great freedom – of naturalisation – could be given to certain priests or groups of priests who would be specifically missionaries and evangelists, and not pastors?

That is what happened in the early centuries. Fr Seumois's book is very interesting on this point; he shows what unexpected freedom in matters of canonical discipline was given in those days to men who were sent out to plant the Church, as distinct from those who were already presidents of local churches and who were bound to a more definite code and to a greater stability; it was accepted that the latter were concerned with Christians who had already entered into the Catholic family.

This would not create two clergies, even if we have got to allow two sociologies in the sphere of the manner of life and of the sociology of the priesthood – the sociology of the pastor and that of the missionary. The unity of the priesthood and of the mission of the Church will guarantee unity in a diversity without diversion.

M. Boulard: But with this difference; that in the first centuries these groups were in different countries, whereas now they are in the same country, side by side every day, and that complicates the problem enormously.

A. Cruiziat: We are indeed in a world of class warfare, we are in a state of war, and I think that all that has been done here, and in C.P.L. particularly, on the Christian assembly – 'Assemblée bigarrée et violente', 'Assemblée, eucharistie et charité' – is far from making clear in the minds of Christians the distinction between the absolutely unique nature of the Church as such and the nature of Christian society.

Fr Forestier: We must hope nevertheless that eucharistic charity will be diffused throughout our social and political life; it ought to be, at any rate, and it ought to be of assistance in reducing the matters of conflict.

M. Martimort: Yes, but then I think we must always have in mind that the work of the Church is eschatological, and that there will always be the drama of that unity which is shown forth in the sacrament, yet which does not come to pass on earth, but is reserved for heaven.

Fr Régamey: The eschatological is not our business; we are concerned with Messianism – we have to bring about the kingdom of God. We know quite well that this is eschatological – but surely that is God's concern.[1]

M. Basseville: I think there is a danger to be avoided, too, in this business of naturalisation; for instance, a priest who is essentially at the service of the bourgeois world, because of his apostolic mission (A.C.I., etc.) must not finish up by installing himself so firmly in this bourgeois social order that he is content with some sort of moral refinement within this order, when he should be pressing, in the name of the kingdom of God, those historical claims which transcend the existing order and social conditions.

I will take an example. It is pointed out – actually it is the role of the hierarchy to get over these problems of 'class' – not only that there is a real growth of a vigorous working class movement, but that it is a duty incumbent on Christians to work for the advancement of the working class.

This is a demand which affects not only the working classes and those who serve them; it must also move all those who are responsible for Christian souls within the kingdom of God. Consequently, a priest, even in an essentially bourgeois environment, must gradually lead all his parishioners to this necessary conclusion even if it offends them. Otherwise his parish may well be open to such things as liturgical adaptation and yet remain a closed world, since it will have no real conception of the problems of the day.

Fr Forestier: Let us not forget, either, in studying assimilation that we have also to become citizens of the kingdom of God, and that this is by no means the easier task of the two; we can only make our bold adaptations in so far as we are at the same time strengthening our own personal adherence to the kingdom of God. Don't you think that at the present time this vision of faith, this profound apprehension of the kingdom of God needs to be strengthened and that it must be always pursued together with the search for a purely human assimilation?

1. On revising the typescript, I see no reason to qualify what I have said. But I think I ought to make it clear in this note that if I had had time for reflection I should have added that a sense of the eschatological ought always to prompt our Messianic effort.

PERSONAL REPORTS

M. VINATIER: PARISH PRIEST OF TREIGNAC (CREUSE)

I ask your pardon in advance for whatever bias there may be in my remarks, and for any words which may seem harsh to people living in Christian areas. I shall not, however, confine myself to my own personal experiences, but I shall appeal to those which many priests are undergoing at this present time, particularly in the least Christian districts of France, since it is clear, from the many confidences I have been privileged to receive, that priests are living through something of the same drama everywhere.

Priests today, particulary the young ones, were sent out into a world which was thought to be, and gave the appearance of being, Christian; yet in this world they find themselves tragically rejected. It is this situation which gives rise to what I call a drama.

During the last few days a priest has been telling me the story of his pastoral vocation. He went to Limousin from the diocese of Lyons. Like every other country priest, he tried his very best to arrange his pastoral life on the traditional basis of the sacraments, in that simple and humble fellowship that easily springs up between priest and people in the heart of the countryside.

In such an environment, where half the people were unbaptised, he soon felt that he couldn't breathe, and came to the conclusion that what had previously been the whole of his priesthood (centring especially on the sacraments) no longer existed. Even when he was administering the sacraments (marriage or any other), he could feel that the faith necessary for the reception of the sacraments was not there.

Things went on like this for a year or two. Then for three whole years he lived, voluntarily, through what might be described as the night. He said to himself: 'I shall have to go into silence, I shall have to try to live – I don't know how – and bear

the burden myself, and perhaps the light will come'. He came to
be afraid of the people in front of him. Particularly after the
gospel, when he turned round to face the few women there in
church, to speak his few, prepared words, he could say nothing
to them. It was very hard.

Then comes the third stage, not yet fully developed; he has
begun to live more 'in community' with his parishioners, so
that they at any rate can discover him afresh. This is just a
simple example I am passing on to you.

Many questions have been raised during these last few days
which I should like to raise again, not from my own point of view
but from that of the people, and the way they themselves look
at the parish priest. 'They always see the official – they do not
see the priest'; these are often their words.

All priests do, in effect, think of themselves as 'set apart' –
there is no doubt about that. They speak Latin, they are the
specialists in that language. They wear a habit which obviously
sets them apart from other men. Their houses are known by a
special name. They are not present at the fêtes and the great
occasions of country life, even the more serious occasions which
have some sacramental reference – for example, they may not be
present at wedding breakfasts. They are never present at those
important discussions which, with us, take place in the cafés,
etc.

But a more serious thing is that 85 per cent of them (that is
a modest figure for these parts, but no matter) are – excuse the
terms – just the leading men in the spiritual folklore. They are
the organisers of the religious folklore, just as the schoolteacher
organises the dances of the Limousin folklore.

But there is a difference: their folklore is so very ordered as
well as being so very sad, since as a rule it has to do with funerals
and mourning (the people are not present on Sundays), and the
heights of this pyramid of sadness are reached on All Saints' day.

Occasionally, however, this 'folklore' is more cheerful, and
then people turn up in greater numbers – Palm Sunday, for
instance, or first holy communion.

I know these are harsh words, but I wish people would realise
how true they are.

And unfortunately there is more to be said. From time to time
the folklore observes an even more important day, when a 'man
in purple' makes his appearance.

If I say these things to you, it is because this analysis strikes exactly the same note as Mgr Garrone when he described the situation in which the Church finds herself in the world of today. Two years ago, at the 'Journée Nationale Catechistique', he said these words, which are very true: 'In this world, the Church is not only a stranger and rejected, but she is foreign as well'.

Another indication of this separation is that the parish priest inevitably votes 'right' (there is no doubt about this in people's minds), and, à priori, defends the established social order.

After these few reflections, I should like, rather tentatively and as an outcome of inquiries which have often been very unhappy, to point out some things which priests see, but to which many others appear to priests to be blind.

As far as the proclamation of the gospel is concerned, they are convinced that the gospel, like everything else, is not merely a question of vocabulary but of mentality. It can only be proclaimed by those who are living its proclamation in their actions.

I find the following example rather striking: the proclamation of the gospel by the travelling missions in those desperate villages of Limousin. The director of the travelling missions told told us only two or three days ago, 'Our proclamation of the gospel only really comes to anything when there is a priest on the spot who is trying to translate our words into deeds'.

I am going to tell you of some of these deeds, for it is through them that their priest's separation is really seen in its true light.

Some days ago, one of these priests told me this: 'Passing through a fair, I noticed a sort of village idiot. The people had got him drunk; they had put him into a wheelbarrow, and were pushing him around: it was the great joke of the neighbourhood.' He said to me, 'My heart leapt into my mouth. I took him in my arms. The people, aghast, lined up on each side, and I felt almost as if I were carrying the Lord, the Blessed Sacrament. I looked after him for the night, and took him home the following morning. He never even said "Thank you". But this action made an impression on the countryside, and provided the opportunity for explaining things to them.'

Another instance: One of the rare Christians in the village came to ask the priest to find him a tenant – but he must have someone dependable. The priest replied, 'No, I certainly will not send anyone to you. You have had four tenants in five years, and we all know how they have been treated.' Everybody heard about this blow!

On another occasion the municipal elections were taking place. Only two parties were contesting the seats – the socialists and the communists – but the candidates went so far as to start shooting at each other in the woods. The priests of the district told the people: 'In these circumstances we are not going to vote'.

Another action of the same kind: the broad-mindedness of certain priests, e.g. in going to the civic funeral of an atheist personality, as against the party spirit of certain people, be they anti-clericals, marxists or anything else.

Another act, which I considered very bold – it concerns a priest who is engaged in special work in his native county. (He has no parochial duties because of his health, and is deeply involved in work for the improvement of the distict.) One day he was asked to sign some petition or other. They even went so far as to provoke him with little notes: 'Are you for us or against us?' He replied in these simple words on the same notes: 'My life is my answer'. And the local people, who knew him well, understood.

Prayer, whether it be the priest's own prayer or that which it is his duty to teach the faithful, is a more serious matter. At the present time, this thirst for prayer is greater than we might suppose, but many are also weary of, and tend to reject, a certain form of prayer.

The following example is a sign of it. At a conference of priests at which the needs of the diocese were being discussed with the bishop, the appointment of certain chaplains were considered, and unanimously the priests asked that the first should be one for themselves: 'We need a chaplain for our prayer', they said.

This is not peculiar to one part of France. You are aware of the real difficulties many priests find with their breviary. This is both dreadful and tragic. There is the language, for one thing; then the progressive apprenticeship of the psalter has perhaps not been served. Again, it all has to be harmonised with the tasks which are entrusted to a young priest today.

I am not sure if it would not be better to look for the answer to this problem not so much in any new departure, but in the burden itself.

I know a priest who, to give meaning to his breviary psalms, reads beforehand either the *Documentation catholique* or the *Actualité religieuse*, not only so that he may feel at one with his environment, but also in union with the universal life of the Church.

Many things could be said about the eucharist as well. As far as the cult is concerned, I should like to emphasise that the efforts of many priests are directed towards what seems to me to be the key to the situation – the preparation of converts for baptism. But here they run into two sets of obstacles. These obstacles come first from the non-Christians, which is only to be expected; but people stick very much to the 'mentality' they had when the priest first found them. For some, preparation for baptism can be extremely profitable, but from the moment they enter into the traditional liturgy one very quickly feels: 'Now we're at a standstill'.

Further – and this is more serious – it is difficult enough converting non-Christians, but it is very hard indeed when we see them not accepted and even refused by Christians. It has been my lot, unfortunately, on several occasions to witness some frightening reactions. The difficulty priests have in getting someone admitted to a Catholic Action movement because he was forty when he was baptised seems to me to be an indication of it: a community which calls itself Christian not welcoming people into its bosom.

A case which also seemed to me striking is that of the priest of not so long ago, whose spirituality had been nourished and built on the sacramental, yet whose whole life is turned towards evangelism.

It is actually one of the points which we have touched on, but which I do not see sufficiently clearly – that evangelisation is indeed a priestly function, an essential and fundamental function at that.

Furthermore, in this sphere of evangelisation the difficulty which priests experience also arises as a result of the present canonical structure of the Church, in which there is no half-way status: there are Christians and there are non-Christians. We don't know where to place the people who are moving towards the Church, who have not attained to faith but are making progress, yet who in certain systems are left completely high and dry. It is most difficult for us to place them, and it is one of the real dramas of the present day.

There are many other things we could say about the laity and about the rural world which is living through a revolution, and which will not hear of our not being in it.

I will refer here to Mgr Marty's pastoral letter (Lent 1954), which is devoted entirely to this sad problem, and looks at it in a quite remarkable way. The Church may, I think, be failing the countrymen at this very moment, as she failed the working classes, because he is falling away rapidly; and the fact is not sufficiently realised.

It was very striking to see, in these non-Christian districts, that when the barricades were going up no problem was created for anyone in these rural areas where we are still very close to the people, if the priests were there; an old archpriest still felt he had to go and ring the bell. . . .

I have exposed this anguish only very briefly. But see how desperately we need light and strength from our bishops and theologians.

M. RÉTIF: BISHOP OF SAINT-FLOUR, EASTER 1954

Here are some reflections on priesthood which are the result of living more than fifteen years in a working-class parish.

First, I am convinced that the working classes – to speak only of them – compel the priest who is making an approach to them to deepen his conception of priesthood itself. The priest finds a de-Christianised world, and discovers that this de-Christianised world possesses its own values, some of which are of an evangelical character. I may add that the majority of priests who come to live among the working classes do not expect to find this, undoubtedly because of their previous training, which is the vehicle for more than one social prejudice.

The priest in a working-class district will feel that he is a stranger in the very environment he is seeking to evangelise, when he makes the effort to be in true harmony with it. This leads to a complete shifting of emphasis in the conception that he has of his priesthood, which gradually gives his priesthood a new accent.

The first stage is the discovery that 'to be a priest, the priest stands in need of the priest'; in this sense, what is fundamentally necessary is clearly the priestly group. The priesthood is essentially a corporate thing. I can no longer be a priest without living and working with other priests. I can no longer recognise in my priesthood now the conceptions of priesthood which were once offered to me, a priesthood which was above all functional in character and, in a way, independent of other priests. So that, it is the priesthood of Christ which assumes a greater reality in this interchange of priestly lives.

In certain cases there is some confusion – compare, for example, militants of the working class who are faced with the business of adult prayer. The adult is essentially one with a sense of personal responsibility, but prayer is an abdication of self. So he attempts two things at once: to be a man who will shoulder responsibility at work, and at the same time to become the 'little child' the gospel expects him to be.

I will take the cross, with its two dimensions and its two directions, as the symbol of this harmonious and corporate priesthood of the Church. In the direction which moves vertically between heaven and earth, I feel that I am God's religious, yet at the same time I feel that I am firmly rooted in the realities of life in my own environment. Then, in the horizontal direction I cannot simply be the priest for those around me in my own parish; I feel, as a priest, that I have a universal mission. I cannot be the Christian's priest completely unless I am the unbeliever's priest too. This strain is in some way quite normal. The mediation of Christ in the Church through the priest is essentially painful. I must accommodate myself to the uncomfortable, and indeed to the unstable.

By calling I am a man of action, yet more and more I feel that I should be a man of contemplation-in-action – to be a parish priest means, to me, that at the fine point of my action I am the contemplative of my community.

A priest living with priests, I am more and more sure that I cannot bring my priesthood to its full stature among priests alone. The laity have become so necessary to me that without them I could not understand and live my priesthood. I do not exercise my priesthood fully save through giving and receiving; the relationship is not merely a paternal one, nor yet that of ruler and ruled. It is a fraternal intercourse, and I realise that the laity, and through them all men, are complementary to my priesthood. In this way I can grasp something of the mystery of Christ's espousals to humanity.

All this expresses itself in our pastoral contacts. Perhaps I am preparing a sermon, or making a point about my ministry, or talking about prayer to the militants. They will ask me: 'What about yourself; how do you pray? How do you live with Christ?' These exchanges, demanding though they often are, help me enormously to get my priesthood into focus.

But for this you have got to have an adult laity. It is not with every layman that you can really establish this 'community of life' – not merely an exchange of views. Only adults in the faith can share in it without confining the priesthood to a sort of spiritual trade union. The diversity of functions in the Church must not be impaired by their complementary nature. And this means more than mere co-existence.

In this sense of 'priesthood laity' I feel that I am a member of a Church in which Catholic Action will from now on be an integral part. The future alone will be able to say what features the laity will bring to the face of the Church which will reveal Christ to a new civilisation.

From this point of view I do not see how one can be a priest in a parish without a minimum of training in Catholic Action. This training, besides promoting a respect for secular values, will encourage us always to be careful to listen to others, to look at life from a fresh angle, and to aim at being able to be with and live with.

Cardinal Liénart recently asked his priests in the *Mission de France* to seek and devise ways of life and approach which the evangelisation of a new world were calling for in priests.

At a session of A.C.O. we recognised that we were out of our element when confronted by the Marxist environment, or by certain difficulties brought to our notice by Christian militants who were at close grips with Marxist influence.

The separation required of the priest who is in communion with the world is not to be found so much in a life apart as in the greater eschatological significance of his presence in that world which he has to evangelise.

It is when we look at things in this way that the future of some vocations to the priesthood seems doubtful. I know young men, some from ordinary homes and some not, who are hesitant about the priesthood. They think of the priesthood, but are acutely conscious of these modern values and are dreading being dragged out of human society and its associations, for one day they would like to minister the presence of Christ in his Church to them. These young people of today could be the priests of the world tomorrow, but I am afraid that their vocations may not come to anything, because there is still, in effect, too large a hiatus between their mentality, the way they go about things, and the clerical training which is laid down for them before they can be admitted to the priesthood. Not a few of us are distressed by this.

These thoughts on priesthood are no more than one priest's reaction to a particular environment, and because of this cannot claim universal validity. But the evidence of other priests with quite different experiences now points in the same direction.

M. F. LELUBRE: PARISH PRIEST OF ST LOUIS, ALFORTVILLE, SEINE

By looking at the fundamentally different roles of the priest and the layman, I should like to indicate those elements which appear to belong essentially to the priesthood. My thoughts are the outcome of a pastorate spent exclusively in a working-class district.

First, a few statements of fact. I have really very few, even occasional or exceptional, contacts with non-Christians. And if the beginnings of faith are not there right at the start, I can safely say that nothing can be accomplished. Of the four or five baptised catechumens which I have in my parish, not one has attached himself to the community.

So at the present time it seems that the laity alone are in a position to be real missionaries, and to evangelise non-Christians. It looks as though we priests are unable to do this at present, and that it will be up to the laity to see that this work is done.

Here another question might arise, but as we should gain nothing from discussing it, I will leave it aside: that of an authentic approach by the laity to the working-class world.

In a non-Christian environment the lay approach is necessary. But, generally speaking, it isn't there. But let us assume that it is – we do occasionally come across it: the laity themselves can start something. But they can't finish it. At best, the result will be a group of catechumens such as I mentioned just now. They are able to prepare catechumens, but ultimately they will not be successful in making a community, and nothing will be created.

It seems that with the laity there is something superfluous and at the same time something lacking.

First, there is something superfluous because they are dependent on an external Christian community to which they are attached as by an umbilical cord. They need the community to live, to be, to remain Christians, to mature and to fulfil their mission; but this community is something extraneous to their environment. Living as they do in the working-class world, they find themselves, of obligation, attached to and dependent on another world, a Christian world which exists outside the world of the working classes.

This struck me very forcibly last year à *propos* Catholic Action. We had got the apprentices together, and a director of Catholic Action had come to discuss with us how they were to to be attached to J.O.C. Now it was clear that on one point there was a lack of harmony, precisely because he was attached to an established Christian community, to another world, although an authentic worker doing authentic Catholic Action among the working class. So real success was not possible.

Christians are heavily compromised by the appearance of the Church, and outsiders regard them as people with bourgeois connections – I am using the word 'bourgeois' in the sense in which it is understood by the working classes – and that is quite enough to rob them of a good deal of their effectiveness.

And then, they can only make converts leave their own world. If they want to lead them to the full practice of Christianity they are compelled to get them to leave the world they live in, i.e. the working class.

It is interesting to examine the position of Christian working-class militants in the absence of priests. They cannot succeed, they cannot cut themselves off from the existing Christian community without dying. They need that community, failing any other truly indigenous one, but it weighs them down and impedes them when it does not render their labours fruitless.

We have only to remember what the Press said about the priest-workmen to understand what desperate appeals the laity themselves made for priests to feed them, to make it possible for them to live and to labour in their own circle. This seems to me to be very important, and shows, secondly, that the laity lack something. Perhaps there is a subjective side to this but I am sure that is not the whole story. We have simply got to state the fact that the priest has surpising significance and position among the workers.

When we look at all the genuine reactions there have been among the workers, even though our contact with them is too indirect to know what they are thinking, we are very struck by the grand place given to the priest-workmen, quite out of proportion to the smallness of their number or the activity which they have been able to carry out. There is something in the very fact that they are priests, something for which there is no substitute, which the layman cannot supply.

But then, I think that fundamentally in people's minds, even in the minds of workers who are completely pagan, there is a vague recognition of what the priest is.

There is an objective side as well: the laity do not give people what they need. There is certainly something lacking in their approach, in their action. They are not adequate.

They cannot give what they do not possess; but why? What do they lack? It is important to know this if we are to try to ascertain something about the nature of priesthood from the facts.

I do not think it can be the sacraments, at least in their practical administration. People do not 'feel' the need of any sacrament – baptism, Mass, penance. I can say that in my parish people who have children at catechism are often believers, and even Christians, although non-practising, but they show no desire for the sacraments. That is not what they are waiting for.

Are they, then, looking for someone to preach the word of God to them? I think in some ways the laity do this as well as ourselves.

We have in my parish an example of this which seems to me to have thrown a good deal of light on this question. For three years a seminarist, who has completed his course in theology and taken tonsure but who has not been ordained priest, has performed, in our group, exactly the same ministry as ourselves to non-Christians, and Christians unattached to the community.

This shows that from the point of view of evangelisation and even of preaching the word of God itself, it is not necessary to be a priest. Laymen could perform the same office as ourselves. For these people, this seminarist was a priest because he brought them the word of God. In fact he had taken tonsure, but even if he had not it would have been all the same.

Perhaps, then, the priest brings the presence of Christ? But it seems that even the layman brings the presence of Christ. In the case I have just mentioned, that seminarist was, in the minds of the people, just as much the 'presence of Christ' among them as ourselves. Why then is there no substitute for the priest? When all these things have been eliminated there seems to be nothing really important left, but we can still make an attempt at an answer.

I think people need a 'founder', someone who will bring them together and unite them in the charity of Christ. The laity can do some things, but are not able to be 'centres'. Now, people need someone among them to be their religious centre, grouping them around the Church. They do not merely need Christians to be the Church present among them, but above all they need a Church, in the sense of the Church focused in a particular community, and they need someone to unite them one to another, someone who is a real head in the sense of a father – not one who gives the orders, but one who gathers them together and is foremost among them.

This ought to be discussed to see if we can draw anything out of it, but on reflection it seems to me the essence of what remains characteristic of the priesthood.

You will say to me that it incorporates all the rest. True enough, but even a priest who does not normally administer the sacraments, who does not exercise any ministry, has none the less even now this character of head, one who gathers together, unites and founds the Church.

M. OSTER: PRIEST OF OFFENDORF, BAS-RHIN

I would like to make a few remarks which are complementary to M. Vinatier's report.

He told us that some of his statements might perhaps be too harsh in the case of Christian areas. I would like to tell him that they have not been too severe for one who, like myself, lives in a Christian area, and who is immersed not only in the general life of the parish, but of the commune as well. On the contrary they were a comfort to me, and I hope that what I have to say will be a comfort to him.

What happens in my own environment if you try really to live your priesthood, or to preach the word of God in truth, or to make the celebration and the sacramental life a living reality, is that you effect what the Germans call 'a discerning of spirits'. There is a whole section of the parish which begins to sense where all this might lead them, and then it takes up a hostile position and opposes it by every means – obstruction, calumny, sabotage and other things.

Such an attitude in people who are in your own assembly and claim to be excellent Christians is perhaps in some ways more lamentable than in people who know no better because they have not been baptised or are pagans.

The gospel message will always remain a scandal, a folly; it will always meet this opposition. I do not think there is anything we can do about it; on the contrary, it seems to me to guarantee the authenticity of our work.

M. CHAMBOUNAUD: PRIEST OF LEMONTEIL-AU-VICOMTE, CREUSE

Here and there we find churches which are quite empty because there are no longer either priests or faithful who come regularly. Failing regular worship and teaching, evangelisation and preaching, even the great essential acts of the Christian life are gradually abandoned. Because it is not frequented the church has become unloved and derelict.

When we see these churches, we have tangible evidence, not of parishes which have been affected by religious strife and brutally destroyed by force, but of parishes which have gradually fallen into decay, like those walls which have nothing to support whose stones are crumbling bit by bit.

I can name such parishes not only in my own region but in others. If they were only isolated cases we need not take them too much into account. But it is here that the shoe pinches a little, for there is a much larger number of parishes which clearly have not reached this last state but which show signs of going the same way. There are hundreds of parishes, usually grouped in regions, where the church still survives. It is open for worship. People have remained faithful on the whole to the great religious acts of life, that is of course, to baptism and burial, since there is a very great falling off of marriages.

There is a similar cleavage in the matter of first communions which no longer take place. In my district, of the one hundred and forty children who go to school, I have thirteen on my register, and only half of them come regularly to catechism.

We see, then, that in theory the parish churches are open but in fact the people who still come, who seek the priest's ministry, do so in a very formal way with long intervals between each call. So much so that the blessing the priest can give in the name of God and the Church he represents seems to be a kind of additional rite tacked on to practices which are really quite sufficient in themselves.

The birth of a baby is a case in point. After the actual event there are the formalities of registration to be attended to, the baby has to be given a name, a godfather and godmother have to be chosen, and then there is a family gathering and a meal. Everybody has all this to do everywhere, but in some families the Church ceremony is added on. So that everybody understands that the words 'to be baptised' are synonymous with 'to be given a name', and for those who call themselves Christians it means, in addition, taking the infant to church for baptism. Consequently, the fact that everyone has a godfather and a godmother is no evidence that they have actually been baptised. It simply proves that the parents have chosen someone to give their child a certain amount of moral support in the shape of presents on certain occasions, or help with his education.

It is the same when anybody dies. They all meet at the house, then proceed to the town, pause at the war memorial if the deceased was an old soldier; there is the procession to the cemetery followed by the interment. And if the family is a pious one, or thinks it is, a Church ceremony is added. So here again, a rite is 'added on' to the other established practices. In other words, even in the case of people who still call on us on such occasions, there is a tremendous devaluation in their conception of what we can do.

Some have mentioned the conflict which faces the priest when his attention is claimed on the one hand by a community which is very 'close' and does not find it easy to open out, but which takes up so much of his time that the many other things he has to do are crowded out; and on the other hand by a multitude he cannot reach at all because of the importance of the community which makes such demands on him. There is so much to do, and there is no time to deal with the others, and even if time were found, the priest would be torn between two very different, almost opposing, outlooks.

For some of us it goes much deeper than this, since we are not absorbed and harassed by the cares of a community in being because it no longer exists.

Many priests have experienced this conflict. Some remain in this state a little while, and it is really very disturbing for personal equilibrium; it makes a genuine 'vocational' work in the country – and many other things – well-nigh impossible.

But the priest will often get over this stage, and I think the difficulty lies chiefly in this: as a result of our training, our family background, our education, we attempt to build our parochial community on the pattern of what we imagine it was in the past, or in our own families and among our own people; and consequently we ourselves forge the chains of that conflict.

What can impede us just as much in such circumstances is obviously the fact that if there is very little parochial work to do in the parish we often tend to multiply that little, and the weeks are taken up with a lot of coming and going for very few people scattered over a wide area.

But I do not think this is such a serious matter. In fact, when we were appointed to our parishes, we received a rather indefinite mandate from our bishop. He simply appointed us to look after our parishes; everything is included in that one charge, and it is up to us to work it out.

Consequently what we have to do has not been determined in detail beforehand. And it is as necessary for us to find a new pattern for our pastoral work as it would be for us to adapt ourselves to snow if we were going into a cold country. This is not a mere theory, an idea or a form of temptation – it is a sheer internal necessity. It is no less than a condition for our very existence. We are compelled to discover a way of life; and we have not been prepared in any way for the situation in which we find ourselves.

I would not wish to formulate any theories about this way of life, but, always bearing in mind that I am speaking from the context of the de-Christianised countryside with which I am fairly familiar, it seems to me that the new way of life of those priests who have received the charge of one or several parishes, must, in conformity with their locality, their individual temperament, their order and the training they have received, develop in three principal directions.

About the first I do not want to say very much. It concerns those priests who take one or two parishes where there is absolutely nothing. Consequently there will not be any outward manifestations of their priestly office, since there are no faithful;

it can only exist in the heart of one who feels himself to be the
father of the people there, but who in fact does nothing for them
as parish priest since he does not preach to them, baptise them,
hear their confessions, etc. But he will try to share the life of the
people by becoming as much as possible one of them.

A second mark of his way of life will be what I call general
contact. The priest who has no faithful in the religious, 'ecclesial' sense of the word, nevertheless thinks of himself as the
priest and pastor of every single person in his parish. He goes
to see them frequently, tries to understand them, but first he
loves them and tries to give proof of the love he has for them;
he shares their indigence – not only their material poverty which
is often very great, but that kind of weariness and despondency
which also affects so many, particularly in very poor country
districts where people really have not enough to live on and are
eventually forced to leave.

Thirdly, there are priests who turn very noticeably to what
might be called a form of Catholic Action, although it is difficult
to employ the expression itself for this work. They keep an eye
on any in their parish, and perhaps even a little beyond its
borders, with personality and courage, who may be capable of
taking things in hand, and hence of shaping not only the present
but the future, whether they are Christians or not.

A little book such as the *Directoire pour la Pastorale des
Sacraments*, however curious it may seem to be when there are
so few chances to administer the sacraments, has given us food
for thought, and some helpful directions on how to do things,
for we must make those actions which people still ask us to
perform for them absolutely vital and real.

I am sure that this branch of parochial work must be well
done, particularly because of its infrequent occurrence: some
will be able to do more than others here, depending on the
number of parishes one has to cope with; but it is not our most
important job, and if we had only this card to play, the cause
would be compromised if not lost.

We must set about something else – the education of the laity.
If they are already Christians they are probably regular com-
municants. If they are not even this yet they must be urged to
act and to be formed in and by this action.

In my own district which is so completely de-Christianised,
for the last three or four years I have been witnessing here and

there in one or two homes (most of them, it is true, belonging to people who have come into the district) the birth of incipient little Christian communities. Their pivot is usually a Christian home, round which are grouped other Christian but less active, or others less Christian but more progressive, homes.

If we wished to make a map of a particular diocese or area showing the state of religion in such parishes, I think it would be a very imperfect guide if it shaded them all the same way and labelled them non-practising. We ought to look again very carefully at those places where Christian communities are springing up, even if they are not obviouly attached to a church, to a parish as such, or even to any organised, official Catholic Action movement. We cannot use the term. We cannot even follow its methods closely, because in the nature of things they are not suited to the conditions under which this form of Catholic Action operates; yet the thing is real, and it exists.

I have certainly schematised a little, but I do think that here we have the beginnings of a new manner of life which we country priests have simply got to find; this is by no means a denial of those ministerial standards which we accepted when we were ordained, but the clear recognition that we can neither surrender nor withdraw, but that we have simply got to adjust ourselves to the situation in which we are placed.

CONCLUSIONS OF THE SESSION

OUR purpose, this session, was to complete what we had begun last year. The scheme, therefore, was necessarily rather different from that of the normal session. But it is important to observe the profound unity underlying the various statements we have heard:

I WE HAVE BEEN CONSIDERING THE ORGANIC LIFE OF THE CHURCH

This is obvious when we consider the papers given by Dom Botte, M. Fransen and Fr Duval. But it is equally true of the papers delivered by Fr Gy (for in and through that vocabulary we can understand something of the life which it expresses) and Fr Lécuyer (there we heard the views of the preachers and the theologians about the nature of the Church and the sacrament of Orders within the Church).

M. Idiart's account emphasises the sense of history in the Christian religion.

Finally, M. Boulard's report and the discussion on pastoral duties show us the Church of today.

In all, the topics we have examined support the conclusions of last year. 'Episcopate, priesthood and diaconate are "Orders" more than ritual functions, and shape the actual structure of the Church in a hierarchical pattern; they are meant to ensure its growth and the sanctification of its members.'

But now we are better able to appreciate that the sacrament of Orders, and in particular the Christian priesthood, was in actual fact lived in the daily life of sinful men through all the vicissitudes of history, before its theology was worked out. The hierarchical structure of the Church was lived before being formulated and it was formulated before being explained.

2 WE ARE AT A TURNING-POINT IN THE HISTORY OF HOLY ORDERS IN THE CHURCH

The facts of pastoral life show us that the conception of the priest as a man who performs the rites of the Church in isolation is being succeeded by the conception of his work as a missionary effort carried out in collaboration with his fellow-priests in a team.

At the same time, a dogmatic decree, the Constitution *Sacramentum Ordinis* of Pius XII, give their privileged place to the imposition of hands and to the consecretory Preface. Now, the Preface states specifically that the priest belongs to a 'college' and to a subordinate Order: priests have no *raison d'être* apart from the bishop; nor can the bishops be thought of as isolated for they form the *Ordo Episcoporum*.

It is in the light of these remarks that we are able to formulate the following conclusions:

1. The priesthood is degraded whenever the ministry of the word no longer occupies a place in it.

The apostles are heralds of the gospel. In the pastoral epistles we see St Paul enjoining Timothy and Titus to 'preach the word'. And if, in the early days of Christianity, priests did not preach it is because this ministry belonged in the first place to the bishop around whom they lived. But the Council of Trent, in its reforming decrees, repeatedly emphasised the office of preaching – the sacraments themselves need to be accompanied by the word of the priest.

We have only to note the importance of the book in ordinations (whether of lectors, exorcists, deacons or bishops) to see the importance which the Church attaches to this ministry.

It would really be stupid to oppose the ministry of the word to that of the eucharist, or the sacraments in general. Every true word is perfected in the Presence. The word of consecration is the realisation, the actualisation of the word of evangelisation.

The ministry of the word continues among men and throughout time; the ministry of the Word of God, Christ himself.

2. In contradistinction to pagan religions, which reserve to their priests acts which are within the power of everyone, the Christian religion gives special powers to its priests. Priests and bishops receive powers which do not pertain to simple Christians.

In particular, the power of consecrating the eucharist has such importance that the name *sacerdos* (which is bound up with the sacrifice of the Mass) has become one of the terms which the Church readily employs to designate those who have this power.

3. The Council of Trent brought out the terminology of the Good Shepherd afresh.

In doing this, it took up again the grand theme of the consecratory Preface, which sees the bishop as absorbed in his charge of ruling the Church, of feeding the flock; it refers directly to our Lord, who alone is the Shepherd of the entire flock.

Priests and bishops do not act in their own name, but *in persona Christi*.

4. The Church is born of Pentecost. The outpouring of the Spirit began with the apostles, and spreads to the whole Church as it grows and develops.

Patristic tradition reflected upon the special place of the mystery of Pentecost, which lays such emphasis on the missionary character of the priesthood.

5. It is in these various functions that the priest's position in the Church is seen in its true perspective. He serves in a ministry which transcends him, for the Christian priesthood simply cannot be understood unless it is raised above the individual.

(*a*) In a diocese, priests are not to be thought of as isolated, but as sharing a common priesthood, and above all as forming, with the bishop, the sacerdotal body, the members of which cannot act independently. In this college of priests the bishop is not a kind of dean or president but the true Pastor. The priesthood of the priest is unintelligible without reference to the bishop.

(*b*) Nor is the bishop alone. He belongs to the *Ordo Episcoporum*. This expression has two meanings:

(i) hierarchically: he is incorporated into an Order; by virtue of this, the episcopate is Catholic.

(ii) historically: he is the heir of a line which goes back to the apostles; by virtue of this, the *Ordo Episcoporum* is apostolic.

The *Ordo Episcoporum* gathered around the Holy See has a collective responsibility.

(*c*) It is in the name of Christ that the *Ordo Episcoporum* acts. On the day of his consecration, the gospels are placed on the shoulders and the head of the new bishop. The priesthood has its origin and its efficacy in Christ the One Priest.

6. We come back now to the title of the session. The sacrament of which we are speaking is that of Orders.

It is called Orders because of its several degrees; each degree contains many members. This multiplicity is necessary to discover Christ. This sacrament serves the Church. It constitutes the essential framework of the Church.

7. Teaching about the priesthood, whether to adults or children, is a permanent necessity. Such teaching will need to be related to the mystery of Pentecost and to the wholeness of the Church, the amazing riches of which are described in the preface for the ordination of deacons:

Thou, O Lord, art the Giver of dignities, who dost assign to each his order and allot to each is office ... whose body thy Church, though adorned by a variety of heavenly graces, and distinguished in a multitude of members, is yet one in the wonderful awe of her being; do thou grant her growth and increase for the extension of thy temple.

In the likeness of Christ the priest, ministers in holy Orders are in the service of the faithful. They are building the Church.

Vanves, 1955.